Creating God

Manchester University Press

The author

Robin Derricourt is an Honorary Professor of History in the School of Humanities at the University of New South Wales and a Fellow of the Australian Academy of the Humanities. He holds a PhD in archaeology from Cambridge University. His previous books include *Inventing Africa: history, archaeology and ideas* (2011), *Antiquity Imagined: the remarkable legacy of Egypt and the ancient Near East* (2015) and *Unearthing Childhood: young lives in prehistory* (2018), which received the PROSE Award for Archaeology and Ancient History.

Creating God

The birth and growth of major religions

Robin Derricourt

Manchester University Press

Published by Manchester University Press
Altrincham Street, Manchester M1 7JA

www.manchesteruniversitypress.co.uk

British Library Cataloguing-in-Publication Data
A catalogue record for this book is available from the British Library

ISBN 978 1 5261 5617 4 hardback

First published 2021

The publisher has no responsibility for the persistence or accuracy of URLs for any external or third-party internet websites referred to in this book, and does not guarantee that any content on such websites is, or will remain, accurate or appropriate.

Typeset in Minion and Avenir
by R. J. Footring Ltd, Derby, UK
Printed in Great Britain
by Bell & Bain Ltd

Contents

Maps

A note on style

The style used in this book may need some explanation. I have found it more appropriate to use the terms CE (Common Era) and BCE (Before Common Era) rather than BC or AD, but I have not added in AH (Muslim) years or years in the Jewish calendar.

I have chosen generally to use variants of people's names that, as best we can tell, were those that applied in the lifetime of the individuals concerned, in preference to those used today. This is in part to help distinguish the historical individual from the figure of modern religious faith: the 1st-century CE Jewish religious prophet Yeshua rather than the 21st-century figure of religious worship Jesus. Thus I generally use Yeshua rather than Jesus/Iesous/Gesù/Isa; Paulos rather than Saint Paul; Muhammad ibn 'Abdullah rather than the Prophet Muhammad; Zarathushtra rather than Zoroaster; and, in the style of his time, Joseph Smith, Jun. Following the styles of the contexts, God may be referred to as male.

What believers in a faith would describe confidently as revelation, outsiders might punctuate as 'revelation'. Here I avoid the extra punctuation. The term applies broadly to the message received or delivered by those who see it derived from the divine. The Mormons' *Doctrine and Covenants* includes revelations to the founding prophet and some of his successors that relate both to matters of theology and to practical aspects of the development of the Church.

Anachronisms are hard to avoid. The name Mormons would be applied to the Latter-day Saints but was not introduced by them; the followers of the Jesus movement were not called Christians until some years after Yeshua's death. The conquerors from the Arabian Peninsula would probably not have described themselves as Arabs. Today, the largest Zoroastrian community, living in India, call themselves Parsees – Persians.

Terms like Israel, Palestine, Syria and Judah/Judaea have had different meanings at different times. Places often have different names in past and present, and there are differing transliterations from Arabic and other scripts, so where possible I have indicated alternative spellings and names the first time a place is mentioned.

I have avoided diacritical marks on transliterated names: they add little for the non-specialist reader and the specialist will be aware of the conventionally transliterated form. I have, however, sought to retain the *ain* ('') and *hamza* ('') of Arabic words and names, and used the conventional 'b.' for *ibn* or *ben* (son of) in names.

To reduce the overall density of notes, references to the sources for different statements within a single paragraph of the text have in places been combined into a single note. I concede that the secondary materials accessed are biased towards those in English. References to websites were live at time of completion of the manuscript in August 2020.

Chapter 1

Introduction: approaching religions' history

In this book I survey the origins and first spread of several major religions. I do so from a definitively secular standpoint, using the debates of historical scholarship and the discoveries of scientific archaeology to ask: what do we really know, once we bypass the myths and later traditions that developed? I consider the landscape of each religion's origins: the place, time and society where it emerged, the material culture of that community, the pattern of contemporary religion and the framework of political history. Here I am interested in religions as the enterprise and activity of human agency, rather than their theology and teachings.

This is not a study of the 'origins of religion', a quite different topic, where hypotheses exceed the bounds of available information and remain largely in the area of untestable theory.[1] Instead I am concerned in each chapter with a specific religion – organised collective movements, with some very different trajectories. The religions covered are those in the tradition of monotheism. That is the belief that just a single all-powerful deity exists, responsive to worship by the deity's followers. It contrasts with polytheism, which is the veneration of many gods, and monolatry, which is the worship of only one god among the many thought to exist.

Chapters discuss the three 'Abrahamic' religions of Judaism (as it became monotheistic), Christianity and Islam, and these are bracketed by chapters on ancient Zoroastrianism (Mazdaism) and modern Mormonism. A feature of the monotheistic tradition is the prophet, the individual who is said to receive direct messages from the divine with instructions or inspiration to spread these widely. There were of course foundational individuals and influential teachers in the traditions of the religions of East and South Asia that recognise multiple deities, but the source of their inspiration is different from the prophetic tradition found across the monotheistic faiths.

Readers may choose to use just those parts of this book that interest them – an individual religion or theme; they may not be interested in the archaeological framework or the geographical setting, or indeed this introduction explaining my approach. Nevertheless, comparison does raise questions and ideas, and these are discussed in the concluding chapter.

Woven through the book is the awareness that texts on religion and history are necessarily subject to the beliefs of the writers. Proselytisers of a religion in its foundational texts were seeking to advance adherence to their faith, not write academic history at arm's length. Later writers inevitably reflect their pious commitment whether they are writing works for a religious purpose or the history of that religion for a broader context. If subjectivity is inevitable then I need to define my own subjectivity, writing from a secular humanist and rationalist position, and explain what I mean by a secular approach.

It is fair to suggest that everyone thinks that the majority of people are misguided and deluded in their religious beliefs and affiliations. Individuals make exceptions just for those with whom they share their own religious faith – it is the others who are deluded. '*I* have knowledge and certainty in my faith, *you* have beliefs, *they* have superstitions, the past has mythologies.' Lucy Mack Smith, mother of the founding prophet of Mormonism, Joseph Smith, Jun., summed this up:

> If I am a member of no church all religious people will say I am of the world;
> and if I join some one of the different denominations, all the rest will say I am
> in error. No one will admit that I am right, except the one with which I am
> associated. This makes them witnesses against each other.[2]

Even my copy of the invaluable classic language reference work *Roget's Thesaurus* lists Christian and Judaic terms under 'Revelation' and those of every other religion (including Mormonism) under 'Pseudo-Revelation'.

Extended to narratives of religions' origins and development, which include divine messages, intervention by deities and the description of supernatural events, the believer may accept all or most of those within their own tradition, while dismissing those of other religious groups as delusions or even fabrications. A secular critical scholarly approach to the narratives associated with a religious group, such as those I outline in this book, merely takes the argument one stage further, to apply equally to all religions. Readers coming from a position of faith may consider the critical approach appears reasonable, even necessary when applied to religions other than their own. A secular and materialist approach such as I adopt assumes that all history, including the creation and development of religion, is exclusively the work of human actors that lies within the setting of a natural world that operates by the laws of nature – the physical and biological properties of the Earth, with no intervention of divinities and supernatural beings, no messages from another world, no supernatural events. To those who say that this is as dogmatic a position as the most extreme religious views, I would say: yes, exactly! Intentionally and deliberately so.

Studying religion on the basis that there is no active deity involved is the opposite of theistic beliefs, and is therefore realistically described as a-theistic. That is different from an a-gnostic approach, since agnosticism by definition 'does not know' if a deity exists and leaves the options open. Such atheism adopted as a necessary working hypothesis is the reverse of Pascal's wager in his 17th-century *Pensées*. There, in essence, Pascal proposed that since one cannot rationally ascertain the existence or non-existence of God, a commitment to adopt and live in line with a belief that God exists is a good choice, since the potential rewards (eternal life) if he exists exceed any minor inconveniences if he does not.

In practice, a non-religious approach to historical process would not conflict with *deism*, the belief in a non-interventionist deity as prime mover and creator of the processes observed in the natural world. In a secular narrative, all preaching, religious texts, announced visions and experiences derive from the complexity of the human personality, and religious movements are social phenomena.

On that basis, there were no golden plates buried in 19th-century New York State for the Mormon founder to uncover; the Prophet Muhammad ibn 'Abdullah did not fly through the sky on a horse overnight from Arabia to Jerusalem in the 7th century; Yeshua (the name by which Jesus was known in his lifetime) was not born to a virgin mother and did not return to life after execution in 1st-century Judaea before a bodily ascent; the Red (or Reed) Sea did not part to let a group of fleeing Israelites pass through before closing down on Pharaoh's troops in the mid-2nd millennium BCE; Siddhartha Gautama (the Buddha) did not levitate, or produce water and fire to reinforce the power of his message. This is different from scepticism (which is merely doubts about such stories): it is a starting point to the secular materialist approach that these events were not historical, that they did not happen.

Miracles are found in the narratives of most religions. In Christianity miracles were reported as performed not only by Yeshua and then by individual apostles, but also by a succession of lay men and women through two millennia. A line can be drawn between miracles, which a secular materialist viewpoint would not accept (e.g. the dead brought back to life), and episodes of faith healing, where someone believes their symptoms to be relieved through their own religious beliefs or the actions of a religious leader, and which continue today.

Some scholars feel they are able to separate their personal commitment to a religious faith from their writing and teaching on the history of their own religion, suggesting they can take a secular interpretation in the latter. Such an approach can be found among Protestant Christian authors, some of whom are cited in Chapter 4. I respect their wish and commitment to do so, although I find it difficult to understand how, say, in one context Yeshua can be described as a reforming Jewish preacher, and in another as the Son of God (or God the Son), who experienced resurrection and bodily ascension. A text is either the word of a god or the word of a human being. It is more common for different Christian and Jewish commentators to identify which parts of the Tanakh (Old Testament) they consider to be historically factual, which to be intentionally allegorical and which to be theologically inspired myths. But such ambiguities are not uncommon: the leading research physicist who holds a lay position in the local church; or the political leader who leads a community in praying to God to bring rain, then proceeds with policies on the assumption that God will not. In this book I note that many of the assumptions of historical events on which religions have based their narratives do not stand up to scientific and academic scrutiny. Those who feel able to distinguish the 'religion of faith' from the 'religion of history' will not be disturbed by this.

Many contributions to critical scholarship on the early history of Judaism, Christianity and Mormonism have come from scholars working from within those traditions. Secular scholars have been vigorous in exploring all aspects of these religions and others – the study of the thousands of New Religious Movements of the modern era is a vibrant academic field of its own. But a view surfaces from time to time that it is not legitimate for non-Muslim 'western' scholars to apply to the early history of Islam the same critical approach applied to other faiths. In part that may reflect practical nervousness: fundamentalists in different religions express their hostility to critical perspectives in very different modes, though many will merely ignore them. Part of the anxiety about outsider views of Islam is traced back to reactions to Orientalism: the approach that came from writers in Christian-dominated cultures with a distanced and even colonialist attitude to societies in the Muslim-dominated world. But the criticism has remained despite the changed intellectual environment of the non-Muslim world. The response by a leading American scholar of early Islam could apply equally to the study of any religion's history:

> I want to make clear that as historians and scholars we must pursue our researches wherever they lead us, even if the results of our explorations seem unsettling to some – whether they be fellow scholars or believing Muslims

4

… the nature of the historian's craft requires that he or she remain intellectu-
ally free to challenge, to doubt, and if necessary to reject, the validity of any
historical source, without exception…. Whereas the believer accepts without
question a certain vision of the past, the historian accepts without question
nothing about the past; his 'faith' is an absolute faith in his methods, not in
the results of his analysis, even though he may be able to defend his deductions with compelling logical argument, for he realizes that his results remain
contingent pending the discovery of new relevant evidence, or the cogent
reevaluation of existing evidence.[3]

Interpreting religion

Is a non-religious approach to religion, taking a secular look at religions'
origins, therefore anti-religious? Not necessarily, I suggest.

Religion can mean many things. In his 2016 BBC Reith Lectures, philosopher Kwame Anthony Appiah distinguished within religion: practice
(what you do); community or fellowship (those you do it with); and the body
of beliefs (the source of most dispute).[4] He noted how much even formal
religion shifts its beliefs over time and place. Religion as a form of community
or identity is how it appears most commonly in past and present – a polytheistic society, a Muslim country, an Orthodox Jewish community, a Roman
Catholic family. The introduction of a new cult or sect or belief system can
have an impact much greater than just the spiritual and personal.

The faith of an individual may permeate their daily lives, both as inner
life and in personal or family rituals: prayers towards Mecca, offerings at the
domestic Hindu shrine, a family meal on Shabbat eve, a spoken Christian
grace said before a meal. An individual's faith may give them comfort in illness
or loss, a source of hope reinforced by prayer, and a set of ethical values. Many
families in western societies who bypass the Christian ritual of baptism and
use a secular celebrant for a wedding may still turn to religion for a ritual to
mark a death, in the absence of a suitably comforting alternative. A contemporary Japanese pattern is to favour a Shinto shrine at birth, a Buddhist priest
at death and some elements of Christian symbolism at weddings.

At another level, the local institutions of religion perform essential social
services. British writer and philosopher Alain de Botton pointed out the many
benefits of an affiliation to an organised religious group that are lost to those
who have abandoned or grown up without formal religion.[5] These include
especially the social and family networks available through religious affiliation when a family moves residence (although these may also reflect ethnic
identity). But equally a minority religious identity can be socially alienating: a

non-Anglican family moving into an 18th-century English village would have faced prejudice and hostility. It helps to describe religion as being composed of different elements and meanings.

Religious affiliation plays a huge role in social, economic and political history. A religious organisation affiliated to the state (or a religious organisation that *is* the state) has immense power, and a power that often has not served humanity well. For example, God's support is often invoked by both sides as they go into battle. Since religious, language and ethnic or national affiliations may partly or even substantially align, we cannot simplify historical (or modern) conflicts as being between one set of religious believers and another. But customary shorthand refers to past or present conflicts in terms of Buddhists oppressing Muslims, Muslims oppressing Christians, Christians oppressing Jews, Protestants fighting Catholics, Catholics fighting Orthodox, Sunni Muslims fighting Sh'ia Muslims, and everyone fighting heretics and break-away groups.

A religion may emerge as that of the ruling group (the cults in city states of the ancient Middle East, for example). A cult may be the cult of the rulers (the deification of Roman emperors, which played a role in the wider Roman Empire). A ruler in one society may be considered deified in another – my brief introduction in Addis Ababa to the then Emperor of Ethiopia Haile Selassie, revered in the Rastafarian movement, was my only direct encounter with the divine. Islamic and Christian monarchs held positions as defenders of the faith as well as rulers of the faithful. Church and state have rarely been two independent historical entities.

A book on this topic can be written and published at this time without official censure because the power and authority of religious institutions and their links with the state are weak. Those of us in western Europe and Australasia are living in societies that are often described as post-Christian, but ones in which the European culture we have inherited (in art, architecture, literature – but also in law and values) requires an understanding of its Judaeo-Christian heritage. Church attendance among those who consider themselves Christians has fallen dramatically in recent decades, while members of other religions and those who declare themselves to be of 'no religion' have grown in number. Definitions and statistical measures differ in reliability, but one survey categorises 11% of the United Kingdom population as 'highly religious', and similarly 12% of the populations of both France and Germany. In Australia the number declaring themselves to be of no religion in the census grew from 13% in 1986 to 30% in 2016, while the proportion declaring themselves to be Christian fell from 73% to 52%, and monthly church attendance fell to 16%. In Canada 29% described themselves as having no religious affiliation. In the United States, by contrast, religious adherence has been more strongly maintained, with only 30% reporting that they did not attend a religious service at least once a month.[6]

An imaginary narrative shows the complexity of how religion's different definitions can still play a role in our society. A man outside a building shoots and kills two people he does not know before being arrested. The parents of one victim react in shock and are helped with medication. The parents of the other turn to prayer, as they often do, and find real comfort from their religious faith. They also get help and succour from the clergyman in a local church to which they belong, although he is someone who now sees his role primarily as social service, having lost his beliefs in much of the detailed theology he once accepted. Political leaders speak out against the shooting and call for all to join in prayer for the victims and their families. This enrages many members of the public, who say forcefully what is needed from their leaders is not prayer but gun control, action against prejudice or more expenditure on mental health. An evangelical church leader from outside the area causes further outrage by saying that an attack like this, which took place outside a nightclub frequented exclusively by the gay community, is yet another indication of God's anger with moral departures from his will. At his court trial the shooter states plainly that he was instructed to undertake the shooting by an angel who had appeared several times with divine messages for him; as a believer he had no choice but to obey. In court the psychiatrist who has analysed the shooter's mental illness recommends he be considered incompetent to plead. Then this scientific specialist takes the oath to tell the truth in court, 'so help me God', with one hand on a copy of the Holy Bible.

Religion, then, can imply a personal faith of succour and ethics and daily practice, or a community sharing their religion in the rituals and association of a structured institution, or a large-scale organisation that is close to, or part of, the state and a dominant element in the body politic. But religions also typically involve acceptance of an historical narrative of events confidently believed to have occurred.

Devotees of the revelations declared in one religion have often described the revelations declared in another religion as deliberately fraudulent. A secular perspective does not need to consider those who proclaim a message from divine sources to be consciously falsifying their experience; a seer's doubts may be eroded once others accept his vision. There are a large number of individuals in every society and at every time who believe that they are receiving messages from God or other divine sources (or sometimes that they

7

are themselves divine), experiencing what the unsympathetic would label religious delusions. A minority of these will persuade their family members that their experiences are indeed divinely inspired, and just a few of these will secure a similar belief and following outside their family, spreading the message or revelation by oral or written means. In the majority of cases a group of followers of such a 'cult' will disappear in less than a generation, many on the death of the individual leader. A few may be acknowledged and incorporated within existing movements. Only a tiny minority develop to be what we can describe as a new religion or religious movement.

History, archaeology and religion

I use material from history and archaeology, geography and linguistics in the chapters that follow. Much of this book focusses on contributions from historical scholarship and historians' debates about evidence, interpretation and approaches. Documents form the core of evidence in such debates, and I discuss the authenticity and role of such texts in individual chapters. It is important to remember the very different categories of historical texts from the ancient and medieval worlds. Some are commercial records – commerce was probably the initial stimulus for the development of writing – in which an agreement between two parties for provision of goods or services was placed on record, whether in cuneiform on a clay tablet or in ink letters on a papyrus sheet, parchment or paper. A second category comprises administrative documents and records of the state or local authorities. A third category is graffiti, effectively 'X was here', from a trader or soldier or passing traveller.

Many texts were intended to establish the authority of the state or to advance the message of a religious leadership (and sometimes both). This is something a critical reading describes as 'propagandist' in purpose and impact, even though the authors may have believed that they were recording facts. Historical documents tell us a lot about the outlook of the time at which they were manufactured. Many texts (and especially religious documents) were copied repeatedly from earlier texts, with a mixture of copyists' errors, changes, combinations and omissions, all of which reflect the different stages in their history. If we know or can reliably determine the dates of their original composition, they can tell us something about the ideas of those times, or even earlier if they record an earlier oral narrative.

But the contents of such texts are rarely unbiased accounts of historical processes and events produced by a dispassionate scribe. Any document has to be interrogated on its purpose, not just its contents. Many modern writers on a specific religion, coming from within the confines and framework of that religion, have set themselves limits to how tough they make that interrogation. As a recent study of early Christian manuscripts notes, when it considers how we should examine and date such objects, an early document is an archaeological object whose date and context can be considered with archaeological questions and methods.[7]

Contemporary debates on the histories of Israel and Judah/Yehud through the later 2nd and 1st millennia BCE have often been defined in terms of an ideological split between 'minimalists' and their opponents. Minimalists are seen as sceptical about using biblical sources for historical description, ascribing typically late dates to the writing or completion of Old Testament (Tanakh) texts. Their opponents criticise them for ignoring the potential of those texts for writing the history of the region, the Jewish people and the Jewish religion. Extreme minimalists assume that historical statements in the biblical texts are true only when there is external evidence that confirms that; their opponents assume that the biblical texts are reliable unless proved otherwise, but they too range widely in how much they accept or are prepared to use in an historical account.

These have been cast as ideological positions reflecting preconceived approaches. But there is a strong argument that all good historical work should be consciously 'minimalist' in the sense that it should not assume the accuracy of a narrative of historical event or process without adequate support. In a court of law that would be corroborative evidence from independent sources supported by trustworthy expert witnesses. Wishing that something was reliable or true does not make it so; saying we have to make do with what texts we have does not change possibility into probability or certainty. A commercial text may be taken as a mutually agreed statement of a contract, but a propagandist text in imperial policy or a declaration of religious guidance is there for a different purpose. Those who edited the books of the Tanakh or wrote the Greek New Testament gospels or who transmitted the *hadith* of the Prophet Muhammad were not seeking to record objective history for scholarly purposes. Why would they? Nor were they seeking to create a fraudulent document and deceive. They were engaged in advancing the religion to which they were faithfully committed.

Historians examine, dissect, compare and interpret the documents available to them and the context of their creation and recovery. The work of scholars involves constant debate, reassessment and the interchange of ideas. In my discussion on the sources, the traditional and revised historical narratives of religions' origins and early history, I have sought to indicate where there is a range of contemporary views, some complementary, but often competing in lesser or greater details. However, I have also suggested what I find the most persuasive and compelling in these arguments, consistent with the evidence brought forward. In that I am influenced by many decades in history and archaeology, reading and research, writing and editing and publishing. Others may read the same discussions and come to different conclusions. Without continuing debate there would be no need for continuing scholarship.

Some of my consideration, and indeed interest in researching and writing this book, involves a continuing engagement with the related topics of the invention of tradition and imagined histories, on which I have written two books and a number of papers published in international academic journals.[8] This reflects a prejudice for truth in the sense of events in the human story, interrogated and revised by the tools of investigative scholarship. While I recognise that all historical scholarship is written within the social and ideological context of its authors, there remains a difference from invented traditions and imagined histories, which serve primarily to reinforce or establish a political, ethnic or religious viewpoint. The writings that develop and expand over time within religious movements may be the most lasting and powerful in the latter category.

Historical documents tell us what people think; archaeological data show us what people do. Whereas new historical documents are rarely uncovered for the periods discussed in this book, there is a constant flow of new data available from archaeology. There is caution about the anomalous: an unexpected date requires testing, an object in the 'wrong' stratum inspires checks, a new kind of find or enquiry stimulates research to match it. A broad interpretation in archaeology requires evidence from a range of sites and finds.

Archaeological surveys show how people have fitted into their landscape and used its economic potential at different times. Excavations plot human settlement and activity in detail, and reveal trends in material culture. Studies of objects found on sites explore technology and help explain the context for that technology, while studies of animal bones, plant remains and pollen grains reveal economic life. Increasingly the work of bioarchaeologists provides information on migration, family relations, health, diet and more from human skeletal remains.

An archaeological site with 100 features of construction and settlement, 1,000 small finds, 5,000 animal bones and 50,000 potsherds may still not prove as useful to historical reconstruction as a single inscribed stone monument. But overall, archaeological evidence, continuing studies and debates can supplement and balance historical studies, and at times refute assumptions based only on a few textual records.

While archaeology can provide information on the society and cultural background in which different religious movements began and spread, the 'archaeology of religion' is a problematic concept. Most archaeology focusses on the material world and the clearly functional. Religion as a matter of spirituality or beliefs can rarely be studied unless it shows up clearly as a temple or artwork or in burial practices. A classic witticism about archaeology suggests that an object, building feature or construction that cannot be explained is traditionally described as 'ritual'. The division between the material and the religious, between the functional and non-functional, is largely a perception of the rationalist modern world.[9] If religion forms part of identity and cultural identity sets the norms by which social and economic behaviour operates, then distinguishing an 'archaeology of religion' may be unrealistic.

Two interesting themes emerge in these chapters. One is the 'absence of archaeology'. We do not know whether Mecca was indeed an important trading town of 6th-century Arabia, or received its emphasis in the Islamic traditions because it had been the home of the Prophet Muhammad. Excavation could clarify this issue, but excavation does not take place. In Jerusalem, archaeology is forbidden on the Temple Mount (the Haram al-Sharif), where tradition places a mighty Temple of Solomon. Commentators have observed that the absence of archaeology there may suit two religious or political groups: Muslims, who fear such a temple might be found, and Jews, who fear it might not.

Another important theme is the 'archaeology of absence'. Where there has been a substantial amount of archaeological work undertaken, reported and discussed, it is significant if something is found not to exist. So the archaeology of the first period of Muslim conquests in western Asia does not show major changes in the material culture of the conquered people, indicating greater continuity than once perceived. The persistence, even extension, of Christian and Jewish religious buildings through the time of the first Islamic conquests gives us an image of the impact of the arrival of the Muslim armies that contrasts with the once held assumption of a rapid imposition of religious and associated cultural changes. Christianity, whose earliest documents are ascribed to authors in the first two centuries CE, is otherwise archaeologically invisible throughout that period, suggesting Christians were a small community before the 3rd century, though they had become highly significant by the early 4th century. And although the Achaemenids ruled the region around Jerusalem where the post-exilic Jewish religion was developed, there was no sign there of those Persian rulers' adherence to the Zoroastrian cult of Ahura Mazda.

Reports of archaeological field surveys and excavations typically separate detailed descriptions of what they have found and recorded from discussion and interpretations, which are open to debate, especially as new questions develop. These exist within a framework of nationality, ethnicity, gender, class, time, place, ideology – and, yes, religious affiliation. This does not make archaeology unreliable; it means that archaeological interpretation itself may need examining in terms of the background of the author, and it also means that some key questions may not be asked in a particular time and place. Some in archaeology have argued that multiple alternative interpretations of the past from different sources can have equal value, yet, in practice, when scientific approaches are bypassed in favour of subjective and unscientific hypotheses, the enthusiasm for such alternatives is diminished and the word 'pseudoarchaeology' is invoked.[10]

Our understanding of major events and processes in human history, such as the beginnings of major religions, can best be understood when we look critically at historical sources and their interpretation, and bring in the evidence, analyses and discussions of scientific archaeology. In this book, I seek to explore what that understanding is today for the origins and development of five major religious movements, and what they might suggest about religions more broadly.

The structure of this book

In the chapters that follow I consider the framework in which individual religious movements began and spread to other regions. Each religion emerged in a distinct social, economic and political setting, in a framework where other religions and other religious movements existed, and in a landscape of human settlement past and present. These issues can inform and illuminate how, when and where a religion originated and gained followers. So in this book I ask what is the key narrative? What are our textual sources on the origins of the religion? What were the broader historical background and the environment of other religious activities and ideas? What was the geographical setting?[11] And what was the material world of the societies in which the religion originated and developed?

I am focussing on religions that belong in the tradition we broadly classify as monotheistic rather than polytheistic: the worship of a single, all-powerful deity. The major feature of Islam is the emphasis on Allah, the single god, with a message revealed to his final Prophet in a region said to be then widely polytheistic. Mormonism identifies itself as a branch of the Christian faith. Christianity has had many theological and organisational schisms, including disputes over the nature and concept of the Trinity as a three-in-one deity, but it remains a monotheistic faith. Judaism developed from worship of Yahweh alongside other gods, to adherence to Yahweh alone among the gods, and finally to the belief that Yahweh is the only God. We have less evidence of the stages that led to Zoroastrianism, which identifies Ahura Mazda as the powerful and benevolent deity alongside his antithesis, Angra Mainyu (Ahriman), but the development of the cult from an early focus on this deity in a polytheistic framework seems most likely.

These religions are different from those from South Asia and East Asia: chiefly Hinduism and Jainism, Buddhism, Taoism and Confucianism, and, later, Sikhism as well as many younger religious movements that trace their ancestry to earlier sources. These belong outside the monotheistic tradition, though at times elements of syncretism may have emerged, combining elements of ritual and belief from different religions. Where these Asian religions have individuals associated with their development, their inspiration does not typically come from direct contact with, identification with or dictation of a text from a divine being. Fascinating though their origins and development are, they lie outside of the subject matter of this book.

I have chosen to start from the modern era and work backwards in this narrative, just as an archaeologist excavates down from the modern and known, layer by layer to the deeper past. I believe this helps us interpret older phenomena and narratives. If we seek to understand religious development from old to new, starting with Old Testament (Tanakh) prophets such as Elijah and Elisha (or even earlier figures, like Moses) we would be confronting a profoundly unfamiliar world: distant in time and society, in which fire could be called down from heaven, the dead raised, waters divided and a prophet (like Elijah) could ascend in a whirlwind. Noting how New Religious Movements begin in the 'ordinariness' of more familiar times, we can track back to earlier movements with less of a sense of wonder and puzzlement.

There have been many thousands of New Religious Movements in the modern era, with their own prophets, followers, successes and failures, and sometimes foundational documents. We could have begun with Scientology or Falun Gong, Jehovah's Witnesses or Theosophists, Cao Dai or the Unification Church, the Shakers or the Branch Davidians, the Christadelphians or Kemetists or a thousand more. There are several reasons for my choice to describe the beginnings and first spread of Mormonism (the Church of Jesus Christ of Latter-day Saints) as a basis and model for considering earlier major religions.

Firstly, the Mormons belong in the linear development of monotheism, with proclaimed links back to more conventional Christianity and to the Old Testament (though not to Islam). Then they have a strong and clear record in accessible printed sources from their very beginning. Also, their origins are marked by the activities of an individual prophet, and the publication of a foundational document in *The Book of Mormon*. To modern 'western' readers, the time and place where the movement began feel less unfamiliar than the Middle East of many centuries ago. And, most significantly, they were not just a phenomenon of one time and place but built up a substantial following which has developed into many millions across the world today. Other details in the story of Mormon origins have comparable elements with older religions, as discussed in the concluding chapter. If we come to terms with how an individual prophet, document and movement began in New York State in the 1830s and 1840s we might find earlier movements a little less enigmatic.

The founder of Mormonism was compared to the founder of Islam in hostile terms by his Christian critics. In considering the origins of Islam, I note modern approaches that have questioned some of the traditional interpretations. The remarkable spread of Islamic power out of Arabia in the 7th century CE has been the subject of much historical study but the archaeology of the period of conquests has provided nuanced pictures that contradict older views.

The founding texts of both Islam and Christianity reflect the contents of the Tanakh (or Old Testament), the literary canon of Judaism. Interpretations of Christianity as a reform movement within Judaism, set in 1st-century CE Galilee then Judaea, contrast with the success it achieved among non-Jews in the eastern Roman Empire. There the theology developed by Paulos (Saint Paul) and the outreach by him and his associates had a more lasting impact than the Judaea-based apostles. Archaeology can tell us a great deal about the context of Galilee and Jerusalem in which Yeshua (Jesus) preached and died but shows little sign of the first two centuries of the religion's slow growth and development.

The influence of Judaism on Christianity and Islam lay especially in its monotheism. Monotheistic Judaism itself originally developed from a cult in the Palestine region, which had seen Yahweh as one among many gods, but a god who required exclusive adherence by his chosen people. Jewish monotheism – its practices, central temple and religious leadership – was forged between the late 6th and the 4th century BCE by a group in Jerusalem, within a marginal area of the Persian Empire, who traced their background to an exile in Babylonia imposed by Neo-Babylonian conquerors. Not least, this group brought together and edited the books of the Tanakh, which would go on to form the canonical works of the monotheistic Jewish faith.

Now with a relatively small following, Zoroastrianism is considered by many as the oldest monotheistic religion, with core texts and a founding prophet, Zarathushtra, that some place as far back as the later 2nd millennium BCE, while others consider he lived in Central Asia in the 7th-6th centuries BCE. The powerful deity of Zoroastrianism, Ahura Mazda, was the cult of the Persian Achaemenids, under whose rule the Jerusalem group developed the Tanakh and their Second Temple Judaism. Influences from Zoroastrianism have been identified in passages of the Tanakh and within Christian ideas. Yet the origins, dating and nature of early Zoroastrianism remain shrouded in enigmas and subject to passionate debates. I explore these questions and ask what light history and archaeology bring. Mysteries and uncertainties remain.

The final chapter in this book considers what the origins and spread of religious movements may have in common, and where they differ. While seeking to avoid reductive conclusions about the nature of major religions and their first stages, I suggest some themes worth further consideration.

Given the broad coverage of this book I have necessarily summarised and simplified a number of issues and arguments. The notes at the end of the book can lead readers to consider a broader range of material, and may stimulate them to take issue with the perspectives of this text and writers I have cited. In surveying and bringing together ideas and information from a wide range of authors, researchers and experts, I have encountered greater detail and discussion on topics I knew well; much information on topics I did not know; and significant new material to challenge and alter my understanding of topics I thought I knew. It is my hope that readers will find this journey as interesting and exciting as I have.

Chapter 2

Frontiers of place and belief:
Mormon origins and journeys

New religions, the individuals credited with their beginnings, and their foundational texts are not just phenomena of ancient worlds and the distant past. Among the religious developments of the modern era, the Church of Jesus Christ of Latter-day Saints – the Mormons – is one of the most successful, with millions of members throughout the world today. In 1846–1847, tens of thousands of adherents of the Church of Jesus Christ of Latter-day Saints took themselves away from their own societies to create a New Zion by the Great Salt Lake. When the Mormon pioneers travelled west they found a niche in the lands of Ute and Shoshone Native Americans to occupy and build their city and temple. The Mormons were the most prominent and lasting of the new religious movements of the 'Second Great Awakening'; as a part of the westward spread of white families in North America they were the most American of religions. The Mormon movement had reached such substantial growth in just 17 years, since the publication of *The Book of Mormon* in western New York State in 1830. The new movement was founded and organised, and its founding document was dictated, by 24-year-old farmer's son Joseph Smith, Jun., in a region regularly visited by evangelical preachers and religious innovators. Less than two generations earlier this had been Iroquois territory; *The Book of Mormon* gave a special role and history to Native Americans in God's plan, and a special role to those who followed its teaching and the new Church. Mormon origins, then, lie in two settings. One was a land with its newly arrived residents looking for new commitments of faith in this new society. The other was a region well beyond the control and culture of the United States, a New Zion set in the midst of indigenous peoples.

In the newly industrialising world of the early 19th century, the United States of America began a phase of massive economic progress, accompanied by the westward spread of white settlement. But this was also an era when new and sometimes independent forms of revivalist Protestant Christianity were preached, part of what is known as the 'Second Great Awakening'; an earlier burst of evangelism had been seen in the 1730s and 1740s. There were travelling preachers and unconventional prophets, individuals proclaiming their personal revelations and the right path to God, especially influential in rural areas, which were beginning to define their identity. Some had an impact locally and even further afield before their influence waned. Others developed into successful international religious organisations, like the Seventh Day Adventists or the Church of Jesus Christ of Latter-day Saints – the Mormons. The Mormon faith, whose origins lay in western New York State in the 1820s through to the 1840s, became a world religion. Today, the Church of Jesus Christ of Latter-day Saints, with its organisational and spiritual centre in Utah, is a widespread movement of some 16 million members.

Mormon origins lay in a somewhat liminal time and place. Western New York State sat between the lands long developed by white people and newer regions acquired after independence of the United States. Fifty years before the publication of *The Book of Mormon* in 1830, this land had been the territory of Iroquois farmers; 50 years later it was part of the rich industrialised world. The Mormon religion began in the farmland occupied a generation earlier by the white settlers of the United States, though its development took its members far beyond those frontiers in order to thrive. While much of America was forging its destiny as a strong modern nation trading on equal terms with Europe and indeed globally, Mormonism and other new movements reflected and sought earlier and simpler forms of religion and identity.

Although Mormon roots lay in Christianity, its proclaimed sources were not just the familiar biblical narratives but also new texts dictated, published and proselytised by Joseph Smith, called in the early Mormon writings Joseph Smith, Jun. (rather than the modern Jr), to distinguish him from his father Joseph Smith. The Church of Jesus Christ of Latter-day Saints (or LDS) is commonly referred to as the Mormons, after the founding document, *The Book of Mormon*. Its new texts placed the Americas solidly within but also beyond the narratives of the older Judaeo-Christian tradition. Describing an ancient history of migration from Israel to the Americas, the book gives a special respect and role to the physical land of America, implying a place where faith could overcome the spiritual failings of European settlement there.

Mormonism began in an area where Native Americans were no longer a threat to white settlement. Their historical occupation was visible in scattered artefacts and 'Indian mounds'. Mormonism moved on to Utah, an area then still occupied by Native Americans. To readers of *The Book of Mormon*,

American Indians were the descendants of migrants from Israel, given a spiritual and central role in the history of God's plan for humanity. The presence or absence of Native Americans is important in the material and historical context of the development of Mormonism.

Joseph Smith, Jun. (like Muhammad ibn 'Abdullah before him) was both theological innovator and organisational driver. He led the new religious movement for 14 years until his death in 1844. Thereafter others led the movement in theological development, in organisational development and, importantly, in regional development as a large group of Latter-day Saints moved west to settle in what would become Utah.

The world in which Mormonism originated less than two centuries ago may appear to us more familiar than that of ancient religions, and we have the advantage of more independent historical data on Mormon origins. But with its core in a source text and a newly inspired organisation we can draw some parallels with older religions. Its influences were from more conventional (and specifically Protestant) Christianity, just as Islam and Christianity reflect a monotheistic Judaic heritage, Greco-Roman gods echo Egyptian deities and Buddhism emerged in a Hindu context.

Christianity is derived from a marginal area of the Roman Empire but became a metropolitan and imperial creed. Islam with its origins in the arid Arabian Peninsula soon came to rule and in due course convert the cities of the Middle East, Central Asia and North Africa. Mormonism began in areas that had until recently been pioneering farms and townships; it then moved to flourish beyond the contemporary boundaries of the United States in what was to become the Utah Territory, and later the State of Utah. Between Mormon origins in upstate New York and the settlement in Utah, increasing numbers of Church followers moved west: first to Kirtland, Ohio, then to Independence, Clay County, and then to create a new settlement they named Far West, in Missouri, and to Nauvoo, Illinois, before the final journey westwards, to the Great Salt Lake area.

If it is valid and useful to consider the material conditions within which a new religious movement began, this should apply to recent as well as ancient faiths. Other chapters of this book consider the material context in which new religions emerged, and such an approach can be applied to a recent movement like Mormonism too. Understanding Mormon origins requires us to study the specifics of time and place. We can consider the broader framework of North American history within (or despite) which this new religion emerged, and the material world and changing nature of western New York State and the subsequent centre of Mormon growth.

Joseph Smith, Jun. and *The Book of Mormon*

When Joseph Smith, Jun. was born in Sharon, Vermont, in December 1805 (as the fourth of nine children) the independent American nation was just 29 years old, its 13 states having now expanded to 17 with the statehood of Kentucky and Vermont, Tennessee and Ohio. On both his father's side and his mother's side he was descended from long-established North Americans: families who had migrated there in the 17th century.

Farming in Vermont faced poor years in 1814–1816, with crop failure followed by a year of 'no summer'. The Smith family, who had earlier tried leaving Vermont for New Hampshire, set out in late 1816 (Joseph Jun. being almost 11 years old) some 320 miles (510 km) from Norwich in Vermont westwards to the promising area of western New York State, which had been opened up for individual settlement about 25 years before. In the fast-growing US economy if this was pioneering it was relatively prosperous pioneering; despite the growth of farming, much of the area was still heavily forested. The Smith family settled first in Palmyra, a settlement of 2,200 people in Ontario County, near the route where construction was about to start for the Erie Canal, linking the Hudson River to Lake Erie.[1] Within two years they would leave the rapidly expanding Palmyra to acquire 100 acres of land to farm two miles (3 km) south between the townships of Palmyra and Manchester, clearing and fencing the land, planting orchards, tapping sugar maples and growing cereals.[2] They lived through the US economic depression of 1818–1821, and in 1822 began building an improved wooden-frame house.

Joseph Jun. was home schooled, with the study of the Bible an important part of that. His mother and brothers were active in the Palmyra Presbyterian Church in the 1820s, but the town had competing Protestant Christian groups.[3] While Joseph Jun. was influenced by them it seems he and his father did not adopt a firm commitment to any denomination, though Joseph Jun. was part of a debating club that met in the school house. Flexible allegiance to different competing Protestant churches was far from unusual in this context, with a storm of itinerant preachers and evangelical excitement.

Amid other youthful activities, in 1822 Joseph Jun. acquired (reportedly while digging a well) what would be described as a 'seer stone', described as enabling him to see things invisible to normal vision. This gave him a role with treasure hunters in the area seeking the location of a supposed ancient Spanish mine thought to contain hidden gold and silver. Lack of success in this project led to Joseph Jun.'s court sentence as 'a disorderly person and an imposter' in 1826.[4]

Meanwhile, Joseph's parents had run into difficulties: financial issues led them to sell their farm in December 1825, though they continued as tenant farmers. Joseph Jun. left to work in southern New York State in 1826, and then returned to Manchester in 1827. That year he married Emma Hale of Harmony, just across the state line in north-east Pennsylvania (whom he had met on a treasure-hunting excursion). Harmony, now part of Susquehanna, had been formalised as a township in 1809. After a period in Manchester Joseph Jun. and Emma moved to Harmony, where they lived in a small house owned by Emma's brother. Here he began narrating the text of *The Book of Mormon* (he could read but seems to have had limited education in writing). After its 1830 publication he bought the house and 13 acres of land.[5]

What was the origin of this text, which formed the basis of the Church he founded? In the histories that he would later narrate to describe the beginnings of the movement, Joseph stated that in 1823 an angelic being named Moroni told him of the 'golden plates'. These were buried three miles (5 km) south-east of his father's farm, but accessibly close to the main road that led from Palmyra via Manchester to Canandaigua, at a site named (Hill) Cumorah. Joseph did not collect these plates and bring them home until September 1827. Now, helped in part by the seer stone, he began to dictate his translation of these plates, which was published as the 584-page *The Book of Mormon* in March 1830. The style of this text is very reminiscent of the 17th-century King James Bible, the 'Authorised Version' of the Church of England, whose authority long remained among US Protestants. The same literary style and its archaisms can be found in the revelations about the organisation of the new Church that Joseph Smith, Jun. subsequently announced and that appeared in the *Book of Commandments* and in the collected *Doctrine and Covenants*.

He would in due course claim that he had already begun receiving direct religious visions from 1820, when he was 14, and that his encounter with Moroni dated from September 1823 (when he was aged 17). In 1820:

> I was enwrapped in a heavenly vision and saw two glorious personages who exactly resembled each other in features, and likeness, surrounded with a brilliant light which eclipsed the sun at noon-day. They told me that all religious denominations were believing in incorrect doctrines, and that none of them was acknowledged of God as his church and kingdom.[6]

The publication of *The Book of Mormon* marked the beginning of active proselytising, which led to the rapid development of a community of believers with Joseph Smith, Jun. as its inspired and highly effective organiser.

Key dates

1783	American Independence
1788	Phelps and Gorham purchase
1805	Joseph Smith, Jun. born
1816	Smith family move to western New York State
1826	Joseph Smith, Jun. court case
1827	Dictation of *The Book of Mormon* begins
1830	Publication of *The Book of Mormon*
1831	Move to Kirtland, Ohio
1839	Establishment of Nauvoo
1844	Death of Joseph Smith, Jun.
1847	Trek to Great Salt Lake

Our sources on the origins and early development of Mormonism are numerous, and have been collected and edited with dedication.[7] Joseph Smith, Jun. compiled his own history of his revelation, and documents from the early converts as well as statements from his family contribute to give us a thorough image of the early stages of the Church, the conflicts it faced and the events that led to the creation of new settlements. The proximity of these documents to the period they describe helps us use Mormonism as a baseline for comparison with older religions, whose source documents, as discussed in later chapters, can be more problematic in constructing reliable history.

Time, nation and the birthplace of Mormonism

Mormonism addresses spiritual questions and the Church organisation sought to develop a practical living movement and community around these. But what was the wider context in which this successful movement was set: the United States of the early 19th century?

At the start of the 19th century the United States was still predominantly an agricultural economy. Its population in 1800 was a third the size of Britain's and a fifth that of France, with just four cities having a population over 20,000. But in the succeeding decades it was to expand in population and area with development accelerated by new roads (especially privately funded turnpike roads), canals linking natural waterways, then steamboats (the first commercially successful operation dates from 1807) and railways (developing after 1827). All of these could bring, at significantly reduced cost, agricultural products to urban markets, manufactured goods to rural areas, and new populations westwards. By 1830 there were 11,000 miles (18,000 km) of turnpike toll roads in the United States.

While Europe was facing the political and economic challenges that followed the Napoleonic Wars of 1803–1815, the United States could redefine itself and prosper. American industrialisation in the northern states generated dramatic economic growth. This growth was not altogether a smooth, however: an economic depression and financial crisis between 1818 and 1821 especially affected the cotton-growing areas of the south. Between 1800 and 1840 the population of the nation grew from 6.3 million to 17.1 million. By 1860, on the eve of the American Civil War of 1861–1865, a country of 31.5 million people had 1.2 million employees in 140,000 manufacturing operations, which represented a third of the nation's economic output, although half by value was concentrated in the states of New York, Pennsylvania and Massachusetts.[8]

Over the half century from 1815, the proportion of the population engaged in agriculture fell from 80% to 50%. Nevertheless, agricultural output (now augmented by mechanisation) continued to be the largest economic sector, albeit changing from 41% of gross national product in 1840 to 35% in 1860. Resistance to the nature and rate of industrialisation came from some whose role had become that of powerless employees (with trade union organisations from as early as the 1830s), and there were politicians' warnings too about the dangers of such rapid development.

But a quite different feature of the first decades of the 19th century was the burst of numerous religious movements, strongest in rural areas and particularly strong in western New York State, the area where Mormonism began. While the Church of Jesus Christ of Latter-day Saints grew to become a major world movement, its origins lay where much other new and extreme religious fervour was developing. And while the origins of Mormonism lay in this time and place, it awaited migration away from upstate New York to build strength and solidity.

By the time the Smith family lived in western New York State the area was no longer a frontier region. Not only relatively prosperous, its society was as well educated as that of other rural regions and was confident in its growth and development.[9] Population growth was marked by a sequence of subdivisions, as new counties were created, divided into administrative districts ('towns') comprising landholdings and a village providing facilities such as shops, schools, churches and services. Thus Manchester was both a district and a village in Ontario County, as was Palmyra (though from 1823 within the new Wayne County): the Smith family lived first in Palmyra then farmed just across the boundary in Manchester. Cumorah, site of the golden plates, lay within the bounds of Manchester.

The pioneer era had brought white residents into the area singly or in small groups but once the land was acquired for settlement in 1789–1790 its population grew rapidly and the infrastructure of American civilisation was firmly and quickly put in place. Whereas the US census of 1800 counted only one-third of a million residents west of the Appalachians, by 1820 this had grown to 2 million.[10]

A key to success was land: the productive capacity of land, the cost of land and the cost of getting goods to market. The value of land would of course increase as it was cleared and farmed, as a neighbourhood grew in prosperity, access improved and the potential income from a farm increased. The rate and nature of territorial disposal had been a hot topic for debate since the first years of the United States. Despite the economic development of the nation and pressure for new land, there were some limitations on its allocation for new settlement. Indeed, a resolution put to Congress in 1829 – the Foot Resolution – proposed to limit the sale of public land (that owned by the federal government) to that surveyed within the original colonies. The resolution was not passed and sales expanded massively. Public land sales totalled 800,000 acres (3,250 km^2) in 1820–1821 and reached a height in 1836 of 20.1 million acres (81,000 km^2); there was another boom in the mid-1850s. The federally legislated minimum acreage of public land that could be bought decreased in stages from 640 acres in 1796 to 40 in 1832, when the minimum price per acre was $1.25.[11]

The areas where the Smith family had settled, though, had not been public lands but were bought and sold as a private deal. In 1788 a group represented by Oliver Phelps and Nathaniel Gorham made a purchase from the Seneca Iroquois of land between Lake Ontario and the Finger Lakes in the western part of New York State, in what would now be no longer the 'Great Western Wilderness'. It was divided up into separate units and disposed of in 1789–1790 and the new farms were acquired by settlers from the east, with village communities developed to service them. The rapidity (and formality) of this development was dramatic: 'Land was abundant, cheap and fertile'.[12] Iroquois retained hunting and fishing rights for eight years, but their settlement now lay to the north and west, although there was one violent clash between a few individuals near Palmyra in 1789. In 1794 another treaty was concluded with the Seneca and other Native peoples.

Although the ready availability of land drew settlers west, its development required forest clearance (of timber that could be sold). The forest was dominated by beech and sugar maple but with many other species present.[13] Hunting also provided food while farms were being developed. The rich soil supported cereals (wheat, rye, barley) as well as vegetables and tobacco and sustenance for livestock. The former Indian trails could be used, and quickly roads were constructed between farms and villages, between communities, and linked to major markets. A generation after the first farms, the Erie Canal would add convenient transport and wealth to the area.

The initial settlement in 1790 brought 1,075 people of European descent (294 families) to the 6 million acres (2.4 million hectares) of the new territory. Twenty years later there were over 15,000 people in a smaller New York county of Ontario, and 10 years later still the further reduced county area had a population of 42,000 and in 1821 some 60,000.[14] The original county of Ontario (including the large towns of Buffalo and Rochester) grew from 1,075 to 217,000 people in the 33 years between 1790 and 1828, when the Smith family had just begun to farm in the region.

The area of Palmyra had particularly good soils and it attracted substantial and committed settlement quickly after the land division of 1790. By 1810 Palmyra 'town' (i.e. farms and village) had about 350 families comprising 2,187 people.[15] A first school was established in 1793, and significantly in 1811 a building was opened to be available to all denominations for their religious meetings. Spafford's *Gazetteer* of 1813, three years before the elder Smith moved into the area, recorded Palmyra as two townships of the Phelps and Gorham purchase, and stated:

> The soil is of a superior quality, and the settlements of a date to give much of farming ease and independence to the inhabitants. There is a large meeting of Quakers, and here is one Episcopal church, with a competent number of common school-houses and schools.[16]

The Episcopal church was a congregation but as yet without its own building.

It was here that Joseph Smith Sr arrived in 1816 to open a shop before he moved to farmland he was acquiring to the south. The first local newspaper, *The Palmyra Register*, began in 1817 and others would soon follow, and by 1830 the local printery was fully able to typeset, print and bind for a paying client *The Book of Mormon*. In fact, the consumption of printed works – newspapers, journals, pamphlets and books – was a central part of the evangelical enthusiasms of the time and region.

The Smith farm lay just within the boundary of Manchester with Palmyra, but as they had begun their stay in Palmyra village that is where their focus lay. The village of Manchester, 11 miles (18 km) to the south of Palmyra, sat on an outlet of Canandaigua Lake, and was initially part of Farmington; it gained its separate identity in 1821. It provided facilities for the local farming

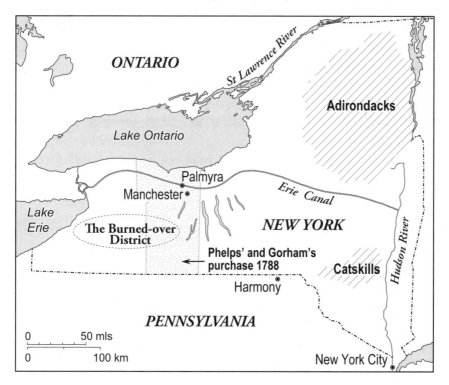

1. The landscape of Mormon origins

community. In 1813 a decision was made to start a school, and a year later a library with 600 volumes was formed.

While it may have been poverty and need that drove the father of Joseph Jun. to western New York in 1816, by 1830 land was cultivated, farms were prospering and the market easy to reach, aided by the turnpike roads and the Erie Canal. The use of the Erie Canal from 1822 and its completion in 1825 brought new strength and opportunity to Palmyra.

In the very year of 1830 that Joseph Smith, Jun. published *The Book of Mormon* a British visitor recorded his journey through the area. John Fowler encountered not angels but farmers and land with rich potential. Travelling up the Hudson River to Albany, his journey took him past the nearby settlement of the Shakers, the followers of English prophet Ann Lee, who had migrated to New York in 1774. He noted the cost of land changing with distance west rather than just with quality. He was struck by the fine public buildings in the western settlements. In the Finger Lakes area he reported good-quality land

and strong commodity prices, and contrasted this picture with a report from 30 years earlier. Canandaigua, to the south of Manchester, gained particular praise: 'The private residences, both in the village and vicinity, are uncommonly elegant, laid out with courts and gardens, and every way worthy of the affluence and respectability of their occupants'.[17] To the north-west he noted a mixture of uncleared land and high-quality farms, before he reached the town of Rochester. But travelling south and west from there the development was more limited: perhaps an image of what had been the Manchester and Palmyra area a generation before. On arriving at Buffalo he noted a Seneca reservation, containing only 'a few hundreds'.

Religion in the Burned-over District

Joseph Smith, Jun. announced his revelation at a time and place of active religious evangelism, to a community and region accustomed to such enthusiasms. His commitment was far from unique, but the lengthy document he dictated and published certainly was, and the passion and organisation he and his immediate followers put into proselytising the new message quickly produced a substantial following.

By the late 1830s and early 1840s the area of Palmyra and Manchester was no longer a pioneering frontier region and no longer one dominated by poor citizens. Palmyra was a confident and even prosperous-looking settlement. It has, though, been suggested that there were elements of economic poverty among individuals drawn to the religious message and new organisation of Joseph Smith, Jun. The willingness of the initial followers to abandon their current homes and travel westwards to new areas implies that the new faith was more powerful than any ties to farm or business.[18] But while a secular and sceptical viewpoint might assume that acceptance of Mormon doctrines arose from ignorance and superstition, it was arguably one more set of alternative beliefs among competing evangelisms of the time, and need not imply a lack of education on the part of those attracted to it.[19]

As an area of comparatively recent development, upstate New York could be said to have combined an energetic community-minded settlement with a non-hierarchical and democratic lien. This showed itself in the lack of obeisance to the structures of the traditional churches, suspicion of Catholicism and, among some, active anti-Masonry. The relatively young age of the populations also played its part, although the United States as a whole was young, with only one in eight people aged over 43 in 1815 and a median age in the nation of 16.[20]

There were formal churches, of course. As noted above, Palmyra village had a church building from 1811, available for use by different religious traditions. Presbyterians were numerous enough to have separate communities in Palmyra and Palmyra West by 1817, with congregations of perhaps 60 people each. Work on an Episcopalian church building began in Palmyra in 1825. The Baptists were active early but did not have their own building until 1841. The Catholic Church came even later: 1848–1849. But a Masonic lodge existed in Palmyra from as early as 1816.[21]

Across the whole western New York region, religious movements were numerous, often independent, individualistic and enthusiastic. Preaching new ideas and placing limited authority on the governing bodies of established churches was the norm – although, as the Mormons found, the framework that allowed new religious passions to be advanced did not necessarily lead to tolerance of their organisational development.

Individuals preached their visions and ideas; followers came and went; people were admired and denounced, welcomed and exiled. They formed part of what is termed the 'Second Great Awakening' – from the very end of the 18th century through to the early decades of the 19th century. The so-called 'First Great Awakening', in the 1730s and 1740s, had wider distribution, incorporating an evangelical Protestant movement in England as well as the movements in the American colonies.

The proportion of the US population who were active church members is estimated to have doubled between 1800 and 1835, with growth especially at the end of that period.[22] Western New York State – far from the urban centres of the United States but no longer a pioneering frontier land – was an especially strong location for these multiple movements. Many of the preachers were young – some very young. Joseph Jun. was just 22–23 years old when he began to dictate the text of *The Book of Mormon*.

The descriptive phrase 'Burned-over district', applied since the later 19th century to describe the area of New York State west of the Catskill and Adirondack mountains in the period 1800–1840, indicates that it was scorched by the fires of competing revivalist faiths and evangelical movements.[23] It is a term that can be used both as praise and as critique of the phenomenon. In his magisterial survey of US history in the period, Daniel Walker Howe has suggested 'The religious revivals of the burned-over district reflected in part a longing for stability, a moral order amidst rapid social change'.[24] In this model the 'ultraists' were seeking a restoration of a supposed early form of religious experience and faith rather than a new and future development of Christianity.

This burst of religious preaching and innovation could arise because of the commitment of the still relatively young United States to religious freedom: the freedom to belong to an established church, or to a newly distinguished denomination, or to act as an independent preacher of faith. The upheavals strengthened after the war with Britain of 1812–1815, and were at their most vigorous in the period 1825–1837, by when the Burned-over District was a region of established farms and townships, a generation or more past its pioneering settlement.[25] The 1825 completion of the Erie Canal brought new prosperity to the area, though to the south and south-west of the canal area farms and communities were not generally so rich. The appeal of the new religious extremes was not so much to the poorest families, but to those established in an area of economic maturity and relative stability. Movements such as Mormonism were not 'frontier' movements.

Residents of the older cities might be more conservative in their institutional loyalties than those living in rural and newer settled areas, but these areas could seem attractive places to which the different Protestant denominations could despatch itinerant preachers. The pattern and familiarity of such preachers could fit alongside individuals who had broken from the orthodoxies of their original affiliation. In such contexts, an appeal to individual salvation could trump that of institutional allegiance; a model of restoration to a supposed early Christianity could outweigh the sophistry of traditional church theology.

During the decades of the Second Great Awakening in the western parts of upstate New York there were Episcopalians, Presbyterians, Methodists, Congregationalists, Baptists, Quakers, Unitarians, Roman Catholics and more. Preachers (sometimes called home missionaries) were sent there from outside the district, notably by Presbyterians, Methodists and Congregationalists. With the rise of evangelical Christianity, splits and schisms took place, new alliances and other external groups gained followers. Rogue members of the existing denominations preached their own path to salvation or exhorted their audiences to new forms of religious experience and declamation. There were Freewill Baptists, Disciples of Christ (also called simply Christians or Christian Connection), Universalists, Arminians, Shakers, Pentecostalists, Calvinists, Mormons, Fourierists, Swedenborgians, Perfectionists, Millerites, faith-healers, spiritualists, proponents of separate communities sharing property or even of 'spiritual wifery', as well as the members of other millenarian movements and unaffiliated or dissenting Evangelical associations. Woven into all this were movements of temperance, anti-Masonry, anti-slavery and social reform.[26]

Originating further east in New York State, former carpenter Robert Matthews travelled and preached under the names of Matthias the Prophet and Joshua the Jewish Minister, inspired by visions he had received in Albany. In 1835 he sought out Joseph Smith, Jun. in Kirtland, Ohio (where the Mormons had settled), and unsuccessfully sought to persuade him of his own mission.[27] To Matthews the New Jerusalem was to be built in western New York.

Preachers and religious movements in the region went beyond appeals to commit to a new degree of faith. There were Pentecostal-style gatherings in which personal links to the divine were demonstrated. There were mass millenarian movements, awaiting an imminent Second Coming of Jesus Christ on Earth, which the Millerites expected for 1843–1844. They could influence each other directly or indirectly: in 1843 a member of the Shaker movement, Philemon Stewart, revealed his own text, which, like that of Mormonism, came from ancient plates buried in a hillside.[28] The origins of today's Seventh Day Adventists can be traced back to millenarian movements in the 1840s.

Evangelical Protestant preachers might have different social impacts in different contexts. In a manufacturing town like Rochester, to the west of Palmyra, a movement of moral uplift among the ordinary working citizens might well suit employers seeking reliable, disciplined and sober employees.[29] That was not a primary role but a by-product of religious enthusiasms in towns, village and countryside.

The revelations proclaimed by Joseph Smith, Jun. in *The Book of Mormon* and his own further preaching and organising led to a movement of remarkable resilience. But they originated in a time and place where 'religious ultraism' was at its peak – extremes of ideas, practices, expectations, beliefs and hopes.[30] This complex was specific to the human geography, the material world and the economy of western New York State in the 1820s, 1830s and 1840s. And while the influence of most preachers came and went, that of Joseph Smith, Jun. had a resilience that led to the mass religious movement of today, despite the initial setbacks it faced.

Iroquois and Indian mounds

Palmyra and Manchester, as part of the Phelps and Gorham purchase of 1788, were on land long settled by the Iroquois, and specifically the Seneca nation (or Onondowaga in Seneca language). For the settlers of European descent in Palmyra and Manchester, the areas' past indigenous occupation would have been irrelevant historical background. They were not pioneer traders and had not themselves negotiated (or seized) land from the Native Americans.

That had been done by others. They were living in part of the United States of America, land now set aside for colonial development in a democratic settler culture of church, state, commerce and education. The American Indian might be an occasional dispossessed figure in the shops and roads but was no threat to the current residents. Native Americans could therefore be given a new role within a Mormon theology.

A white trader in the 17th or earlier 18th century might have viewed Native Americans differently. Iroquois conflict with French adventurers and settlers had led many of them to ally with the British but when such alliances continued during the American Revolution their position weakened as they clashed with the Americans in 1779–1780. A series of meetings and treaties defined and imposed their relationship with the new nation after its birth in 1783, as new boundaries were recognised.

The long tradition of myths about the 'Lost Ten Tribes' of Israel had seen claims in print that the American Indians – or at least some of them – represented such a group.[31] Where *The Book of Mormon* differed was in giving them a conscious role in God's plan and a detailed history of their settlement. The Native Americans were far enough away from a daily presence or threat in Palmyra to be reintroduced in a narrative placing their distant ancestry in North America as a divinely ordained migrant from ancient Israel. But this does imply awareness of the indigenous people on whose former territory Mormonism emerged. The land on which the Smith family settled was traditionally Iroquois: land they had lost over time as a result of military, political and economic factors.

Native Americans and the idea of ancient conflict loomed large in *The Book of Mormon*. In that text, Levi had left Jerusalem in the 6th century BCE and travelled to America by ship. There his descendants became different and sometime warring communities: lighter-skinned Nephites, who fell into unbelief and evil ways; mainly darker-skinned Lamanites, who attacked and slaughtered them and became the ancestors of many Native Americans; Jaredites; and Mulekites. The Nephites built defensive forts of timber palisades on earth mounds but this did not protect them from the aggressions of the Lamanites. Mormon religious goals included not only making a New Zion in North America but converting the descendants of the Lamanites to be part of the new order.

As Hill Cumorah lay at the heart of the spiritual story of pre-settler America, the region of western New York State could provide Mormons with a specific geography.[32] But they found they would need to move westwards to create their own City of Zion. While the settlers expanded westwards they encountered more evidence of the Native American past – the earthworks in the east (from the Hopewell tradition) were familiar and the more dramatic Mound Builder sites further west had long been reported by travellers, though associated with unknown peoples.

If the area of upstate New York might no longer witness conflict between Native Americans and white settlers, it had plentiful evidence as reminders of the American Indians who had occupied it, such as finds of stone arrowheads and pots. Fortified palisaded settlements on high ground were a familiar part of the landscape.[33] Low mounds were recognised as the signs of indigenous inhabitants, with a presumption that these 'Mound Builders' were a race that preceded the historically attested Iroquois.

Burials were uncovered from such sites of indigenous people, and there were many settlers who believed that buried treasure lay within such pre-European sites. Joseph Smith, Jun., armed with his seer stone, was not the only treasure seeker to be active in the area. Excavations such as that underway for the Erie Canal inevitably uncovered pre-European archaeological remains.

Modern archaeological evidence indicates cultural changes in the centuries preceding European occupation. In the period before about 1500 much of the area in western New York held dispersed Iroquois settlements where several families lived together in longhouses grouped in villages of 1,000 people or more, and villages were linked in tribal groups. Horticultural activity (beans, squash and maize especially) was supplemented by fishing and hunting. At some stage before white settler contact – possibly well before – a Confederacy (or league) had been agreed between a group of Iroquois tribes (Seneca, Cayuga, Onondaga, Oneida and Mohawk, to be joined later by the Tuscarora) to end feuding and fighting between them. Archaeological evidence demonstrates the contrast between the five tribes: they were not identical in material culture.

From the mid-16th century European trade goods and French traders had begun to enter the area, as well as Jesuit and Protestant missionaries.[34] The arrival of whites and traded weapons stimulated some return to warfare in the earlier 17th century. Traded goods from white settlement increased substantially from about 1600 and had replaced many indigenous manufactures by 1640.[35] By the mid-18th century the five tribes in the Confederacy could raise almost 2,000 fighting men.[36]

A map drawn up in 1771 is valuable in showing the Iroquois settlements in the area of western New York.[37] An Indian village named Canadasegy lay south of Palmyra, close to Manchester, and an Indian trail ran past it,

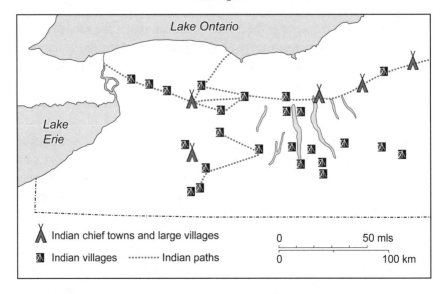

2. Territory of the Iroquois, 1771

linking in the west to a village called Canadaragey, the route parallel to today's Interstate 90 highway. Further villages lay around the region and a major settlement, Cayuga, is marked at the north of Cayuga Lake, the longest of the Finger Lakes.

Archaeological work undertaken at the 16th-century site of Corey on Cayuga Lake gives a nuanced image of the life of Iroquois people before European contact. The settlement was on a defensible stretch of high land with a constructed earth bank and ditch. It was abandoned two centuries before the Cayuga people suffered destruction of their homesteads and crops at the hands of the US Continental Army in 1779. Corey village was organised around specialised zones of activity.[38] Rubbish disposal and a bank and ditch (50 metres long) were at one end; small longhouses built with rigid poles set alongside each other bordered another side of the village, with an area for stone working in its own part of the village. A track led down to areas of garden horticulture and 15 herbs with known medicinal uses were recovered.

When groups had sided with the British against the French, this gave them some stability and power but when some (but not all) sided with the British against the rebellious American colonies their fate was sealed. Villages and crops were destroyed during the conflict and the new US government dictated their future. A population of perhaps 9,000 Iroquois was reduced to around 6,000.[39] Some Iroquois settled in Canada, and those remaining in the United States found their territories condensed to reserves far smaller than their traditional lands and areas of activity. By 1790 the Oneida, Onondaga and Cayuga held only three small reservations, representing 4% of their previous territory.[40] These lands were further reduced over the next two or three decades. Western New York had been occupied by the Seneca branch of the Iroquois, who associated their origins at Canandaigua, some 15 miles (24 km) south of Palmyra.

Iroquois access to land for hunting was now substantially limited. When they did agree to sell land – as the Seneca sold the area that included Palmyra – they received annuities that came over time to have symbolic value greater than the financial value. But while the area on which Iroquois now lived might be small, the marks of their previous widespread occupation remained.

It appears that when white pioneers settled in the area around Palmyra around 1789 there were no longer major Native American settlements; Phelps' and Gorham's negotiations with the Seneca had addressed that. Cayuga Lake to the south-east remained an Indian encampment, and Native Americans remained in the Finger Lakes area as settler agriculture spread, entering the area of European settlement to trade and at times to fish or hunt.

The Native Americans of western New York State were no longer what they had been, and were no threat to the white families settled in the region. *The Book of Mormon* gave Native Americans a new role in God's design and in history. The recent past combined with a mythical distant past to support a new future under Smith's revelation.

Locating the New Zion

Despite the religious revivalism of western New York in the 1830s and 1840s, this region did not prove to be the long-term centre for the growth of the Church of Jesus Christ of Latter-day Saints. Instead, its followers travelled westwards and quickly grew their numbers in new areas, with the most dramatic demographic change being the 1847 migration under the leadership of Brigham Young to the Great Salt Lake in what became the Utah Territory, within the Great Basin. This echoes aspects of the history of Christianity, which failed as a proselytising movement among the Jews of Palestine but grew adherents elsewhere; even Islam's greatest strengths developed outside of the Arabian Peninsula where it originated.

Mormonism could be described as a modern religion in its rejection of traditional Christian sects and its unwillingness to mimic them. A utopianism in its theology was balanced by a utopianism that developed in the structure of the movement – the spiritual as well as practical authority that could be spread widely across the community of the Latter-day Saints. The 'democratisation of prophesy' was a key to Mormonism's success.[41]

As the Latter-day Saints movement developed, under the guidance and declaimed visions of Joseph Smith, Jun., a priority emerged to create a New Jerusalem – a Zion in the Americas – where God's newly chosen people could be a 'gathering' and withdraw from 'gentile' (non-believing) society while preparing themselves for a new divinely ordained future. Because *The Book of Mormon* emphasised an origin of American Indians in migrations from Israel, such a location for the new Zion might be to the west, closer to Native American territory lying beyond the Missouri River. Smith in 1831 had already said that the Saints should 'assemble yourselves together to rejoice upon the land of Missouri, which is the land of your inheritance'. Yet converts to the new movement were being made not on the frontiers of white society but among educated and prosperous people in the east (and also in England), people who were looking for a definitive set of religious beliefs they could adhere to, inspired by revelation, although not all might choose to join the migrations to form a unified community.[42]

The importance of place in the Mormon world view has been emphasised in several studies.[43] Mormon settlements were given names that reflected religious meaning. Most significant, perhaps, was Adam-ondi-Ahman, in Daviess County, Missouri. Here, according to an 1838 revelation to Joseph Smith, Jun., was the place where Adam came towards the end of his life, long after he had been expelled from the Garden of Eden, to bless his living descendants, and where a future gathering could be expected.[44]

An early group of followers was established at Kirtland in Ohio, 230 miles (375 km) south-west of Palmyra, and Joseph Smith, Jun. moved himself there; and then to nearby Mentor, despite a physical assault in 1832. But Missouri seemed more inviting as the future Zion, and some Mormon followers had already moved to establish themselves in the far west of Missouri. The upper part of the River Missouri marked a boundary between the United States and Indian territory.

A first group was established in Independence, close to today's Kansas City, on the south side of the Missouri River. Leading a group out of Ohio to Missouri in 1834, Joseph Smith, Jun. stopped to dig into an Indian mound on the banks of the Illinois River, uncovering a 'Lamanite' skeleton and retrieving an arrowhead; some of the bones and the arrowhead were retained by Smith's successor, Brigham Young.[45] The new settlement was seen as a border with Indian territory: where the land of the white man met land currently assigned to the Indian, a religion could thrive that saw a future role for both groups. When the growing community of Latter-day Saints met local conflict with hostile white Americans they crossed to Clay County on the north side of the river and in 1836 created the settlement of Far West. Joseph Smith, Jun. moved there, effectively making it the new centre of the movement.

Local hostilities in this border region grew, fuelled by suspicion of the attitude to the Native Americans implied in Mormon theology. Violent clashes occurred. Smith led the group in the purchase of land in 1839 to the north-east, in Illinois, 250 km (160 miles) away, on the east bank of the Mississippi, and named a new settlement Nauvoo. This was the edge of the state: beyond lay territory controlled by the United States but not yet formalised as the state of Iowa. Here, it appeared for a while, could be the site of the New Jerusalem, and by 1842 Nauvoo had a population of some 10,000.

Pioneering archaeological work since 1961 associated with restoration work on heritage sites, and sponsored by Mormon groups, has recorded aspects of the early town. The work itself was not without controversy.[46] Secular approaches to restoration from the National Parks Service and others initially complemented the approach of the Church of Jesus Christ of Latter-day Saints, but such secular approaches gradually gave way to an emphasis on the religious importance of places. Rivalry emerged with the Reorganized Church of Jesus Christ of Latter-day Saints, the movement (today known as the Community of Christ) that had broken away from the Salt Lake City leadership by 1860, to whom Nauvoo retained significance other than being the departure place of Brigham Young's trek westwards. Each church had interests in the restoration of different sites in Nauvoo.

The political, organisational and theological development of the Mormons was guided by new revelations announced by Joseph Smith, Jun. While internal discords arose over the development of the movement, these were exceeded by external hostility from those who suspected the ambitions of the Mormon community. After a clash between dissenting Mormons and followers of Smith, he and others were arraigned on a criminal charge, and while in jail in June 1844 they were attacked by a mob. Alongside his brother, Joseph Smith, Jun. was killed: aged 38, just 14 years after the publication of *The Book of Mormon* and 14 years into the dramatic development of the Latter-day Saints. Smith's death was followed by splits from and within the Latter-day Saints, with different groups and different leaders.

Just as the movement had been growing, so the United States of America was growing with a westward and southern spread; there were now 26 states in the nation. Settlement west of the United States was already under way before the Mormon migration; by the end of 1844 the Oregon Territory had

5,000 American nationals and 700 Britons – a larger number of Americans than were then living in California.[47]

Migration far west had already been considered and discussed by the Mormon leadership while Joseph Smith, Jun. was still alive.[48] Long-distance migration was, of course, a fundamental theme in the world history presented in *The Book of Mormon*. The pursuit of a Zion in the Americas inspired the largest migration far to the west: that led by the now ordained President of the Latter-day Saints, Brigham Young, to create the basis of the 'gathering' in what became Utah. Seen from a demographic viewpoint this was genuine pioneering. Historians may disagree about the relevant powers of 'push' and 'pull'. A self-governing Mormon community seemed both practically and theologically desirable: it could not be established in the now well settled areas of western New York but needed to go elsewhere. Nauvoo might appear to be a secure and sustainable community but internal conflicts and external pressures determined otherwise, and the New Zion of the west now needed to be much further west.

The Mormon migration to Utah cuts across conventional models in human geography and archaeology, which assume population movements reflect population pressures and technological advantage, and are typically gradual. Here was a leap of distance driven by ideology as well as the need to escape the risk of future persecution. The settlement site by the Great Salt Lake in America's Great Basin lay 1,070 miles (2,010 km) from Nauvoo, Illinois. Its choice as a location arose from the Mormon leaders' study of travellers' verbal and written reports, including a description by John C. Fremont, who reached the Great Salt Lake in 1844. Utah Lake nearby had also been considered as a possible first site. That the area of the Great Salt Lake appeared to be marginal to major Native American groups was an influencing factor, although perhaps involving some wishful thinking.

Around 16,000 people began a westward migration from Nauvoo in 1846. Some would travel via California after taking a ship from New York. But the largest group set off in 1847 by wagon (one group's attempt to replace these with handcarts in 1856 was not successful) and the large flow of Mormon converts who followed made Utah the definitive centre of the movement. In the 1860 census of Utah, there were 40,244 foreign-born and 27,490 American-born residents with widely dispersed origins, but the largest numbers were from the states of Illinois, New York and Iowa.[49]

While Mormonism had achieved, and continued to achieve, converts across and beyond the United States, the appeal of a safe and isolated place for the movement's centre was clear. This was done in open sight of the US authorities; it developed as separation within the nation, not outside it. An 1849 meeting the Mormons discussed requesting Congress to recognise their land with formal territorial status, then went further in proposing statehood under the name of Deseret, adopting a word in *The Book of Mormon*.[50] This was not to happen. A territory (smaller than proposed) was recognised in 1850. But the now extreme form of separation led to extreme forms of antagonism and in a 'Mormon War' conflict between the new community and the federal government was marked by a call by Brigham Young in 1857 to leave the United States, four years before the larger threat to the Union that marked the beginning of the Civil War. After peace was negotiated, conflict between the Mormons and the US government would continue, especially over the issue of polygamy until endorsement of this practice was abandoned by the official Latter-day Saints in 1890.

By then Utah was a major administrative unit of the United States and the leaders of the Latter-day Saints were important public and administrative figures as well as spiritual and religious leaders. A settlement in such a region needed more than faith to survive. Not least its success and importance lay in management of irrigation: such schemes led by Brigham Young established both the security of the settlement and the security of his own leadership.[51] But one gap between religious teachings and practical realities had emerged. The Native Americans, whose historic and future role was described in *The Book of Mormon*, proved less than appreciative of the white people coming into their ancestral lands.

The land of the Mormon settlement

The move west had been part of Joseph Smith, Jun.'s plan, attributed to divine revelation. Mormon literature described western lands in glowing terms.[52] The Great Basin, within which the Great Salt Lake sits, had been suggested as a suitable site, and the Great Salt Lake area itself emerged as a strong possibility, with information gained from trappers and explorers who knew it. The Mormon leadership formed the view that the area south of the Salt Lake Valleys would be the most fertile area. Early impressions of the pioneer Mormon settlers were said to be favourable, although they noted the limited availability of timber and there were certainly some whose expectations of the Promised Land met with challenges.[53] The 60,000 migrants who arrived in the 22 years after 1847 did so in the framework of this description. History was rewritten in a few years with the suggestion that the journey there had not been guided by merely human sources but undertaken under divine guidance.[54] In this model there was a heroic destiny to settle and tame that 'desert' region rather than a human choice of land for sustainable development. The Mormon 'invention' of irrigation agriculture in North America was part of this destiny, guided by their deity. The Salt Lake Valleys were near desert but, as the history of Native American occupation shows, they were not actual desert, whatever later claims might suggest.[55]

Brigham Young arrived at the future site of Salt Lake City in July 1847 and confirmed the plan of settlement. His first small group took occupation (the vanguard party consisted of 143 men, 3 women and 2 children).[56] Young returned east to organise the movement of additional families of Saints whose destination was the new settlement. By the end of 1847 some 1,700 Mormons had reached what was to be Salt Lake City: still a small proportion of those who had set off from Nauvoo.

Practical organisation of the community was required. For the urban settlement, this involved the creation of a town of formal layout of wide streets and square blocks. Perfection in place led to perfection in design: the grid pattern of the new city was based on an east–west axis. Urban plots that initially cost $1.50 could be sold four years later for $1,000.[57]

The Mormon leadership recognised that the key to survival and success in such a challenging region lay in irrigation, which required more than individual enthusiasm. Alongside irrigation and the planning of the city, the priorities in the first winter near the Great Salt Lake were to cooperate in ploughing, planting, collecting timber for construction of log palisades and log cabins, and building adobe walls, and to supplement limited resources with hunting and gathering wild foods.

A photograph of the city in 1853 shows a settlement already beginning to develop within a framework established for a much larger community. In the foreground are fields; public buildings and private dwelling of different qualities and scales have been built, but the mood of the image is still one of a forbidding landscape.[58]

Again, this history challenges conventional models of settlement patterns and development. In a broader context of human history, people migrate to new land, cultivate it and develop centralised facilities to assist in the exchange of their surplus: centres that begin as villages and develop into towns, providing practical, specialised services as well as religious institutions to provide spiritual and ritual services. Salt Lake City did not emerge slowly to meet the needs of pioneer farmers, but was established from the start as the centre of the New Zion, and with a temple at its core, though a temple so ambitious that its completion took decades.

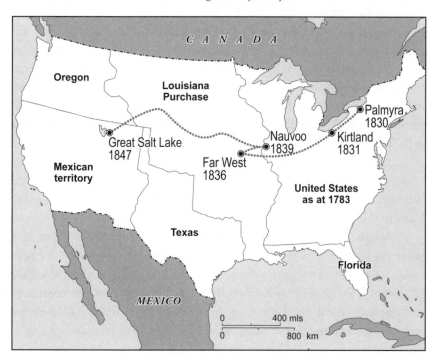

3. Places of the main Mormon migrations up to 1847

Settlement spread in valleys mainly south of the Great Salt Lake, valleys separated by high ridges.[59] All the rivers of northern Utah flow into the Great Salt Lake or the Utah Lake to the south. To the west lay the Great Salt Lake Desert; to the east rose the Wasatch Range and Plateau. Around these, especially to the west and south, were arid lands that did not allow farming or sustainable grazing. This initial settled area was some 15–20 miles wide by 20–40 miles long (22–32 km by 32–65 km). The Mormon leaders insisted on emphasising the south as a direction for further settlement, although this pushed people into increasingly arid and unproductive lands.[60] As the Mormon community of the later 19th century developed its own history, the theological view was that the Mormons had been sent to tame the desert lands; a more pragmatic approach and better advice might sooner have moved settlement further to the north.

Further Mormon settlement began from March 1849 some 45 miles (70 km) south of Salt Lake City, on the Provo River at the east of Utah Lake, where fishing and local foraging could complement irrigated cereal farming, with ploughing reliant on oxen rather than horses. Cattle and sheep were grazed on common land, limited by the threat of Indian raids on livestock. A defensive structure named Fort Utah would develop into the town of Provo; over a decade the settlement grew to some 2,000 people. Other fortified settlements were spread further around the north of the lake. Early houses were mainly of adobe, since wood for construction would require expeditions to the higher land to the east.

At the same time, outpost settlements were envisaged, not just in the broader Utah area but as far as San Bernardino in the Los Angeles basin; however, after the challenge to Mormon political ambitions by the United States in 1857, that location was abandoned.

Although Mormon identity is focussed on the Great Salt Lake area and valleys to the south in particular, and Utah in general, a broader 'Mormon region' is identified by geographers.[61] The growth and spread of Mormon settlement grew rapidly, while Salt Lake City remained its administrative and spiritual centre. By the end of the 19th century around 500 Mormon communities had been established, over a vast stretch of land, from Canada to Mexico.

Native Americans in Utah

The New Zion was not established in an empty land. As with other westward migrations from the contemporary border of the United States (see Map 3), contact and conflict with the Native Americans occupying those areas formed part of the story.[62] The Utah area fell within territory claimed but not actively administered by Mexico (ceded by Spain as a result of Mexico's independence in 1821), and became part of the United States by the treaty with Mexico of 1848. So when Brigham Young first claimed land in Great Salt Lake area in 1847 it was arguably either Native American land or Mexican land – but it was certainly not yet owned by the United States. The local Native Americans' contact with the Hispanic community had been sparse, but included being the victim of raiding and trading for slaves, a feature of inter-tribal contact too.

Latter-day Saints in the west had two conflicting needs. Their religion gave Native Americans a special role in history and in a future saved world, so kindness at least and active proselytising at best seemed priorities. Yet the Mormons were also fundamentally part of the 19th-century expansion of white settlement into the lands of Native Americans and Mormon survival required the confident control, defence and cultivation of these lands. As the Mormon community settled in and beyond the Great Basin, both these issues remained important. In time, a myth developed that Mormons, in taking possession of the valleys near the Great Salt Lake, had encountered an unoccupied and empty land.[63] But in reality it had been territory of indigenous peoples for thousands of years. The regions in which Mormons settled had perhaps 12,000 Native Americans at the time of first contact.[64] Brigham Young's declared intentions to maintain good relations with American Indians while settling in their area met inevitable challenges: by 1850 he was asking the US government (unsuccessfully at the time) to settle Utah's indigenous people elsewhere.

Several specific factors eased the arrival of the Mormons. The local Native Americans (Ute and Western Shoshone) were now foragers with a seasonally migratory life cycle, rather than cultivators with fixed lands and villages. In this particular area of the Great Basin, unlike the Great Plains and some other parts of the Great Basin, it appears probable that the local native peoples had not adopted horses for hunting or fighting and were limited in their ability to challenge the much more mobile white settlers. It was also helpful that this area lay at the boundary of two tribal groups rather than at the core territory of either one (although, as in most such contexts, the identity and affiliation of an individual could change).

People of the prehistoric Fremont culture had occupied Utah, including the areas of early Mormon settlement, since at least the 5th century CE.[65] They may have had links in their origin to the Anasazi of the Southwest. The Fremont combined food derived from hunting and gathering with horticulture (maize, beans and squash) until the impacts of climate change reduced maize yield, increased their reliance on foraging and eventually stimulated their movement away from the region.[66] The Fremont areas had been settled around 1300 CE (there is debate on the chronology of their expansion) by people who already had some presence in the region, speakers of languages in the Numic language group.[67] These were ancestral to the tribal units around the Great Salt Lake broadly classified as part of the Western Shoshone, and to the south-east as part of the Ute.

In 1937–1938 anthropologist Julian H. Steward mapped his understanding of where the traditional divisions of Native American groups had been.[68] West of the Great Salt Lake was unoccupied desert. The Shoshone speakers in the north he classified in groups as Pine nut eaters, Rabbit eaters and Huki (wild grass seed) eaters; those south-west of the lake as Skull Valley Gosiute and he assigned the term Gosiute just to this group. At the south-east of the lake the people called the Weber Ute he considered belonged to the Shoshone language group. For the Shoshone, the pine nut was a major food source but one whose unreliability required much mobility, and poor food resources made for a low population density.

The indigenous population seems to have increased in mobility during the 17th century and somewhat decreased in number, possibly as a result of diseases introduced through encounters with white travellers and with other Native American people whose own economic and social pattern had changed with possession of the horse.[69] Itinerant groups of 'mixed blood' had also begun to visit the area by horseback.[70] Horses had been traded from Spanish territories from the mid-17th century and had a significant impact on the hunting and warfare capacity of Plains Indians. Some groups in the Great Basin had traded and bred horses for similar purposes, but not the Western Shoshone; and the Ute adopted the horse only in better-grassed areas than the Great Salt Lake. Settler contact with Western Shoshone and Ute had been limited: traders and trappers and missionaries passed through their territory but did not threaten to settle there. Expeditions criss-crossed the Great Basin in the 1820s and the Great Salt Lake formed part of their reports. Non-Mormon white men travelling through the region had been willing to trade guns to the Ute of the region.

The nature and size of the Mormon migration was therefore dramatic – and not readily open to resistance by a mobile indigenous group. The Gosiute (or Goshiute or Goshute) group of the Western Shoshone, who lived at the north-east extreme of Shoshone territory, west, south and east of the Great Salt Lake, had little contact with the Ute. The Gosiute, with a relatively low density of population, were among the more impoverished of the Shoshone groups.[71] Their economic pattern was of seasonal migrations in groups of 25–30 people, foraging a wide variety of wild foods, for which the Mormons were not major competitors.

Mormon activity from 1849–1850 in the Tooele Valley south of the Great Salt Lake began significant encroachment on Gosiute lands. A mixture of withdrawal and accommodation to the Mormons became the Gosiute pattern. For a while it was possible for Mormons and Gosiute to avoid clashing but as the Mormon community expanded through the 1850s and early 1860s, conflict over territory and the theft of settlers' cattle became inevitable, until in 1863 the Gosiute signed a treaty with the US government which guaranteed free passage for the white travellers, an end to hostilities and compensation to the Gosiute for their loss of hunting.

It was safer for the very first Mormon settlers initially to settle on the land around the Salt Lake rather than confront the people of Utah Lake to

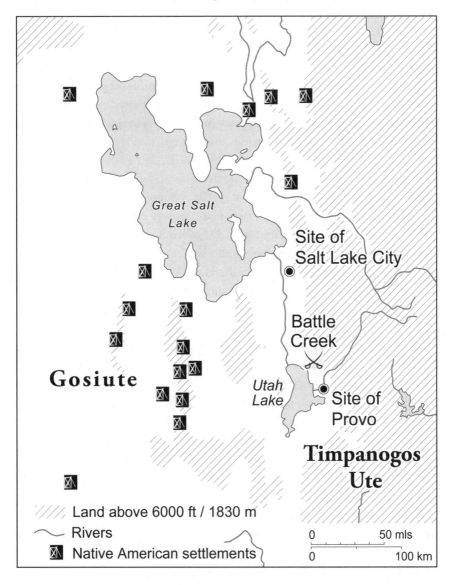

Great Salt
Lake

Site of
Salt Lake City

Battle
Creek

Gosiute

Utah
Lake

Site of
Provo

Timpanogos
Ute

///// Land above 6000 ft / 1830 m
~ Rivers
⊠ Native American settlements

0   50 mls
0   100 km

4. Native American and Mormon settlements near the Great Salt Lake

the south, but from March 1849 they moved there, to what would become the city of Provo.[72] The fish resources of Utah Lake had been important to human settlement for at least six millennia.[73] Mounds from Fremont settlement indicate the density of groups in the area and excavations suggest that fish were probably a greater contribution to diet than their farming, even before the effects of changing climate were felt by Fremont peoples.

The Ute group known as Timpanogos (Timanogots, Tumpanawach) lived in semi-permanent camps towards and beside Utah Lake. Fish from the lake provided a third of their diet, and when dried helped to spread resources over the year. This was supplemented by hunting and food gathering, with a seasonal round that included summer travel to the higher mountain areas.[74] Settlement was on waterside sites on low beaches, with the largest sites situated where streams enter the lake. Such locations were used repeatedly over time; pits were probably used for winter storage. The settlement pattern seems to have been especially influenced by the wish and need to store fish, with chub, sucker and trout the dominant species.[75] Supplementary food included bison, deer, antelope, mountain sheep, rabbit, beaver, muskrat, carnivores and birds, alongside a range of plant foods. The bulrush served different purposes, including construction of dwellings and rafts.

Given the resources of the lake, the Gosiute were a relatively prosperous community, but their resources were attractive to the Mormon newcomers too. After initial coexistence, conflict arose when Timpanogo hunting extended to Mormon cattle. A Mormon expedition in response in 1848 led to the 'Battle Creek massacre', modest compared with some later conflicts, at a site near today's Pleasant Grove. Mormon settlers (some with experience of frontier regions elsewhere in North America) now moved to lands in the Utah Valley among the Timpanogos, and some cooperation, conflict and competition for natural resources continued.[76] Early construction of a fort indicated the settlers' concern, confirmed with bloody encounters in 1850, when a pitched battle was followed by 'mopping up' exercises in which scores of Ute were killed. The Utes were now effectively defeated; as Brigham Young advised, the Indians must now do as God tells them through the Mormon chief (i.e. himself). Compromise reigned, although there were occasional further outbreaks of conflict, until the Ute people were finally removed into the Uinta Basin in north-eastern Utah at the end of the American Civil War in 1865, by treaty with the federal government.

Mormon tradition has it that divine providence protected the loyal members of the Church of Jesus Christ of Latter-day Saints and guided them to an unoccupied arid land that they could tame by their initiative of irrigation and the guidance of their appointed leaders. The reality is that local Native American communities had long settled the region and exploited its resources. And as Mormon settlement grew and spread, new conflicts over land occurred with other Native American groups, but that is part of the broader history of the American West.[77]

Conclusions

The world in which the Church of Jesus Christ of Latter-day Saints emerged and grew was one which presents contrasting images. Mormon origins did not lie in the urban or industrialising regions of a developing and fast-changing United States, but neither was this the America of the early frontier pioneers. The roots of Mormonism lay in the agricultural communities of the next generation, who were constructing farms and creating small and relatively prosperous towns. In one area of these settlements, the 'Burned-over district' of western New York, enthusiasm for new religious ideas presented in person and in print by young evangelists set the context in which Mormonism began its evolution as one of the most successful new religions of modern times. Where multiple evangelical Christian movements (from within and beyond existing churches) were competing for influence, that led by Joseph Smith, Jun. and inspired by his leadership and the text he dictated set the trajectory for its followers to create a substantial new organisation. Established in an area where Native Americans had long lived but no longer thrived, this religion could include messages about a Native American past and their possible future that did not conflict with daily experience.

Once the movement had grown and acknowledged the need to build its 'New Zion' in North America away from conventional society, the Mormons did become a pioneering group. After following the Church leadership away from western New York, and experiencing external and internal conflicts and the death of the founding prophet at 38 years of age, a substantial group of Mormons migrated to settle around the Great Salt Lake at a time when it was on the cusp of territorial claims by Mexico changing to those of the United States. The New Zion was a land in which agriculture was more challenging, and the organisation of civil society was crucial to its success. Although they were motivated by religious rather than economic factors, the Mormons in Utah faced the same issues, challenges and experience of other Americans in colonising and changing the West. As a leading historian of the American West has observed, 'Mormonism is in many ways the most American of religions'.[78]

The area around the Great Salt Lake and the Utah Lake was not empty land: it was territory occupied and exploited by Native American groups. But it did have one advantage to the settlers arriving from the 1840s: it was at the periphery of the land of the two major tribal groups, the Shoshone and the Ute. A marginal group of white Americans could therefore squeeze itself into this region without the full level of conflict seen elsewhere in the story of the American West.

Placing faith in the contents of *The Book of Mormon* and the leadership of the new church isolated the followers of the new movement from the communities within which they emerged. Moving westward temporarily beyond the territory of the United States extended theological and organisational isolation into geographical isolation. But before long the isolation was eroded by the broad sweep of the American occupation of the North American continent, with its impacts on indigenous inhabitants, on the landscape and on the political imperative to hold together the many sectors of a diverse nation.

Mormonism has always described itself as a Christian church, but it is set apart from all other Christian denominations not just organisationally but by the position it takes on *The Book of Mormon*: four times the length of the gospels, more than three times the length of the Qur'an. To Mormons, their church supplements traditional Christianity (and provides an American angle through its foundational text). In structure and the integration of historical narratives and religious injunctions *The Book of Mormon* might be compared more to the Tanakh (Old Testament) than to the New Testament, and it asserts a direct historical link to pre-Christian Israel.

As early as 1834, critics of Joseph Smith, Jun. compared him to the Prophet of Islam, Muhammad.[79] The famous Victorian traveller Richard Burton extended the comparison when he visited and wrote about both Mecca and Salt Lake City. They generally meant it as an insult: two fraudulent inventors of new faiths who challenged the truths of the conventional Christian message. Some critics described both men as sharing sensuousness, even a commitment to violence. An influential international voice in these comparisons was German scholar Eduard Meyer in 1912, who argued there were close similarities between the beginnings of Mormonism and the historical development of Islam.[80] But from an independent point of view, the comparison could also be judged in less negative terms. Each had proclaimed divine insights and had dictated lengthy texts that would form a foundational document for a new religious movement. Each would be the leader and organiser of a successful new movement. Each would provide detailed rules by which adherents of the new group should live. And each would see their beliefs acquire devoted followers quickly and lay the basis for expansion into new territories. To the followers of Muhammad ibn 'Abdullah he was the last and final prophet in a long line of prophets, and the Qur'an the sacred text that needed no further text. To the Mormon community, Joseph Smith, Jun. was the translator and transmitter of a text that told of a distant past and inspired a new future, but one in which the guidance of the movement's leaders would be of great importance.

What is remarkable is that in an era before social media, though an era of print, one movement emerging within an environment of competitive evangelisms could develop in just 17 years from an individual and his family and friends, to a cohort of tens of thousands of followers willing to leave their homes and travel far west to establish a new religiously based community.

Mormonism provides an example of how one man's vision and its communication in words and actions could develop quickly into a successful, large, growing and continuing religious movement. It sets a model for viewing other religious movements, their origins and spread. Joseph Smith, Jun. sits in a long line of prophetic individuals whose insights, inspiration and words were and are perceived by their followers to come directly from the divine: names such as Zarathushtra, Isaiah, Yeshua (Jesus), Muhammad ibn 'Abdullah and others whose different contexts we discuss in the following chapters.

Chapter 3

Vision, faith and conquest:
the source and power of Islam

In the middle decades of the 7th century CE, armies from the Arabian Peninsula achieved the rapid conquest of territories extending from Afghanistan to North Africa, seized from the weakened Sasanian and Byzantine Empires. They created new settlements and fortifications, and taxes were now payable to the new rulers. However, for much of the first century of the conquest it did not transform the material culture, economic or social pattern of most of the peoples of the Levant. The unifying ideology of the conquerors from Arabia was adherence to a new religion, Islam, but the Judaism, Zoroastrianism and different strands of Christianity in newly controlled communities continued to operate, and in some cases further develop, without enforced conversion. Politics rather than religion ruled. Just as Mormonism was forged as an organisation by the individual who had dictated its founding document, so the Islamic community and its military and political strengths were brought together by the man who declaimed the key religious texts. Muhammad ibn ʿAbdullah was a merchant from Mecca in the Hijaz region of western Arabia, who proclaimed from *ca.* 613 to his death in 632 his religious revelations, which would be brought together as the Qur'an. Our main sources for the origins of Islam were compiled by Muslim scholars some six generations after the death of the Prophet. Modern scholarship has considered the context in which Islam emerged, in a world of competing monotheisms and polytheisms, and asks whether Mecca was indeed the important trading town suggested in the Muslim tradition. Historical debates indicate we should be less confident than we once were about the early stages of Islam.

―――――――――――――

The Middle East hosted multiple competing monotheisms before the 8th century CE. Some were Christian in different affiliations, some were forms of Judaism, while Zoroastrianism thrived and the dualism of Manichaeism had emerged in the 3rd century. The worship of individual deities in the Arabian Peninsula included polytheistic and monotheistic approaches. In Arabia new preachers with new religious ideas emerged in the early 7th century. It was the teaching of one such preacher, Muhammad ibn 'Abdullah, and the movement he taught, Islam, that came to dominate the whole Middle East as they united Arabs under one political and military power that could fill a political void left by weakened empires.

In the middle of the 7th century CE the political order and the longstanding rivalries of the powerful empires of Sasanians (Persia) and Byzantines ('New Rome') were broken apart by the military strength and determination coming from the unexpected quarter of the Arabian Peninsula. Within just decades, Islamic Arab conquests had extended through the Levant to eastern Anatolia, eastwards to Iran, and westwards into Egypt and beyond. By the mid-8th century all of the North African coast and a large part of the Iberian Peninsula were under such alien rule, while to the east Muslim conquests had spread into Central Asia and reached as far as Afghanistan.

A key characteristic of these militant conquerors from Arabia was their identification with a new religion, Islam, and adherence to the beliefs whose core statement developed as 'There is no god but God [Allah] and Muhammad is the Messenger of God'. The religion traced its origins to revelations received in the first three decades of the 7th century CE by a single prophet in the Hijaz region of western Arabia, Muhammad ibn 'Abdullah, who by his death in 632 CE had secured the adherence of most of the population of the Arabian Peninsula to the new Islamic community, through a combination of persuasion, successful military campaigns and treaties. A political structure developed in Arabia to serve the new religious revelation of Islam; it organised the body of followers and brought together a military to defend it. Accepting the new religious identity became the basis which identified and united the military and political groups, as Arab rule grew and spread with devastating effectiveness.

The primary impact of Islam on the wider world was not one of migration (as with Mormonism) or proselytising (as with Christianity) but of military force and political power. Initially there was no pressure on conquered peoples to convert: followers of other faiths paid tax, unlike Muslims, and so more converts would mean less tax. But within a century of Muslim rule, it proved politically wise, financially beneficial or culturally popular for many in the newly conquered territories to adopt the religion of those who now ruled them. 'Early Muslims were less religious missionaries than religiously motivated imperialists.'[1]

The newly defined world controlled by the Muslim Arabs emphasised military power, political organisation, economic power (with trade across and beyond a vast pacified region) and, in due course, new styles in art and architecture, as well as religion. Scholarship was held in high regard, producing philosophers and jurists, scientists and historians, but all operating within the framework of religious faith and the model in which religious faith was traced back to early 7th-century Arabia. So historical documents are many, but interpreting them in the light of modern scholarly approaches is far from easy.

We face a number of problems in understanding the context in which Islam emerged. Archaeology is a strong potential source of knowledge of the past because it is not influenced by the selectivity and conflicting interpretations of historical documents, and reflects a stratum of society broader than that of the literate minority. But archaeology is limited by the variable density of field research, and by the periods, places and questions that archaeologists choose to examine. While we know much about the archaeology of developed Islamic civilisation, and increasing amounts about the early background of parts of Arabia, the archaeological record for the time and place in which Islam emerged is limited.

Historical documents, like potsherds or stone walls or rock engravings, are themselves objects created in a specific time and place for a specific purpose. Interpretation of those documents involves detailed analysis, debate and a critical approach. A scholarly critical approach to source documents of Judaism and Christianity has developed within the cultural tradition of those religions. However, some scholarship from writers within the Islamic cultural world can appear to the outsider generally less critical, inhibited by the risk of an accusation of apostasy.[2] Much of the detailed religious scholarship that is a characteristic of Islam remains largely within a framework defined by that religion.

Meanwhile, historians of Islam who do not come from within that religious tradition, primarily those from western universities, have examined early Islam from a range of perspectives. The influential critique by literary academic Edward Said described 'Orientalism' – a Eurocentric sense of superiority and distance that long influenced much western writing about Islam and Arabs.[3] In reaction, many writers seem more cautious about the risk of being considered part of a new Orientalism in their scholarly approach. Western approaches range from those that accept much (but not all) of the fundamental historical narrative that accompanied Islamic expansion, through to critical and sceptical debates about places and dates, with some western historians questioning basic assumptions about the origins of Islam. As modern scholarship has developed, it has suggested we may know less than we thought we knew from historical sources.

The narrative of early Islam

A high florescence of Islamic culture – 'the Golden Age of Islam' – marked the first centuries of the 'Abbasid caliphs, who ruled from Baghdad in Iraq over the five centuries from 750 CE to 1258 CE, when the Mongol Khanate successfully besieged then sacked the city. From the mid-9th century the territory controlled by the 'Abbasids began to reduce, though it would be another two centuries after the sack of Baghdad before the Ottoman sultanate conquered Constantinople to make it their capital, Istanbul.

The 'Abbasid era saw a burst of new literary endeavour (by some accounts, facilitated with the introduction of paper into the Arab world via Chinese captives). New copying of existing texts for distribution inevitably involved some selectivity and redaction to match the real contemporary setting as well as copyists' errors. The rich Arabic literary corpus from the worlds of Islamic civilisation provides plentiful detailed accounts of the origins of Islam for the historian to assess and use.

The first century of 'Abbasid rule, in particular, was a period of unified power and a cultural efflorescence. Islamic religion was central to society and empire. The Arabic language held its position of status and influence, as the language of the Qur'an, but the 'Abbasid dynasty had acquired power with an army that incorporated numerous non-Arabs and a feature of 'Abbasid Baghdad was a focus on Persia – looking east. Being Arab ceased to be as important as it once was.

The 'Abbasids had overthrown the Umayyad caliphate, which had ruled from Damascus the now large Islamic empire for nearly 90 years from 661. The Umayyads established much of the pattern of intertwined Islamic scholarship, religion, politics and creativity. When the subsequent 'Abbasid rule extended from Damascus through to Egypt, separate rulers claiming legitimacy as successors to the Umayyads held control of the western parts of North Africa (the Maghreb) and Spain, sponsoring a no less rich world of arts and learning.

Umayyad rule from Damascus had united vast lands in a single polity, with an increase in the power of Islam and conversion to the new religion. But the period also marked the beginnings of a conflict with those who declined to recognise the Umayyad rulers as the successors to the Prophet, a position that in due course would lead to a split in Islam between Sunni and Sh'ia.

The accession of the first Umayyad caliph in 661 CE followed an astonishing three decades of conquest by Islamic Arab armies under the military control of four successive caliphs, whom Sunni Muslims call the Rightly Guided

Caliphs (*Rashidun*), all of whom were in-laws or relatives of Muhammad ibn 'Abdullah. The Arab armies moved out of Arabia to take control of huge swathes of land in and beyond Iraq and Iran from the Sasanian rulers; moved through the Levant to take from the Byzantines land in Palestine, Syria and Anatolia (present-day Turkey); and conquered Egypt and continued westward to the Maghreb. The world had changed. Because these conquests brought Arabs into the highly literate world of other empires, the historical dates for conquests outside Arabia seem uncontroversial.

The Muslim armies had established a unified control of the people in the Arabian Peninsula. Some may have joined the Islamic Arab community only after the Prophet's death in 632 CE.[4] However, the traditional histories stated that during the Prophet's lifetime he had secured declarations of adherence to Islam from Arab leaders on the eastern Arabian coast – including nominal subjects of the Sasanian Empire[5] – but then a rebellion had followed his death and military action was required in 633–634 to bring the area back into the Islamic fold, with Jews and Christians agreeing to pay a tax rather than convert.[6] That is, the traditional narrative of Muhammad ibn 'Abdullah's life shows major military activity led by Muhammad himself, which persuaded or forced the varied tribes of much of Arabia to acknowledge the authority of a single polity, identified by following the monotheism he proclaimed.

The forcefulness of this movement was, of course, not just the conventional acquisition of land, wealth and power, but was inspired by the belief that Muhammad ibn 'Abdullah was 'the Messenger of God', the final prophet in a line of prophets from Adam to Noah and Moses to Jesus. The religion called Islam (a term meaning 'submission'; 'Muslim' has the same root, meaning one who submits) was asserted through the spoken texts that Muhammad ibn 'Abdullah had declaimed over an extended period, and that were recorded piecemeal by scribes: what would be called the Qur'an (or Koran), a term meaning 'recitation'.

The political organisation and military action to serve it began to unify and defend the community of those who believed in the message of Islam conveyed by Muhammad ibn 'Abdullah. The later recitations that would be brought together in the Qur'an addressed the political and military issues. The politics that had begun by serving a religion developed into a religion that met political needs and was the unifying core around which the Arab conquerors spread throughout Arabia and, after the death of the Prophet, across the Middle East and beyond.

After the death of Muhammad ibn 'Abdullah, his utterances were brought together into the document we call the Qur'an, and over time detailed narratives of his life and actions and sayings were collected, written, copied and developed with the uncertain accuracy discussed below. The core narrative in the tradition was of an orphan from Mecca (Makkah) in the Hijaz of north-western Arabia – by age Muhammad ibn 'Abdullah would have been born about 570 CE – who accompanied his uncle on a trading mission to southern Syria, and then worked for a widow (Khadija, whom in due course he married) as a merchant trading out northwards from the Hijaz. His first religious revelation came near the age of 40, and from around 613 he began to proclaim his vision and the monotheistic religion that became Islam. His wife was the first to accept the revelation and others followed.

One later tradition claimed some of his followers soon undertook a migration from Mecca to Christian Ethiopia. Another tradition has it that, a few years later, around 621, Muhammad ibn 'Abdullah took a night journey from Mecca to Jerusalem and back on the winged creature Buraq under the guidance of the angel Jibril. Medina, Mecca and Jerusalem would become the three holy cities of Islam. Jerusalem had been occupied by the Sasanians in 614 and would remain so until the Byzantines reconquered it in 628.

The traditions record conflict, dated to 622, with members of the dominant Quraysh clans in Mecca (within which Muhammad ibn 'Abdullah himself was born). This led the small community of believers to migrate north to Yathrib (later known as Medina). This event, the *hijra*, marks the beginning of the Muslim calendar. In Medina he appears to have reached a formal accommodation with the significant numbers of Jews there (already monotheistic). Conflicts that would develop with this Jewish community may have been over religious differences, but also over political influence as well as access to land.

From Medina, the Muslim group undertook a familiar feature of Arabia: a raid on a trading caravan from Mecca, with a fight known as the Battle of Badr, dated to 624. A revenge attack planned by the Meccans in the following year (the Battle of Uhud) was successful but a subsequent conflict (the Battle of the Trench, 627) appears indecisive.

As Muhammad ibn 'Abdullah's followers grew in number, the conflict between them and other Arab groups increased. Guided by the leadership and message of the Prophet, his community of believers successfully established military and political control of many areas of the Arabian Peninsula, with enemies old and new suffering substantial losses in battles or in associated massacres of non-combatants (notably Jewish communities). Two years after a negotiated arrangement with the people of Mecca, in 630 Muhammad ibn 'Abdullah's forces took control of that town.

By the time of Muhammad ibn 'Abdullah's death in 632 most of Arabia was said to be unified in a political unit with Islam as its binding force. With the growing number and strength of his followers, it is not crucial to distinguish what groups in Arabia were brought into the newly emerging power by conquest, which by treaty, or which by enthusiasm to join an apparently rising force – or which by persuasion of the power of the Prophet's religious message over that of competing monotheisms and polytheisms. Adherence to the political power of his followers seemed, however, to require acceptance of his message from God and of his role as God's Prophet. Even the now divided chiefdoms of the formerly rich and powerful Yemen area, south-west Arabia, were not strong enough to resist the power of the north. After Muhammad's death, the speed with which some Arab tribes broke their loyalty to his successors suggests their adherence to the new religious faith had been more pragmatic than spiritual.

These groups were soon brought back into the community of armed and committed Arabs, who now proceeded with a rapid movement of successful conquests. The Arab control of areas under the now weakened claim of the Sasanian and Byzantine Empires swiftly followed Muhammad ibn 'Abdullah's death. From the beginning there were thus intertwining and interdependence of the ethnic, religious and the political: unifying areas politically with the power of a religious message and military might. Arab and Muslim identity combined to inspire military might and political power, but neither religious conversion nor demographic replacement of native populations was a priority to the conquerors from the Arabian Peninsula.

Sources and their problems

The editor of a recent major reference work on Islam began by noting 'the realisation that what we know about early Islam is less certain than what we thought we knew'.[7] But contributors to that volume varied in the credibility they gave to the traditional Muslim sources. Our Islamic historical documents on the life of Muhammad ibn 'Abdullah are plentiful but they were not contemporary with his life, and modern scholars ask 'What do we actually know about Muhammad?'[8]

Our sources for the biography of Muhammad ibn 'Abdullah mainly date from the early 'Abbasid era. That period was marked by the quantity and quality of its scholars, in Baghdad and elsewhere, who poured over every detail of the traditions and documents provided or edited by their predecessors. The substantial and remarkable scholarship during the 'Abbasid era has provided us with a vast corpus of literature, including that derived directly or indirectly from earlier writings. The scale of available literature is huge: one 10th-century public servant owned 400 camel loads just of theology books.[9] But the 'Abbasid rulers' claim to power lay in their overthrow of the Umayyad dynasty, whose historical rule they necessarily disowned. As a result of all these early medieval Muslim scholars' work, we know a great deal of what the 'Abbasid era believed about the preceding two to three centuries, and we can surmise what the Umayyads believed about this history, but we remain uncertain about the accuracy of the detail in the accounts. That is, we do not necessarily know what actually happened in the Hijaz in the early to middle 7th century CE.

As an historical source for early Islam, the most useful, because it is seen as the core of Islam, is the Qur'an. The Qur'an is not a sequential document. Islamic scholars agree that the present arrangement of the Qur'an is artificial – almost all of the text was ordered by length of the surahs, or chapters, some years after the death of the Prophet. The reality behind the composition of the Qur'an is complex; it was debated in the early centuries of Islam and remains debated in modern times.[10] Although they are generally said to represent a single voice, the different sections of the Qur'an were acknowledged by the early Islamic scholars to derive from different times in the life of the Prophet.

By tradition they were the subject of revelation over a period of some 23 years, beginning from when Muhammad ibn 'Abdullah was a religiously inclined merchant about 40 years of age, and continuing when he was a powerful and successful military and political leader. Detailed scholarship has sought to classify the surahs into a chronological sequence. Critics see in it repetition, many ambiguities, and a shift from the early visionary revelations of faith to more pragmatic (and often polemical) revelations related to the practical issues of the Islamic community fighting its enemies in the Arabian Peninsula.[11] In the Qur'an, the voice is sometimes directly that of God and sometimes that of Muhammad ibn 'Abdullah making the recitation of his revelation.

There had been (and continued into the medieval period) a strong Arabic tradition of oral literature – declaimed, learnt and repeated – much as we assume for the Homeric epics of Greece. As Muhammad ibn 'Abdullah was consistently described as a merchant he would almost certainly have been literate (despite early Muslim traditions), but he lived in a culture where literacy was functional, for business transactions and records and the like, while poetry was an oral literature.[12] Hence the Qur'an as 'recitation'.

The emergence of a consonantal alphabet in the Middle East had been a valuable advance for traders (and graffiti) on the use of cuneiform on clay tablets, which had dominated official correspondence.[13] But although Arabic was already a written language by the era of Muhammad ibn 'Abdullah, we have relatively few examples dating from the period; and indeed most of our written sources of Umayyad and pre-Umayyad Islamic materials come from copies made in the 'Abbasid era.[14]

The Qur'an is in rhyming prose – a rhetorical form, though not fully poetic in style.[15] Pre-Islamic poetry survived and was long admired (and in due course recorded in writing) through Islamic societies; and non-religious poetry blossomed throughout the Islamic world. It is from the archive of pre-Islamic poetry written down in the 'Abbasid era that much of our imagery of pre-Islamic Arabia is derived.

Writing down the Prophet's separate revelations must have become important as his movement grew, and the decision to make a complete compilation is traditionally attributed to 'Uthman, the third caliph (ruled 644–656). Nevertheless, despite this tradition, the Qur'an as a unified document cannot be confirmed any earlier than the Umayyad period and the end of the 7th century, though, as noted below, there are some possible earlier fragments.[16]

As late as the 'Abbasid caliphate there were still multiple variant versions of the Qur'an in circulation, although the differences were not of the significance of the distinct canonical and non-canonical Christian gospels, or the contradictory stories included in the biblical book of *Genesis*. In 934 CE seven variant versions of the text were declared officially acceptable (canonical), although arguments were maintained for others.[17] The theological differences were not substantial, but the issue was an important one because of the belief that the Qur'an is the literal word of God, dictated word for word in Arabic by the angel Jibril (Gabriel), with Muhammad ibn 'Abdullah merely the agency by which God's words were delivered for all humankind. Within Sh'ia Islam there is a view that the Sunni version of the Qur'an has omitted important elements, but there was also debate about the correct text of the Qur'an in the early Sunni community itself.[18]

Because the Qur'an is seen as God's direct message through his Prophet, Muhammad ibn 'Abdullah, it is the core of Islamic communities. Its importance increases the likelihood that its contents come largely or entirely from the lifetime and mouth of the Prophet. The substantial references to Jewish scriptures, prophets and themes has raised the question of whether some of the text may be drawn from other sources and requoted by the Prophet or incorporated in the definitive version of the Qur'an used by his followers. Others have suggested a use of Christian texts within the Qur'an, but this remains a minority view.[19]

An even more radical suggestion was raised in the 1970s but meets with little acceptance today. In this model, because the earliest definitive written version of the Qur'an appears in copies from the early 'Abbasid period, the present text owes its formation to that period, being constructed and compiled not in Arabia (nor Syria), but in Iraq, where the 'Abbasid state needed documents to underscore its power.[20] In 2015 the parchment of a document owned by the University of Birmingham carrying surahs 19–20 of the Qur'an was dated by radiocarbon assay, in which it had a 95% probability of a date between 568 and 645 CE, with a midpoint at 606 CE.[21] Critics, however, note that this dates the parchment, not the writing, so that significantly later writing could well have been placed later on an older parchment.

A parchment bearing a very early version of texts in the Qur'an comes from the Great Mosque of Sana'a in Yemen; radiocarbon assay dates it to between 578 and 669.[22] Discussion of this source has supported the idea that the compilation of revelations into individual surahs (though not the ordering) of the Qur'an was earlier than the third caliph, 'Uthman. But again, the dating is of the parchment rather than the writing. Another radiocarbon-dated parchment of the Qur'an studied in Tubingen has been claimed to date (with 95% probability) from between 649 and 675 CE.

The Qur'an, with its 77,000 words in 114 surahs, seems our best source for the history of Islam's origins because it spreads across the later years of Muhammad ibn 'Abdullah and can be related of events in his life. Its theological and political importance means it was less likely to have been altered and augmented than other documents.

More problematic in the use of sources is identifying the historical material within the vastly greater collections of traditions that reported what the Prophet had said or done in his lifetime. These *hadith* (what in a secular context we would describe as 'anecdotes' and 'sayings') came to have respect and authority in Islam second only to the Qur'an itself. They grew in number over the decades, creating a challenge for the early scholars. It was common to cite *hadith* in response to some practical, legal or ethical issues, and some had clearly developed to suit the changing politics of the Islamic world. Questions of the authenticity of individual *hadith* therefore came to the fore among scholars in the early medieval Islamic world. Compilations early in the 'Abbasid era brought together 1,720 *hadith*, then 2,767 *hadith*, and finally tens of thousands as the numbers of *hadith* gradually increased in the

'Abbasid collections.[23] The commitment to track authenticity relied on tracing the chain of transmission (*isnad*): those whose chain of transmission could be traced back to individuals alive in the time of the Prophet had the best claim to authenticity. Where legal ruling referenced the words and examples of the Prophet this was particularly important. Studying, selecting and providing editions of *hadith* with the detailed chains of transmission formed a major industry for early 'Abbasid scholars.

Modern scholarship echoes the Islamic scholars in scepticism about many of the *hadith*, in the search for those which can be traced back to the life of the Prophet. Some western analysts go further, in seeing the construction of the first lines of transmission as no earlier than 70–80 years after the death of Muhammad ibn 'Abdullah, with many much later. An additional complexity is that contemporary western scholars have suggested some of the *hadith* whose *isnad* was considered in antiquity most authenticated now appear to be later fabrications.[24]

While the contents of authenticated *hadith* were traced back directly to the lifetime of Muhammad ibn 'Abdullah himself, Islamic sources for the actual history of the life and work of the Prophet were derived from information of other contemporaries. There developed numerous biographies of Muhammad ibn 'Abdullah and accounts of military expeditions led by him and by others during his lifetime. This substantial *sirah* literature using *hadith* as an important source provided the greatest detail, although with 'thousands of conflicting accounts'.[25] Distribution of such works served to reinforce the religious and political heritage of the caliphs and so, as with any such sources, modern historians treat them with care. 'The narratives of the *sirah* have to be carefully and meticulously sifted in order to get at the kernel of historically valid information, which is in fact meagre and scanty'.[26]

The first histories we possess were compiled or edited in the 'Abbasid period, five to six generations and more after the death of the Prophet, and many other histories followed. They face the common problem with religious traditions, as noted in the numerous developing accounts of the lives of Christian saints: that over time the details provided can become greater, not fewer. Uncertainties and conflicting statements noted by medieval historians in the Muslim world would develop into facts when reported by later historians.[27]

The learned and dedicated scholars of the 'Abbasid era could work with the histories provided by earlier scholars, back to the Umayyad period.[28] Those Umayyad writers in constructing their history relied on narratives obtained not from historians but from oral testimony, with all the strengths and weaknesses, bias, selectivity and imagination that oral testimony inevitably involves. Additionally, scholarly historians in 'Abbasid and other Islamic contexts sought to interpret the documents that they had before them – especially the often ambiguous surahs of the Qur'an – to construct an historical explanation and interpretation. Rather than history setting a context for the Qur'an, the Qur'an itself, though not a work of history, could stimulate historical explanations and interpretations that lacked other sources, as Islamic scholars sought to suggest historical events in the Prophet's life that would explain the significance of Quranic references.

Attempts by the early Islamic historians to fill the gaps with possible or probable explanations could be seen as acts of piety and religious devotion, and do not help the later secular historian. Reconstruction of historical events therefore becomes a matter of assessing probabilities, and historians' own perspectives inevitably mean they take widely differing views.[29] The question for modern historians is to consider which of the historical elements in 'Abbasid documents can be traced back to pre-'Abbasid times, which of these are reliable in general, which are reliable in detail, which are invented and, even more difficult, what aspects of the history of the emergence of Islam have been omitted entirely from the 'Abbasid histories because they were in conflict with the interests of the ruling groups of the era.

> As the Muslim authors themselves realised, a great deal was forged, or at least re-written to suit the interests of a particular party, cause, family or theory. How can one distinguish what is basically authentic from what is not, the true from the false? There is no absolutely sure criterion.... There is nothing of which we can say that it incontestably dates back to the time of the Prophet.[30]

The early Muslim historians focussed on political and urban life. With scholars coming from, and working within, urban elites, their narratives give us little if any information on rural society and the lives of the common people in the early history of the Islamic world.[31]

Some historical records are unambiguously inventions. An example is the insertion of an 'Abbasid ancestor in a crucial meeting with Muhammad ibn 'Abdullah.[32] Copies of correspondence between the Prophet and other contemporary rulers may date from early in the caliphate to back-date the relationship with the newly conquered world.[33] Undoubtedly the combination of revealed religion and successful empire that began in the lifetime of Muhammad ibn 'Abdullah required historical support that matched the memories of those who had participated or who knew participants. But by the 'Abbasid period, historical writing served to justify the claims of the religion to universal authority, the claims of the caliphate to widespread terrestrial power and the claims of the ruling 'Abbasid family, which had overthrown the Umayyad rule of the Islamic world.[34]

Those we describe as scholars in early Islamic society were not pursuing abstract knowledge: they were functional members of a complex society, performing functional roles and providing functional interpretations.[35] That does not suggest they were cynically distorting history or inventing facts; it merely reminds us that all writing and publication take place in specific social contexts. 'There is no generally accepted and foolproof method for distinguishing what might be true from what might be false.'[36]

Many non-Muslim historians have accepted the majority of the core traditions of the Prophet's life, even if they consider some of the details of his military victories amplified over time. Yet they still decline to accept as history that the angel Jibril transported Muhammad ibn 'Abdullah at night to Jerusalem on a winged animal, or other 'supernatural' events (and acknowledgements of his religiosity) attributed to the earlier life of Muhammad ibn 'Abdullah when he did not yet have 'Companions' in his religion to remember events.

That all the major events in Muhammad ibn 'Abdullah's early life were said to have happened on the same day of the week, a Monday, is a reminder of the issues with the sources.[37] So too is the attempt by early Muslim historians to attribute other symmetries to the Prophet's life, with 10 years of revelation while resident in Medina exactly balanced by 10 years of revelation while based in Mecca.[38]

It might be noted that this is not very different from western historians' use of documents such as the 8th-century *Ecclesiastical History of the English People* by the English monk Bede. His accounts of English history form an essential source for historians who nevertheless discount and edit out his accounts of 52 miracles that he reported with equal confidence and certainty.

While we lack non-Muslim contemporary sources for the life of Muhammad ibn 'Abdullah we do of course have sources from the nations subsequently attacked by the Arab armies. The term 'Arabs' was not necessarily used to describe Muslim armies from Arabia who conquered territories of the Byzantine and Sasanian Empires in the 7th century: they may have been described as Saracens, or *Muhajirun*, or *Mawla*, Hagarites or Ishmaelites, or followers of the new religion.[39] The Muslim community is not known to have used the term 'Arab' for itself until the Umayyad period of the early 8th century. It must therefore be conceded that when, as in this chapter, we use 'Arab conquests' this risks being anachronistic terminology.[40] However, our use of the terms 'Muslim conquests' or 'Islamic conquests' does not imply that religion was the purpose of the Arabian armies.

These external sources provide us with some details and chronology.[41] In a document from Syria two years after the conventional date of the Prophet's death, the *Doctrina Jacobi* of 634 noted 'A false prophet has appeared among the Saracens'. The patriarch of Jerusalem, Sophronius, who died in 638, wrote of the 'Saracen' advance on Palestine, before he surrendered Jerusalem to the Arab caliph. A text in Syriac possibly dated to 636 wrote of the Arabs of Muhmd, probably the earliest reference to the Prophet known today.

In the changing historiography concerning Islam, contexts of critics and writers have been highly influential. There have always been polemicists from an Islamic religious viewpoint. There have long been (and continue to be) anti-Islamic polemicists from a Jewish or Christian viewpoint. Many non-Muslim western scholars of modern times have sought to apply their linguistic, literary or historical skills to the documents of early Islam in a way that would not offend their fellow scholars from within the Islamic world.

But more independent critical views have been published over recent decades, which affirm their authors' priority to critical intellectual endeavour without formal respect to religious sensitivities. Books by a number of scholars have examined anew some of the sources on early Islam to propose interpretations at variance with those of their predecessors, as noted in this chapter. These were before and independent of the lay hostility to Islam that has emerged since the revival of radical militant 'Islamist' political movements. Given the gap between the available 'Abbasid manuscripts and the events they describe, such attempts at 'revisionism' are unsurprising. Debates will continue on what aspects of the traditional early Islamic histories of the life of Muhammad ibn 'Abdullah and his immediate successors are accurate and reliable statements of what happened in the late 6th and early 7th centuries.

The Middle East before Islam

The rapid successful Arabian conquests in the three decades after the death of Muhammad ibn 'Abdullah in 632 demolished much of the duopoly that had governed and fought over the Middle East for centuries: dynasties derived from Persia and the successors to the Greco-Roman world. Their most recent conflict had weakened both powers, the Sasanians and the Byzantines. The speed with which their territory was taken by the armies from the south shows how fragile their control had become. It seems likely that the Arabian armies included fighters experienced in warfare within the armies of those they conquered, but the combination of a new world faith and a succession of victorious occupations of Sasanian and Byzantine possessions made the Arabs' will and ability to unite and conquer ever greater.

The Sasanian Empire was Iranian (Persian) by origin but its political centre lay in Iraq (Mesopotamia), with its capital, Ctesiphon, on the Tigris, 22 miles (35 km) from where the successor city of Baghdad would be founded. Byzantium (ruled from Constantinople or 'New Rome') had struggled against the Sasanians for 300 years. While the Byzantines would focus on retaining their lands in Europe and western Anatolia over the successive centuries, their control of the Levant and Egypt quickly fell to the Islamic newcomers from the south.

The borders between land controlled by the Sasanian Persians and lands controlled by the Greek-speaking Byzantines had shifted one way then the other during their conflicts, but neither had established control over the Arabian Peninsula, and neither seems to have anticipated, or taken action to prevent, assault from this direction.

Arguably the Byzantine–Sasanian rivalry was an extension of the clash between the classical (Greco-Roman) world of Europe and the eastern world of Persia that dated back to the 6th century BCE. The Median rulers from Persia (Iran) had replaced the power of Assyria in the late 7th century BCE, extending their control through much of Mesopotamia and north as far as eastern Anatolia. In the mid-6th century BCE, with the rise of Cyrus II, 'the Great', and Achaemenid rule, Persian control extended across Anatolia to the Ionian Greek settlements in its west, was consolidated in Mesopotamia, and reached to Palestine and Syria. Cyrus's successor, Cambyses, expanded the empire to Egypt in 525 BCE. Arabia remained outside Achaemenid rule; perhaps it was seen as a predominantly arid area, of interest only for its trade routes.

In direct conflict in 500–479 BCE between Greece and Persia (ruled by Darius I, then Xerxes I), which followed revolt by Greeks in Ionia, the southern Greek city states held the Persians at bay. Something of a stand-off between Greeks and the Persian Empire characterised the next century and a half, with minor clashes. The conquest of the Persian Empire by Alexander the Great (334–330 BCE) brought Achaemenid power to an end. The Greek successors of Alexander's expedition established their own power. Rule by Greek-speaking Macedonian families (the Ptolemies) continued in Egypt until the Roman occupation of Egypt (30 BCE). The Seleucids, of Hellenistic descent, who ruled Persia, Mesopotamia, Anatolia and the Levant, gradually lost territory to the Romans in the west and from the mid-3rd century BCE to the Arsacid dynasty of Parthians from Iran in the east.

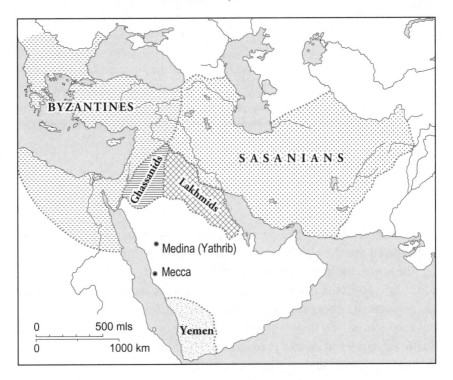

5. The Middle East *ca.* 600 CE

The rise of the Sasanian dynasty of Persia from the 3rd century CE and their defeat of the Parthian rulers gave them four centuries of control, not just of Persia but of Mesopotamia. This brought them into conflict with the Roman Empire and specifically with the Eastern Empire ruled from Byzantium from 330 CE. While Rome or Byzantium would never occupy Iraq nor Sasanians possess Constantinople, the two powers fought across territory west and east of the intermediate area. A treaty of 'Eternal Peace' was signed in 532; then war broke out again eight years later.

To the south, Arab client kingdoms provided an effective buffer with the Arabian Peninsula. The Lakhmids, west of the lower Euphrates at the north of Arabia, were periodic allies of the Sasanians and the alliance between the Sasanians and the Nasrids who ruled the Lakhmid territory gave them both political advantages and safety for essential trade goods. Influence (but not control) may have extended for a period as far south as Medina.[42] Despite the alliance with the Sasanians, the historical suggestion that the Lakhmid capital of al-Hira(h) had a substantial Christian population was confirmed

Key dates	
532	Byzantine–Sasanian treaty
541	Justinian plague begins
570	Birth of Muhammad
613	First public recitations
632	Death of Muhammad
632–661	Rightly Guided Caliphs (Rashidun)
636	Battles of Qadisiyyah, Yarmuk
637	Surrender of Jerusalem
661–750	Umayyad dynasty
750–1258	'Abbasid dynasty

by excavations there.[43] After an attack by the Muslim armies in 633, al-Hira surrendered and this allowed its Christian tradition to continue.

The Sasanians' annexation of the Lakhmid territory in 602 (shortly before Muhammad ibn 'Abdullah's emergence as a religious and political leader) may have weakened rather than strengthened their protection from the threat that emerged successfully from within Arabia. Sasanians effectively controlled the south-western tip of Arabia (Yemen) in the last decades of the 6th century, replacing Christian allies of Byzantium.

To the west of the Lakhmids but east of the areas of Palestine and Syria, the Jafnids, who ruled the Ghassanid kingdom (a community who traced their origins back to a 3rd-century migration from Yemen), were allies of Byzantium, and then from the late 6th century a client state, providing a further buffer zone from Arabia.

The spread of the bubonic plague across the Middle East in the mid-6th century, named the Justinian plague after the ruling Byzantine emperor, took its toll on states and populations in the most densely settled areas, and there is reason to suggest climatic events from the mid-6th century onwards (the 'Late Antique Little Ice Age') had a significant impact. One example is the site of Elusa, in the Negev region, where a collapse of the urban social order is dated to coincide with the period of these crises.[44]

The final conflict between the two empires lasted through much of Muhammad ibn 'Abdullah's lifetime, from 602 to 628. It must have inspired awareness among the Arabs that the weakening of the two great powers gave an opportunity to establish a new order. As Byzantium sought to regain control of western lands in the Roman sphere, Sasanian military expeditions between ca. 613 and 619 gained control of Byzantine territory in Anatolia, Syria and Palestine before securing Egypt, which they occupied for less than a decade. New Rome struck back with Byzantine emperor Heraclius regaining control of Egypt and much of the newly occupied areas, and negotiations were undertaken in 628 between the two weakened nations. The stay in long-term hostilities between the two powers proved irrelevant, for by then the followers of Muhammad ibn 'Abdullah to the south had set in train the religious, political and military developments that would undo the power of both empires in the region.

History and Arabia

Although the 7th-century incursion of armies from the Arabian Peninsula was a dramatic change to the political order of the eastern Old World, they were far from the first power based in Arabia. Historians of late antiquity may have long expressed wonder that major states were overthrown by forces from an unexpected source to the south. Islamic historians have emphasised that it was only through the power of the new religious revelation of Islam that the Arab people could rise to impose God's will in victories over the established great powers. But although the Hijaz itself had not been a powerful region, Arabia before Islam had been much more than just a barren wilderness occupied by nomads and traders.

The final Neo-Babylonian king, Nabonidus, had travelled to Yathrib (the future Medina) and made the Hijaz oasis of Tayma his personal base for a number of years around 552–543 BCE. His return to Babylon did not save him, as Cyrus the Great captured him and ended his rule. Tayma, as well as Dedan and Duma, are oases of the Hijaz mentioned in early Islamic sources.[45]

The east coast of Arabia on the Persian (Arabian) Gulf had cities and settlements of significant prosperity from as far back as the 3rd millennium BCE, reflecting their relationship to the great powers in Iraq and Iran, and maritime trade eastwards. Their gaze looked away from the Arabian Peninsula.[46]

Relations between eastern Arabia and the Sasanian Empire fluctuated. Arab incursions into Iraq were recorded between the end of the 2nd century BCE and the early 1st century CE.[47] After initial Sasanian military incursions in the early 3rd century CE, the Lakhmid polity as a Sasanian client exercised some control but by the early 4th century it proved necessary for the Sasanians themselves again to take the military initiative. By the 5th century, control had lapsed again before a final Sasanian push in the mid-6th century.[48] The archaeology of the region indicates that this control was modest and largely indirect. The opportunity arose for Arab tribes in the area to operate independently from Sasanian control, until the power of the Muslim forces eroded that opportunity.[49]

In the far north of the desert region, Palmyra (today's Tadmur in Syria) was long a prosperous city on east–west trade routes. Through its ancient history it played roles in clientship to a succession of empires in the region. Its greatest independent role lay in the later 3rd century CE (with the famous queen Zenobia a regent) when Palmyra made war on the Eastern Roman Empire. The city was an early conquest by the Islamic Arab armies in 634.

The Nabataean state in the far north-west of the Arabian Peninsula, extending as far as the Dead Sea, was a powerful polity. It is famous for its city of Raqmu (Petra in modern Jordan). The Nabataeans were described as 'Arabs' by the Roman writer Diodorus Siculus. Emerging by the 4th century BCE, the Nabataeans had acquired regional prominence in the 1st century BCE, by when their power and influence extended southwards. They were conquered by the Roman armies of Emperor Trajan in 106 CE and became a province ('Arabia Petraea') of the Roman Empire. By the time the Islamic conquerors overran these lands, they were largely Christianised and no longer an area of riches, but traders from the south could be well aware of the ruins that reflected a once great Arab state.

The ancient societies of Yemen and south-western Arabia were well known through the ancient world. Classical sources referred to the different peoples of south-west Arabia; in the 3rd century BCE these were described as Sabaeans, Minaeans, Qatabaeans and Hadramites. The languages of South Arabia were from a quite different branch from those, including Arabic, to the north.[50]

With origins possibly as far back as the later 2nd millennium BCE, Saba' developed into a powerful and wealthy trading nation. Archaeology shows the monumental constructions they erected; the Marib Dam, built in the 6th-century BCE to control the region's seasonal waters and manage irrigation, is considered a pioneering work of civil engineering.[51] Saba' is commonly (though not universally) identified in the later biblical narrative as the homeland of the Queen of Sheba, who arrived at Solomon's court in Jerusalem with gifts.[52]

The numerous inscriptions from South Arabia in Sabaean script (though in different languages) extend from the 8th century BCE to the end of the 3rd century CE; then the numbers significantly reduce, and there are no more after the mid-6th century.

The Yemen region is important not least because of trade routes: the Hijaz and Medina lay on the trade routes between Yemen and the rich areas of the Levant and beyond. In turn, the Yemen area was a trading gateway to Ethiopia and East Africa, and to the Indian Ocean. The main traded products north from Yemen in antiquity were spices: myrrh and frankincense especially, both used in ritual in the Greco-Roman world. But between the 1st century BCE and the 1st century CE, when Rome ruled over a vast area, sea trade was secure and more important than the overland trade seen on the eve of Islam.[53]

One tradition claimed that peoples from Yemen had migrated north to the Hijaz in the 1st or 2nd centuries CE, some remaining there, some continuing north.[54] Other traditions suggest migrations of this kind in the 3rd century. A revealing short inscription from the later 3rd century CE, found at Jabal Riyam in Yemen, records the political entities of Arabia as experienced by a traveller northwards.[55] An interpretation of the text placed Ghassanids in the Hijaz and the Lihyan to the north and south.

Civil war brought down the existing Sabaean power, and rule by the neighbouring Himyarite kingdom was established in the 1st century BCE but did not last long. The Sabaean temple of the god Almaqah at Marib remained a shrine of central importance, before the power of the Sabaean state declined again. Himyarite rule resumed in the late 3rd century CE. An historically interesting aspect of the Himyarites is the rulers' conversion in the late 4th century CE to a form of Judaism, sometimes called Judaeo-Monotheism or Rahmanism.[56] This was perhaps a reaction to the Christianisation of the Ethiopians across the Red Sea. There was a century of conflict between the Himyarites and Ethiopians from the Christian Axumite kingdom, which had already held a settlement in southern Arabia. This conflict led to the Himyarites' defeat around 525 CE and the imposition of Christian rule in the Yemen, during a period marked by further rebellion, until removed by Sasanian activity. In the Islamic histories, an expedition from Yemen reached as far north as the region of Mecca about the time Muhammad ibn 'Abdullah was born, before retreating south.

Sasanian control of the coast and parts of south-west Arabia was established about 570 CE. A substantial silver mine in Yemen was operating in the 6th century CE, and mining continued as a source of wealth in Islamic Arabia. The collapse of the Marib Dam in Saba' around 575 CE (a date confirmed by archaeological work) was a practical and symbolic marker of the decline of Yemen, an event at the beginning of Muhammad ibn 'Abdullah's life that secured a reference in the Qur'an itself.[57]

The area remained under Persian influence but the weakness of the state laid it open for a new role as part of the Islamic Arab world, and the Islamic armies took control at the very end of Muhammad ibn 'Abdullah's lifetime. It appears that Yemenite communities did not accept the classification as 'Arabs' until after the arrival of Islam.[58]

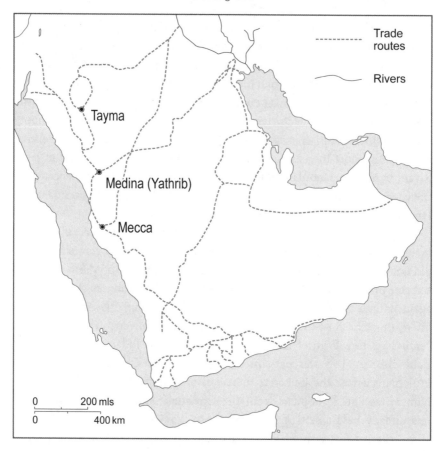

6. A reconstruction of pre-Islamic Arabian trade routes (after D.T. Potts)

There were numerous active trade routes in the Sasanian era: 'constant movement throughout the entire peninsula'.[59] These continued to pass through the Hijaz, and the Arab residents of Yathrib and other settlements near oases along the trade routes could remain prosperous and secure.[60] Mecca was traditionally described as benefiting from such trade too, an image not without challenge from some modern historians.[61]

Thus Arabia was host to an extended sequence of change and development, the shifting power of local kingdoms and wealth from trade, agriculture, pastoralism and the economy of urban settlements. The wealth of the towns on the Gulf was substantial; the Yemeni states attracted widespread fame; the Nabataean kingdom and Palmyra were major entities in the ancient world. But the Hijaz region of western Arabia was central to none of these states, large or small, as they rose and fell. The residents of this relatively arid region focussed on what mattered most to traders: material wealth. Because the Hijaz lacked the kind of ports that provided deep anchorages for trading vessels, it is likely that most of the traditional trade was by north–south land routes. In the model given by later Islamic historians, trade within Arabia was dominated by central markets at which seasonal gatherings would be the most important times for both exchange and also for religious activity.[62]

If an educated and informed citizen of one of the great powers in the year 600 had considered the ebb and flow of politics, they would be aware that the strength of the Persian/Mesopotamian world and the Greco-Roman world was affected by what happened in intermediate areas like the Levant and Anatolia, and by who controlled the 'gift of the Nile', Egypt. They could be aware that far away from the 'civilised' world kingdoms existed or had existed in the far south-west of Arabia and in the highlands of Ethiopia. They would not expect that from settlements along the trade routes in the west of the Arabian Peninsula a new force (backed by the ideology of a new religion) would emerge to sweep away the powers that had long controlled the Middle East.

Religion at the brink of the rise of Islam

The new rulers from the Hijaz were united by a new monotheistic faith with a strongly defined set of rules for personal, social and public life. But the areas around them were far from culturally coherent. There was substantial variety in languages, in ethnic identity and in religious observance. The Arabian Peninsula in the late 6th and early 7th centuries CE was bordered by, and penetrated by, a range of religious ideas as well as political and economic changes. The religious pattern of the Middle East helps in understanding the emergence and success of Islam.

Under the 'Abbasid caliphate, historical and theological writings emphasised the role of religion in the founding of the Islamic empire. In this narrative, guided by a God who had sent humankind messages through his final earthly Prophet, Muhammad ibn 'Abdullah, those who accepted the message he delivered were destined to replace polytheisms and false monotheisms with true religion. In particular, the sources emphasise a widespread idolatrous polytheism in the Arabia of Muhammad's youth, from which Islam provided a salvation. Other monotheisms, accepted in the early Islamic conquests, were now subject to criticism – Christianity's trinitarianism had been condemned in Quranic verses.

Most religious groups like to establish classifications to contrast their own movement and followers with others. These descriptions may be binary (the faithful and the heathen) or they may be more nuanced (Islam's 'People of the Book') and these simple classifications can be extended back to apply to past societies. Reality is more complex: 'conversion' does not mean a wholesale abandonment of previous beliefs; a community described as Muslim or Christian or Jewish may have families and individuals with quite different loyalties and beliefs; and the religious affiliation of the ruling groups may be very far from the beliefs, rituals and loyalties of their many subjects. In considering the religions before, during and after the rise of Islam in Arabia, the broader Middle East and neighbouring regions, we need to avoid assumptions that group large numbers of people into a single category, and be aware that most societies would include in differing proportions people with different religious devotions, even if these societies were not formally recognised as pluralistic.

There has been much discussion about the religious background to Islam. It does seem likely that at least until the 4th century CE the majority of the inhabitants of Arabia – settled and nomad – were polytheists in one or another definition of that term.[63] The influences of Christian and Jewish communities were limited. But many areas of the Middle East and beyond were seeing the growth of Christian communities of one kind and another; influential Jewish families and groups were to be found in many locations in the region; and Sasanian tolerance of their subjects' diverse religions beyond their own Zoroastrianism provided their empire with strength rather than weakness.

Within the Arabian Peninsula a wide range of monotheistic and polytheistic religious ideas and practices seem to have been practised at the time of Muhammad ibn 'Abdullah's revelations, although our use of the concept of 'polytheism' may be a simplification of adherence to a hierarchy of divine beings.[64] Many may have already perceived Allah as a supreme deity. One argument suggests that the emphasis of Muhammad's preaching was to attract those adhering or attracted to other monotheisms. In this model, the narrative that Islam was revealed to Muhammad ibn 'Abdullah as a major contrast to his own world of idolatrous polytheism was a later construction, or at least a later emphasis, although the Muslim traditions would report his interactions with Jews and Christians.[65]

The Sasanian rulers, like the Persian conquerors who preceded them, were adherents of Zoroastrianism. The Qur'an has numerous references that echo Judaism or aspects of Christianity but no apparent Zoroastrian influences. The 'Magians' (*majus*) referred to once alongside Jews, Christians and Sabaeans are generally considered to be the only reference in the Qur'an to the Zoroastrians.[66]

Within Sasanian territory other religions thrived. In upper Iraq there was a substantial Christian population. Christians in the Sasanian heartlands were predominantly Nestorians: followers of a theology that orthodox Byzantine Christians saw as heretical. Christian communities found themselves in something of a buffer zone between the Arabian Peninsula and the Zoroastrians, away from the main trade routes of the Hijaz or western Arabia. Smaller groups of Christians were present in lower Iraq and Persia. Jewish communities could be found within the Sasanian lands and some Jewish individuals played important roles in the Sasanian polity.[67]

When the Sasanian Persian army conquered Jerusalem in 614 they seized from the Byzantine Christians the relic believed to be fragments of the 'True Cross' on which Jesus had been crucified. But when they took this back to Ctesiphon it was put in the hands of the Nestorian Christians. The later Byzantine victory of 628 returned to Jerusalem what were considered to be the same fragments.[68]

Churches of Eastern Christianity dominated the Byzantine territory: Anatolia and the Levant. The Ghassanids of northern Arabia ruled a Christian community by the time of the rise of Islam. In Egypt the Coptic Church claimed its origins from Saint Mark and the apostles. From the 5th century it took a different organisational path from the churches of Byzantium, with a dispute over theological ('Monophysite') interpretations. Of substantial antiquity was the Christian church in Ethiopia (Abyssinia), where Christianity had become the state religion of the Kingdom of Axum in the 330s. On the other side of the Red Sea, individual Christian communities, influenced by Monophysite missions, were scattered across the Arabian Peninsula.[69] Ethiopian political influence in Yemen was matched by religious influence.

After the religious revelations announced by the 3rd-century CE Mesopotamian-born prophet Mani, followers of Manichaeism had spread through the Persian, Greco-Roman and Egyptian worlds and beyond; the Christian leader Augustine (from Roman Numidia, in modern Algeria) had initially been an adherent in the late 4th century. Although facing active hostility from the Roman, Byzantine and Sasanian states, there were still followers of Manichaeism in the Middle East into the 'Abbasid era of Islam.

No region of the Sasanian or Byzantine Middle East was exclusively Jewish, although Jewish religious and ethnic communities had been spread across the Middle East since the Achaemenid era. Jews and synagogues were present in Iran and Mesopotamia (Iraq), in Anatolia, Syria and Palestine, in Egypt, in Ethiopia and in Yemen, as well as along the trade routes of the Hijaz.[70] Iraq had remained a centre for Jewish communities; the 'Babylonian Talmud' had its source in this area, probably completed under Sasanian rule during the 4th to the 6th centuries. Jews in 6th- and 7th-century Arabia were merchants and traders, date palm cultivators in the Hijaz and elsewhere, living in towns and settling around oases.

Jewish individuals were documented in the Hijaz at Hegra and also at Dedan in the first centuries CE, and the form of Judaism of the Yemen began with the conversion of the Himyarite king, perhaps around 380 CE, and continued until the conflict with Ethiopia about 520. A more traditional Jewish community seems to have lived in the area before this conversion.[71] The significant presence of Jewish communities in the Hijaz is emphasised in the early Islamic histories of the Prophet's life, with Yathrib (Medina) especially identified as the location of a Jewish population. Muhammad ibn 'Abdullah's relations with the Jews of Arabia formed an important part of his biography (as well as a visible element in the Qur'an).

The important Jewish population of Yathrib in the narratives of the Prophet's life raises the question of their origin. While they have been considered as part of the substantial Jewish diaspora of the Middle East, there are also reasons to suggest some may have been Arab converts.[72]

The Qur'an contains numerous references to Jewish prophets, Old Testament episodes and Jewish cultural norms. It has fewer references to Jesus, while considering him the last of the prophets before Muhammad ibn 'Abdullah, and it lacks any mention of the influential Christian evangelists and apostles. The name Musa (Moses) has 143 mentions, Ibrahim (Abraham) has 70, Nuh (Noah) has 45, Adam has 25, Dawud (David) has 16, Sulayman (Solomon) has 16, Ismail (Ishmael) has 12, whereas the name of Isa (Jesus, Yeshua) has 27 mentions. Yahya (John – the Baptist) is mentioned 5 times, Zakariyya (Zechariah) 7, while Maryam (Mary, mother of Jesus) is mentioned more frequently, on 35 occasions. The references to individuals (though not to theology) from the Christian tradition indicate the contact of Muhammad ibn 'Abdullah with the Christian communities he encountered on his travels. Some may have been orthodox Christians in the Syriac tradition, although it has been suggested that a specifically 'Jewish Christianity' was a significant influence.[73]

The common occurrence of these references, but also the style and context of their presentation, implies that Muhammad ibn 'Abdullah's audiences were familiar with these narratives and their religious significance.[74] This contrasts with the emphasis on Arabian polytheism given by Muslim historians. We thus have conflicting images: were those to whom the Prophet addressed his recitations steeped in the falsity and ignorance of tribal polytheism, or were they well aware of the monotheistic traditions and narratives on which he built?

We envisage Muhammad ibn 'Abdullah as a merchant, born and working on the trade routes that linked the southern Red Sea to the Levant and beyond. In that context he would have frequently encountered Christian communities of orthodox Eastern churches, Nestorians and Monophysites. He would have interacted regularly with Jews as minorities in the region and solid in their own faith and identity. He would have met all kinds (and degrees) of polytheists in the areas of Arabia that were not part of the Byzantine or Sasanian world. He would have experienced other degrees of monotheism within Arabia, and monolatry – the dedication to one single god while others were believed to exist.[75]

He would also be aware of other contemporary individuals who had religious ideas to challenge the range of current norms. In early 7th-century Arabia, another prophet emerged declaring a revelation from God delivered through the angel Jibril (Gabriel). This revelation was announced in poetic form and included guidelines for daily life as well as belief. Followers of this new faith started to exert political power in much of Arabia. The prophet's name was Maslamah (also known as Musaylimah, and al-Rahman), and we know of him through later Islamic denunciations.[76] Other such prophets and proselytisers included Khalid b. Sinan and Hanzala b. Safwan.[77] They too were mentioned, and denounced, in the later Islamic texts. Monotheistic ideas at least initially independent of those of Muhammad came from his contemporaries Abu Amir Abd Amr b. Sayfi, Abu Qays b. al-Islat and Zayd b. Amir.[78] Some like Tulayha b. Khuwaylid or the female Sajah, both also living at the same time as Muhammad ibn 'Abdullah, would combine a role as a prophet with political leadership. A contemporary of Muhammad ibn 'Abdullah, a boy from the Jewish community of Medina, Saf b. Sayyad, claimed prophetic insights and uttered incantations that demonstrated this. However, the question remains whether some of these were in fact imitators of Muhammad, inspired by his initial success. Additionally, three non-biblical prophets of ancient Arabia are cited in the Qur'an: Hud, Salih and Shu'ayb.[79]

This information shows that Muhammad ibn 'Abdullah was not the only proselytiser of new religious ideas in the Middle East of his era, nor unique in combining religious and political authority. As with the context that produced Joseph Smith, Jun., or Yeshua (Jesus of Nazareth), the times produced the prophets but history decided which prophets would secure long-term followers. Although Muhammad ibn 'Abdullah was not the only preacher of new religious ideas in the early 7th-century Middle East, it was his message that succeeded in uniting a large following, strong enough to become a new political and military force.

A different interpretation of the relation of Muhammad ibn 'Abdullah's Islam to other monotheisms is advanced by US scholar Fred M. Donner. He notes the predominance of the term *mu'minun* (singular *mu'min*) – the 'Believers' or the faithful – in the Qur'an and early Islam, rather than references to Muslims. This suggests that the initial formation of Islam may have included monotheists with broader beliefs than came to be defined as the Islamic faith. In this model, Jews and Christians could also be considered in the Qur'an as 'Believers'.[80] Details of the Jewish and Christian communities in Arabia during Muhammad ibn 'Abdullah's time are not well documented, and contradictions and uncertainty surrounding the historical narratives of the period do not help to resolve this question. But this model would suggest how the Arab polity managed so readily to build allegiance from different groups across Arabia and meet limited opposition in its early conquests; early caliphs called themselves 'Commanders of the Believers'.[81]

Donner further notes that while later traditions told of the military success of violent conquests, archaeology does not show evidence of destruction accompanying the arrival of Arab/Islamic power. This would extend the view that the Muslim conquerors did not force conversion on monotheistic Jews or Christians, to an idea that they were initially accepted as part of the community of 'Believers', awaiting the last judgement they all considered would happen, and perhaps expected to happen soon. The argument suggests that Islam started as 'an apocalyptic oriented pietistic movement'.[82]

This argument implies that the religious identity of Islam in opposition to other monotheisms, as well as the emphasis on Arab identity, may have emerged only at the very end of the 7th century, when we first see the role of Muhammad ibn 'Abdullah emphasised.[83] Another bold, earlier and somewhat experimental study discussed a transition to formal Islam during the reign of the fifth Umayyad caliph, 'Abd al-Malik (685–705), and emphasised Judaic influences on early Islamic doctrines visible in the Qur'an.[84] These contributions to debates have not been widely accepted to replace more conventional views of the nature of early Islam.

A corpus of the earliest Islamic inscriptions indicates the process of change.[85] Although the name Allah is found in inscriptions before the 690s, the first inscribed name of the Prophet does not appear until some 60 years after his death.[86] The earliest Muslim tombstone known, from 651–652, makes no mention of Muhammad.[87] Quranic phrases are found within inscriptions that appear to date as early as the 650s and 660s. Two coins dated 690–691 state 'In the name of God, Muhammad is the messenger of God', but these coins were found at Fars in Iran and minted by a leader rebelling against the Umayyad rulers.[88] An inscription at the Dome of the Rock in Jerusalem constructed under 'Abd al-Malik's rule in 691–692 (the date may refer to the start or completion of the work) states 'There is no god but God alone … Muhammad is the messenger of God' and this site has the first mention of Muslims. The Prophet is mentioned on tombstones after this period.

Given the limited sources from the period of early Islam, our historical knowledge of the religious context of Islam's origins remains subject to diverse interpretations, and vigorous debates are sure to continue.

Geography and the puzzle of Mecca

Islamic civilisation would rule and flourish in the most prosperous and productive areas of the Middle East, but its origins lay in environmentally much poorer places. The great civilisations of the ancient Middle East developed and thrived in the Nile Valley; in the Fertile Crescent, which extended from Mesopotamia through to the Levant; and in upland but still agriculturally productive areas of Iran and Anatolia. Here over the millennia hunter-gatherers had created intensive semi-permanent settlements, wild plants had become cultivated, hunted animals domesticated, village life developed into town and city life, and states with hierarchies, craft specialisation and writing had emerged. Through these regions lay trade routes that linked Asia, Africa and Europe, and it had access to the maritime trade of the Mediterranean. The Arabian Peninsula was marginal both geographically and to a large extent culturally to these developments. If it had been an area of substantial and accessible mineral wealth, of rich agricultural potential, or with large populations, it would have attracted greater attention from the competing empires that conquered and reconquered territories across the Middle East. Yet Arabia was not an arid wasteland of nomads – it had a geographical diversity and a strong history and prehistory of its own.

The Arabian Peninsula is far from unvaried, and the concept of 'Arabia' is an artificial and historically determined one. Arabia proper has an estimated area of 1.2 million square miles (3.1 million km²) but the desert regions to the north – the Syrian desert, the Negev, Sinai – can be considered an extension of the peninsula.

Topography in the peninsula changes dramatically, geology and rainfall create patterns of vegetation that have offered different economic potential over time, and therefore different and changing patterns of human settlement.

Trade within and beyond Arabia was a key to prosperity and the peninsula was positioned for the control not just of land trade routes but also of the maritime trade linking the region with East Africa and the Red Sea to the west and South Asia and beyond to the east.

The east of the peninsula held its historical importance from proximity to the Persian (Arabian) Gulf, along which travelled trade goods. These lands faced Iran, and and the role of eastern Arabia was determined by development across the Gulf, but especially in lower Mesopotamia; therefore its focus lay north, beyond Arabia. The sand desert of the Rub' al-Khali (the 'Empty Quarter') separates the east from minimally watered inland regions of sand and rock, where sparse nomad populations travelling between oases were the most that the land could support.

But south-western Arabia provided a different range of opportunities. The Yemen region, through which pass the Asir Mountains, guarded entry to the Red Sea, and is only 20 miles (30 km) from the coast of Africa. The annual rainfall, brought by the monsoon and trapped by the mountain range, which reaches as high as 12,000 feet (3,600 m), is much greater than in any other part of Arabia. This gave the region fertility, a benefit over the rest of Arabia, and gave it the classical name 'Arabia Eudaimon' or 'Arabia Felix' – Fortunate Arabia. To the east of Yemen the area of Hadramaut (Hadramawt) is far more arid than western Yemen, but at times historically had links with Yemeni states.

The mountain soils remain semi-desert northwards along the coastal region as far as the Gulf of Aqaba, but with patches that permitted irrigation as well as larger areas where nomadism could thrive. While the desert and semi-desert regions might look forbidding to residents of the more fertile lands to the north, those who grew up in western Arabia knew how to manage the land, its resources and also how to use their location to trade with the prosperous northern lands.

Stretching along the western Arabian coast south of the Gulf of Aqaba, the Hijaz (or Hejaz or Hidjaz) region is marked by uplands parallel to the Red Sea, with heights ranging from 5,000 to 8,000 feet (1,500–2,500 m), which mark off a coastal region from the inland desert. Although the word 'Hijaz' means 'divide' or 'barrier' – the watershed – the term has come to mean the region that includes the Tihama coastal plane, the mountain escarpment itself and the part of the Nejd plateau immediately east of the range.[89] Despite its aridity, it was from the Hijaz in the 7th century that Islam began as a religion and Arab power emerged to create a world empire.

Ancient rocks rather than windblown sands mark the landforms, here exposed in the broken ridge line. With low rainfall, the soils are generally poor and unproductive, especially in the north (from Sinai and the Gulf of Aqaba south towards the latitude of Medina), where rainfall is minimal. South from there, the rainfall is better and the vegetation could be described as semi-desert rather than desert, with a few oases. On slopes facing south-west, especially south of Mecca, more productive land is aided by water from mountain springs. There is thus more cultivation in general in the southern Hijaz.

In the core of the Hijaz there are wadis (seasonal watercourses), some flowing east of the range but important ones flowing west into the sea. Before modern times the oases provided the water necessary to support life but since natural vegetation in the Hijaz is scrubby, cultivation at the oases was crucial. This pattern meant a divide between nomadic Bedouin herders and those whose lives focussed on the larger settlements, where trade was the primary economic driver. Of course, since the rise of Islam, the passage of pilgrims contributed to, and then transformed, the economic life of the holy cities of Mecca and Medina.

Although the Hijaz is known historically for its role in trade, much of this was by land routes, primarily between south and north. Trading access to the Red Sea from small ports may well have existed: al-Shu'ayba is cited in the early traditions as important to Meccan trade but this could be a later rationalisation. The old port of Rabigh lacks a true harbour so that larger trading vessels there needed their goods to be transferred to the shore by smaller craft.[90]

While Mecca lies on the western side of the range, at an altitude of just over 900 feet (277 m), Medina, at almost 2,000 feet (over 600 m), lies higher in the plateau, some 95 miles (150 km) from the coast. The travelling distance from Mecca to Medina is about 200 miles (330 km). Around and north of Mecca, in the arid coastal lowland, sandy plains and occasional wadis mean very limited water and very poor vegetation. In the higher areas around Medina, the soils are deeper and there are some natural terraces with deposits laid down by the seasonal watercourses, although rainfall is sporadic, unpredictable and unreliable. But on the rising land between the two locations, the wadis carry more water run-off, the alluvial soils are richer and deeper, and in this area the natural vegetation is more abundant and the possibilities for plant agriculture strongest, with underground water accessible from wells.[91] Summer temperatures rise to 45°C in Mecca and 40°C in Medina.

Medina (Yathrib in early sources) seems to have been a major location on trade routes of pre-Islamic Arabia. It appears to have been a cluster of communities in Muhammad ibn 'Abdullah's time (including the Jewish groups recorded in the histories), an 'oasis complex' rather than a consolidated town, spread over perhaps 20 square miles (50 km²) on flat ground in a relatively well watered oasis location. Wadis pass through the region from north to south. There were many wells and springs, so agriculture (notably date palms but also cereals) could complement Yathrib's role in trade. The third of the Rightly Guided Caliphs, 'Uthman, was reported to have built a dam wall as protection against seasonal floodwater. A dam from the early Umayyad period has been studied 9 miles (15 km) east of Medina.[92]

Mecca (Makka) by contrast is not set in a fertile section of the Hijaz. It lies in a wadi between two ranges of steep hills; its role as a settlement was made possible by underground water sources. It was not an agricultural area and according to the 10th-century Arab geographer al-Muqaddasi it had 'suffocating heat, deadly winds, and clouds of flies'. The occasional flooding in the wadi by seasonal rains was addressed by early Muslim caliphs with flood prevention engineering.

In the traditions recorded in the medieval Islamic histories, Mecca was sited at the crossroads of trading routes south to Yemen, north and north-east to the Fertile Crescent (including Syria and Mesopotamia) and west to the Red Sea,[93] and it contained an important cultic shrine (or shrines) that Muhammad ibn 'Abdullah transformed to make Mecca a centre of Islamic religious life. If this information is accurate, it would explain why a town grew up in such an otherwise unpromising location. The 'Abbasid histories claimed that the trading wealth of the Quraysh and of Mecca itself owed much to Muhammad ibn 'Abdullah's great-grandfather, who brought both into international standing. But doubts exist as to the historical veracity of these images and in modern critical studies pre-Islamic Mecca remains an enigma. Notably, Mecca was unknown in history until after Islam had spread. None of the ancient sources on Arabia collected in a recent 600-page survey mention a place called Mecca.[94]

If Mecca was not at the junction of major trade routes and did not have an important shrine, as per the traditional account, is it possible that the birthplace of Muhammad ibn 'Abdullah and site of his religious revelations developed in the writings of Islamic history into a place of much greater importance than it actually was? A comparison would lie in the Tanakh's image of a Jerusalem of David and Solomon far grander than it was in reality. If Mecca had been a smaller, less important settlement when Muhammad ibn 'Abdullah began to experience his revelations, that might have fitted less well the later theology and practice, in which pilgrimage to Mecca is one of the pillars of Islam. It has even been suggested that the Prophet may not have come from the town, or that his town was not the site of modern Mecca.[95] Archaeological exploration would be the best means to understand the true nature of Mecca in the lifetime of the Prophet, but such exploration has not taken place.

One exhaustively documented study asked 'what do we actually know?' and concluded 'Nothing if not a problem'. This argued that Mecca was not at a crossroads of trade routes, and not even on a north–south trading route, so not a natural stopping place for merchants; Ta'if, to the south, would be much more of a destination.[96] The prosperity attributed to Mecca in the histories and the role of the Quraysh as wealthy merchants (in some but not all of the traditions) trading incense, spices and other luxury goods to the north would thus be a later construction.[97] By this argument, Meccans were trading in leather, clothing, livestock and perhaps food, dominated by local products rather than imported luxury items.[98] Another suggestion is that the Meccans (with perhaps limited adequate ports) were primarily trading raisins and leather in a mainly local trade.[99] This trade would be with Arabs, including those further north, but not a prosperous long-distance trade network of goods stretching between Yemen and the Byzantine and Sasanian heartlands.

The Islamic traditions cite Mecca as the location of a shrine or temple, with walls of loose stones, and containing the black stone that marks the site today. There is a substantial narrative in the Islamic sources extending the history of the Meccan *ka'ba* back through Muhammad ibn 'Abdullah to pre-Islamic polytheists and to a tradition of its origination with Abraham and his son Ishmael.[100] Another important site of pre-Islamic religious activity appears to have been Arafat, some 11 miles (20 km) east of Mecca, which remains a key location for the Islamic Hajj.[101] A corollary of the critical perspective outlined above would question whether pre-Islamic Mecca was already a sacred location or housed an important shrine for pilgrims before Muhammad ibn 'Abdullah's time, but clearly it gained central importance quickly with the new religious ideas.[102] Historical documents alone seem inadequate to confirm the nature of Mecca before and during the life of the Prophet, and in the absence of a full archaeological record the questions are hard to resolve and conflicting opinions will remain among historians.

Archaeology of the Arabian Peninsula

In the first century of archaeological research in the Middle East, the Arabian Peninsula was largely ignored. There were early excavations in Yemen in the 1920s and 1930s, and more widespread pioneering professional work in the

1960s began to reveal parts of the area, both as extensions of the activities of ancient empires and as a territory with a strong heritage of its own.

Arabia is now considered the route through which anatomically modern humans spread out of Africa to colonise Asia and then New Guinea and Australia. Widespread finds of Stone Age sites across Arabia indicate its past economic potential during varying climatic periods, while the rock art of the region shows the activities of hunter-gatherers, nomadic pastoralists and traders.

Personal interests as well as national and religious affiliations have influenced the emphases of research projects.[103] As a result we know more of the archaeology of the 2nd millennium BCE, when eastern Arabia was an important part of the Mesopotamian Bronze Age polity, than we do of Arabia in the era of Islamic origins. The coast of the Arabian Gulf has been explored in major surveys, excavations and analyses that demonstrate its role in trade and in relation to the Mesopotamian civilisations to the north.

In the Yemen region of south-west Arabia, substantial archaeological work was undertaken over the decades before recent civil strife, both on its prehistory and to complement the historical narrative of Sabaean, Himyarite and other states. The deserts north of the Hijaz – within Jordan, Israel and Syria – have been intensively visited by archaeological expeditions, recording their early and later prehistory and their role in the long history of competing powers. But in the Hijaz, archaeological work is still under-represented and provides no information about the towns of Medina and Mecca at the beginnings of Islam.

Archaeology does echo history in suggesting that the prosperity and urban complexity of both eastern and southern Arabia had experienced serious decline in the period immediately before Islamic conquests. The coast of eastern Arabia bordering the Gulf had seen significant settlement and prosperity in the Seleucid and Parthian periods before the emergence of Sasanian power in the mid-3rd century CE. Sasanian interests in Arabia lay in the economic benefits of trade and in security; but the indirect control effected through the Nasrids in the Lakhmid territory was enough to complement a line of forts that stretched west of Mesopotamia, from Basra to Hit.

Although Sasanian trade goods spread more widely, archaeology suggests the Sasanian period may have been one of reduced active settlement along the coast, and relatively sparse in the southern part of the Gulf. Historical sources imply that Arabia – and specifically north-eastern Arabia – was more important before and after the 5th centuries, but was less so in the 5th century itself.[104] Some settlement during the late Sasanian period is known at individual coastal sites but otherwise the area of south-eastern Arabia seems to have had much reduced Sasanian influence by the period in which Islam emerged on the other side of the peninsula. Other than in north-east Arabia, Sasanian coins are rare in the peninsula.[105] Distracted by their conflicts with Byzantium, the Sasanians' lack of focus in eastern Arabia, indicated by the paucity of archaeological materials from the period, suggests how the earliest Islamic influence over this part of Arabia could readily have been achieved.

The large urban site of Ed-Dur (Umm al-Quwain) at the south of the Arabian Gulf, whose prosperity and development had been closely linked to the different Mesopotamian states, was of particular importance in the 1st and 2nd centuries CE, but had been largely abandoned by the 3rd century. The population of the long-occupied site of Mleiha in what is now the United Arab Emirates was much reduced by the 4th century; indeed, it may have been abandoned in a sudden and violent episode.[106] At both sites, after their fall in size and strength, fortified residences until the 5th century suggest that local Arab elites had taken up occupation, perhaps as clients of the Sasanians, and with trade actively continuing. An early Islamic burial was placed into an older (4th-century) burial chamber at Mleiha, and other 'intrusive' Islamic burials are found elsewhere in the region.[107]

Excavated levels at Kush in the same region spanned the period of Islamic origins, with material from the 5th to 13th centuries CE.[108] Late Sasanian-period constructions, including a defensive tower, were abandoned but some settlement continued. The transition of control of the area in the early Islamic period was not marked by a major disruption of material culture, although Kush does not seem to have become an Islamic settlement of major importance.

About 100 miles (160 km) inland, work around the Buraimi oasis has traced settlement from late Bronze Age to modern times. A village of mudbrick was present from *ca.* 1300–300 BCE, and an Islamic-period settlement was dated *ca.* 750–900 CE. Excavations at al-Ayn (al-Ain) in the same area has revealed a water tunnel and other material from very early in the Islamic era.[109]

At Sir Bani Yas on the Arabian Gulf (near Abu Dhabi) a Christian monastery was constructed after the Islamisation of the area, in the 7th to 8th centuries CE.[110] This indicates more than tolerance of Christian communities by the Muslim rulers – indeed, historical evidence suggests the Christians came to play an important continuing role in the area in the 8th to 9th centuries.[111]

Fulayj near Suhar on the Gulf of Oman was a military fort built around the 5th to early 6th centuries CE. It continued in use (possibly after a period of abandonment) until about the mid-7th century, after which it was permanently abandoned.[112] It thus spans the late Sasanian period and the rise of Islam, which led to Sasanian defeat. The residents of the Oman region in the early 7th century CE seem to have followed political expediency. Loyalty to the Sasanian Empire could be readily enough replaced by agreements with the Islamic polity during the Prophet's lifetime. But after his death the military presence of the Islamic forces ensured the region's inclusion in the new Arab power.[113]

In south-west Arabia, which includes the Sabaean heartland, the historical picture has been complemented by survey and excavations of settlements from the 3rd millennium BCE onwards, showing relatively dense occupation in the more productive higher areas.[114] The civilisations of southern Arabia are highly visible in the archaeological record, but so is their decline before the rise of Islam.

The Awam temple from the Sabaean period at Marib, east of the urban centre Sana'a, was in use from the 8th century BCE into the 1st century CE, serving the cult of the moon god Almaqah.[115] Located within an oval surrounding wall, the temple was built primarily of limestone quarried nearby. Its rectangular form of high walls enclosed open areas bounded by pillars and many inscriptions have been recovered from the site.

A survey of the Dhamar region of the Yemeni highlands, south of Sana'a, traced the substantial human settlement of the area over several millennia.[116] Sites from the 1st millennium BCE, the period that included Sabaean domination and subsequent Himyarite rule, included naturally fortified settlements on high rocky outcrops with significant monumental construction. Masonry dams showed Himyarite efforts at water control of the seasonally flooded wadis. Possible domestic bath structures were found at the Himyarite site of Busan.[117] Settlements from the Islamic period suggest a denser occupation.

Najran, on the border of today's Saudi Arabia and Yemen, shows continuity of Christian settlement across the period 300–700 CE.[118] In the early Islamic era, Christian churches in Sana'a were only gradually changed to serve as mosques, similar to a pattern noted below in the Levant.[119]

At the western edge of Arabia's Empty Quarter, the site of Qaryat al-Faw was an important urban settlement from the 4th century BCE, and became the main town of the Kindah people and polity of pre-Islamic Arabia, who, according to tradition, had converted to Judaism in the 5th century BCE, following their Himyarite neighbours. Its prosperity was based on its position on trade routes, and the fortified site also served as a religious centre. Qaryat al-Faw demonstrates inland urban development in Arabia before the rise of

Islam. Yet this site, too, seems to have lost its role and population by the 4th century CE.

Temples in the area of the Hadramaut to the east of Yemen can be traced from the mid-1st millennium BCE, if not before, and are found within and outside domestic settlements. Archaeological work at the Hadramaut capital, Shabwa, revealed settlement from the Bronze Age onwards. The site fell victim to the predation of neighbouring states and had been abandoned by the beginning of the 5th century CE.[120] The urban settlement of Makaynun in central Hadramaut was developed before the 6th century BCE and had major fortifications and temples constructed in the 2nd to 1st centuries BCE. Recent archaeological work located a prosperous residential building dating to the 2nd to the 4th centuries CE, and evidence for the trade routes from this part of southern Arabia across to the north-east.[121] Bi'r Hamad was an apparently unfortified settlement north-east of Shabwa. It thrived during the 1st millennium BCE and into the first century CE, a date when other Hadramaut sites were abandoned. An agriculturally rich area around al-Guraf was also abandoned after the first centuries CE.[122] The inland settlement of Jujah had occupation from as early as the 9th century BCE to the early centuries CE.[123]

The seaport for Hadramaut, Qani', was developed in the 1st century BCE, and grew as trade expanded. However, by the beginning of the 5th century CE the main period of prosperity was ended; from then until its final occupation in the early 7th century the settlement was much reduced.[124] The Muslim domination of Arabia seems to have ended the port's importance, as the focus of the early Islamic empire was further north, but other ports in Hadramaut were active from the 9th century onwards.[125] Further east, the settlement of Sumhuram in modern Oman was a coastal town dating from the early 1st century BCE to the early 5th century CE, whose massive monumental buildings affirm both Hadramaut's wealth and the value of maritime trade.[126]

Much less archaeological work has been undertaken in the western parts of the Arabian Peninsula, within which were the places that played such an important role in the rise of Islam. Surveys within Saudi Arabia have included sites on the trade routes between the Hijaz and southern Arabia, as well as later sites on the pilgrimage route to Mecca from the north.[127] Studies east of the Hijaz in the arid interior of Arabia around the oasis of Jubbah recorded prehistoric occupation affected over time by increasing aridity, with numerous rock inscriptions from hunters and then from nomadic cattle herders. There were also a few Islamic inscriptions in Arabic that were considered to be early, though they cannot be dated more specifically.[128] In the region around Medina, rock engravings probably represent a range of periods as far back as the 5th millennium BCE, including Arabic inscriptions and engravings from later Islamic communities, but not from the time of Islam's origins.[129]

An Islamic inscription found 23 miles (37 km) south of al-Hijr, itself some 190 miles (300 km) north of Medina, on the trade and pilgrimage route from Syria, appears to date from 644–645 CE, 12 years after the death of Muhammad ibn 'Abdullah. This makes it the earliest dated known Islamic text.[130] The text is incised on a sandstone rock face and is translated as 'In the name of God I, Zuhayr, wrote this at the time 'Umar died, year four and twenty'. Another nearby text also contains the name Zuhayr. The opening phrase matches the pattern of earliest Islam; its occurrence so soon after the death of the Prophet asserts the establishment of the religion as well as the nature of the early Arabic script.

The area of the Hijaz had been significant in the late Bronze Age and early Iron Age of the late 2nd to early 1st millennia BCE, reflecting the region's role as a source of minerals for Egypt and Mesopotamia.[131] There may then have been a period of relative underdevelopment before the Neo-Babylonian occupation of the desert town of Tayma in the 6th century. Tayma, 250 miles (400 km) north of Medina, with origins dating back to the 3rd millennium BCE, was as a centre for trading incense and spices between their origin in south Arabia and markets to the north, with dramatic buildings marking the town's importance.[132] Tayma fell under Nabataean control but only after Roman conquest did its architecture follow that of its rulers.[133] Muslim historians suggested Tayma had contained a significant Jewish community. But by the 8th century CE settlement at the site was just that of scattered domestic buildings.

Mada'in Salih (Mada'in Saleh, al-Hijr) in the northern Hijaz, about 200 miles (320 km) north-west of Medina, lay at the south of the area of Nabataean settlement.[134] Numerous rock-cut tombs attest to the importance of this town up to the 1st century CE, set on the trade routes to southern Arabia. But as with other Nabataean sites, by the era when Islam emerged its significance seems to have ended, despite the text in the Qur'an that associated the site with the pre-Islamic prophet Salih. Later Arabic rock inscriptions are found in the area and a fort was built there in the Ottoman era, in the 18th century.

Excavations at al-Rabadha (al-Rabadhah, Abu Salim), 125 miles (200 km) north-east of Medina, revealed a continuity of settlement from pre-Islamic to 'Abbasid times, with numerous camel bones reminders of its role in trade. In the Islamic era, fortified buildings were distributed among residential areas, and a complex water storage system was constructed.[135] Archaeology and history appear to agree it was destroyed after nearly three centuries of Islamic occupation.

The silver and gold at Mahd al-Dhahab, 100 miles (165 km) south-east of Medina, had been actively mined in the Bronze Age, and again in the 'Abbasid period from the 8th century (with a revival today).[136] There is no evidence for its use in the era of Islamic origins: the idea that minerals may have been an important trade item in the Hijaz of the time would need more conclusive evidence than citations in some later Islamic histories. Clearly, mining became important from the 9th to 10th centuries CE. Dams near Ta'if and Khaybar in the Hijaz seem to date from relatively early in the Islamic era – one dated by an inscription as early Umayyad (677–678).[137]

Missing from the archaeological record are a detailed examination of Medina and an archaeological assessment of Mecca that would examine and test the validity of their descriptions in the traditional histories of Islam and help set a cultural and environmental framework in which to understand the origins of Islam and the Islamic polity. As long as excavation is prohibited in Mecca or the city of Medina for religious reasons, there is no prospect of recovering an archaeological image of the material culture or settlement from the period of Islam's origins.[138] One scholar suggests that by comparison with later hamlets in similarly arid locations, early Mecca may have consisted of modest stone houses set above the wadi.[139] Medina, with its scattered homesteads, would have carried a larger population; by 682 the Umayyads had constructed a town wall to encompass these homesteads, as part of their development of the Hijaz.

With the decline of the ancient states of south-western Arabia, and the limited influence of the later Sasanians in eastern Arabia, settlements in the peninsula had become more modest in wealth and complexity by the early 7th century. Many of these became allied to the newly emerging Islamic power in the lifetime of Muhammad ibn 'Abdullah, and if they withdrew their loyalty after the death of the Prophet, they were quickly brought back into the fold. Yet, as the focus of the Islamic polity was towards conquests to the north, major impacts of Islamic culture and prosperity within the peninsula are visible in archaeology only later, and some places that had lost populations before the rise of Islam would regain their role and size only in 'Abbasid times.

History and archaeology of the conquests

The impact of the Islamic Arab conquests in just a few decades of the 7th century CE was dramatic. But just as the Muslim armies did not emerge from a barren Arabian wilderness without history, neither was Arab military strength just an indigenous development. Arab mercenaries ('Saracens' in

Greek and Roman terminology) had been useful to the armies of the great empires while they were fighting each other or elsewhere. In 378, Arab soldiers were crucial in defending Byzantine power from attack by Goths to the west.[140] A document from about 400 lists cavalry units of Saracens based in Egypt, and in the mid-6th century the Byzantine emperor Justinian rewarded an Arab chief from the Hijaz with a political position further north.[141]

When the Muslim armies moved out of the Arabian Peninsula to acquire control of lands within the Sasanian and Byzantine Empires in the middle decades of the 7th century, they could benefit from knowledge gained by those among them who had earlier served in those empires. An important example is the use of chainmail body protection, learned from the armies with which they had been active, and not a traditional feature of the military conflicts and local raids within Arabia. The tribes from Arabia who fought under the banner of Islam had before them the record of Arab groups – the Lakhmids, Ghassanids and others – who had been closely involved with the empires whose power was now being supplanted. While Romans applied the term 'Arabia' to their colonised land, it was language and religion rather than external classification that provided identity and unity.[142]

The early Islamic community did not comprise nomadic pastoralists. 'Islam was born among town-dwellers and started out with a town-dweller's stereotyped image of nomads as unreliable and deceitful.'[143] Within three decades of the death of Muhammad ibn 'Abdullah, Muslim Arab rulers had within their empire the large cities of the Middle East, living in or near them, and had created new urban settlements of their own.

The first caliph following Muhammad's death, Abu Bakr, focussed on adherence to the newly proclaimed religion of Islam to unify Arabs, urban and nomad, in a single polity; with its combined military strength it could now occupy territory to the north.[144] But that conquest itself appears to have been made easier and more speedy by the weakness of the existing empires, by their strategic focus away from the unexpected source of the attacks, and by the willingness of newly controlled communities to accede to new rule.

The arrival of the Arab armies and the political control of huge areas did not involve the settlement of large numbers of migrants from Arabia: one estimate is of 250,000–300,000 Arabs settling among the conquered populations.[145] The size of the Byzantine Empire has been estimated as 20–25 million subjects, and the Sasanians some 12 million, but these suggested figures are hard to test.

Islam eventually became the dominant religion for much of this population. The Umayyad caliph 'Abd al-Malik in the 690s made Arabic (as the language of the Qur'an and of the ruling elite) the official language of government, although Persian and other languages were significant in parts of the Islamic empire. The designation of 'Arab' as applied to the broader Islamic community is seen three caliphs later, under Umar b. 'Abd al-'Aziz.[146]

In the centuries before and during the expansion of Islam, the history of the Middle East was dominated by a sequence of conflicts and changes of power. These affected armies and those who fought; they affected cities and the authority of urban elites. But we can presume that pastoralists continued to travel with their flocks; that peasant agriculturalists continued their lives much as before; and that traders continued their travels and livelihoods with whatever adaptations proved necessary. Archaeology generally indicates continuity more than interruption. Disruption of the power of ruling families and the control exercised by distant imperial capitals may not have been the most important aspects of ordinary people's lives, at least outside of major cities.

Historical narratives described cataclysmic change as Arab Islamic armies overcame mighty empires in a matter of decades, to rule huge areas of land. But many residents of those lands may just have continued their lives without major disruption, while paying taxes regularly to whoever was currently in power. To many communities, rule by Persians, Byzantines or Arabs could be judged more by its direct impact than by traditional loyalties, and the Arabs may have appeared to some a lesser burden than existing rulers. There was inevitably a variety of responses, from armed resistance to treaties involving payments under new rules for taxation, from declared conversion to fighting in armed alliance with the Arab forces, or just temporary domestic adjustment, like hoarding coins or valuables.

By making treaties with local elites under threat of military action, and allowing them to retain their position, the Arab military leaders could establish control without battle. In particular, pressure for conversion to Islam was not a priority – local Jews, Zoroastrians and Christians of different affiliations could retain their religious identity and practices, but they had now to pay taxes to the Arab authorities (followers of Islam were exempted from the *jizya* tax in the early Arab empire). Until the later part of the Umayyad period, the rulers of the new world order might have been seen by many of their subjects as 'Arab' rather than 'Muslim', just as earlier rulers had been seen as Persian or dynastic rather than 'Zoroastrian'.[147]

The Arab forces operated separately in campaigns to the central and southern regions of Sasanian power.[148] It is a possibility that the first Arab attacks on the Sasanian Empire in Iraq were not by Muslim armies but by other Arab groups taking advantage of Sasanian weakness, and whose

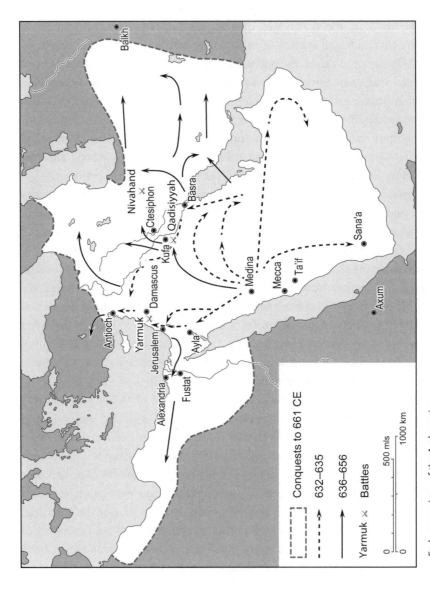

7. Early campaigns of the Arab armies

endeavours were included by the later Muslim historians in the general narrative of unified Islamic victories. The historical sources note that some Jews and Christians were fighting alongside the Muslims.[149] One recent and controversial interpretation has suggested that Muslim conquests in Iraq can be dated to 628–632 CE, that is, earlier than generally accepted and within the last part of Muhammad ibn 'Abdullah's own lifetime.[150]

The battle of Qadisiyyah in 636 – just four years after the death of Muhammad – was followed by occupation of the Sasanian capital, Ctesiphon, the following year. Further military conflicts occurred as individual parts of the Sasanian world determined their own fate, some finding Arab rule less of an imposition than Persian rule. The battle at Nihavand in Iran in 642 effectively ended the dynasty's power (the last Sasanian ruler survived but was murdered nine years later). By the 650s, the Muslims were in Afghanistan, occupying Balkh in 651. By 656 most of the important towns of the Sasanian Empire were under the control of the Arab armies; the countryside may well have been more gradually assimilated. In southern Iraq, cities negotiated their own treaties with the Arab armies, which assured them continuing rights.[151]

Arabian conquests and successes in Iraq and beyond were paralleled by military conquests to the west in many areas of Byzantine control and influence.[152] Muhammad ibn 'Abdullah had already led some raids in his lifetime in the north of the peninsula. The apparent ease with which the Muslim Arab armies could take possession of Byzantine lands reflected the reduction in defences that had allowed earlier defeat at the hands of the Sasanians. When the Muslim armies headed north towards their victory at Yarmuk in 636, 'they rode by numerous but now empty forts falling slowly into decay', in the evocative phrase of one historian.[153] Archaeology does indicate that the defensive locations on the eastern flanks of the Byzantine Empire were already in decline by the late 5th century, and many were abandoned by the late 6th century.[154]

Westwards, the Muslim forces occupied much of Egypt in 640–641, making their base at the newly developed site of Fustat (within modern Cairo) and taking control of Alexandria in 642–643, and Tripoli in 643. Such achievements imply – indeed would require – little or no resistance from local populations. In the Umayyad period the Arabs reached Bukhara by 674 and Toledo by 712 but were halted at Toulouse in France in 721 and Poitiers in 732. Their attacks on Constantinople itself (in 674–678 and 717–718) failed to seize the city, but demonstrated the power and determination of the Arab empire.

Although some non-Muslim sources would suggest huge armies had been involved in the conquests, the Muslim sources indicated otherwise. We cannot be sure of the actual numbers: one estimate suggests Arab forces of 30,000–40,000 confronting a large Byzantine force at Yarmuk, and a smaller army, of 12,000–15,000, against the Sasanians at Qadisiyyah.[155] This was remarkable considering the substantial area of the occupation and the short time involved (although the conquests by Alexander the Great had taken only 11 years).

Control of the desert east of Syria and Jordan – geographically an extension of Arabia itself – was quickly followed by the towns of the Levant (Syria, Jordan and Palestine) coming under Arab control. While the Battle of Yarmuk in 636 and the rapid domination of the area may have signified the end of Byzantine authority over the Levant, the change of rulers did not initiate a dramatic transformation of society. The now substantial amount of archaeological work on sites that span the later Byzantine and early Muslim periods in the Levant demonstrates continuity in material culture, and the lack of immediate impact on society and economy in the first period of Muslim conquests.

Rural life continued initially largely without change; the many towns whose bishops or other leaders negotiated terms of surrender with the Arabs continued without damage and operating much as before, building and developing their churches while paying taxes to the new rulers.[156] Communities took advantage of new economic and trading opportunities, without the need for religious conversion or social upheaval, although some areas of the Levant did experience economic decline in the early centuries of Islamic rule.[157] Settlements already in existence before the Arabian conquests showed the 'virtual absence of a Muslim material culture' to mark the early period of the historical transition of rulers, and such continuity has been noted in areas newly occupied by the Arab conquerors as far apart as Central Asia, the Levant, North Africa and Spain.[158]

We cannot be certain of the numbers of Arabs who migrated into the newly conquered territories of Syria, Jordan and Palestine under either the Rightly Guided caliphs or the early Umayyad rulers.[159] However, they were not present in numbers that would dominate in the lands the Arab armies now controlled. While their conquests gave them rule over a vast area of cities, towns and the rural economy that supplied them, the Arabs' own occupation initially seems to have largely focussed on creating garrison towns.

In the early decades of the occupation they established new settlements (*misr*, plural *amsar*): in Iraq, Kufa and Basra: in Egypt, Fustat; in Tunisia, Qayrawan (Kairouan); in Algeria, Tagrart.[160] Umayyad rulers added buildings to some major towns (notably Jerusalem) but the Umayyad elite also constructed their own fortified residential homesteads on large estates in more arid areas of the Levant called *qasr/qusur*, which marked a dramatic new style of settlement away from the military encampments or the older towns.[161]

There were exceptions to the pattern of new independent settlements. New populations from Arabia settled in Homs and Qinnasrin in Syria. The long-established city of Damascus would become the centre of the caliphate from 661, and the major Christian shrine (supposedly containing the head of John the Baptist) that had been welcoming both Muslim and Christian worshippers was replaced by the great mosque built between 706 and 715.

On the Gulf of Aqaba, a new settlement (Ayla) was established during the reign of the third caliph, 'Uthman (644–656). Sited next to a former Byzantine settlement, this town continued in importance until the 12th century. In the hinterland of Ayla, new settlements flourished to provide produce and craft items.[162] The Ghassanid town Jabiya was redeveloped as a major military and administrative centre.

A later new town was al-Ramla, on the coastal lowlands of Palestine between Jerusalem and the coast. This was constructed to be the administrative centre of the province of southern Palestine, and developed in the mid-Umayyad period, in the early 8th century, on a site with no prior settlement.[163]

We can trace the patterns of continuity and change in the early Islamic Levant northward in many locations in modern Israel and the West Bank, Jordan to Syria. Jerusalem, with perhaps 15,000 inhabitants, was considered a holy city in Islam.[164] The narratives of early Levantine conquests are contradictory but the occupation of Jerusalem with a treaty of surrender following a siege was a landmark event.[165] A nine-line inscription found at the south-west corner of the Haram al-Sharif (the Temple Mount) in 1968 with a reference to year 32 AH (652 CE) could be a text to mark this treaty, witnessed by followers of the Prophet.[166]

The al-Aqsa Mosque was initially a construction on the Haram al-Sharif by Umar ibn al-Khattab, who was caliph from 634 to 644, to mark the site where tradition now placed the night journey of the Prophet Muhammad. A more solid construction under Umayyad rulers 'Abd al-Malik and al-Walid was built from 690 but it was heavily damaged by an earthquake, as was its successor built in 780, in which the wood workmanship that has survived suggests the use of Christian craftsmen. The present form and structure reflect (though with many changes and additions) the construction that dates from the 1030s.

The architectural wonder of the Dome of the Rock shrine was first built *ca.* 687–691, under caliph 'Abd al-Malik. It too suffered from earthquake damage and was rebuilt in the 1020s. The dramatic external decoration has been renewed periodically since.

Under the early Muslim control of Jerusalem, the religious buildings, rites and religious visitors of Christianity continued alongside the new religion of Islam, and there was a revival of the city's Jewish population. Jerusalem's overall layout saw little change until a decline in the 10th and 11th centuries.[167] Leading Jewish authorities moved from Tiberias to a base in Jerusalem after the Islamic conquest. The Umayyad rulers constructed a palace compound immediately south-west of the Haram al-Sharif in the caliphate of al-Walid I (705–715). Under 'Abbasid rule, the economy of the city maintained wine-making despite the Islamic prohibition on alcohol, perhaps an indicator of its continuing religious diversity.[168]

At Ramat Rahel, 2½ miles (4 km) south-west of Jerusalem, a 7th-century Byzantine church flourished on the site of an earlier construction and continued in use into the 8th century. Studies of six Byzantine towns in the arid Negev region showed how little changed in the early Islamic period.[169] Subayta in the Negev added a mosque to its existing churches but otherwise maintained cultural continuity.[170] From the middle of the Umayyad period is a mosque at the northern Negev settlement of Rahat, whose discovery was announced to the media in 2019. Here, settlement in the early Islamic period followed on from Byzantine farming.

Similarly, archaeology at the long-established city of Beth Shean in the Jordan Valley south of the Sea of Galilee (Kinneret, Lake Tiberias) showed no immediate sign of change as a result of the Islamic conquest.[171] The first Umayyad caliph, Mu'awiya, constructed a residence on the site of Byzantine settlement at al-Sinnabra (Khirbet al-Karak) on the Sea of Galilee itself, presumed to be a winter retreat.[172] Tiberias, a Byzantine town of modest size on the Sea of Galilee, flourished under Islamic rule, developing as a regional administrative centre while retaining much of its established layout.[173]

Not all the transition to Islamic rule is invisible in the archaeological record. At Beit Shemesh, some 19 miles (30 km) west of Jerusalem, those involved in recent excavations consider destruction is indicated between the Byzantine level and evidence of Islamic settlement. But most sites in Palestine, Jordan and Syria have no evidence of destruction in the early 7th century; indeed, many saw growth in economic prosperity and population numbers between the mid-6th century and the mid-7th century. Antioch remained prosperous through the transition of rule, as did Caesarea Maritima. This would contradict the argument that economic decline in the region had fa-cilitated Muslim conquest. Such views arose because of assumptions that the arrival of Islamic wares marked the time of Islamic conquest, whereas such material should be dated up to a century later.[174] However, some small forts disappear from the archaeological record after the 7th century, implying greater security across the region.

East of the Jordan Valley, the Christian site at Deir 'Ain 'Abata in Jordan to the south-east of the Dead Sea continued to develop after the period of Islamic conquests: a 5th-century church and a building considered to have been the Monastery of Lot was affected only after earthquake damage, when an Islamic construction was built. One feature in Jordan where Islamic settlement did make a difference was in the development of some industrial activity. A copper-smelting site in the Wadi 'Araba dates from early in the Islamic period – provisionally the late 7th century.[175]

The large city of Jerash (Gerasa) in northern Jordan had seen some decline in its prosperity in the later 6th century, but with Islamic control economic prosperity grew, and mosques developed while churches continued in use by the Christian community.[176] The same pattern of cultural continuity is seen in other sites areas of northern Jordan, with greater adoption of Islamic pottery styles noted only from the early 9th century.[177]

The Jordanian site of Pella (Fihl, Tabaqat Fahl) had seen major religious and secular construction in the 6th century and there was no break in the archaeological record through to the 7th century to mark the change of ruling power. The town, lying on the route between Jericho and Damascus, had signed a pact with Arab general Abu Ubaydah in 635 after the defeat of a Byzantine army nearby, and agreed to pay a tax. The final Byzantine period (Phase V) can be dated to the period of Islamic rule and lacks defensive structures. The common presence of wine amphorae indicates that it had not taken up Islamic religious rules on alcohol; Christians faced no such prohibition. The town saw rejuvenation in the early 8th century (when coinage suggests the growth of wider trading networks) before destruction by an earthquake in 749. The settlement was redeveloped in the 'Abbasid era.

Umm al-Jimaal in northern Jordan, which had first developed as a Nabataean town, continued as a Christian settlement, and showed little effect of the Muslim imperium in the 7th and 8th century, other than improvement of public buildings, perhaps to serve in administration.[178] Further north, archaeology at the site of Déhès, in north-west Syria, excavated in the 1970s, showed sufficient continuity to allow the description of a 'Byzantine-Umayyad period' but with gradual innovations in ceramic styles.[179]

Some Ghassanid sites in Syria and northern Jordan, which had been important in the period of rule by the Jafnid allies of the Byzantines, were redeveloped under the Umayyad rule of the late 7th to the early 8th centuries.[180] Religious transitions were slow: the were churches later used as mosques, but the area of Jordan showed no significant social disruption at the time of the conquests, the Byzantine and Islamic phases being described as 'smoothly interlinked'.[181] Indeed, in areas of the Levant, archaeology shows renovation works (and even new constructions) of both churches and synagogues in the years of the early Islamic period, continuing to function well into the 8th century.[182]

In Syria, the Muslim Arabs arrived where rural life had thrived in earlier centuries: prosperous Christian villages in large numbers, often in areas that had seen little occupation in the earlier classical period. The economy here may have seen some decline ahead of the Arab invasion.[183] Construction in many locations of Syria had slowed by the 6th century CE and after the incursion by the Arab Muslims occupation there was mainly in existing buildings, with little growth even in the 'Abbasid period.[184]

Excavations revealed pig bones remaining through Umayyad levels of settlement at sites in the region of Syria but pigs were rarer in the 'Abbasid period.[185] There was no requirement that Christians should not consume pork; a change could indicate the rate of conversion to Islam, with its strict dietary requirements. Both the production and the trade of items showed relatively little change for two generations after the Muslim conquests.

Recent studies of Anatolia under late Byzantine rule have eroded a long-held image of the destructive impact of Arab attack.[186] The threats from Persian then Arab conquerors had stimulated defensive urban development, and the strength of these settlements of Byzantine Anatolia was sufficient to hold the Islamic armies at bay, although the economy of rural regions suffered.[187]

It is a matter of active debate how much the Byzantine territories of the Levant were in serious social and economic decline by the time of the arrival of the Muslim armies.[188] Although the power of the Byzantine state had been weakened by the extended conflict with the Sasanians, both the rural and the urban populations may have continued to prosper alongside the arrival of new rulers and a relatively small number of followers from Arabia.

The Byzantine cities that now fell under early Muslim rule had already changed since the era of the classical Roman Empire. Temples and their precincts had decayed or been raided for building materials; churches had been constructed; and patterns of urban life had adapted to the reduced prosperity in parts of the Byzantine Empire.[189] Changes made under the Umayyads were therefore in towns that had already begun to lose their 'classical' feel, and new religious, administrative and trading structures complemented the existing streetscapes.

Our image of the impacts of Arab Islamic conquests in and beyond the Levant has gradually altered though the archaeology of recent decades, though there remains much research to undertake and many questions to consider.

> Excavations and surveys have revealed considerable evidence of ... seventh-century occupation in the Middle East and North Africa. The overwhelming impression is that the Arab conquests did not bring about radical and sudden change in the daily lives of the inhabitants of these regions.[190]

One explanation proposed for the absence of archaeological evidence of the Muslim conquests is that the 'Islamic state' itself did not fully emerge until the caliphate of Umayyad 'Abd al-Malik (685–705); state monumental buildings would be irrelevant and unlikely until then.[191] The greatest changes to both urban and rural societies and economies would come with the processes associated with the shift of rule to the 'Abbasids and Baghdad from the mid-8th century, and that period saw a growth in the number of newly constructed mosques.

In early studies, when excavators assumed that the arrival of Islam would necessarily be marked by a change in material culture, the presence of Byzantine pottery types was used to date an occupation level of a site to before the 630s. In reality, Byzantine-style pottery commonly continued after the changes in political control, with dominance by Islamic styles later, sometimes much later.[192] And archaeological work in the areas of early Islamic conquests, as elsewhere, would be influenced by the specific interests of the researchers, such as Byzantine studies, or the established architecture of the 'Abbasid era, and would concentrate on what promised the best return for time and money spent addressing the archaeologists' research priorities.[193]

Older conventional history, focussing on rulers, armies, conquests and political empires, cast the period from the early 7th to the mid-8th centuries as one of quick and dramatic change as Muslim Arabs replaced Byzantine Christians and Zoroastrian Persians in control of the Fertile Crescent from Iran to the Levant and Egypt and beyond. Modern archaeology suggests a much more nuanced and gradual process of change to the economy, society and daily lives of the people of the region. Most of rural life, much of urban life, and traditional religious allegiances in many areas continued much as before, transforming only gradually as the influence of the Arab state, the Islamic religion and the Arabic language penetrated the vast region in which in which the caliphs had replaced Byzantine and Sasanian rulers.

In particular, the record of church construction shows that Christianity continued to thrive alongside the new faith for several centuries, and Jewish communities clearly continued to practise their religion.[194] Muslim rulers continued not just to tolerate Christians, Jews and Zoroastrians but to incorporate them into the administration and structure of the societies they controlled. Unfolding research demonstrates the nuances of relationships between groups of different religious adherences and the limits that lie in assuming sharp divisions between these communities.[195]

Conclusions

Historical study and debate, as well as archaeological field research and interpretation, have developed to review and question some longstanding images and assumptions about early Islam: its origins and the world of initial conquest by Muslim armies from Arabia. Critical scholarship has served to suggest how little we know with certainty of Islam's origins and has raised questions about the nature of the time and place in which Islam emerged, and the initial form and impact of the worlds of the Islamic conquests.

Islam began in revelations recited by a middle-aged merchant, Muhammad ibn 'Abdullah, from Mecca in the Hijaz region of Arabia. He perceived these as coming from a divine source, and requiring him to declaim them more widely. Their contents, later gathered together as the Qur'an, reflected aspects of Christianity and especially the monotheism of Jewish tradition, with prophets acknowledged from Adam and Noah to Jesus (Yeshua).

We still await – and may long await – an archaeological picture of the region where and time when Islam itself emerged: the Hijaz of the western Arabian Peninsula in the 6th to 7th centuries. Later traditions would attribute to Mecca an important role on major trade routes, but as no archaeological work has been undertaken in Mecca, the nature of the settlement in the lifetime of Muhammad cannot be examined. However, its role in the traditions as the home of Muhammad and place of his first revelations contributed to its emergence as a holy place for Muslims.

In the setting of multiple competing religions of the Middle East, other new ideas and prophets had emerged in Arabia but it was the message of Islam, and the organisation of believers that he led in the early 7th century, that would survive. As the followers of the message grew in number, they found themselves in conflict with others within the Hijaz, and this conflict led to the development of a military and political force organised and led by Muhammad to defend the Islamic believers. Medina (Yathrib) became the centre of the movement. Texts in the Qur'an belonging to this period reflect the political and military conflicts.

That force grew into a powerful political and military organisation that within decades (and within Muhammad's lifetime) appears to have gained influence over much of Arabia; it proceeded to conquer vast areas of declining empires. Politics had taken over from faith but the successful Arab armies declared that they were held together by their belief in the one God proclaimed by Muhammad and the identity of Muhammad as the true and final Prophet of God.

This combination of politics, religion and military power could take advantage of the weakened authority of the Byzantine and Sasanian Empires without initially confronting the beliefs and religious practices of their citizens. As the Muslim Arab armies seized from their former rulers control of the lands to the north and east and west, archaeology indicates little initial impact on the social, economic and material lives of rural and most urban inhabitants, notably in the Levant region. The rise of Islamic power transformed the societies it controlled only slowly. Jewish and Christian communities continued to flourish and worship in their religious buildings. It appears that proselytising Islam was not a priority for the Arabian conquerors: non-Muslims contributed taxes to the new rulers. Conversion to Islam was a gradual process, and followers of other monotheistic faiths continued to serve the Islamic rulers for centuries.

The previous chapter noted how rapidly Mormonism gained its followers, but soon hostility from others combined with the opportunity of a new land to settle, and inspired a westward migration. Mormonism gave an imperative to its followers to leave their familiar setting to establish a New Zion in the west, in land generally less inviting than their places of origin.

Within its Arabian heartland, Islam attracted adherents with comparable speed. Islam provided a binding force by which Arabian armies could conquer more prosperous regions and create a great empire of their own. They retained their Muslim identity but lived alongside the other monotheisms of those they ruled. Over the next centuries, increasing numbers of their subjects adopted Islam, and the cultural, artistic, technological and intellectual elements of Islamic civilisation continued to develop. The emergence of Christianity presents a different picture. Unlike Islam, it did not establish itself as the dominant faith in its place of origin, nor did it become the religion of a state or empire until three centuries after the death of its founding prophet.

Chapter 4

Rural Galilee to imperial cities: the beginnings and spread of Christianity

In the middle of the 1st century CE, a new religious movement slowly developed in parts of the Roman Empire. Those who would be called Christians included members of the widespread Jewish diaspora and non-Jews, responding to travelling evangelists, of whom an Anatolian-born urban Jew, Paulos (Paul), was a leading figure. At the core of the new religious beliefs was a narrative of salvation through Yeshua (Iesous, Jesus), a preacher from Galilee who was executed in Jerusalem, was said to have returned to life before ascending to heaven, and who was now considered to have divine status as the Son of God. Paulos had never met Yeshua, had never heard him preach, and had not joined the group of his followers in Galilee or Judaea, but he shared their beliefs in Yeshua's resurrection and role in personal salvation for those who believed in him. Yeshua's direct followers had initially considered the movement as specifically for Jews and were expecting an imminent apocalyptic change, but they achieved only modest success within Judaea itself. In the 1st century CE, Palestine was at the margins of the Roman Empire. There had been other Jewish individuals in the area who presented unorthodox ideas, preaching in public, undertaking faith healing and attracting followers. Most had no long-term impact. Although Yeshua's preaching was mostly in and around his native Galilee, his message attracted Jewish followers from beyond that territory. On travelling to the religious centre of Jerusalem, in Judaea, he was executed by the Romans after about 30 CE, with support from Jewish religious authorities. By the later 1st century, a set of traditions had been recorded about Yeshua, including birth to a virgin mother, details of his teaching, his performance of a range of miracles, and his resurrection. The archaeological record begins to show the existence of Christian communities within the Roman Empire only from the late 2nd century, which suggests that the growth of Christianity was both gradual and widely dispersed.

There has been no shortage of debates and discussions published in western languages about the era in which Christianity emerged. A challenge is to distinguish contributions that seek to support a preconceived position of faith from those that apply critically the disciplines of independent scholarly method in the historical sciences.[1]

Critical studies by scholars with a Christian background have paid a major part in debating and reinterpreting the narratives and reviewing the chronology and understanding of the events around Christian origins since the late 19th century. Many of these writers started from conventional religious positions but developed nuanced and revisionist analyses of sources and their reliability. By contrast, relatively few secular historians have focussed their work on interpreting and reinterpreting these events.

To most people in medieval and early modern Christian Europe, the time and place of Christian origins must have seemed far away: lands occupied by Islamic rule for all but a Crusader century, with events in the distant past, in a deeply unfamiliar society, which could be perceived only through the writings of the New Testament, supplemented by interpretations and presentations of priests, as well as pictorial images in churches. But today millions of tourists have travelled to Israel, Jordan and the West Bank. Archaeologists can hold in their hands numerous objects from 1st-century Palestine (the region that includes ancient Galilee, Samaria, Judaea and Idumaea), and have excavated and documented in detail the urban developments and rural settlements of the time and place. The 'Holy Land' of the 1st century CE is no longer distant or a mystery. However, its interpretation remains more complex.

Every detail of the literary sources relevant to the study of Christian origins has been examined exhaustively by scholars in every interpretative model, while still leaving issues for a critical understanding. The locations of Christian origins were mainly in Aramaic-speaking areas of Galilee and Judaea, with Hebrew as the language of the biblical texts a second (and probably widely understood) language. These lands were, however, ruled by speakers of Latin and Greek, and the early historical and religious sources are all in Greek, written to be read by Christians far from Judaea (or, rather, read *to* – in the small Christian community of the first two centuries it is likely only a minority were literate).[2]

The sequence of items in the collection of writings we call the New Testament is very different from, and in significant places the reverse of, the date of its major books. The four canonical gospels were traditionally (though incorrectly) attributed to Matthew, Mark, Luke and John; they were supplemented by the Acts of the Apostles. Despite questions of actual authorship, scholars retain these conventional references for the biblical books. They tell of the life and death of a Jewish preacher whose name in Hebrew and Aramaic would have been Yeshua (the version we use here). In Greek his name is converted to Iesous and in Latin this became Iesus, in English Jesus, in Arabic Isa or Yasu and in other languages Jesu, Gesu and variants. His death was followed by active proselytising among the Jewish population in and around Judaea, by those who had associated with Yeshua in his lifetime. The religion gained greater impact further afield, among both Jewish and non-Jewish communities spread through parts of the Roman Empire, especially through the activities and associates of Paulos (the Greek version of the Hebrew name Shaul, and Anglicised as Paul). He was the most influential proponent of the new religion and was active in its development as a religion outside of Judaea and beyond Judaism, although he had never met Yeshua, had never heard him preach, and had not joined the group of his followers in Galilee or Judaea.

In addition to the four gospels, Acts of the Apostles and Revelation, 21 letters are included in the New Testament, traditionally attributed to Paul (Paulos), James, Peter, John and Jude, with one anonymous. Scholars agree the four gospels and Acts were written *later* than the majority of the letters in the name of Paulos. If the letters of Paulos represent a Christian theology as developed by him in the 50s, some 20 to 30 years after the death of Yeshua around 30 CE, the gospels represent the oral traditions, accepted narratives and developed beliefs of Christianity from 40 to 70 (or even 80) years after Yeshua's death.

There have been numerous modern reinterpretations of the life of Yeshua, from the pious and evangelical to the analytical, from the measured to the wildly hypothetical, seeking to understand his life and the movement that followed him within the political and religious uncertainties of the 1st-century CE world. Some academic theologians, such as Rudolf Bultmann in the 1920s, have advanced the argument that the pursuit of historical detail is irrelevant to the validity of religious faith, and they have separated the 'Jesus of history' from the 'Christ of faith'. In practice, we can see contemporary church leaders who appear to follow the same line.[3]

Most historians, secular as well as religious, accept that Yeshua was a real individual who preached in 1st-century Palestine, even if they disagree on details of his biography, context and theology. A contentious, minority view advanced by some scholars has suggested that the narrative of a Jesus who lived, preached, died and was resurrected was an invention of those in the mid-1st century who developed what became the Christian religion, and who generated a myth of Yeshua's incarnation as well as reincarnation.[4] But if, as most secular historians would argue, it was not reality that the death of this reforming preacher was followed by his resurrection and bodily ascension, then the historicity of other details in the traditional narratives remain open for debate.

Questions we face, therefore, include the following. What was the context in which Yeshua lived and died? What was the context in which early Christianity arose in Galilee and Judaea? And what was the framework in which it spread elsewhere in the Roman Empire? New documents have only occasionally been found to complement the long-known manuscript sources. Archaeology continues to uncover new material from the relevant period, although sometimes scientific study sits alongside optimistic and biased claims for the significance of new finds.

Sources and their problems

The absence of contemporary sources for the life of Yeshua is matched by the lack of independent information on the earliest activities of his followers. Christians were mentioned by Roman writer Tacitus, whose *Annals*, dated from about 116, recorded a story of Emperor Nero victimising Christians in Rome more than 50 years earlier, in 64 CE. And Suetonius, writing *The Twelve Caesars* in about 121, also recorded punishment of Christians by Nero, and referred to an expulsion from Rome of Jews making disturbances 'at the instigation of Chrestus' under Emperor Claudius, who ruled 41–54 CE, a possible reference to early believers. The great Jewish historian Josephus, writing in Greek in the early 90s, referred to John the Baptist and made one brief reference to the execution of the brother of Iesous, with a further reference to Iesous, which historians consider may have been amplified by later Christian copyists.

This limit of complementary historical evidence is not dissimilar to the issues for early Islam discussed in the previous chapter. Brief mentions of Islamic attacks on the Byzantine Empire soon after the death of Muhammad gave us a political framework, but the histories of the Prophet were written much later. Whatever the accuracy of details in the Muslim histories, the Qur'an is considered to be a reasonably authentic collection of revelations declaimed by Muhammad ibn 'Abdullah.

The preaching and sayings of Yeshua, recorded in the books of the New Testament, may have a similar authenticity, forming the basis of the belief system that developed as Christianity. Non-Muslim historians of Islam long accepted the major historical narrative of the biographies of Muhammad, while filtering out the miraculous events attributed to his early life, or his aerial flight to Jerusalem. Similarly, European historians filtered out the miracles in order to use Bede's *Ecclesiastical History of the English People* (from *ca.* 731). So secular historians following a materialist paradigm could see in the gospels a record of a Jewish preacher, his radical theology and his sayings, without accepting miracles that changed water to wine and raised the dead, or supernatural events that returned him to life after execution and had him ascending bodily into the heavens (quite apart from a virgin birth).

The four canonical gospels present different accounts of the virgin birth, baptism, miracle working, preaching, acquiring followers and final death and resurrection. Although scholars in the Christian tradition acknowledge the contradictions between the narratives in the four gospels, and their composition two to three generations after the events described in their collective 65,000 words, they examine and interpret every name, phrase and event within the texts.

All four gospels in the New Testament associate Yeshua's death with the period when Roman rule of Judaea was exercised by the prefect, Pontius Pilatus, known historically from early Jewish historians Philo and Josephus, and mentioned on an inscribed stone found in 1962 at Caesarea Maritima on the coast of Israel. A ring from the Herodium near Bethlehem was recognised in 2018 as bearing a name 'Pilatus'.[5] However, those reporting this find gave good reasons why it would not belong to the prefect: a crude ring with the name roughly inscribed does not have the gravity of an imperial delegate, and the context in which it was found suggests a Jewish owner (though perhaps a member of Pilatus's staff). Pilatus was prefect of the Roman province from 26 CE, that is, under the imperial rule of Tiberius – before being recalled to Rome in 36. The year 36 thus appears a *terminus ante quem* for Yeshua's death.

The gospels concur that Yeshua was baptised by John the Baptist (Yochanan in Hebrew, Ioannes in Greek). John's death at the hands of the Romans' local client ruler, Herod Antipas (Antipatros), was also recorded by Josephus, who located the execution at the Herodian fortified palace of Machaerus, east of the Jordan River.[6] Herod Antipas held office until year 39; there is no agreement on the year of John's death.

Of the gospels, only Matthew and Luke describe Yeshua's birth, placing it in the period of client rule by Antipas's father, Herod 'the Great', who is generally considered to have died in 4 BCE. But Luke contradicts its own chronology, placing the birth at the time of the census ordered in 6 CE by Quirinius, the Roman governor of Syria. The more ambitious narrative in Matthew attributes to Herod the massacre of all children under two in the Bethlehem area, whose historical improbability is confirmed by its absence from Josephus's critical history of Herod. Neither the earlier gospel of Mark nor the later one of John mentions Herod's reign, and, given the date of Matthew and Luke (some 85–95 years after the implied time of Yeshua's birth), no certainty or even confident estimate can be assumed for Yeshua's actual birth date. The phrase in Luke that Yeshua was about 30 when he began his preaching has been used to create a timeline for his ministry, although it is possible this was only indicative (it marked an age when most males in the culture would expect to have married). Estimates based only on the gospel of John, which mentions three Passovers, could suggest Yeshua's ministry lasted no more than three years; the texts of the other three gospels would certainly not imply any longer period. Luke states that John the Baptist began his (earlier) preaching in the 15th year of Emperor Tiberius's rule (i.e. 28–29 CE), which could put the death of Yeshua at around 31–32 CE.[7]

The longstanding debates over the date of Yeshua's birth seem flawed, if not pointless, to the secular historian. Knowledge of religious leaders comes from the time of their adulthood. Joseph Smith, Jun. began his religious outreach at the age of 24, and would subsequently claim visions from the age of 14 and meetings with the angel Moroni from 17. Muhammad ibn 'Abdullah's revelations began around the age of 40, yet the Muslim biographies generated substantial details of a birth (including miracles associated with this time), childhood and early career. The gospels of Mark and John focus on Yeshua's teaching and adulthood and have no interest in stories of a miraculous birth; nor do the letters of Paulos. The placing of his birth in the period of Herod's client rule relies on the other two gospels, one with a contradictory chronology, one reporting a massacre that seems not to have happened. Without the stories that tied the birth to Herod, Yeshua could have been born within a range of years: while the consensus, using Herod's reign, gives a date of 6 BCE or 4 BCE, it could be before, after or even at the time boundary we use to distinguish the eras of BCE and CE.

Irrespective of the unknown and unknowable date of Yeshua's birth, a death by execution in the prefecture of Pontius Pilatus seems sufficiently central to the Yeshua narratives that a date of Yeshua's death after 26 and before 36 CE is enough to provide a framework for the beginnings of Christianity. Least useful to the historian are attempts to link references in the gospel accounts of the birth and death of Yeshua to actual astronomical phenomena: an exercise in faith not science, even though Isaac Newton was a pioneer in this approach.

The first manuscript copies we possess of New Testament books are significantly later than the period when they are thought to have been written. There are no documents that can be confidently dated back to the 1st or 2nd centuries. Most fragments with claims to be early lack an archaeological context or other method to provide a reliable date and are more safely attributed to the 3rd or early 4th centuries.[8] A systematic review of the question notes 'the degree to which scholars are susceptible to the overwhelming temptation to weave fragmentary bits of papyrological evidence into coherent, even compelling stories'.[9] We do have a Christian parchment from Dura Europos on the Euphrates that must predate the town's destruction in 256, but this manuscript is a fragment from a combination of the contents of the gospels. The persecution of Christians by Emperor Diocletian in 303 may have been an incentive to hide documents away.

As noted above, the writing of the gospel narratives we possess date later than the letters of Paulos, but their authorship and the context for their writing remain areas of debate. The gospel of Mark is generally considered the earliest, from around 70 CE, a date suggested because it would tie in with the time of the Jewish Revolt against Roman rule in 66–73 CE. A shared resource common to both Matthew and Luke was proposed in the late 19th century (named 'Q', for the German *Quelle* – source). Both these gospels are most commonly dated to the period 80–90, and Acts, being a sequel to Luke by the same author, perhaps only a little later. Acts presents a range of traditions concerning the activities (and miracles) of early apostles, including the conversion of Paulos, before changing voice to 'we' for a detailed account of Paulos's travels and preaching. Following these three gospels, our surviving version of the gospel of John is placed by most scholars within the range 90–110. All were written not in Aramaic or Hebrew but in Greek, for an audience who could read or understand Greek, wherever they may have lived. A current perspective suggests the gospel of Mark may have been written in Syria, Matthew also (in Antioch), Luke in Anatolia and possibly Ephesus, and perhaps John there also.[10]

The differences between the four canonical gospels are not just in style and temporal scope. They differ substantially in their choice of events in Yeshua's life and the preaching they quote, despite the description of the gospels of Matthew, Mark and Luke as 'synoptic' – sharing a common theological approach – with Matthew and Luke thought to derive largely from Mark and Q[uelle]. Even the 'beatitudes' (delivered in the Sermon on the Mount) are included only in the gospels of Matthew and Luke. The topics common to all four are: the story of Yeshua being followed by a large crowd with the consequent feeding of the 5,000; incidents immediately preceding Yeshua's death (the entry into Jerusalem, prediction of his betrayal, Peter's denial, the release of Barabbas); events on the cross; the release and burial of his body;

and the experience of some women after his body has left the tomb.[11] Clearly, by the times the gospels were written, different aspects of the inherited story had acquired different emphases.

Most of today's conventional dating of the four gospels, to the later 1st century (and possibly the early 2nd century for John), is based primarily upon their contents. It therefore accepts the antiquity of their text, even though our oldest surviving manuscripts are much later. The versions we have clearly include copyists' errors, but it is assumed they did not reflect significant redaction by the scribes who copied them after the initial generations of Christian development, because of the belief and reputation that the text dated back to early apostles or their immediate successors.[12] Some contradictions between the versions of the history of Yeshua's life in the gospels and the events in early Christianity in Acts and the letters were allowed to remain. The *Codex Sinaiticus*, dated to the middle or later 4th century, includes all four gospels, though with textual variants from the version adopted by the later church. For each separate gospel, 3rd-century texts have been recovered.

Definition of the canon which forms the familiar New Testament developed by stages. The text known as the First Epistle of Clement, thought to date from the mid-90s, mentions no canon of gospels and includes quotes from Iesous that are not included in the New Testament texts.[13] The Second Epistle of Clement (probably a different author, in the 2nd century) also makes no reference to a fixed set of source books. Irenaeus (the Turkish-born bishop of Lyon in France) in his *Adversus Haereses*, written around 180, refers to the four New Testament gospels by name, implying that by this time their authority was clearly established. The 4th-century church leader Athanasius emphasised a binary division between acceptable and unacceptable books; others had seen works as accepted, false or the category of disputed reliability and acceptability.[14] The Synod of Hippo in northern Africa in 393, which brought together senior figures in the Christians churches, formally adopted the present list of canonical books, while there were some differences within the eastern churches.

Several issues arise for historical interpretation of the gospels, being our major documents on the life of Yeshua, but written between 40 and 70–80 years after the death of Yeshua. By this period, the sources of narratives are no longer the testimony of those who had encountered and heard the teacher but those of a second and third generation of followers. The details of the narratives had diverged: the stories of miracles vary and, as noted above, stories around his birth are in only two of the four gospels. A core belief was that Yeshua had been executed but had returned to life and met with some of his followers before a bodily ascension. The theological significance of this is presented in all four gospels alongside his teachings, though with different emphases, and it would play a key part in the teaching of Paulos. By two generations after Yeshua's death it was essential for Christians to have written accounts of the life and teachings of Yeshua, and to have this in a language accessible to them, even if this meant that different versions were in circulation. The spread of Christianity was an incentive to replace oral traditions with written reference sources.

Oral traditions, of course, reflect the settings in which they are narrated and the context and needs of these.[15] Memories can be edited and omitted over time. They can also be created, not just by an individual, but within a group whose members believe they have personally shared in what some are confident they experienced.

Yeshua's origins and most of his preaching lay in Galilee, where he attracted from other regions those who wished to hear him or join his followers. His execution appears to have been designed to prevent a larger following developing in Judaea. The arrival in Jerusalem of a popular Galilean preacher, one whose Judaism suggested minimal respect for the religious authorities, made the Jewish authorities more than willing to secure Roman agreement to his death before he could cause further disruption.[16]

The gospels describe crowds of people welcoming him into Jerusalem, but also a number rejecting Pilatus's offer to free him in favour of Barabbas. If Yeshua's preaching lasted only three years, this was far less than Muhammad ibn 'Abdullah's 20 years and Joseph Smith, Jun.'s 14. The success of the Christian movement depended on a different image of Yeshua. A secular materialist interpretation would assert Yeshua that did not return to life after death, appear to his followers and ascend to heaven. But this narrative was essential to continue the 'Jesus movement' beyond the message of an inspired and influential preacher and to distinguish him from other Jewish charismatic figures of the era. The story of the resurrection, 'the risen Christ', is at the core of early Christianity, and of the theology advanced by Paulos. From an historical viewpoint it is not particularly important whether it was deliberately invented by the earliest proselytisers, or quickly built as a perception of their common experience, or developed more gradually as a tradition.

Given the dating of the gospels, we cannot know what history the first Christians believed in the years immediately following the death of Yeshua, but the letters of Paulos show a theology that had developed within 20–30 years after Yeshua's life. By the later 1st century there was a central narrative of a period of Yeshua's preaching and miracles, his execution and a resurrection witnessed by a group of his followers, which indicate what the church fathers of the 2nd century believed to be the historical origins of their religion.

Numerous 'gospels' – narratives of the life, words and deeds of Yeshua – were in circulation in the early centuries CE. Some of these belonged to what would we now see as mainstream Christianity; others emerged in what is called the Gnostic tradition. If history is said be written by the victors, that is true of religion as well as politics. One person's faith is another person's apostasy, and what is a core ('canonical') document to one organisation is false ('apocryphal') to another.

The early Christian movement experienced early schisms and divisions, as most religions do after the death of their founder. Mormonism experienced splits soon after the death of Joseph Smith, Jun.; conflicts over the leadership of the Islamic world emerged within 30 years of the death of Muhammad. Early divisions of opinion in Christian theology and organisation are described in the New Testament. The apostles of Yeshua in Judaea promoted their new movement as a reform of Judaism, with the expectation initially that its followers would follow the requirements of Jewish law and practice. Others, like Paulos, worked to develop Christianity as a religion for gentiles and Jews alike, without a requirement for adherence to Jewish religious and social practices.[17]

What became the established church leadership acknowledged the orthodoxy of just four canonical gospels, as noted above. That is, they were formally distinguished from the many other gospels in circulation, even though some of these, like the four in the New Testament canon, had been attributed an authorship which gave them an authority of transmission from early apostles. Most Christian scholars place the canonical gospels earlier than the apocryphal ones, seeing those as mostly dated to the 2nd century, though a minority are later still, and by the 6th century a long list of apocryphal writings was known.[18] Manuscripts containing these alternative gospels, most of which were first written in Greek, were translated into Syriac, Aramaic, Coptic and other languages, and some are known only by early references to them rather than by manuscript fragments. In addition to gospels (i.e. books on aspects of the life of Yeshua) there were non-canonical accounts of the lives of the apostles and early followers of Yeshua, and apocryphal letters attributed to them. The multiple competing versions of Christianity and multiple competing documentary sources were reduced to the canonical New Testament by the successfully established church organisations.

Among the early variants of Christianity, Gnosticism was the source of a number of these gospels and other writings.[19] The height of Gnostic beliefs lay in the 2nd century and reflected Jewish and Hellenistic influences as well as Christian. Gnostic influence is seen in the gospel of Thomas (discovered in manuscript only in 1945). Thought by many (but not all) scholars to date some time in the early 2nd century, it is unusual among apocryphal books in being primarily sayings of Yeshua rather than an account of events. Some are similar to sayings in the canonical gospels, but others are quite different. A more recent find, the gospel of Judas, shows the development of Gnostic ideas later in the 2nd century. Another early Christian writing omitted from the canonical New Testament is the *Didache*, a presumed late 1st-century document of religious teaching and religious practices to be followed by a largely gentile community of believers.[20]

The New Testament includes 21 letters which by tradition appear in the names of early Christian evangelists. The attribution and dates of these have also been widely debated. Letters traditionally ascribed to James, Peter, John and Jude are now considered to be from other writers in the later 1st century or early 2nd century, and therefore no earlier than the gospels. Some see the anonymous Letter to Hebrews as earlier.

Thirteen of the letters are conventionally attributed to Paulos, and while some seem to have been created by others later using his name (in the late 1st to 2nd centuries), the majority of these (seven, and possibly nine) are considered by modern scholars to be copies of genuine writings of Paulos from the decade of the 50s.[21] This would be more than 20 years into Paulos's evangelical work. They thus represent a formulated theology of this most influential organiser and innovative preacher. Alongside his own evolved religious outlook we can consider what he had come to believe about the history, life and death of Yeshua himself. These would represent our earliest text relating to Yeshua's life, but these early documents in fact say very little about the life and works of the religious leader in whose name Paulos was preaching.[22]

In Paulos's writings there is no story of a virgin birth; Iesous (Yeshua) is described as from the line of David. Much emphasis is on the return of Christ to judge the world. The 'last supper' narrative is recorded, as is the crucifixion. Quotations from Yeshua are not a feature of the letters.[23]

The key narrative of Yeshua's resurrection is featured in Paulos's texts. But otherwise Paulos says little about the man, his activities and the detail of his sayings, and barely a mention is made of the leading disciples; he is more interested in Christianity and in Christ in heaven than in Christ on earth. The letters of Paulos present plenty of quotable material in his own words but relatively few of Yeshua's words.

In summary, we have no historical data on Yeshua dating from his lifetime, and in the letters of Paulos, 20–30 years later, we have only minimal information on his life. Then, beginning from around 40 years after Yeshua's death, we have the beginnings of narrative accounts in writing, as oral traditions were turned into the Greek-language accounts in the New Testament (and the undated inferred Q source), and the probably later 'apocryphal' texts. We therefore have limited 'history' to illuminate the details of the origins of Christianity. But we can seek to understand it more by considering the political context, the broader religious patterns of the time and the geographical setting, as well as the archaeology that shows directly the material world of 1st-century CE Galilee, Judaea and neighbouring regions.

The historical context of the Yeshua movement

How did the activity of Yeshua as a religious teacher and figure fit into his environment, and attract a following in the period immediately before his death in the early 30s CE? How did a movement built around his life, work and teaching begin among Jews of the region, in the period after his death – and why it did not succeed as a Jewish reform movement within the Judaean heartland of the Jewish religion? And how did it grow as a movement among Jews and gentiles elsewhere in the Roman Empire? It is useful and important to consider the emergence of Christianity in the social, political and religious context of Galilee, Judaea and the region.

The Roman Empire plays an important part in the New Testament narratives: Pontius Pilatus (Pilate), the Roman execution, experiences with soldiers and references in the gospels and Acts to the power of Caesar. Political boundaries shifted several times in the period before, during and after the rise of Christianity.[24] Judaea was on the margins of the Roman Empire: geographically marginal and marginal to its political power and economy in the 1st century BCE through to the 1st century CE. However, as a province at the border of Roman rule, its security mattered, especially given threats that might develop from the east.

Jewish independence from Hellenistic rule had not long existed. The Seleucid rulers, who were of Hellenistic descent, faced the Maccabean revolt in the 160s BCE; that revolt established the Jewish Hasmonean dynasty, whose power gradually expanded. Fully independent from the Seleucids by 110 BCE, Judaean statehood lasted less than 50 years beyond that.

The Roman Levant – the easternmost Mediterranean – came under Roman control almost incidentally. Roman armies led by Pompey defeated the Pontic ruler of Armenia and Anatolia. As a result the western part of this empire became the Roman province of Syria from 64/63 BCE, with its administrative capital at Antioch (today's Antakya). This conquest gave Rome control of eastern seaports. Pompey proceeded south to Jerusalem to intervene in a conflict between two rival Hasmonean figures; he besieged Jerusalem, and left Hyrcanus as High Priest and Judaea with reduced independence, under Roman influence but not yet direct rule, and with tribute payable to Rome.[25] Rome effected indirect rule with the appointment of Antipater from Idumaea, south of Judaea, and Julius Caesar granted him greater power in 47 BCE. His son, Herod 'the Great', was named as King of Judaea by Rome in 40 BCE and established his rule through military action, conquering Jerusalem in 37 BCE. His Idumaean ancestry contributed to the uneven relationship he had with Judaism; another contributory factor was his encouragement of non-Jewish people to settle in the towns he developed. Herod turned part of the heavy taxation he collected into dramatic and ambitious building projects, including the substantial rebuilding and expansion of the Temple in Jerusalem.

On Herod's death in 4 BCE his area of control was initially divided between his three sons as Roman client rulers. Until 34 CE, Philip ruled the area north of the Decapolis – the ten cities which remained relatively self-governing, under Roman protection. Archelaus ruled Idumaea, Judaea and Samaria (north of Judaea) until 6 CE, when this area was taken into direct rule by Rome as the Province of Judaea, with a Roman prefect governing from the coastal city created by Herod the Great, Caesarea Maritima, and responsible to the government in Syria. Pontius Pilatus was the fifth such prefect. Herod Antipas ruled Peraea (east of the Jordan) and Galilee north of Samaria, and continued to do so until 39 CE. In a pattern of indirect rule, Rome allowed Agrippa, grandson of Herod the Great, to control increasing parts of Herod's territory and named him King of Judaea in 41; he died in 44. Direct Roman rule then resumed, with the governor now at the rank of procurator, which was higher than prefect. Agrippa's son (Herod Agrippa II) for a period served as a Roman client ruler in different areas.

The Maccabean revolt, which led to much of Palestine being under Hasmonean rule, has been described as based on an alliance between numerous independent farmers and rural priests. But the era of Herodian rule was marked by large wealthy landowners and numerous free but impoverished farmers. Jews under Herodian rule faced not just the burden of taxes collected for Herod and for the Romans, but the tax that supported a priesthood as well as the Temple tax payable to Jerusalem, which was an obligation also on Jews scattered across the diaspora of the eastern Mediterranean and Middle East.[26]

8. Palestine in the early 1st century CE

In the lifetime of Yeshua and the two generations that followed, political unrest underlay Judaea and beyond. It is unclear how much the movements of protest were linked. There were rebellions around the end of Herod the Great's rule, including an attack on Herod's palace in Sepphoris led by 'Judas the Galilean', who would be identified by Josephus as a leader of the religious group known as Zealots. Judas's two sons were executed for rebellion about 46 CE. Pilatus's response to a rebellion in Samaria that broke out in 35 CE led to his recall to Rome.[27]

This complex, changing and unsettled set of events placed the religious leaders of Judaism under the sequence of client rulers of the Herodian family and Roman delegates. Appointment and removal of local client rulers was in the hands of the Romans; Jewish political independence was not for most a realistic option. The Zealots, as described by Josephus, were the exception, taking as a religious view that only God could be their ruler; their hostility to the Roman regime showed itself in the Jewish Revolt of 66–73 CE, which saw the Roman army besieging Jerusalem, destroying its Temple in 70, and punishing many Judaean Jews for their support of the rebellion. This was a significant symbolic defeat for Judaeans, for Jewish identity and for the Jewish diaspora already widely spread through the Middle East and the eastern Mediterranean. But it neither destroyed Judaism nor the rural economy of Judaea. Nevertheless, the Jews were probably around half the population of the Palestine region before the revolt, and it seems their proportion may have started to fall soon afterwards.[28] Judaea was subsequently administered under a Roman legate, with a greater military presence. Following a further revolt in 132–135, the province was renamed Syria Palaestina.

The geography of Yeshua's life, as presented in the synoptic gospels, placed him primarily in Herod Antipas's Galilee, with some visits suggested to different polities of the region: the area ruled by Philip, and to the Decapolis, into the Province of Roman Syria, and Peraea, and Samaria before reaching Jerusalem in Judaea. In the very compressed chronology of the gospel narratives, his arrival in Jerusalem saw the religious leaders there complaining to the Roman governor (by implication visiting from Caesarea Maritima), who (in Luke) referred the case to Herod Antipas (also, by implication, present in Jerusalem for the Passover) before an execution by the Roman authorities in that city.

In such a situation, religious identities, religious affiliations and religious arguments can take the place of politics. When the three synoptic gospels were written in the later part of the 1st century they all quoted Yeshua advising that dues to Caesar should be paid – a direct warning against political

Key dates

64–63 BCE	Pompey's victories in Syria and Palestine
40	Herod the Great named client king of Judaea
37	Herod conquers Jerusalem
4	Death of Herod the Great
6 CE	Judaea placed under direct Roman rule
6	Census of Quirinius
17–23	Construction of Tiberias
26	Pontius Pilatus prefect
28–29	John the Baptist preaching
31–32	Estimated dates of Yeshua's death
36	Pontius Pilatus recalled to Rome
39	Herod Antipas exiled
41–44	Agrippa king of Judaea
50–57	Letters of Paulos
ca. 62	Josephus's report of James's execution
64	Tacitus's date for Nero's victimisation of Christians
66	Jewish Revolt begins
70	Destruction of Temple in Jerusalem
ca. 70	Gospel of Mark
ca. 80–90	Gospels of Matthew and Luke
ca. 90–110	Gospel of John
112	Pliny's report of Christians present in north Anatolia

involvement. These writers were not living in Judaea but would be well aware of the events that followed the Jewish Revolt.

But an unorthodox preacher, undertaking exorcisms and miracles, building a large following and speaking of a new and imminent kingdom of God on earth would be a threat not just to Jewish religious authorities but to the political stability of Rome's frontier province. The gospels might lay the blame for Yeshua's execution on the Jerusalem hierarchy, but it was the Roman authorities that chose to execute him, as a warning to others whose ideas they might consider a danger to the state.

Religious orthodoxy and dissent

Studies of Yeshua have tended to focus on the specifics of his theological and ethical teaching, his apocalyptic message and his conflict with the Judaic religious authorities of the 1st century CE. A wide variety of religious ideas accompanied the political turmoil of the 1st century, with competing Jewish hierarchies, varying patterns of Roman direct and indirect rule, and the changing roles and powers of members of the Herodian family. The high priests, who maintained religious authority from Jerusalem, and those who held political influence or control were subject to criticism from other 'prophets' than Yeshua.[29] Some of the voices against authority can be described as 'messianic', especially about the time of the great and fatal Jewish Revolt against Rome. The 1st century saw a range of dissenting public figures, ranging from those whose message was primarily religious to those whose message was primarily political (challenging Rome, or the Herodian dynasty, or the priestly hierarchy).[30] A common theme of many was a message preaching the potential renewal or revival of Israel in a model echoing that within the Tanakh (Old Testament). The position of Yeshua and his early followers within this continuum has been widely debated.

One interpretation sees the apocalyptic message of 1st-century preachers as of interest primarily to the Jewish upper classes, who had lost their power and influence under Roman rule. What appealed to the rural poor, who did not have any power to lose, in contrast, was the charismatic side of prophesy, together with miracle working. The threat to the Roman state came from those whose message addressed the elite, not those who introduced new religious ideas to the poor.

Miracles are a persistent part of the gospel narrative of Yeshua and the story of the early apostles in Acts. Faith healing, in particular, was a feature of the era, making Yeshua 'a charismatic wonder-worker whose profile has some parallels with fairly well-known Jewish saints and sages of his period'.[31] The early Christian leaders are also credited in Acts with powers to undertake miracles of faith healing, no less than Yeshua himself.

At the core of Yeshua's preaching, as recorded in the New Testament, was the apocalyptic vision of the kingdom of God on earth, the end of the current world by divine intervention with a judgement of individual humans. While there has inevitably been much analysis and debate, there are strong arguments that Yeshua expected this 'end of days' to be within his lifetime and that of his listeners; and that when he died before it came, his immediate followers still expected it within their own lifetime. Gradually Christianity developed to retain the importance of the final judgement day but without necessarily specifying a time – although throughout two millennia of Christian movements there have been plenty of prophesies that the apocalypse, the 'second coming' of Christ', is imminent.[32]

Close reading of the early Christian literature supports an argument that Yeshua never declared himself to be divine, but that his identity as the Son of God developed after his death.[33] The concept of 'the Trinity' of God the Father, God the Son (Yeshua) and the Holy Spirit would develop more slowly, and be argued over in successive centuries. So, while the first canonical gospel,

Mark, suggests that Yeshua was a human who became divine, John suggests a divine being who became human. The divine status achieved by humans who became emperor was, of course, a feature of the Roman Empire. The theological arguments of subsequent centuries were fierce around the divine nature of Yeshua and his relationship to 'God the Father'. Human saints (especially Mary as the mother of Yeshua) would become the posthumous recipients of prayers, but with status distinctly below the rank of the Trinity.

John the Baptist is known to us through the gospels and the writings of Josephus in the late 1st century CE, both as a religious prophet and as someone who made political criticisms of Herod Antipas. But we know of other religious innovators and teachers in the same period. Theudas was a figure whose religious preaching to a substantial following and the hostile response to this (mentioned by Josephus and in Acts) led to his death about 15 years after that of Yeshua. Other religious movements challenged orthodoxy in the decades before the destruction of the Temple.[34]

A Galilean figure named Hanina ben Dosa, known from narratives some centuries later in the Talmud of Rabbinic Judaism, is an example of a man who combined ethical teaching with miracles in the middle of the 1st century CE, while keeping away from political issues.[35] He came from the same region as Yeshua – perhaps 12 miles (20 km) to the north of Nazareth. Talmudic stories of other charismatic figures include Judaean miracle worker Honi ha-Ma'age in the 1st century BCE, who, like Yeshua, met a violent death. Two of Honi's grandsons were also recorded as miracle workers.[36] Not all fell foul of the authorities as did Yeshua and John the Baptist. Some were ignored. 'Jesus son of Ananias', actively preaching the impending doom of Jerusalem from around 62 CE to the fall of Jerusalem in 70, was handed over by the religious authorities to the Romans but released on the grounds that he was insane.[37]

Josephus in his *Antiquities of the Jews* identified the major Jewish religious groups in 1st century CE Judaea as Pharisees, Sadducees, Essenes and a fourth group, who, by the time of the Jewish Revolt of 66–73, were known by the name Zealots. The Essenes, though not mentioned in the New Testament, have become perhaps the best-known of the variants of Judaism in the era of Christian origins. The Dead Sea Scrolls archive has amplified our knowledge of the beliefs and practices of this community if, as most scholars accept, it represents a library of Essene writings.

Over much of two millennia, Christian religious groups have maintained ambiguous attitudes to Judaism: incorporating the Tanakh as the 'Old Testament' in the Christian Bible while rejecting the image of Israel as God's chosen people. Christianity's first debates were between those who expected the followers of Yeshua to adhere to Jewish religious laws and those, like Paulos, who saw the potential for Christianity as a religion for gentiles and Jews alike. But as scholars such as Geza Vermes have shown, the religious preaching represented in the books of the New Testament, and the life of the preacher Yeshua reported there, sit comfortably as a development within, not beyond, Judaism, from an individual following Jewish religious practices. To Vermes, Yeshua was a 'charismatic healer and teacher and eschatological enthusiast'.[38] In this, what was unique was not what he said or did but in the posthumous following that developed.

Our understanding the life and work of Yeshua becomes clearer becomes clearer when we see the consistent description of a religious life led mainly in Galilee. With Bethlehem a later invention (as noted below) and Jerusalem a final destination, Yeshua's primary preaching was in an area that was not at the time central to religious Judaism and its elites. Galilee was a Jewish enclave but had the Decapolis and Roman Syria (Phoenicia) on its borders, Samaritans further to the south (whom the Jews of Galilee and Judaea clearly distinguished from themselves) and the relatively Hellenised towns of Tiberias and Sepphoris within its boundaries. Galilee's own Jewish traditions may indeed have been strengthened in the earlier 1st century BCE under Maccabean/Hasmonean rule.[39] About three years of religious preaching from a Galilean base were followed by a journey to the religious and organisational centre of Judaism, Jerusalem, where a quick response by the religious authorities led to Yeshua's execution. His followers, however, considered that the potential success of their movement lay in moving its core from Galilee to Judaea. Remaining focussed on Jerusalem, they established the movement in which Yeshua the person – not just the ideas he had preached – was central. But Paulos, whose conversion came from contact neither with Yeshua nor with his apostles, developed the religion by extending his message elsewhere in the Hellenised world of the eastern Roman Empire and laid the basis for much of its success.

The geography of Christian origins

To the medieval Christian cartographers and illustrators of a *mappa mundi*, Jerusalem sat at the centre of the world, as devised by God. Central to the 'Holy Land', Jerusalem was and is a holy city to the three Abrahamic religions. But it was also a marginal (if troublesome) place at the edge of the Roman Empire.

The lands of Judaea and its neighbours loom large in religious consciousness. In broader secular history it appears a major region: fought over between ancient Egyptian, Mesopotamian and Anatolian kingdoms, land contested by European Crusaders and Saracens, and one of the regions whose troubled and conflicted history over the past 70 years has influenced world affairs. Yet the small size of the region can come as a surprise. The land area of today's Israel and the West Bank together are just 10,300 square miles (26,630 skm²), to which the Negev desert region contributes 4,650 square miles (12,000 km²). That is a total size between Vermont and Massachusetts in the United States, between Wales and Belgium in Europe, and 40% of Tasmania.

In 2010, I stood looking out north from a high point at Umm Qais in the north-west of the Kingdom of Jordan. Below was the Golan Heights, part of Syria until the 1967 war, while today's actual Syrian border was just eight miles (13 km) to my right. The most distant hills I could see extended into Lebanon; below me was Israel and the Sea of Galilee (Lake Kinneret, Lake Tiberias), and sharply left, to the south-west, out of sight but less than 35 km away, was the West Bank – Palestine. Five countries in one broad sweep.

The topography of Israel is dominated by a central Judaean range running north--south – a watershed separating the Jordan Valley from watercourses running into the fertile coastal plain and the Mediterranean. Jerusalem sits at the top of the range; Samaria spans the range to the north and further north still the topography is lower between the Sea of Galilee and the west (Lower Galilee) before the high land of Upper Galilee. The vegetation and land use zones of Israel and the West Bank range from the higher-rainfall and more productive areas of north and west to the increasing aridity to the south and east, dominated by the Negev.

Jerusalem (with perhaps 20,000–30,000 people if not more in the early 1st century CE) was the largest settlement in a region that was primarily a rural economy. The more populous and agriculturally more productive area was Galilee, not Judaea, while the other territory ruled by Herod Antipas, Peraea, was the most arid and least populated.[40]

The setting for Christian origins is spread through and then beyond this area. In creating a narrative from oral traditions for Greek-speaking Christians, the authors of the gospels (and the Q source) were writing theological works, not historical analyses, and were not likely to have events in Yeshua's life set in an accurate order consistent within or between each gospel. All gospels mention Yeshua as coming from the village of Nazareth, west of the Sea of Galilee. The area around Galilee in the north of modern Israel is identified as the locality of his major preaching and activities. Jerusalem, as the ritual and conceptual centre of Judaism, played an important part at the end of the sequence.

The identification of Bethlehem, 5½ miles (9 km) from Jerusalem, as Yeshua's birthplace in just two gospels, Luke and Matthew, would appear to be a myth designed to link with a prophecy in the Old Testament Book of Micah that the Messiah would be born there, as it was the city associated with King David. Describing the birth of the Messiah in the city of David reinforced its authority to Christians of Jewish background, with Matthew and Luke specifically linking Yeshua's father, Joseph, to the line of King David. The narrative in Luke moved Yeshua's family there for the birth by the highly improbable suggestion that his family, as paternal descendants of David, needed to travel from Galilee to Bethlehem for the Roman census of 6 CE (despite them living outside the area of Roman Judaea), and anachronistically linked this also to Herod the Great, who had died 10 years before this census. Bethlehem does not therefore seem a real part of the historical story.

Christian origins lie firmly in the Lower Galilee area, which extends westward of the 'Sea of Galilee' – the freshwater Lake Kinneret/Tiberias, which is 64 square miles (166 km²) in area and lies on the path of the River Jordan. Extending north from the fertile Jezreel Valley, Lower Galilee reaches 2,000 feet (600 m) above sea level.

As noted above, Galilee was not under direct Roman rule but was the client kingdom of Herod the Great and then Herod Antipas, who built Tiberias on the lake as his administrative centre and residence from around 20 CE (with non-Jewish as well as Jewish residents). Such a development would have provided much work for any craftsman living in the area: Yeshua's father, Joseph, is described in Matthew as a *tektōn*, meaning artisan, craftsman, builder or, as conventionally translated, carpenter. But trade in goods was an essential part of Galilee's economy: a network of roads facilitated communication within Galilee and beyond to its neighbours: to coastal trading and administrative towns, south across the Jezreel Valley, along the Jordan Valley and east across the Jordan Valley to cities of the Decapolis.[41]

Nazareth lies about 5½ miles (9 km) by road from Sepphoris (an important town under Herodian rule that also saw rebuilding under Herod Antipas, before he turned his attention to constructing Tiberias), and it is 19 miles (30 km) by road from Tiberias. Gospel references to Yeshua's early preaching place this at Capernaum, on the lake edge, 7 miles (11 km) beyond Tiberias. The area was not therefore one with visible Roman dominance or occupation; but it was a region that, according to Josephus, had experienced tension between religious Jews and Herodian rulers, whose faithfulness to Jewish practices was suspect. Nazareth sat at a distance from Jerusalem in Judaea, a journey of about 80 miles (130 km) through Samaria or of 95 miles (150 km) down the Jordan Valley, so the area was not under the direct gaze of the religious elites, though a devout family from Galilee would have visited the Temple at Jerusalem from time to time, despite this being perhaps a week's journey by foot if avoiding the riskier passage through Samaria. It is suggested tens of thousands of Jews would have visited Jerusalem on pilgrimages each year in the 1st century CE, though that would still have been a minority of the Jewish population of the Palestine region.[42]

All four canonical gospels identify the beginning of Yeshua's religious life with a symbolic immersion by John 'the Baptist'. John was a religious figure who is mentioned by Josephus as an influential preacher, and whose death at the hands of Herod Antipas was cited by some as the source of Herod's subsequent divine punishment by losing a war with the Nabataeans in 36–37 CE.[43] John's execution indicates he was active in Herod Antipas's territories – possibly in Galilee as well as in Peraea, along the eastern side of the Jordan River, where by Josephus's account he was put to death. These two territories were separated by the Decapolis, outside of Herod's control. In the gospels baptism was a ritual undertaken in the River Jordan; Christian tradition has placed the baptism of Yeshua in southern Peraea.

The New Testament accounts suggest Yeshua's period of active preaching was brief, about three years between his baptism and his execution. His activities began in Galilee and many of the activities cited in the gospels they located in Galilee, with his first followers recruited on the banks of the Sea of Galilee. Incidents at other places in Galilee are mentioned: Capernaum (preaching), Cana (a miracle of turning wine into water), Bethsaida, just outside Galilee proper (a miracle), and Nain (a miracle), 8½ miles (14 km) from Nazareth. The Sermon on the Mount was located in the period of preaching in Galilee, as was the 'Feeding of the 5,000' miracle and the miracle of walking on water.

Places further away were included in the traditions incorporated in the gospel texts: a visit to the region of Sidon and Tyre in Roman Syria, miracles in Tyre and in the Decapolis, preaching in Caesarea Philippi (in the northern area where Philip was client ruler) and a visit to Sychar in Samaria. But the emphasis of the gospels is that people came to Galilee to hear him preach: according to Matthew and Luke from Syria, the Decapolis, Judaea and across the Jordan.[44]

But Judaea becomes important at the end of the narrative, as Yeshua journeyed to his final preaching and death in Jerusalem. The latest canonical gospel, John, reported other journeys to Jerusalem in addition to the final one, but the synoptic gospels bring Yeshua to Jerusalem only for the end of the story. His activities in Roman Judaea recorded in the gospel narratives include a miracle at Jericho and a miracle in Bethany, considered to lie just east of Jerusalem.

The implication is that Yeshua's preaching remained focussed on Galilee and away from both the Roman colony and the religious centre of Judaism until the final (and fatal) journey. And if it was believed that an apocalyptic end of days was imminent, Jerusalem would be seen as the focus of this. There is thus a contrast between Yeshua's ministry in the territories controlled by Herod Antipas – rural communities whose lives were affected by the political activities of the Herodian family – and the final ministry focussing on Jerusalem, the religious centre of Judaism operating under direct Roman rule.[45] As the Temple city, Jerusalem was a natural (if dangerous) place to preach a reformist version of the religion. When the Jewish authorities asked the Roman authorities to punish this challenging figure, according to Luke Pilatus recognised that he was classified as a Galilean in referring his case initially to Herod Antipas.

After Yeshua's execution in Jerusalem, his apostles were reported to have returned to Galilee: Matthew writes of a vision of the risen Yeshua there and John narrates a sighting on the Sea of Galilee itself. Before this, the gospels of Mark, Luke and John described encounters with a risen Yeshua in or outside of Jerusalem. The author of Luke is the author of Acts, and Luke leaves the apostles in Jerusalem, not returning to Galilee as do Matthew and John. Only after Yeshua's death did Jerusalem apparently become central to the small nascent Christian movement. The leaders now included not just Galileans but also Judaeans.

From the documents, the simplest historical construction thus places Yeshua as a highly persuasive and visionary religious teacher in Galilee who built around him a group of local supporters, and whose fame attracted listeners from much further afield. His success, influence, following and challenges to Judaic conventions attracted the hostility of the religious authorities in Jerusalem in the Roman province of Judaea, and when he travelled there to preach his message his arrest led to his death. If the core of his message was an expected imminent apocalyptic change by divine intervention, as many have argued, then he was as much a threat to Roman power as to the Jewish religious leadership.

Compared with the 270,000 words of *The Book of Mormon*, or the 80,000 words in the Qur'an, the recorded words of Yeshua are relatively few: under 25,000 in the Greek text of the four canonical gospels (including words in more than one gospel). The apocryphal gospel of Thomas contains just sayings of Yeshua, 114 in all. As noted above, the letters of Paulos, dated earlier than the gospels, have very few direct quotes. In his writings it was the message of Christianity rather than the words of the teacher that counted, in contrast to the traditions that led to the gospels.

The loyal disciples of Yeshua's teaching proceeded to promote his theology and ethics, challenging the impact of his execution by making it a central part of their message that Yeshua had risen from the dead and shown himself to his key followers before ascending into heaven. The narrative in Acts shows the apostles performing their own miracles, extending their preaching and having a major debate over whether converts to their religion needed to follow Jewish practices. While numbers of adherents did build in Judaea, as well as in Samaria and Galilee, success with gentiles and diaspora Jews in cities outside of Judaea, influenced especially by the activities of Paulos and his associates, led to the view that this would not be necessary.[46]

A critical historical perspective on the sources and setting of the beginnings of Christianity allows a relatively straightforward picture of the beginnings of the Christian religion. This can be supplemented by the study of the material world of the 1st century CE provided by archaeology.

Archaeology of the world of Yeshua

The professional fieldwork, excavation and analyses of archaeology bring us direct images of the time and places of Christian origins. But excluded from the world of early Christianity are the archaeology and sites that reflect later *tradition* rather than the formative period itself. Thus in Bethlehem the Church of the Nativity, constructed from 327 under instruction from Emperor Constantine and his Christian convert mother Helena, marked a location that had entered Christian tradition as the specific site of a Bethlehem birth of Yeshua. The Grotto of the Nativity (subject of a 19th-century conflict between Catholics and Orthodox) is at a lower level than the church itself. The Shepherds' Field to the east of the town further reflects the tradition in two gospels of a Bethlehem birth.

With the lack of continuity between the Christians of 1st-century Jerusalem and the Byzantine pilgrims from two centuries later, gospel references to locations in Jerusalem took on their own significance. So Gethsemane and the Mount of Olives to the east of the city and nearby Bethany are among core sites in Christian heritage.[47] Elsewhere sites have been claimed as locations of events in Yeshua's final days in Jerusalem, or associated with the differing gospel traditions of resurrection followed by bodily assumption to the heavens.

Several archaeological finds from the 1st century CE have been cited as relevant background to Yeshua's life. These include an ossuary (a chest of stone or wood used to store human bones) found in Jerusalem in 1990 and thought by many to include the bones of the high priest Caiaphas, who plotted for Yeshua's death; the inscription mentioning Pontius Pilatus found in Caesarea Maritima; and the bones of a crucified man named Yehohanan found in 1969 in Givat Hamivtar in East Jerusalem, showing that a victim of Roman execution could still receive a formal burial.[48]

There has been intensive archaeological research in Galilee, the region of Yeshua's birth, preaching and early followers.[49] This indicated major changes at the end of the 2nd century BCE, with a shift to a distinctly Judaised community, probably as a result of the settlement of Jews from Judaea as Hasmonean rule expanded northwards. Population continued to grow in the Herodian and early Roman era.[50] The Herodian dynasty sought to balance the rule of the Jewish community and their role as clients of Rome, and this divide is reflected in the material culture of 1st-century CE Galilee, whose administrative centre under the rule of Herod the Great was Sepphoris.

Beginning soon after local uprising that followed the death of Herod the Great in 4 BCE, Herod Antipas's rebuilding (and fortification) at Sepphoris incorporated Hellenistic-Roman architectural and planning elements, including the Eastern Basilica building on the main public street, which became a market for luxury goods.[51] Sepphoris combined administrative and commercial buildings, homes of the prosperous and more humble dwellings, and a aqueduct system developed in the 1st century CE to bring water into the city from nearby springs.

While part of the town's population clearly remained Jewish, there are dissenting views on how culturally Jewish, and how culturally Hellenistic, was the town.[52] Jewish-style lamps found in Sepphoris seem to have been traded from the Jerusalem area. The population of the city has been estimated at between 8,000 and 12,000, spread over a wide area, with Tiberias of roughly similar population. But an alternative calculation suggested populations for Sepphoris as 18,000, Tiberias 24,000 and all Galilee in the 1st century CE about 150,000–175,000.[53]

Herod Antipas's subsequent construction over the period 17–23 of Tiberias as his administrative centre, 19 miles (30 km) away from Sepphoris, was more definitively in Hellenistic-Roman style, with roads on a grid pattern, public buildings around public spaces, theatres, bath houses and other features of classical urban life.[54]

The historical emphasis placed on the scale and importance of the two large Galilean towns of the Herodian dynasty is reinforced by archaeological work in both. Yet none of the gospels places Yeshua in either Sepphoris (never mentioned) or Tiberias (cited just once, as a source of some followers), despite their emphasis on his Galilean origins, preaching, travels and followers.[55] Was such an omission deliberate? Of course the gospels are not history and were not compiled until long after Yeshua's life. Written in Greek for a Christian community spread through the eastern Roman Empire, the emphasis of the narrative of Yeshua's preaching was on smaller and mainly Jewish settlements, not the towns in Galilee (or Caesarea Maritima) reflecting Hellenic-Roman culture.

Archaeological survey suggests that the Hellenic-Roman cultural pattern in these towns had not spread significantly to the countryside of modest farms and small villages between and beyond them. These retained a Jewish identity and material culture, possibly even reflecting political opposition to Roman rule.[56] Most pottery was in local style apart from some specialist vessels; oil lamps were traded to the area from Jerusalem; stone vessels include those matching Jewish purity laws. Overall, the material culture of rural 1st-century CE Jewish Galilee seems not very different from that of Judaea.[57]

The Herodian towns would provide markets for craft, produce and services from the rural communities of Lower Galilee.[58] Archaeology has suggested an unusually dense pattern of small villages developed in the hinterland of Sepphoris; the area around the city is fertile land. A large urban settlement and administrative centre requires fresh food from farmers of crops, herders of animals, fishermen and producers of other supplies from outside the metropolis. An extreme suggestion is that the main contribution of rural Galilee to the Herodian towns was in the form of taxation: a tributary political economy rather than an open market economy in goods and services.[59] But if taxes are collected, in turn they are spent on purchasing products and purchasing skills, not all of which will be obtained within the walls of the metropolis.

Today, the edge of the spreading city of Nazareth, biblical home of Yeshua, is visible from Sepphoris. In the 1st century the small settlement of Nazareth would have lain across a low ridge to the south-east of Sepphoris, about 5½ miles (9 km) distant: perhaps two hours by foot, or less on a motivated donkey. Such a journey would be quite feasible for a farmer seeking to sell produce to the most lucrative local market, and at least as attractive for a Nazarene craftsman selling products or services. If Joseph the father of Yeshua was a craftsman and if his son was brought up in the same trade, then

Sepphoris would have been part of their economic world. Yeshua would have been well aware of the uprising that took place there around the time of his own birth.

The long-established village of Nazareth lay on the lower part of south-east-facing slopes of a valley in a well-watered fertile part of Lower Galilee. The land around was very suitable for cereals, grapes and olive cultivation, and it was well connected to other villages in the area.[60] Archaeology has shown some of the world of Nazareth in which Yeshua grew up. Its population at this time has been estimated at around 1,000.[61]

Excavations uncovered residential locations and ossuaries from the early 1st century CE. Near a Byzantine church built to mark the tradition of the 'annunciation' of Mary were found tombs from the early Roman period. Beneath them was a rectilinear structure of a 'courtyard house' with stone walls (some coated with plaster) built to incorporate a rock-cut area, dated to the 1st century CE or perhaps a little earlier.[62] A second house nearby, mainly of stone walls, had two rooms as well as a storage silo and a rock-cut tunnel. Jewish ritual baths were found at the site of the major churches that developed in Nazareth. No 1st-century or earlier synagogue building has been found, suggesting the common pattern of religious activity focussed on people's homes. Despite proximity to Sepphoris, the pottery in Nazareth was utilitarian wares of Jewish traditional style.[63]

Yodfat (Yodefat), in central Galilee to the north of Sepphoris, has provided a visible parallel for Yeshua's Nazareth, since the excavated 1st-century CE settlement of 1,500–2,000 people on slopes of a spur had not been covered by later occupation.[64] Simple houses set on narrow alleyways were constructed from rough stones with mud plaster walls and packed-earth floors, and showed evidence of olive-oil production, wool weaving and pottery manufacture. Pottery finds were of local type, not Roman, and oil lamps were traded from Jerusalem. Some houses had small ritual baths. Meat bones from sheep outnumbered those from goats and there were also cattle and some chicken bones. An elite area of the community had large fine houses whose walls and also floors bore painted frescoes.[65] Roman coins from mid-1st century CE indicate the links of the village to the wider world. In 67 CE, besieging Roman forces conquered Yodfat, whose residents had fought them in the Jewish wars, led by Josephus.

In the gospel narratives Yeshua moved from Nazareth and the hinterland of Sepphoris to the hinterland of Herod Antipas's new town Tiberias, on the shores of the Sea of Galilee (Kinneret), beginning his religious mission in Capernaum on the lake. By this time Tiberias would have transformed the local economy, creating a new market for skills and produce, not least fish from the lake itself.

Ancient Tiberias extended along the shoreline in an area between the lake and a low range of rocky hills south of the present town of the same name. As the political capital of Galilee, its establishment acquired the importance in Herod Antipas's dominion previously held further west, at Sepphoris. The migration of Yeshua to the Sea of Galilee following the migration of the regional capital sounds logical in that context, whether initially in search of work as a craftsman like his father, or in pursuit of an audience to preach his religious message, or both.

Capernaum (Kefar Nahum) on the Sea of Galilee, about 10 miles (16 km) north of Tiberias by foot, and less by boat, is cited in the gospels as the site of Yeshua's early preaching. The community had grown significantly with Jewish settlement after the Hasmonean conquest; the 1st-century CE population has been estimated at between 1,000 and 1,700.[66] Capernaum had the characteristics of a typical Jewish large village of no great prosperity, with modest homes of stone and mud, many with thatched roofs, and without plaster surfaces, frescoes or ceramic roof tiles. The homes were spread randomly without the planned grid of the Hellenic towns. A Byzantine church was built on the site of an early stone-built house, said to have belonged to the apostle Peter, and the tradition of the 'house of Peter' has continued into modern times.[67]

Some 3 miles (5 km) north of Tiberias, a lakeside site has been suggested by scholars to be the Magdala of the gospels, and also identified as the Tarichaea mentioned by Josephus.[68] Excavations underway since 2009 suggest it was a settlement and fishing base of some importance in and after the Herodian era, with a wharf of stone, a warehouse and a working area for fishermen, as well as a large marketplace. A 1st-century CE building has been interpreted as one of the earliest Jewish synagogues.

South of Capernaum and 6 miles (10 km) north of Tiberias, along the lake near Ginosar (Ginnesar), the discovery in 1986 of a boat probably dating from the Herodian period gave a direct image of the lives of fishermen on the lake. Referred to as 'the Galilee boat' or even 'the Jesus boat' it is over 26 feet (8 m) long, had a very shallow draft, and incorporated a single mast as well as positions for up to four rowers.[69] Twelve different types of wood were used to construct or repair it.

The site of Et-Tell, just east of the Jordan River, inland of where it enters the Sea of Galilee today, has been identified as the probable site of the town of Bethsaida, which is mentioned in the gospel of John as the home town of three apostles: Andrew, Peter and Philip. Subsequent landscape changes from silting have blocked the site from direct access to the lake. This location places it just outside of Galilee proper, in the territory controlled by Philip, the son of Herod the Great. There were modest domestic dwellings before and after the Herodian period, over which time the population of Bethsaida changed in number.[70] The archaeological finds suggested an influx of migrants from Judaea moving north into the area in the early to middle 1st century BCE. Although it developed with some Hellenistic-Roman influences, evidence of Jewish religious and cultural practices show its fundamentally Jewish character and there were no archaeological signs of gentile cults.[71] Closer to the entry of the Jordan River into the Sea of Galilee, El-Araj (Beit Habeck) is an alternative site for biblical Bethsaida. There was a Roman-period settlement here, and the discovery of a church at the site supports the view that this was considered by Byzantine Christians to be the location of the home of the three apostles.

The gospels place Yeshua firmly in the society and culture of the rural and fishing communities of Galilee. Archaeology emphasises the cultural difference between the Jewish rural communities and the towns in the period of Yeshua's life, with their Hellenic-Roman pattern. Conservative and overwhelmingly Jewish rural Galilee appears to have held the culture of outsiders at arm's length.[72] The Herodian towns and their lean to the culture of the Hellenistic-Roman world are omitted from the gospels, despite their economic and political dominance. 'All groups, Jewish and non-Jewish, were agrarian communities dominated by Hellenistic development accelerated by Roman society.'[73]

When Yeshua moved his focus from smaller communities, he and his followers went not to the local towns of Sepphoris or Tiberias, but to Jerusalem. After his death, his Galilean followers and others seem to have thought and hoped Jerusalem should be the centre for their movement's long-term development, while in Christianity's place of origin, rural Galilee, a commitment to traditional Judaism seems to have remained dominant.[74]

Many locations in and around Jerusalem were linked in Byzantine Christian and later Crusader pilgrimages to places named in the gospel accounts of Yeshua's final days on Earth. The Roman destruction in Jerusalem and expulsions of its residents in 70 CE during the Jewish Revolt had undermined the direct the direct link of familiar places to the early Christian oral tradition. The 4th-century church leaders Eusebius and Epiphanius recorded a story that the leaders of the Christian community in Jerusalem had moved across the Jordan by the time of the destruction of Jerusalem, relocating to Pella in Peraea.[75] Although Pella has been subject to 40 years of intensive excavation and study without locating support for this tradition, a small Christian community at Pella may have linked their origins to the events of the Roman destruction of Jerusalem.

The central place of Byzantine pilgrimage was to Jerusalem's Church of the Holy Sepulchre. This location had been a quarry into the 1st century CE, though containing much earlier material. Debris filled in the quarry before a Roman building (possibly a temple) was constructed on a raised platform covering earlier deposits during the reign of Emperor Hadrian in the 2nd century CE.[76] A drawing of a Roman ship found below the level of the church is considered by many to date from the 2nd century.

The gospel of John (19:41) makes reference to 'a garden in the place where he was crucified, and in the garden there was a new tomb'. This tradition of the location as the site of both Yeshua's crucifixion and his burial was established (or reinforced) when the Empress Helena, visiting from Constantinople about 325, was shown a place with fragments suggested to be from the 'True Cross' of the crucifixion. Emperor Constantine authorised excavations at this location, which were undertaken by Macarius, Bishop of Jerusalem. These removed the Roman constructions and beneath the Roman rubble fill they uncovered rock-cut tombs, one of which was then interpreted as the rock-cut tomb in which Yeshua had been placed at the behest of its prosperous owner, Joseph of Arimathea. The Church of the Holy Sepulchre, including the 'Tomb Chamber', was built at the site on Emperor Constantine's instruction to mark both death and burial of Yeshua; it was completed in 335. Construction of a Christian church on the site of a pagan temple reflects the widespread tradition of reassignment of religious sites. After centuries of damage, construction and repairs, its 11th-century destruction was followed by a major reconstruction in 1042–1048, with further additions during the Crusader era, and modern restoration work since a damaging fire of 1808.[77] Archaeological study, which has been permitted at the site for over a century, has included finds from the 4th-century church, and has then focussed on the sequence of subsequent religious buildings and the stages of construction at the site of the Tomb Chamber.[78]

Jewish burial practices would require a tomb to be outside the walls of the city (most commonly to the east or south, occasionally north), making this location within the Old City, and just a quarter of a mile (400 m) west of the Temple Mount, initially puzzling, but archaeology has suggested the city wall was extended west of this site around 41–44 CE.[79] So the tomb uncovered in the 320s would have pre-dated that time and become incorporated within the city by the latter's expansion. Evidence of tombs has been found less than

300 yards (250 m) west of the Church of the Holy Sepulchre, and it is logical to think of tombs in the area as flattened and emptied to make the surface for the Roman temple.[80]

The majority of Jewish people of the period were buried in simple graves excavated in the ground. Rock-cut tombs were the privilege of the wealthy, and just 900–1,000 rock-cut tombs (for multiple family burials) have been identified in and near Jerusalem from the Herodian period, for a population whose size is estimated at 20,000–30,000 upwards.[81] Bones would eventually be gathered and placed in an ossuary (typically of stone, many with external decoration and some inscribed with people's names, but sometimes of wood or clay).[82] While criminals executed under Roman law would elsewhere have their bodies discarded without ceremony, Jewish law was strict about the disposal of the dead and there is some evidence to suggest this extended to executed criminals.[83] The body of a crucified man might therefore have found deposition in line with normal Jewish burial practice.

The Romans used crucifixion as a warning to others and so these executions were sited in a highly visible place; the execution of Yeshua beyond the city gate, on the road westwards, would appear more realistic than the site of the Church of the Holy Sepulchre.[84] But the idea of a single location for both the crucifixion of criminals and an elite tomb, near to the core of the old city of Jerusalem, served theological purpose rather than being practical and realistic. Furthermore, it fitted the religious and practical needs of the period well to have the Constantinian church built inside the city and to mark both the death and the burial of Yeshua.

For pilgrims – and those to whom the flow of pilgrims provided economic benefits since the 4th century – its importance has remained, irrespective of historical authenticity. Visitors today queue to see the location of a rock-cut bench from the tomb uncovered in the 4th century, a stone from the tomb entrance, a second tomb associated by later tradition with Joseph of Arimathea, and other sites linked to the death and resurrection narrative. They visit a rock on which the cross of Yeshua's crucifixion was said to have stood, although this low area lacks the topography to support the hill with three crosses of biblical tradition. This is the archaeological study of places of traditions as they had developed in the 4th century rather than the archaeological study of Christian origins.

Both the Catholic and the Orthodox Churches accept Constantine's church as the location of Yeshua's tomb, but Protestant Christians from the 19th century described this as a 'pious fraud' and proposed, often with passion, an alternative site, some 200 yards (200 m) north of the city wall, which provided for modern pilgrims a quiet location for prayer and reflection.[85] They also accepted the concept that the tomb where Yeshua was laid stood close to the place of his execution. The shape of a rock face at this location was compared by German scholar Otto Thenius in 1842 to the biblical reference of the execution at a 'place of a skull'. A two-chambered burial place found here in 1867 was suggested to be that of Yeshua's burial and resurrection, and became known as 'the Garden Tomb'. It attracted detailed debate combining emerging, if still amateur, biblical archaeology with confidence in the literalism of the biblical descriptions.

Other claims for Yeshua's tomb have emerged from time to time. A tomb in the East Talpiot area of south Jerusalem excavated in 1980, containing ossuaries typical of the 1st century CE, became the subject of later popular claims to be the burial of Yeshua and members of his family, despite the observation that the names associated with this multiple burial were common in the period.[86]

Differing routes have developed over many centuries to mark a *Via Dolorosa*, a path linking 'Stations of the Cross', the events leading to Yeshua's crucifixion. The present route, as followed by tour parties through the narrow streets of the Old City, had been fixed by the 16th century. It begins near the location of the Antonia Fortress, the military barracks built by Herod the Great but destroyed by the Roman army in 70 CE after it had become a stronghold of the Jewish Revolt and leads to the Church of the Holy Sepulchre, from the Lions' Gate below the Mount of Olives. Near the start of the route are two rival subterranean sites and associated religious buildings (dedicated to St Anne) at a location which became identified by tradition as the site of the birth of Mary, mother of Yeshua. Close by are remains of the Herodian and Roman water reservoirs named Bethesda, where the gospel of John located a miracle of healing.

More informative than the archaeology of sites important to later tradition, the scientific archaeology of Jerusalem itself in the later 1st century BCE and the 1st century CE (before its sacking in 70) gives a useful framework for Yeshua's time in the city and the important period in which his followers sought to develop a movement there in his name. This era of Jerusalem, commonly referred to as the Herodian period, is also described as the late Second Temple period or the early part of the Roman period.

Jerusalem had grown significantly in size and population under Hasmonean rule. On the eve of its destruction in the later 1st century CE, a cautious estimate calculates that it may have reached 20,000 residents, but other estimates have put its population as far more.[87] In the last decades BCE

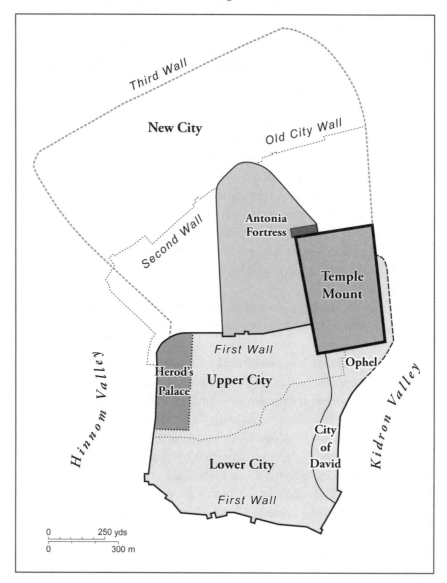

9. Jerusalem in the early 1st century CE

Herod the Great constructed a palace at the western edge of the ancient city, with fortifications incorporating Hasmonean towers and walls (the Citadel, which today, following a Crusader tradition, is called 'the Tower of David'). Ramparts (now excavated) associated with the palace served to strengthen the city walls; further excavations have uncovered a sewage tunnel near the

Citadel and have exposed some of the Herodian walls in the interior of the Citadel itself.[88]

Herod's main construction was the substantial rebuilding at the Temple site.[89] With the Temple Mount (al-Haram al-Sharif) today dominated by the Islamic Dome of the Rock and the al-Aqsa mosque, systematic modern archaeological excavation has not been permitted. Controversial construction work in 1999 led to the uncovering of some early material which has been subject to continuing examination. A small works project in 2007 allowed more careful monitoring, and some architectural elements of the Herodian Temple have been identified.[90] Salvage excavations in 1997–1999 to the south of the Temple Mount confirmed how the Herodian works had been extended in that direction.[91] A site adjacent to the western wall of the Temple Mount, which revealed a paved road from the mid-1st century CE, gave a marked image of dietary practices, with pig bones almost absent from the Jewish era, then with pigs accounting for almost 11% of the animals from the later Roman and Byzantine periods, and back to a nominal presence in the Islamic era.[92]

The ancient city dump excavated to the south-east provides an image of material culture, including pottery, stone-vessel pieces, glass, animal bones, seeds and coins. The coins provide specific dating.[93] The size and content of the dump imply an organised civic pattern of rubbish removal from the densely packed population of Jerusalem. The deposit here is up to 33 feet (10 m) in depth and estimated as 260,000 cubic yards (200,000 m³) in volume. Attempts had been made to shore up the dump with stone walls in antiquity. Most of the deposit is thought to come from the mid-1st century BCE to the beginning of the Jewish Revolt that led to the destruction of the Temple in 70 CE. The city dump included plaster from houses, mostly white with occasional fragments from painted walls, and tesserae from the floors of elite homes were also found.[94]

Animal bones from the city dump show a diet that was definitively Jewish, not Roman. Pigs were absent and the fish remains matched Jewish dietary practice (pigs were found in the Roman military settlement of Binyanei Ha'umah on the outskirts of Jerusalem).[95] Sheep or goat dominated the meat in the diet but cattle provided a significant contribution, and all suggested an age of killing soon after they had reached full growth. There were also numerous chicken bones, but plant foods probably formed a major part of the daily diet.[96] The presence of deer showed that hunted fauna augmented the diet in a small way. The pattern and frequency of pilgrims coming to Jerusalem for religious celebrations is indicated by the numerous cooking pots. The goat and sheep bones demonstrate widespread origins, which suggests that trade in livestock for religious sacrifice was a major part of the Jerusalem economy in the period. Stone-vessel manufacture was also an active industry in Jerusalem in the late 1st century BCE and especially in the 1st century CE.[97]

Archaeological work has shown how the elite in the late 1st century BCE and first part of the 1st century CE lived in fine housing in the Upper City – in marked contrast to the lives of rural Judaean communities. This area on the western hill of Jerusalem became identified in the Ottoman city as the Jewish Quarter and the Armenian Quarter. The painted frescoes on the walls and the mosaics on the floors of these elite houses, cisterns, steam rooms and rich material items reflect strong Hellenistic-Roman style, even though their inhabitants included Judaism's religious leadership, whose houses looked down towards the Temple.[98] Formal dining rooms containing luxury vessels show the influence of Hellenistic-Roman lifestyles but Jewish dietary laws were respected, and homes included Jewish ritual baths. Domestic dwellings of richer Jewish homes were largely in terraces of two-level houses: a functional basement and a ground living area, with a possible second storey for some houses.[99] One two-storey house covered an area of around 6,500 square feet (600 m²).

Such studies in Jerusalem continue to show the dynamism and relative prosperity of the largest city of Judaea: the religious centre where Yeshua spent his final days and where his immediate followers decided to extend his teaching and their developing beliefs. Scientific archaeology can illuminate the context; and can be pursued despite the sensationalism and claims that sometimes accompany a discovery from New Testament times.[100]

Paulos and the spread of the new religion

After the execution of their leader, Yeshua's followers sought to develop their movement from a base in Jerusalem in Judaea rather than back in Galilee. They were influenced by the belief that the 'second coming' of Christ and the judgement that would mark the end of the world was imminent, in which case Jerusalem would be its expected locus. Their influence on the local Jewish community was relatively modest. The Jewish Revolt of 66–73 and the sacking of Jerusalem 40 years later would impact the small Christian community that had developed in Judaea.[101]

They also assumed that theirs was a reform movement for Jews only, not gentiles, a perception which changed with experience to a willingness to convert non-Jews. The apostles' initial focus lay on preaching to the Jewish community within Palestine, then, according to Acts, further afield, in Roman

Syria and Cyprus. Over many centuries, numerous myths and legends would develop to suggest a deep history for local Christian communities – creating stories of travels by Yeshua's immediate family, his apostles and leading disciples from his time to engage in active preaching across the world, from India to Spain, from Egypt to England, or even further.[102]

There are indications in the letters of Paulos that his influential journeys were not the only means by which the new message of the Yeshua movement spread beyond the Levant. But the impact of the outreach by him and his associates, both to members of the diaspora Jewish communities and to gentiles who might be attracted to the appeal of a Christian message, does seem substantial, if not dominant. Other preachers would move or emerge through parts of the Roman Empire to spread an understanding of the new religion, even if, as Paulos wrote, 'there are some who are confusing you and want to pervert the gospel of Christ'.[103] By the time he reached Rome it seems others had made converts there first.

By his own admission, Paulos never met Yeshua or heard him preach and his letters rarely quote from Yeshua's sayings or his life. But neither was Paulos converted to the new faith by the apostles of the Yeshua movement. He developed away from them in his new religious beliefs and in his confidence that it was his mission to preach them to a wide audience. At what is traditionally dated as just a couple of years after Yeshua's death, Paulos, an educated devout Jew and active opponent of Christians, perceived that he had received a revelation of Yeshua, and this led him to preach and develop Christianity, indeed, to take a lead in extending its reach to the gentiles as well as Jews. His theology is reflected in his letters included in the New Testament.

Many future saints would experience visions of the Virgin Mary; Muhammad ibn 'Abdullah would receive dictation from the angel Gabriel; Joseph Smith, Jun. would be guided by the angel Moroni, and Paulos perceived that his vision was direct from the risen Christ, Yeshua.[104] Paulos therefore acquired his commitment to religious teaching in a manner comparable to Muhammad and Joseph Smith, Jun., rather than that of Brigham Young or the Companions of the Prophet, who all had personal acquaintance with the founder of their religious faith.

In the letters attributed to Paulos, he claimed that following his vision he began preaching immediately and did not make contact with the apostles in Jerusalem for another three years, when he saw only Simon Peter (Cephas) and James the brother of Yeshua. He travelled to Jerusalem with Barnabas and Titus after 14 years, where he met with Peter, James and John to reach agreement on territorial responsibility: he would preach to the gentiles, they to the Jews. The tradition reported in Acts, composed some 50 years after the relevant events, brought Paulos to meet the apostles earlier, and reported the later meeting when they discussed the question of preaching to both gentiles and Jews. Paulos's proselytising work kept him away from Judaea and the main area of the apostles' activities.[105] In practice, though, the work of Paulos, his associates and their successors led them to the Jewish diaspora and gentiles alike.

We see the nature of Paulos's theology and the focus of his proselytising activity in those letters in his name which scholars consider authentic copies of his writing, dated to the decade of the 50s. That period is still 20 and more years after Yeshua's death and Paulos's vision of Yeshua, a period in which both the theologies and organisations of the early Christian movement had developed. It would be a further one to two generations before the traditions associated with Yeshua would be recorded in the four canonical gospels, written in Greek for an audience who understood that language. As early Christianity developed, the documents we hold are mainly from gentile Christian rather than Jewish Christian sources: the views of the gentiles had come to dominate by the late 1st and 2nd centuries.[106]

Paulos, a man of urban origins and urban life, made cities his focus. While Yeshua's preaching as recorded in the gospels is full of references to farming and rural life and the poor, Paulos's frame of reference in his letters is largely urban.[107] Paulos was cited as 'from Tarsus', in southern Anatolia, but this may have been only his birthplace or family's origin and he had spent time living in Jerusalem.[108] He recognised and affirmed the symbolic importance of Jerusalem to the followers of Yeshua but seems to have made Antioch, capital of Roman Syria, the base for his early mission, and then spent time working in Ephesus, on the western coast of Anatolian Turkey, with his final preaching in Rome while under limited house arrest. Antioch, Ephesus and Rome were three of the largest cities of the 1st-century Mediterranean and Middle Eastern world, although there is no consensus on their actual sizes in the 1st century. The Book of Acts mentions no mission of Paul or others to Alexandria, despite its relative proximity to Palestine, its large Jewish community and its population of perhaps 250,000–400,000, making it the second largest city of the Roman Empire; Christian origins there are still not well understood.[109]

Since the letters attributed to Paulos give differing accounts of his visits to Jerusalem from those in Acts, there may also be inaccuracies in the geography and chronology of Paulos's journeys detailed in Acts.[110] However, contemporary scholarship still generally accepts the spread of Paulos's journeys outlined there. What seems clear from both sources is that in his travels to proclaim his faith, he focussed, unsurprisingly, on the urban concentrations: towns which lie today in the Levant, Turkey, Cyprus and Greece.

Although Paulos is thought to have pursued studies of Judaism while in Jerusalem, his home might then have become Damascus. His revelation came near Damascus and he returned there after an initial visit to 'Arabia' – arguably to the Nabataean capital, Petra. The Nabataeans had ruled Damascus before it fell within the Roman Empire, when the Nabataean ruler was a Roman client, and the links between the Nabataeans and Damascus remained strong in Paulos's time. He then went to preach in the regions of Syria (the Roman province with its administrative centre in Antioch) and in Cilicia beyond, the region of southern Anatolia (Asia Minor), which included Tarsus. Apostle Simon Peter would later visit Paulos in Antioch, where Acts suggests others, beyond Paulos and his associates, had preached, and where the followers of the new religion were first called Christians.[111]

Antioch appears to have become the primary operating base from which Paulos and his associates undertook missionary work. The narrative in Acts details four journeys.[112] One took him from Antioch to Cyprus (Salamis and Paphos), on to the region of Pisidia in southern Anatolia (Perga, a different Antioch, Iconium, Lystra and Derbe) and via Attalia back to Antioch. Another journey took Paulos from Antioch to Tarsus and back by land to Derbe and Lystra again, then westward through Anatolia without preaching until he reached Troas and crossed by sea to resume his activities in Philippi in Macedonia. He preached further in Thessalonica, then a little further south in Beroea, before travelling on to Athens, followed by Corinth in the Greek Peloponnese. Sailing across the Aegean he spent time in Ephesus before sailing on, returning to Antioch via Caesarea Maritima and Jerusalem. After that he spent time active in the areas of Galatia (central Anatolia) and Phrygia (west-central Anatolia).

In another journey reported in Acts Paulos left Antioch and crossed Anatolia to Ephesus before spending time in Macedonia and Greece, returning across the Aegean to Troas. Then Paulos travelled home via Miletus on the coast, Cos, the island of Rhodes, Patara to Tyre, meeting Christians in Ptolemais, south of Tyre, and proceeding via Caesarea Maritima to Jerusalem. Arrested in Jerusalem, he was transported to Rome (possibly around 60 CE) but on the way preached in Caesarea Maritima and in Rome itself for two years after his arrival. The Acts narrative ends here but later Christian tradition recorded by Clement in the mid-90s and Ignatius in 110 held that he was executed in Rome.

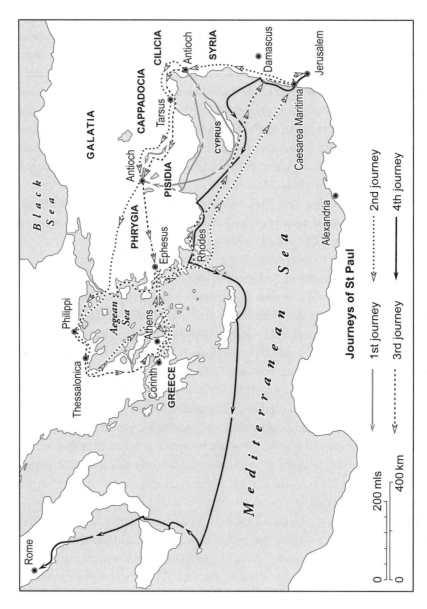

Journeys of St Paul

— 1st journey
······· 2nd journey
- - - - 3rd journey
—— 4th journey

10. Journeys of Paulos according to the Book of Acts

Jewish Christians outside of Palestine – those who followed Jewish precepts and practices while seeing themselves as followers of Yeshua – would be a significant part of early Christianity. Their distance from Judaea made them less susceptible to the pressures of the Jerusalem hierarchy, or the impact of the Jewish Revolt against the Romans. Jews were spread through the eastern part of the Roman Empire as well as Rome, where they had been able to maintain identity and religious affiliation from the late Republic into the early imperial era.[113]

A sociological discussion of early Christianity suggested that it would be more likely to have succeeded among the Jewish minority than a pagan majority; and be more successful among the more skilled and educated classes than among the poor and dispossessed.[114] The Jewish population of the Roman Empire has been estimated by some as reaching 10% or even 15% of the total (with only a small minority of these resident in Palestine) but these claims are hard to test. With a feasible figure of 50–60 million people as the total population of the Roman Empire of the 1st century CE, and an urbanised population of 11–12 million, including Rome, with population estimates from 650,000 to 900,000, such arguments have led to suggestions ranging from 3 to 7 million Jews across the empire.[115] The probable size of Jewish communities in the towns of Syria, Anatolia, Greece, Cyprus and Rome gives a dramatic impression of the context of Paulos's mission. Gentiles too attached themselves to these Jewish communities, attracted by their religious values.

Our image of the Jewish population of the Roman Empire is made more complex by genetic studies of the mitochondrial DNA of Ashkenazi Jews that suggest their ancestry included many European females at around 2,000 years ago, implying a movement of Middle Eastern males migrating and marrying non-Jewish women.[116] After the Persian (Median) Empire conquered Babylon and the Neo-Babylonian Empire, Jewish communities were spread widely across the region. Their religious focus was towards Jerusalem, to which they might make a pilgrimage, just as Catholics would focus on Rome and Muslims on Mecca and Medina. But their residence was spread through the Persian Empire and its successors; by the 1st century BCE, the Jewish communities represented huge numbers in the countries that bordered the Mediterranean, while the population of Judaea represented a minority of ethnic and religious Jews.[117]

Our historical sources on the expansion of the 'Jesus movement' and the development of Christian communities are limited. The mid-1st-century letters of Paul, and the later 1st-century gospels, are complemented by the mention by Josephus in the 90s that Yeshua's brother James was executed (around 62 CE) and by Tacitus's statement from around 116 that Emperor Nero had executed Christians after the great fire in Rome of 64. Suetonius's reference to earlier disturbances caused by a 'Chrestus' in Rome is ambiguous. By the text of a letter of Pliny from 112 we see Christians established on the Black Sea coast of Anatolia. Two centuries later, Christianity would acquire its leading position in the empire, now ruled from Byzantium (Constantinople). The lack of independent sources suggests the growth of Christian groups was neither dramatic nor generally, in political terms, highly subversive. We can therefore ask if archaeology provides more direct evidence of early Christianity.

Early Christianity and archaeology

Archaeology reveals the presence of material culture and a picture of economy and society. Importantly, intensive survey can also reveal absences: as described in Chapter 3, the archaeology of the Levant and beyond suggests that Islamic conquests did not alter the fundamentals of communities there for many decades.

Archaeological studies in the areas of the first Christian communities have been substantial, yet, perhaps surprisingly, they have revealed no identifying signals of the Christians of the 1st and 2nd centuries CE. Until the end of the 2nd century, Christianity is invisible in the archaeological record – what Christian families, communities and congregations existed left no visible signs of their beliefs in domestic buildings, symbols of their faith or even in burials.[118]

There has been a long and vigorous programme of what was called 'Christian archaeology'.[119] Since the 19th century, scholars have searched the Middle East and the Mediterranean for evidence of Christianity in its first centuries. Amateur approaches inspired by religious fervour were followed by professional studies: an International Congress of Christian Archaeology met regularly from 1894. Contemporary work has expanded this research, even if less commonly now driven specifically by religious motivations. There can, nevertheless, remain tensions between those prioritising scientific and scholarly research and those writers whose interests have been primarily to provide a background to faith.[120] 'Christian archaeology' and 'classical archaeology' are closely overlapping fields.

Yet despite all this research, a visible archaeology of Christianity and a Christian community has not been uncovered before the early 3rd century, suggesting that the numbers of active committed Christians may have remained modest.[121] Numerous details are now seen of the expansion of Christianity that immediately preceded, accompanied and followed Constantine's repositioning of Christianity in the centre of the Roman Empire in the early 4th century, and from the 4th century onwards the archaeology of Christianity is rich in detail.[122] So although Christian archaeology has become a well established field, in practice most of its attention is on the visible remains of established communities in centuries later than the religion's origins.

As with the remains in Palestine from Byzantine and Crusader times, some of the archaeology is archaeology of Christian *traditions*. It studies sites marking a tradition of the life or work of a proselytising apostle or early disciple or sanctuary around their bones; an example is the supposed burial place of New Testament apostle John in Selçuk, in western Anatolia. In the 19th century, a house in the same area was claimed as the home that Mary, mother of Yeshua, occupied in her old age.

Since we have no manuscripts from the first two centuries of Christianity, history relies on later copies of texts originating in that period. Papyri from Oxyrhynchus in Egypt dating from the 3rd to 6th centuries include texts from early church theologians, the New Testament and apocryphal works. Also from Egypt are Coptic documents from Nag Hammadi mainly from the 3rd and 4th centuries, many of which reflect a Gnostic tradition. The Dead Sea Scrolls of the Essenes found at Qumran in the West Bank have contributed to today's reinterpretations of the religious life of the 1st century CE. In 2019 the University of Basel announced the publication of a private letter from a Christian author in central Egypt on a papyrus dated about 230.[123]

There may be several explanations for the absence of early Christianity in the archaeological record, but lack of searching is not one. In some times and places Christians may have needed to hide their faith, but this does not seem an adequate explanation for the widespread absence of Christian symbols in private houses or burials in the eastern Roman Empire. There were local administrative acts against Christian groups at times and a major persecution under Emperor Diocletian in 303, by when Christian numbers had swelled.

Over the first two centuries of their religion, Christians may have remained in fairly small groups, growing their numbers slowly, and following their faith within the context of the larger community in which they lived, worked and were buried. Christian material culture started to be visible almost two centuries after the beginning of the missions of Paulos and his associates.[124] Given the image of Christianity as an all-encompassing outlook on God, humanity, ethics, salvation and the coming kingdom of heaven, it is hard to think of the religious movement as just another set of personal beliefs that did not affect the way its adherents planned their lives and deaths. Yet it appears indistinguishable in the archaeological record from the wider society, whether deliberately or through an absence of distinct self-identity, until the late 2nd and especially the 3rd centuries.

The slow growth of the Christian community suggested by archaeology correlates with population studies, one by a sociologist and one by an historian of the ancient world, extrapolating an annual growth rate from the religion's origins to its flowering in the 4th century.[125] A constant rate of increase arising from proselytising and family growth would suggest a Christian population of under 10,000 at 100 CE and 210,000 at 200 CE; an alternative estimate gives 7,500 Christians at 100 CE. If there were 7,000 Christians in Rome by the year 200, that could be approaching 1% of the city's population. The actual number of Christian communities cannot be stated: estimates of as few as 50 in 100 CE and 100 in 180 CE, based on recorded references, are subject to doubt. One suggestion is that by about the year 300 some 10% of the population of the Roman Empire was Christian (perhaps 6 million individuals).

We cannot use archaeology to show where early Christianity had greater or lesser success and impact. It is noted that there are no signs of Christianity in Galilee, even in the 3rd century, until the period of Constantine.[126]

The initial successful spread of Christianity seems from historical sources to have been largely an urban phenomenon.[127] We can see through the lens of archaeology aspects of the cities and towns in the period when they first saw Christianity preached. Finding direct evidence of early Christianity in these settings, like burial and mortuary inscriptions or Christian symbols on walls, has proved more difficult.

One challenge to finding early Christianity in the archaeology of the region is that our historic sources imply Christian meetings were taking place in private houses, and this seems confirmed by archaeology. Churches and chapels were not a feature of earlier Christianity. The growth of constructed churches follows Constantine. We can therefore think of a home regularly used by the early Christians as a 'house church' (*domus ecclesiae*).[128]

This is comparable to the position of Judaism, where scholars consider that buildings constructed to be dedicated synagogues were not a core and essential feature of Judaism until after the destruction of the Temple in Jerusalem of 70 CE. Communities could follow Jewish practices with meetings in domestic settings. Only a limited number of buildings found by archaeology have been identified as community meeting halls suitable for religious use as synagogues from before the 3rd century, although those discovered are important finds.[129]

In the Roman-era settlement at Dura Europos on the Euphrates, archaeology has recorded from the 3rd century CE both a Jewish synagogue and a 'house church' used by the Christian community for religious gatherings, and other religious communities in the town also used domestic buildings for their meetings. The house church was constructed around 232, and renovated for religious purposes from about 241 to 256, decorated with frescoes of biblical scenes.[130]

At the Legio site near Megiddo, in Israel, excavations in 2005 uncovered a building dated to about 230 which was described as a Christian prayer hall (effectively a church). An inscription on a mosaic, with abbreviated words, has been interpreted as stating 'The God-loving Akeptous has offered the table to God Jesus Christ as a memorial'.[131]

With the growth of Christian numbers by the 3rd century, house churches must have been many and congregations within a large city numerous and separate.[132] It would have been impossible to bring all the Christian community of such a town together for services and meetings. Given the crowded conditions revealed in many Roman cities, only the wealthy would have been in a position to host such gatherings in their homes. Tradespeople with industrial premises might have been able to provide equivalent space for Sunday gatherings. One alternative is that those living together in crowded tenements would have met in shared common areas – but this implies all these residents shared a religious affiliation, something that would develop only over time. Given this demographic reality, it is perhaps not surprising that a variety of religious viewpoints coexisted in early Christianity.

The religiously symbolic term *ichthus* (fish) is first found about 180 to honour Aberkios (Avirkios), Bishop of Hierapolis, in Phrygia (Anatolia). A Phrygian find from west central Anatolia dated about 200 may be the earliest Christian representation: the tomb of a man called Eutyches, it is thought to represent the bread (marked with a cross) and wine of a communion service.[133]

What of the large cities of the eastern Roman Empire that seem to have served as a base for Paulos and others in the earliest spread of the Christian message?[134] Antioch, as a prosperous Hellenistic city, became a centre of Roman administration, with a population of perhaps as many as 250,000–300,000 (including a significant Jewish community) in an urban area of 1,500 acres (600 hectares).[135] The region around Antioch became especially densely populated in the 1st century CE.[136] Modern archaeological work on the details of Roman-period Antioch has been limited, while work from the 1930s concentrated on some major monuments. So we know relatively little from archaeology of the community of early Roman Antioch – 'pagan', Jewish or Christian – though important Christian finds from the late 4th and early 5th centuries have been recorded from the city.

By contrast, Ephesus has been subject to a vast amount of archaeological survey excavation and recording for over a century, although, given the size of the city, still only a part has been uncovered. In the 1st century CE it became Rome's administrative capital for western Anatolia (Asia Minor). There is plenty of material from the era when Paulos was present and the earliest Christian community developed, yet there are no archaeological signs of this group of perhaps 92,000 people, although smaller and much larger estimates have been made.[137] While many of the famous buildings associated with Ephesus date after the period of Paulos, in his time the State Agora and Square Agora would have dominated city life, with housing spread widely in terraces, giving a dense urban environment.[138]

In a large cosmopolitan city of the eastern Roman Empire, numerous religious cults and civic associations could coexist, continue and develop, without making an impact on the city life as reflected in its archaeological profile. Antioch and Ephesus were of great importance to early Christianity, but Christianity was not of great importance to those cities until much later. The 5th-century construction of the Church of Mary in Ephesus and the 6th-century Basilica of Saint John nearby are reminders of the significance of the Christian tradition that developed in Ephesus.

Rome housed a sizeable Jewish community at the time of Yeshua and Paulos and the early presence of Christianity is indicated by Paulos's Letter to the Romans (dated about 57). Locating early Christians in the archaeology of Rome is a challenge. Scholars have accumulated a corpus of inscriptions reflecting early Christianity but dating only from the beginning of the 3rd century.[139] A sarcophagus of Marcus Aurelius Prosenes, dated 217, with the text 'led back to God' may imply he was a Christian. Christian symbols have been identified on tombs dating from the 3rd century, including a burial dating from 266; the *ichthus* (fish) symbol on some 3rd-century tombs is assumed to indicate a Christian individual.[140]

A large quantity of evidence of Roman imperial society comes from the burials in underground catacombs which began in the second half of the 2nd century CE. Christian burials seem to have been placed alongside others, a practice which continued into the 4th century (to which two-thirds of the catacombs belong).[141] Jewish or Christian symbols are not normally marked on these burials before the 3rd century, with many Christian images dating from the 4th century. In catacombs such as that of San Callisto in Rome,

Christian burials are marked with both Old Testament and New Testament themes.

Twentieth-century archaeological work at St Peter's Basilica in Rome, encouraged by the Vatican, searched for a possible tomb of the apostle Peter, reflecting the tradition which developed that the apostle travelled to Rome, and was executed and buried at the site where Constantine would later build a church.[142] While non-Christian tombs from the 2nd to early 4th centuries CE were found in the area, a small building from around 160 has been claimed as a possible Christian marker of this tradition.[143] A mosaic showing Christ and pre-dating Constantine has been identified from Mausoleum H at the site of St Peter's.

Conclusions

This review of the history and archaeology of the period and context of Christianity's origins reminds us of how limited is our knowledge of Yeshua, his first followers and the initial impact (or lack of impact) of the Yeshua movement. With Mormonism we have contemporary historical accounts of the dramatic growth of the Latter-day Saints and their journeys: these enable us to critique the documents of the movement's founder. The spread and conquests of the Muslim Arabs are well documented, even if we need to interrogate and reinterpret the substantial number of documents that developed in the century and a half after Muhammad's death. But Christianity developed slowly, without establishing an early mass movement of followers, and did not make enough impact to generate a range of independent contemporary historical sources. Christianity's own history of its origins has relied heavily on words and phrases in a few documents from two and three generations after the death of Yeshua. Thus, the birth narrative, bypassed in two of the four canonical gospels, is represented in 900 words of one gospel and 2,000 words of a second, which, despite some internal contradictions, have together created a major tradition.

To seek a reliable sense of events and processes we need to strip away overlays from the two millennia of development of the Christian religion. Medieval Crusaders identified places in Palestine with those in biblical tradition. Byzantine Christians, beginning with the travels of Helena, the mother of Emperor Constantine, around 325, built churches and monasteries in locations which local people helpfully suggested were linked to places in the New Testament texts. A pattern of pilgrimage inevitably followed. The freeing of Christians to pursue their religion in 311–313, and its declaration as the official religion of the Empire in 380, succeeded the Diocletian persecution at the beginning of the century; this indicates how vigorous and significant the movement had then become. In the 4th century, church leaders wrote their accounts of the history of Christianity. The different widespread Christian communities would then or later (and sometimes much later) link their local origins to one or another of the companions of Yeshua mentioned in the biblical texts. Between the *Ecclesiastical History* of Eusebius in the 4th century and *The Golden Book* of Jacobus de Voragine in the 13th century, traditions of apostolic voyages (and their distributed bones) would see spirited development.

Despite vigorous searches for archaeological evidence of early Christianity, symbols of the religion emerge only around the end of the 2nd century, when, as noted above, it is estimated that about 210,000 Christians were distributed across the Roman Empire. The success of the movement lay in effective and impassioned proselytising using the collection of books which represented not just accounts of the life and teaching of Yeshua and his disciples (the four gospels and Acts) but theology and guidance contained in letters dating from early Christianity, of which the larger number were (and are) considered those of Paul – Paulos.

The documents of the New Testament books but also writings of early Christian leaders imply that it emerged as a reform movement within Judaism, and one focussed on the Jewish communities in regions of Palestine, but that its success and development happened outside those regions, among both gentiles and Jews living elsewhere in the Roman Empire. And the source of that success leads us back especially to Paulos and those who followed on with his work and mission, from the mid-30s to the 60s CE.

Paulos, an Anatolian Jew who never met Yeshua and did not join the group of his followers after Yeshua's death (though he would meet with them later), preached in his own words, not those of Yeshua, and developed a complex theology. At the core of this theology, held in common with Yeshua's followers in Judaea, was salvation through the death and resurrection of Yeshua and acknowledgement of his divine nature.

The Jewish disciples of Yeshua back in Judaea and Galilee came to concede that becoming a follower of Yeshua and believing in his divine mission did not require adherence to Judaism or adoption of Jewish practices. Their initial commitment to develop an alternative movement within the Judaism of Judaea had only limited success.

What is remarkable, though, is that the preaching over a short period by one individual, Yeshua (for perhaps three years until his execution), had such a powerful and lasting impact. The power and message of the words and actions of Yeshua quoted in the New Testament outstripped those of other contemporary charismatic preachers and Jewish reformists, though his miracles and faith healing had parallels in the same area and period. But the account and belief in his resurrection and the theological perspective placed upon him as divine gave the Yeshua movement something unique, and something which those who accepted this new faith – and especially Paulos and those working with him – could use to develop a faith which would build its numbers steadily over the successive centuries.

Whereas Paulos's religious inspiration did not come from encounters with Yeshua, that of the Jewish reform movement based in Jerusalem did. And many, if not most, of these followers began their participation in the Yeshua movement in his native Galilee. The simplest and clearest history indicates a background as a rural villager from Nazareth, a traditional Jewish community but one physically and economically close to the Herodian town of Sepphoris. The Herodian capital of Galilee moved to Tiberias on the Sea of Galilee, and Yeshua also moved to the lakeside, where his preaching began and his following developed. His alternative approaches to Judaism (and, it appears, his forecast of an imminent end of days) attracted followers from outside of Galilee and therefore opposition from the religious establishment. When he came to the Jewish Temple city of Jerusalem, their opposition led them to secure his execution by the Roman authorities, but his followers, staying in Jerusalem, proclaimed he had risen from the dead. Such a message formed part of the developing beliefs of Christians as the movement slowly spread through the Roman Empire to build the Christian churches, until it became the official religion of the Empire in the 4th century.

Chapter 5

Scribes, priests and exiles under foreign rule: the emergence of monotheistic Judaism

Between the late 6th century and the 4th century BCE the religious practices and beliefs of Judaism developed under a group of religious leaders (without political power) based in the former capital of Judah, Jerusalem, at the time within the small and marginal province of Yehud in the Persian Empire. They developed a monotheism which identified Yahweh as the sole creator god, whereas earlier exclusive worship of Yahweh had perceived him as one deity existing among others. They assembled the canon of the Jewish religion, the Tanakh or Old Testament, with new books alongside edited and augmented versions of earlier texts and oral literatures. The new religious leadership focussed on the area of Judah and the Temple they built in Jerusalem as the centre of the religion, applying the name of the former northern kingdom, Israel, to the larger Yahwist community. As background they emphasised their families' exile when the Neo-Babylonian rulers had followed their conquests of Judah in 597 and 586 BCE by removing to Babylonia groups of the political, religious, mercantile and craft elites. The exile provided the context for a theological move to a strict monotheism. The conquerors had left behind the larger part of the Judaean community, and the archaeology of Judah indicates much cultural continuity but with a dramatic reduction in Jerusalem's position as a major urban centre. In 539 BCE Persian ruler Cyrus the Great conquered Babylonian territory and allowed his new subjects to resume the worship of their own religious cults and, it seems, to return to the lands from which their families had been removed. Some of the Judaean community took the opportunity to move back, and over time they were joined by additional returnees. Others who did not return to Yehud would nevertheless still recognise the Jerusalem Temple as the centre of their religion and the collection of biblical literature brought together by its priesthood as the basis of the Jewish faith.

The religions discussed in previous chapters – Mormonism, Islam and Christianity – are clearly inheritors of Jewish religious beliefs and marked by their monotheism (even though the Christian concept of the Trinity left its claim to monotheism challenged by others). Monotheism (belief in the existence of just one god) as distinct from monolatry (devotion to only one of multiple gods that exist) developed from the 6th century BCE onwards in the 'exilic' and 'post-exilic' periods of Jewish history, with the latter also referred to as the early Second Temple period.

A common assumption is that the people of Israel and Judah were much earlier believers in one sole and supreme deity. There have been scholars who asserted true monotheism can be traced many centuries earlier, even back to the biblical figure of Moses; another view is that the words of biblical prophets mark significant steps between monolatry and monotheism, while definitively monotheistic statements remain fewer and later. One assessment identified only 25 passages in the Tanakh (Old Testament) as explicitly monotheistic, and these all from the 6th century or later.[1]

Our term 'monotheism' emerged in the European Enlightenment, as part of a debate about natural religion, and 'monolatry' was probably used only from the 19th century. The sharp distinction might appear artificial when applied to ancient societies. It is more realistic to consider than, even as the new leaders of Judaism in Jerusalem emphasised a belief that its own deity, Yahweh, was the only deity, others in the same community made such a transition from the Yahwist cult more gradually.

A traditional but flawed image was that after the conquest of Judah by the Neo-Babylonians in 597 and 586 BCE, 'the Jews' were sent into exile in Babylon, from which they were freed by the Persian conquerors to return to Judah, restoring the Judaic cult of Yahweh in a rebuilt Jerusalem with its Temple rebuilt on the site of a great predecessor, where they remained centred until a dispersal after the destruction of the Temple by the Romans in 70 CE. Such a model underestimates and misrepresents the theological developments and innovations of the 6th, 5th and 4th centuries BCE, when monotheistic Judaism was defined; and it downplays the continuity and widespread distribution of Jewish communities after the exile to Babylon. The picture established from scholarly history is much more complex, and archaeology has clarified the image of the world in which Judaism developed its monotheistic character and crafted the familiar version of its literature.

It is reasonable to describe as one of the most inspired periods in theological and literary history the two centuries when the Persian-ruled province of Yehud – the region around Jerusalem – saw Judaism developed and the canon of its literature defined. Yet many histories of the religion and of the Jewish people give relatively little attention to these two centuries, while emphasising the legends of previous eras and the religious developments of later times.

While the Old Testament accounts of the rule of David then Solomon, conventionally placed in the 10th century BCE, and the stories of an earlier 'Exodus' from Egypt have dominated narratives of Jewish ethnic identity, it is later centuries that are central to the development of Jewish religion. 'Scholars have emphasised that the time when Judah and the Judaeans were under Persian rule was the single most important period in the development of Jewish thought and practice.'[2] Combining critical historiography and archaeological studies can provide a nuanced (although still far from perfect) image of the period and the social and economic setting of the developments of Judaism, even though 'Religion is hard to define and harder to identify in material culture.'[3]

The Judaism that proclaims the existence of only one deity, with whom the Jewish people have a direct relationship, was defined in the Persian province of Yehud by a Jerusalem elite who emphasised their background of exile in Babylonia. The Jerusalem 'Second Temple' (that which was later substantially rebuilt and expanded by Herod), the priestly hierarchy, forms of religious worship and social practice, definitions of monotheistic belief, and notably the compilation of religious, historical and literary writing into the Tanakh (or Old Testament) can be dated largely to the two centuries of Persian rule of Yehud from 539 to 332 and the conquest of the area by Alexander the Great; nevertheless, under the period of Hellenistic rule further developments in Judaism and its literature did take place.

The Babylonian exile in the 6th century BCE played a major role in the ideology and literature of the Jewish elite of Yehud. For the first who returned to Yehud, this exile had lasted for two generations; other 'Judaeans' left for Yehud some generations later. Among the impacts of exile was the emergence of monotheism from a Jewish tradition in which Yahweh had been worshipped with greater or lesser loyalty as one of many deities. The figure referred to as Deutero-Isaiah ('Second Isaiah'), considered to be a religious prophet during the Babylonian exile, may have played a significant part in this transition, as illustrated by his definition of Yahweh as 'the creator of the ends of the earth' and the statement 'I am the first and I am the last; besides me there is no God.'[4] In historical as well as religious terms, therefore, it is useful to write of pre-exilic, exilic and post-exilic times, although recognising that for many inhabitants of rural, agricultural Judah and their neighbours, life continued much the same through these stages, whether ruled by Jerusalem monarchs under Assyrian control, by Babylonian kings or by Persian emperors.

While modern scholarship tends to locate the emergence of monotheism in the Babylonian exile, and in a post-exilic framework, there is continuing debate about the nature of pre-exilic beliefs. Did the post-exilic editing of biblical texts seek to imply that monotheistic beliefs were more commonly the norms in earlier Judaism, with departures from these readily condemned by the biblical prophets? Or did the edited texts acknowledge that Yahweh worship had been extensively held within a polytheistic framework, and now aim to move the Yahwist community to recognise a sole deity?[5]

Works presented in the Tanakh as those of pre-exilic prophets and writers contain ideas that intimate strict monotheism but we cannot be sure which parts of these texts were affected by the editing processes of post-exilic times.

Historical, literary and archaeological studies have coalesced to demonstrate the complexity of beliefs in the Yahwist communities of Palestine in the pre-exilic world. Communities acknowledged the existence of multiple deities, referred to their major deity as Elohim or El or Yahweh (though this one deity sometimes had a divine consort), but at times also paid homage to the other deities, as acknowledged (and condemned) in prophetic writings.[6] As discussed in the next section, the proportion and identity of pre-exilic texts included in the canonical Tanakh is debated. But whatever the proportion, the evidence of polytheism remains. Psalm 82 speaks of Yahweh's superior position: 'in the midst of the gods he holds judgment'. Psalm 89 records him 'feared in the council of the holy ones'. The origins of a deity named Yahweh are still debated: a source among semi-nomadic groups to the south or southeast of Palestine is a strong possibility.[7]

Displacement and exile in Babylonia forced a Judaean group to address the theological implications of their fate, and gave a framework for a transition of ideas towards a 'radical monotheism'. It has been observed that 'it takes the concentration of intelligentsia in an urban centre to generate, sustain and communicate the new ideas of a monotheistic faith'.[8] Persian rule of Yehud provided the opportunity for such an 'intelligentsia' to settle and act in Jerusalem in the region from which their families had been exiled.

Sources and source criticism

Discussions of the places, people and times in which Judaism developed its monotheistic theology are dominated by the written texts that were brought together as the Tanakh (the Jewish Bible, the Old Testament). Modern scholarship concedes that the versions we hold were edited, combined, revised and in some cases first written long after the events they purport to describe, reflecting the developing religious leadership of the Jewish community of the time. Despite this, even small details included in the texts are cited in historical discussions. Long and intensive critical study of the books that comprise the Tanakh have been used to interpret and debate the nature of Jewish beliefs in pre-exilic Israel and Judah, in exile and under Persian rule.

The broader historical context is documented in key written texts from the ruling civilisations of the Middle East. The Nabonidus Chronicle is a cuneiform tablet (now in the British Museum) narrating the annals both of the reign of the last Neo-Babylonian king, Nabonidus, and of his conqueror, Cyrus II ('Cyrus the Great'), detailing the transition of power in Babylon itself, and therefore setting the scene for the end of the Judaean exile. The Cyrus Cylinder, discovered at the site of Babylon in 1879 (and also now in the British Museum), is a document in cuneiform boasting of the role of Cyrus, describing him as a liberator and invoking the support of the Babylonian god Marduk.[9]

Our sources independent of the Tanakh have been supplemented in recent years by the discovery and publication of a valuable resource, the al-Yahudu tablets.[10] These clay tablets with cuneiform text are dated to about 572 to 477 BCE, thus extending from the period of deportation through to times when the Temple had been re-established in Jerusalem. The 103 tablets reflect three communities with populations of Jewish background in Mesopotamia (one named al-Yahudu or al-Yahudaia, 'town of the Judaeans', the others Alu-sa-Nasa and Bit-abi-Ramr), thought to be in the area of Nippur, about 50 miles (80 km) south-east of Babylon. The texts of the tablets focus on commercial activities, including house rental.

Another important collection, the Murašu archive, discovered in the late 19th century at the site of Nippur, is an assemblage of business documents from about 454 BCE. It includes personal names that incorporate the name of Yahweh, which is confirmation that the Jewish diaspora continued in the Persian period.

While complete manuscripts of the Tanakh in Hebrew are known only from the 10th century CE, the Dead Sea Scrolls, discovered in the 1940s near Qumran in the Judaean Desert of the West Bank, contain numerous texts from the 1st centuries BCE and CE with elements from the majority of books in the Tanakh. (Another fragment from Ein Gedi nearby is dated to the 3rd or 4th century CE.) The Greek translation from the Hebrew – the Septuagint – is known in full from the 4th century CE but parts have been recovered in manuscripts of the 2nd to 1st centuries BCE. The writings of the early 2nd-century BCE Jewish scholar Ben Sira (or Ben Sirach) refer to contents of the biblical text which correspond well enough to those of the Tanakh we know, so it can be assumed that the canon was well formulated by this point.[11]

There is a large and learned industry of scholarship seeking to identify and date the different elements that make up the texts of the books of the Tanakh. These discussions reflect changing contemporary perspectives on language and literary forms, but they also reflect assumptions about the nature and timing of historical narratives, mythological stories, legal precepts and creative writings. The Tanakh texts inform the understanding of religious history, but religious interpretation and assumptions can also influence historical construction.

A majority of scholars consider that most of the books in the Tanakh we have today had been redacted, edited and brought together by the end of the Persian period. For many individual sections of books in the Tanakh there is no consensus on their sources or on the degree of their later editing. Challenges, and continuing debates, have been over which texts have their origins in the period of Palestine before the Neo-Babylonian conquests and the deportation of the elites which followed; and how much such texts were edited and changed over time. To some scholars, a text may reflect a Yahwist monotheism dating from before the defeat of Israel by the Assyrians, while to others it was fundamentally a construction by the Jerusalem elite to consolidate their religious leadership late in the Persian or even in the subsequent Hellenistic period.

Understanding the nature and context of the texts in the Tanakh involves attempts to uncover the layers of its construction through time. A safe historical method is to consider the dating of historical documents as we do the dating of archaeological finds: moving from the latest to seek the earlier, making cautious judgements about time depth based on external and direct evidence and comparisons rather than unprovable assumptions. Describing these approaches as 'radical' or dismissing them as 'minimalist' when applied to books of the Tanakh can at times sound like special pleading, since historians recognise documents generated in other contexts as designed to achieve specific political and religious goals, and interpret them through that lens. Israeli scholar Israel Finkelstein expressed this critical approach when he wrote:

> I tend to give archaeology a central, independent role and treat the text as a stratified literary work whose layers are embedded with the ideological goals of their authors and the realities of their time.[12]

These debates may ultimately be unproductive. The editing, redaction, writing and compilation that took place in the Jerusalem of Persian Yehud necessarily reflected the agenda of the religious leaders of the time. Those who developed the Tanakh to form the Jewish canon were not undertaking an academic exercise in literary editing: they were creating a body of literature to consolidate the beliefs, traditions, power and authority of the Jewish religion and its religious leaders. But, equally, they were not attempting to forge a unified document: discrepancies, contradictions, omissions and differing narratives remain. The Tanakh was compiled from previous written and oral sources, edited, augmented, copied (inevitably with copyists' errors) and edited further, and it was presented as the cumulative literature of the Jewish people, an anthology of historical, prophetic and literary works, not as a single coherent narrative. References in the Tanakh to other writings demonstrate that there are some texts that have not survived, or that were not considered sufficiently in line with current religious orthodoxy to be included within the canon.[13]

The contents that appear to derive from earlier sources report the early Israelites acknowledging their deity (Yahweh and in some contexts Elohim) as one god among the many that existed. The transformation that took place during and after the Babylonian period moved this belief to a belief in one universal deity, and thus laid the basis for future monotheisms. A dominant narrative in the Tanakh is the covenant between the 'children of Israel' (defined by patriarchal ancestry) and Yahweh: they should worship only him and if they did their god would protect them. The defeat of the 10 tribes of the northern kingdom of Israel by Assyria in 722 BCE, then of the southern kingdom of Judah and Benjamin by the Babylonians over a century later, therefore required theological explanation: this was that dedication to Yahweh had been weak. Such a message is present in the historical books of the Tanakh and a major emphasis of the books of the prophets.

Therefore the dominant and unresolved debate is over what texts were composed in Persian Yehud by the Jerusalem religious elite leading and preaching a monotheistic religion, which earlier texts were heavily edited and changed in that era, and which texts are more closely related to pre-exilic sources (written or oral), even if they were later combined with other materials.[14] Since the 1870s, scholars have worked to disentangle the different sources incorporated and adapted in the Tanakh, distinguishing material that came from both northern and southern kingdoms of pre-exilic Palestine as well as the conscious additions of the post-exilic compilers.

In primarily non-literate societies, narrative oral traditions as well as memorised and repeated oral literatures (especially in poetic form) are all important. Such declamations can help maintain the content of a narrative over long periods, as seen in Zoroastrian traditions (discussed in Chapter 6) or indeed the Jewish traditions compiled in the Mishnah of the 3rd century CE. But oral narratives can develop and be changed over time more readily than a definitive written record. While the highly literate scholars of modern times have intensively analysed possible written sources and their integration into our versions of the Tanakh, the fluid oral tradition and oral literature have been given a lower priority. A challenge in understanding the development of the Tanakh is the issue of the combination of written sources with oral traditions and oral literature: the process by which oral literature from different sources became written literature, augmented with new written literature, before then being amended, edited and copied. Many sections of the Tanakh – the Psalms and the Book of Proverbs, obviously, but also many poetic sections of other books – have the feel and form of an oral literature passed from generation to generation, though not necessarily without change.

Like elsewhere in western Asia, early writing in Hebrew emerged to meet secular needs, commercial and administrative, rather than literary or religious roles. However, it is possible that by the mid-9th century and especially by the later 8th century BCE a cohort of scribes would have been able to record longer texts in Hebrew.[15] A limestone block from a Judaean burial cave dated to the first half of the 8th century BCE, and now in the Bible Lands Museum in Jerusalem, has an early Hebrew inscription translated as 'cursed be Hagaf son of Hagab by Yahweh Ṣebaot'.

The first written texts that in later edited form found their way into the Tanakh may date from the late 8th century BCE, and include records of the words of prophets. Elements of biblical texts have been compared to the style found on inscriptions from the late 8th to early 6th centuries, although the deliberate use of archaisms within the Tanakh cannot be excluded.[16] Ink inscriptions found at the desert site of Arad from about 600 BCE, shortly before the first Neo-Babylonian victory, show the activity of different scribes.[17] Perhaps puzzlingly, after that there is little direct evidence for much scribal activity until the end of the 3rd century BCE, leading some to consider whether the work of constructing the Tanakh in written form was later than most historians have believed likely.

Those removed into Babylonian exile would be the rich and powerful, the religious elite and some of the commercial, craft and military cohorts. As in the world of early Islam and early Christianity discussed in previous chapters, literacy would be limited to a minority in both pre-exilic Judah and post-exilic Yehud. The majority, including the urban poor and rural families, remained in Judah. This is significant because it is reasonable to suggest that the most literate were among those sent into exile, and the least literate stayed behind. The community left in Judah would have the strength of oral traditions (legends, myths), which, like all traditions, would develop and alter to fit the dramatically changing world.

The written texts of early 6th-century Judah would be retained in the possession of the exiles. With a new post-exilic priestly class in Jerusalem bringing together the written documents of the Jewish religion, their authenticity would be reinforced by making connections to existing beliefs and oral literatures of the non-literate majority, rather than by a scholarly comparison with the details of previous written texts. And because religious leadership lay with a Judaean elite in a Judaean town, Jerusalem, those leaders could emphasise a history in which Jerusalem played a central role, including a story of a united monarchy once ruling from there over both Israel and Judah, the lands of 12 tribes unified by ancestry and devotion to Yahweh.

It has long been thought that the books of Deuteronomy, Joshua, Judges, 1 Samuel, 2 Samuel, 1 Kings and 2 Kings, which are in historical sequence, were based on material from a single source (sometimes referred to as the Deuteronomist, even if from more than one author). This source is often attributed to the southern kingdom of Judah in the 7th century BCE, when the northern kingdom had been defeated by Assyria, and not long before the conflict with Babylon. How 'monotheistic' and how 'monolatrous' were the beliefs behind these original text cannot be ascertained. Other than three verses that may be late additions, the narrative in Deuteronomy would fit a society where Yahweh was one deity among others.[18]

The covenant between Yahweh and his people is central to the narrative. The histories in the Tanakh place religious reforms and the emergence of hostility to cults other than Yahweh in the reign of Josiah, king of Judah *ca.* 640 to 609, and many scholars have identified his reign as the time of writing of several of the texts later redacted into the Tanakh, and a period within which some consider monotheism began to emerge.

The first four books of the Torah (the Pentateuch) as we now have them – Genesis, Exodus, Numbers and Leviticus – are effectively an anthology within an anthology. The construction of this narrative in its present written form was undertaken within Persian Yehud, when different oral and possibly written sources were drawn together to forge a sequence of linked stories. Some, such as the flood story, have clear parallels in Babylonian mythology, and there are Mesopotamian counterparts to the story of the Tower of Babel, as well as Mesopotamian images reflected in the Garden of Eden.[19] Oral traditions merged from different groups included patriarchs arriving in the Levant from Mesopotamia, linked to another story of a group seeing themselves in exile in Egypt before being led across Sinai and through Transjordan by Moses. The legends of the biblical patriarchs and their territorial occupation have parallels with the claims made by the 'returnees' from Babylonian exile, an analogy which could have supported the returnees' perspectives and claims for authority.

Themes such as those in Genesis imply the literary work of the Yehud religious leadership in editing the text we know today. But a recent study of the language used in the Tanakh has argued for a more traditional chronology, distinguishing the Pentateuch as well as the Deuteronomical books as written in Classical Biblical Hebrew and dating them to the late monarchical (i.e. pre-exilic) period, perhaps after the Assyrian conquest of Israel. Such a model would tie in with the image of Josiah as a religious reformer.[20] It implies a greater proportion of earlier written sources for the later edited texts, but would not preclude some late additions. However, it excludes the idea of deliberate archaisms introduced into the texts (Chapter 2, on Mormonism, notes how Joseph Smith, Jun. presented *The Book of Mormon* in a style heavily influenced by the King James Bible of two centuries before.) The differences in theological emphasis and in historical detail between the Pentateuch and the Deuteronomist history suggest different origins. Debates will continue.

Editorial work and additions are seen in the books of the prophets, and these have been used both to provide additional perspectives on historical events and to help in tracing the transition to monotheism. There are inevitable disagreements on which texts reflect the concern of the times when a prophet is thought to have lived, and which reflect a later construction, to give current perspectives the authority of antiquity.[21] The Book of Jeremiah is of particular importance, since it is set primarily in the three decades leading up to (and just beyond) the 586 conquest of Judah and exile of the Jerusalem elite. A core theme is the breach of the covenant between Yahweh and his people. Much of the book Jeremiah is presented as a message to those exiled in Babylonia, and highlights the salvational role set for that group. The poetic Book of Lamentations has similar themes, with the destruction of Jerusalem at the centre, and was traditionally associated with the author of Jeremiah. Both books, then, serve to emphasise the importance of the exile experience in the development of post-exilic Jewish identity. The very brief Book of Obadiah also appears to be placed around the fall of Jerusalem. Ezekiel is a prophetic text set within the early years of the Babylonian exile but also looking forward to the restoration of Yahweh's chosen people in their land.

The 66 chapters in the Book of Isaiah present three distinct voices. The first (Proto-Isaiah) includes prophetic messages placed in the period of the

Assyrian conquest of the northern kingdom of Israel, as seen from Judah. It is with Deutero-Isaiah (chapters 40–55) that a statement of monotheism emerges. The setting is the Babylonian exile and these chapters make the most specific presentation of the exilic outlook. The final section, Trito-Isaiah, is from the Persian period. If the core text of Deutero-Isaiah does date from within the Babylonian exile period, its author can be considered one of the major contributors to the changing theological views.

Of the other, shorter, Tanakh books in the name of prophets, Hosea is set in the 8th century BCE, that is, before the Assyrian conquest, and reflects the departure of Yahwist devotees to worship other deities, and is seen by some to be the first text to emphasise the worship of Yahweh alone. With a setting slightly earlier, but in both northern and southern kingdoms, is Amos. Micah (source of the reference to a future ruler from Bethlehem, mentioned in Chapter 4 above) includes material which spans the defeat of the northern kingdom. Nahum, with its denunciation of the Assyrian city of Nineveh for its moral failings, is framed in a context of the end 7th century BCE. Habakkuk has a late 7th-century setting, that is, before the fall of Jerusalem. The Book of Zephaniah places its text in Judah at the end of the 7th century. There is no agreement on the date of material included in the brief Book of Joel.

Whatever the 'setting', the editing of these prophetic texts emphasised the importance of adherence to Yahweh, and frequently to interpret political disasters as a failure to maintain that worship. A future in which punitive exile from the land is followed by a restoration and renewal indicates the editing by the religious elites of Yehud, although some religious authorities would still see the predictions of exile as genuine prophecies before the event.[22]

Compositions commonly agreed as originating in Persian Yehud, and possibly very late in the Persian period, include the historical books 1 Chronicles, 2 Chronicles, Ezra and Nehemiah, all reflecting a perspective that privileges a Judaean priestly class and extending the period described by the Deuteronomist histories. Ezra and Nehemiah record a history of Yehud in the first century after the exile, in just over 14,000 words. However, arguments have been advanced that both books may owe much or all of their origins to the Hellenistic period (after 332 BCE), and that they serve to create a narrative to explain the development of Jerusalem, the Temple and the ruling group.[23]

Prophets within the Persian period with works attributed to them are Haggai, Zechariah (probably two separate authors, the second post-Persian), Malachi and the author of Isaiah 56–66 ('Trito-Isaiah'), while the Book of Ruth reflects the concerns of Judaism in Persian Yehud. Additions to the canon were made in and after the period of Hellenistic rule. Such later compositions include Job, Ecclesiastes, Jonah, Daniel, Esther (whose setting is Persia), the Song of Solomon (Song of Songs), as well as books classified as apocryphal. The Book of Psalms, like Proverbs, collects works of widely different dates, many considered to have pre-exilic origins.

In summary, many decades of historians' debates have not resolved questions of how much of the Tanakh was first composed in the Persian and Hellenistic periods, and which sections were redacted and edited from earlier written documents or oral traditions of the pre-exilic southern kingdom of Judah and the northern kingdom of Israel.[24] The framework of these debates is often influenced by preferences relating to religious beliefs and ethnic identities, rather than critical scholarship. The matter is complex (and biased) when a writer starts from the older position, that a biblical text gives a reliable historical portrait unless and until it can be shown otherwise (by literary critical methods, or by contradictory evidence from other historical documents or from archaeological sources). Such an approach cannot deny that polytheism was present in pre-exilic Israel and Judah because accounts of such falling away from devotion to Yahweh are a theme of the histories and prophetic writings. But using the later texts to define early history – as noted in our chapters on Islam and Christianity – can be a matter of faith more than historical certainty.

Most books of the Tanakh in broadly their present form are widely accepted as having received their final editing in the Second Temple period, with most of this undertaken by the religious leadership based in Jerusalem within Persian Yehud. That the edited versions reflect the theological and practical role of this group is not contested; that this group of people had an ancestral background in exile in Babylonia is generally (though not universally) agreed. But, clearly, those copying, editing and disseminating a religious document would do so in the light of the authority and beliefs of their time and place – the world of change that was Middle East in the 6th to 4th centuries BCE. As an authoritative survey of the development of biblical literature concludes, 'the purpose of the major works was the search for identity during and after the exile and the need for "Israelite" self-assertion in the difficult situation in the Persian period of Yehud'.[25]

The historical background

The books of the Tanakh provide information relating to the history of the Middle East, inevitably presented through the lens of religious ideology. Written sources from the succession of regional empires record or proclaim their achievements in documents typically created for political ideology and propaganda. Together with archaeology, they offer the basis for constructing a reasonably coherent account and chronology of events in the ancient Middle East.

The Levant was home to many different peoples, including Aramaeans, Phoenicians, Israelites, Philistines, Ammonites, Moabites, Edomites and Judaeans.[26] The region provides links between Egypt, Mesopotamia, Anatolia and the Mediterranean littoral and was a magnet for conquest, and so the history of the lands of Israel and Judah is one largely of foreign domination. A succession of Egyptian, Assyrian, Babylonian, Persian, Hellenistic, Roman, Byzantine, Arab/Muslim, Crusader, Ottoman and British rule meant that between 722 BCE and 1948 CE the independence of the land of greater Israel lasted only the 77 years of Hasmonean rule, from 140 to 63 BCE.

The Assyrian Empire, ruling from Nineveh in northern Mesopotamia, had expanded its territory during 300 years from the early 10th century BCE, conquering lands or enforcing tribute from local rulers. Assyria described its conquered lands as the provinces of Megidu (Galilee), Samerina (Samaria) and Ammon. In Galilee, the archaeological evidence suggests some decline in settlement and population in the period after the Assyrian conquest.[27]

In 722–721 BCE the land of Israel (the 'northern kingdom' of the inland Palestine region) was conquered after a period of siege of its capital, Samaria. Studies in archaeology have demonstrated the economic strength and social complexity of the northern kingdom of Israel before the Assyrian conquest, in contrast to that of its contemporary southern neighbour. Before the defeat, Israel may have had up to three times the population of Judah and more urban settlements. One estimate puts 8th-century Israel at 250,000, Judah at 110,000 and the coastal area of Philistia at 50,000.[28]

Following the conquest, much of Israel's population was dispersed to elsewhere in the Assyrian Empire: the biblical text specifies areas of upper Mesopotamia and 'cities of the Medes' to the east. This led to the many later legends surrounding the 10 'Lost Tribes of Israel'.[29] Assyrian policy is interpreted as dispersing the people they displaced from their land, whereas the Neo-Babylonians seem to have permitted those they exiled to remain together. Following the conquest there were new settlements in the south-western parts of the region.[30] Evidence that the Assyrians brought outsiders into their conquered land came from excavations at the site of Hadid, reported in the media in 2019, where clay tablets recording land sales had 19 names, none of which appeared to be of local origin. Excavations show destruction in parts of the northern kingdom but there is no confirmation in the material culture of a large replacement population coming in from elsewhere in the Assyrian Empire.

As with the later exile affecting the southern kingdom, it is improbable that the productive land of conquered Israel was deprived of its peasant farmers. More realistic is that the ruling groups and their families were removed and their lands seized, to prevent the risk of revolt. Since the record comes from Tanakh texts edited later by the religious leadership in Jerusalem, at a time of some hostility to Samaria and to demonstrate the historical failings of Israel, details in the narrative are open to question.[31] Because the religious leadership was located in Judah, the literary tradition gave the south greater prominence in Palestine's history. By the time the Book of Nehemiah was completed, it reflected rivalry between those around the Temple of Jerusalem and those to the north, who constructed their own temple at Gerizim (dated by archaeological work to the mid-5th century BCE). The community around the Gerizim temple formed the basis of the Samaritans, whose distinction from the Judaism centred on Jerusalem had grown greater by the 1st century CE.[32] This temple was, according to Josephus, destroyed by the Hasmonean leader Hyrcanus in 128 BCE.

The Assyrian defeat of Samaria and the northern kingdom of Israel had lasting effects on its then poorer southern neighbour, Judah.[33] Both Israel and Judah were primarily adherents of Yahweh as their tribal deity. The defeat of Israel implied they had lost the protection of their god, a situation which would require theological interpretation of political and military events by the Yahwists of Jerusalem.

The later writings from the Judaean leadership in Jerusalem would use the term 'Israel' to mean not just the former northern kingdom with its capital, Samaria, but a broader (and by then monotheistic) religious and ethnic identity of Jews, and this usage became entrenched.[34] This literature would present a tradition that kings based in Jerusalem, David then Solomon, had once ruled both Israel and Judah as a united kingdom. In the myths of Genesis the patriarch Jacob, father of the brothers whose names were those of all 12 tribes of the northern and southern kingdoms, was given the name Israel, meaning 'he who strives with God'.

During the 8th century, fortresses were constructed within Judah, the southern kingdom, whose capital was Jerusalem and which included the tribal area of Benjamin.[35] In the Assyrian campaigns around 701 there were successful attacks on many towns of Judah. One estimate is that of numerous Judaean settlements that suffered destruction in the late 8th century, only a minority were rebuilt in the 7th century.[36] Benjamin, north of Jerusalem, did not experience such a downturn. A siege of Jerusalem was not successful (as recorded both in the Tanakh and the cuneiform annals of the Assyrian king Sennacherib, discovered in 1830), but Judah fell under effective Assyrian control, although, with payment of tribute, it avoided formal incorporation into the Assyrian Empire.

There may well have been a move of some of the Samarian population south to Judah after their defeat by Assyria. Judah saw substantial growth in the late 8th century BCE and more in the 7th, and this led to major expansion of the area and population of Jerusalem.[37] Following the defeat of Israel, rulers of the southern kingdom of Judah maintained the Yahweh cult. As noted above, Josiah – king of Judah from about 640 to 609 – is credited in the Tanakh with religious reforms, including destruction of temples to gods other than Yahweh, and the writing (or least the editing) during his reign of several source texts of the Tanakh.

In the late 7th century, the Assyrian power fell, impacted by the rise of the Medes in Persia and of a dynasty from southern Mesopotamia we call the Neo-Babylonians, who had gained power in Babylon in 625. Like the Assyrians, the Neo-Babylonians sought to expand their power and territory, and challenge the pharaohs of Egypt for the control of the Levant. Their activities in Judah developed over several stages. Initially, Judah acceded to a role as a client of Babylon but the ruler Jehoiakim rebelled, an action that invited swift and successful response under Babylonian king Nebuchadnezzar II, who took control of the city of Jerusalem in 597. Tanakh texts state that some thousands of Judaeans (the king, the elite, the military and the craftsmen) were removed from Judah but not the poor, who would have been the majority.[38]

Within a few years, the new vassal king left by Nebuchadnezzar, Zedekiah, rebelled, perhaps expecting to have Egypt support him, and the Babylonian response this time led to the destruction of Jerusalem and its Temple in 586. To reduce the power of religious and political elites, more citizens were exiled from Jerusalem, but not from the agricultural lands. Five years later another group was removed from Judah.[39] 'Exile' remained the condition of these people and their descendants until the options made available after the defeat of Babylonia by the Persian ruler Cyrus in 539.

Unsurprisingly, Babylonian authorities did not remove 'the Jews' from Judah, where most residents were peasants living in agricultural settlements. There was no reason why Babylon would wish to weaken rural productivity in its empire. In fact, the Babylonian Empire both desired and required the produce of the lands it conquered, including especially the harvests from the

Key dates

722 BCE	Fall of Israel to Assyria
ca. 640–609	Reign of Josiah
597	Babylonian conquest of Jerusalem; first exile
586	Destruction of Jerusalem; second exile
581	Third exile
539	Victory of Cyrus
515	Date given for completion of Temple
445	Nehemiah governor of Yehud
332	Conquest by Alexander
167–160	Maccabean revolt
140	Hasmonean rule

olive groves and vineyards of Palestine.[40] Babylon needed prosperous and stable territories able to contribute to the economy of the empire; agriculture, trade and the production of traded goods continued.

With the religious and political leadership from Jerusalem removed, it is not surprising that the allegiances of much of Judah changed, to the point where the religious leadership of exiles returning after the fall of Babylonian power met resistance in their planned rebuilding of the Temple.[41]

The setting of the Babylonian exile

The biblical texts present a detailed account of Israel and Judah – the northern and southern kingdoms of Palestine – up to the time of the Babylonian deportation, and describe the reconstruction of Yahwist religion and Jerusalem after the return of those who chose to do so. They are very limited in their information on life during the 'exile' itself, so we have to consider this in a broader context.[42] Our reconstruction can be only partial and much is surmised.

Moving the elite of a conquered territory away from that land had a clear political logic. Once the religious, political and economic leaders had been moved from Jerusalem they were no threat to Babylonian rule. Although 'Babylon' through into modern times has taken on a symbolic meaning of loss, exile and despair, the lives of the deportees was not that of prisoners.[43] Unlike the people removed from Israel in the earlier Assyrian deportation, this group (or at least enough of them) retained their identity and their observance of Yahweh as their divinity. Some adopted Babylonian names, while others retained Hebrew names, which can be found in Babylonian cuneiform records of work payments.[44] The skills the deportees brought with them into the multicultural word of Babylonia would serve them and the society in which they now lived.

In addition to the information that can be obtained by dissecting the Tanakh, our image of the Jewish community in 6th-century Babylonia is augmented by Babylonian sources. Tablets from the royal archives noted rations granted to a royal captive thought to be the Judaean king Jehoiachin (Jeconiah), together with five of his sons. As those who had been forcibly taken from Judah to Babylonia in 597 or 586 or 581 would have died in exile, another generation was born and grew up there, followed by a third, with Jewish identity maintained by many despite a continuing presence of intermarriage. The proclaimed end of the Babylonian 'captivity' around 538, following Cyrus's victory the previous year, meant that the exilic period had lasted for 59 or 48 or, for the latest group, 43 years, while for the many families who formed the widespread Jewish diaspora, this relocation was permanent.

The al-Yahudu tablets mentioned above demonstrate that at least some of the Jewish community remained together in Babylonia well into the Persian period. This group included many whose livelihood lay in agriculture, while others led lives of greater prosperity. Our other sources emphasise the decision by many to remain there and in other areas of the Persian Empire outside of Palestine after Cyrus's conquests. The image of 'exiles' choosing to remain in exile contrasts with the religious message of the Tanakh.

One interesting explanation of the Judaeans' willingness to remain in Babylonia is the suggestion that improved climatic conditions – a period of warming in the 6th century – made the river plains of Mesopotamia more appealing for agriculture than Palestine.[45] In fact, recent studies suggest that the area of Judah was affected by dry climatic conditions that extended from the 6th to the mid-5th centuries, conditions that would dramatically reduce the agricultural productivity of the marginal environments within Judah, and make them more appropriate for nomadic pastoralism.[46] Increased rainfall from the late 5th century to 4th century improved its agricultural potential.

The concentrations of Jewish communities in Mesopotamia recorded centuries later in the Talmud were in towns mainly to the north of Babylon (with a few to the south) and this may in part serve as an indication of one region of their settlement during the 6th century BCE.[47] The Babylonian Talmud of ca. 500 CE has had great lasting importance in the history of Judaism than the earlier Jerusalem Talmud. But the contemporary archives noted above were of settlements around Nippur to the south. The documents show a community settled into the new context – what they do not provide is an explanation for the religious movement that developed in the exilic period.

The elite of Judah had lost power, wealth and roles in both political and religious leadership. The destruction of Jerusalem and its Temple by the followers of other gods appeared to conflict with Yahweh's covenant with the Jewish people: the people must have broken their pact with Yahweh. This experience required a new interpretation of history and of Jewish religious beliefs. Exile provided a context which both required and allowed the emergence of new religious ideas, away from the popular cults of the Judaean and Israelite peasantry. Biblical references to the exile from post-exilic Yehud, from both the Persian and the subsequent Hellenistic periods, inevitably present the exile in instrumental terms, as a religious message (the impact of a fracture in the covenant with Yahweh) rather than an historical narrative.

Direct influences from the Babylonian exile can be seen in elements of Genesis, but other Babylonian themes in the Tanakh are harder for scholars to agree on. Comparisons can be made between some texts in the Tanakh and stylistic elements in other regional writings, including those of Babylonia, and a Babylonian presence in the texts of Ezekiel and Deutero-Isaiah has at times been suggested.[48] The theme of exile is emphasised not only in references in prophetic books, psalms and histories in the Tanakh, but by the prominence placed in the texts and in Judaic practice on another exile story: that of Israel in Egypt, rescued not by Cyrus but by Moses, with this community identified as the ancestral group of all Israel and Judah: the historic northern and southern kingdoms. Deutero-Isaiah implies a parallel between the two experiences of exile.[49]

The books of prophets, as later edited and included in the Jewish canon, were designed to support concepts and models of religious adherence and ethnic identity, not to present a record of people and events. The majority of the prophets whose words and works are included in the Tanakh are said to have lived in the pre-exilic period of Israel or Judah, or the post-exilic Persian era. Yet if the exile was a period when major religious ideas developed, we should expect powerful individuals to have led the movement.

Some prophetic literature on exile has been dated within the exilic period: Ezekiel's message reflecting the early decades of exile, and Deutero-Isaiah (chapters 40–55 of the Book of Isaiah) the last part of the exile.[50] But as with all other texts, we do not know what editing and adaptation took place in post-exilic times to finalise these books into the text we now have, and some sections were clearly additions.

The Book of Jeremiah, a prophetic work set in Judah before and during the exile, has Jeremiah urging the exiles in Babylonia to build houses, cultivate and consume their produce, marry and raise families and seek the welfare of the place in which they were exiled.[51] The same text states that the Babylonian power would last just 70 years, after which they would return – an indication that the text was finalised with editing in the Persian period, and thus can be presumed to represent the experience and view of the exiles. A warning 'do not let the prophets and the diviners who are among you deceive you' also points to the ideological turmoil of the exiled Jewish community. By tradition Jeremiah was also considered the author of Lamentations, which addresses the destruction of Jerusalem and its Temple, and the end of the kingship of Judah.[52]

The Book of Ezekiel identifies its author as a first-generation exile living at Tel-Abib, 'by the river Chebar',[53] which may be a location near Nippur, in line with the Murašu archive, mentioned above, which recorded people of Jewish descent still present there in the mid-5th century BCE. An emphasis of the text is on religious failings as a cause of the exile and the destruction of Jerusalem. The book also emphasises Jewish rituals as an important way to retain identity in exile. The description of the restoration to Judah and the future Temple to be built in Jerusalem indicates its post-exilic editing and additions.

The text of Deutero-Isaiah is conventionally located in Babylonia within the exile. This is often cited as a mark of the emergence of monotheism among the Jewish community, with the individual who wrote Deutero-Isaiah a highly influential figure of the new monotheism in the exilic period, by excluding not just (as before) the *worship* of other deities, but the *existence* of other deities. But this text is focussed on religious revival not in exile but back in Judah ('say to the cities of Judah "here is your God"') and specifically Jerusalem: 'it shall be rebuilt'. References to Cyrus as the liberating agent of God position this at the earliest at the very end of the exile, as inspiration and briefing notes for the returning Judaeans: 'in the wilderness prepare the way of the Lord'.[54] As such, a date in the period between Cyrus's victory and the return of Judaeans is feasible, but it could equally be placed somewhat later, to give the movement authority. In this context, denunciations of idol worship and the need to confront it would imply the continuance of these practices in Judah and Israel. References to the sea coast may imply greater territorial ambitions than in riverine Mesopotamia.

The period of exile, then, seems to have produced prophetic writings from figures whose influence is suggested by the prominence given to their writings (in edited and expanded form) in the development of post-exilic Judaism. We cannot determine who may have been the practical activists in the maintenance in Yahwist religious practices or the development of Jewish religious ideas. But it could be said that the exile of the Judaean elite, which they saw as a tragic event, provided the opportunity and incentive for religious developments which might not have happened so readily with the continuity of the monolatrous Yahwist cults of pre-exilic Israel and Judah. And in the text of Deutero-Isaiah, whether its author wrote in Babylon at the very end of the exile or early in the period of the return of exiles to Jerusalem, we have a powerful voice that would continue to be an inspiration to Judaism, and one cited widely in Christian contexts.

The new world of Yehud

The defeat of the Babylonian Empire by Cyrus, from the Achaemenid dynasty, provided a context in which descendants of the Judaeans relocated to Babylonia could travel to what was now the Persian province of Yehud, settle in and around Jerusalem, and in due course establish religious institutions, practices and a literature that would define a monotheistic Jewish religion.

Cyrus 'the Great' had moved from his position as the Persian client king of the Median Empire to overthrow Median rule in 550–549, extend his conquests into Anatolia, then finally overthrow the last Neo-Babylonian king, Nabonidus, in 539, capturing Babylon. Given the power and spread of the Babylonian Empire, its defeat was of major importance to the new Achaemenid ruler.[55] Now reigning over a substantial territory, Cyrus sought loyalty from its diverse citizens by affirming their rights to their own religious cults and cult centres. The Nabonidus Chronicle records how the idols of different gods that had been brought into Babylon were returned to their home cities. The Cyrus Cylinder proclaims that Cyrus restored both inhabitants and cults to their former locations. A similar experience is recorded in the Tanakh, where Cyrus is cited as Yahweh's 'anointed'.[56]

Jerusalem was identified by the Judaean families in exile as their cult centre and the books of Ezra and Nehemiah in the Tanakh, which we possess in redacted and edited form, purport to present a detailed account of events in the development and reconstruction of the Temple and the town.[57] It now lay within (but was not the administrative centre of) the Persian province of Yehud Medinata. With Persian permission, but also under Persian administrative guidance and control, those descendants of the deported Judaic elite who chose to do so went from 538 and after to the city from which their families had been exiled, where they would define the religious and cultural world whose ideological origins had developed in Babylonia.

Just as the narrative in the Tanakh emphasised an exile, it emphasised 'a return', but it seems likely that the migration from Babylonia to Yehud by people of Judaean ancestry took place over some time, in small groups, though perhaps with a major movement in the mid-5th century, in the time of Nehemiah.[58] Although the biblical books of Ezra and Nehemiah list in detail communities and numbers of people said to have returned from Babylonian exile, these do not represent the real world of Yehud; this discrepancy suggests the text may have a late compilation, either Hellenistic or even Hasmonean.[59]

Just as only a minority of the population of Judah had been removed to elsewhere in the Babylonian Empire (though leaving Jerusalem itself largely desolate), only a proportion, probably a minority, of the descendants of these exiles chose to return to Persian Yehud, with Jerusalem initially a small settlement and the population of Yehud itself of modest size.[60]

The biblical texts mourning the Babylonian conquest of Judah and emphasising the significance of exile and return are powerful, but they reflect the perspective of those who took the opportunity to go to Judah after the Persian conquest. A significant proportion of those from exiled families remained outside Yehud; some stayed where they had been displaced, others moved elsewhere, and some returned at different times to the area they identified as their place of origin. Those who worshipped Yahweh would recognise the Jerusalem Temple and its religious leaders as the centre of the Yahweh cult, and Jerusalem may have become an important place of pilgrimage before it became a large and important place of settlement.

The many Jews who remained outside of Yehud were widely distributed and performed many roles. A Yahwist community may have lived in Egypt by the early 6th century.[61] The Jewish community of Elephantine, working primarily as mercenaries at the southern border of Egypt with Nubia, is the subject of an archive of surviving documents from the 5th century BCE. It is uncertain if this community originated from the exile period, or perhaps even earlier, with an origin in the northern kingdom.[62] These texts give direct evidence of a group who identified as Yahwists, had their own temple yet recognised the primacy of the Temple in Jerusalem and the religious leadership around it. Excavators in 1997 interpreted a building 20 feet (6 m) wide as the temple or shrine of this Jewish community.

The groups who moved from Babylonia to Yehud had the authority of the Persian administration to settle in the former Judaean capital of Jerusalem, re-establish their religious cult and rebuild their Temple. They were given (and required) no political power. The region which had been the Babylonian province of Yehud had been administered from Mizpah, some 7 miles (12 km) north-west of Jerusalem, and it is quite possible that the Persian administration of Yehud Medinata retained Mizpah as the administrative centre. Not until the governorship of Nehemiah (himself one of those of Judaean descent who had remained in Mesopotamia) in 445 did Jerusalem resume a role as the administrative centre for Yehud. Religious authority would remain separate from political authority, as Persian rule was succeeded by Hellenistic rule in 332 BCE.

The initial Judaean move from Babylonia back to Yehud would present many challenges to the new arrivals in a region their families had left some two generations back. The leaders of the Yahwist community at the time of Cyrus would be the grandchildren of the leaders at the time of the Babylonian deportation. That allowed both continuity and change: the traditions of the old and the vigour and priorities of new generations. We can see the Babylonian exile as a period that inspired revolutionary changes in attitudes and ideas. But we should also remember the possibility that an individual's life could span the whole period: a child aged 10 at the first exile of 597 would be 69 in the year when the return began; or 58 if their family was from the second exile, of 586. So the exile can be considered as a transformative episode rather than a period in itself. A parallel here lies in the massive changes effected in the modern 'colonial period'. It would be possible to be born in pre-colonial Africa and die in newly independent Africa, with colonialism just a phase.

The importance of this return was represented by numbers given in the Tanakh as 42,360 returnees plus slaves and 'singers', but this is a statement of symbolism rather than history.[63] The archaeological evidence implies a much smaller population growth of Jerusalem, which remained a settlement of very modest size until at least the mid-5th century BCE, and very possibly into Hellenistic times.

The new arrivals who travelled from Mesopotamia to Yehud found themselves at a distance from those still living in the area, in both religious and political terms. They needed to establish their religious control of the land since they were unable to re-establish political control. The Tanakh books of Ezra and Nehemiah make it clear that they met local resistance to establishing their role and religious leadership, including from those who would form the basis of the Samaritan community to the north and build their own temple to the north at Gerizim. Towns in Samaria, as indicated by archaeology, showed cultural continuity from the 7th to the 4th century BCE. Samarian adherence to Yahwism remained, but with no ready acknowledgement of the Jerusalem hierarchy. Under Persian administrative organisation Samaria was separate from Yehud (as was Galilee).[64]

A large population had remained in Judah, primarily in agricultural villages, and had their own loyalties and cult beliefs, even if these foregrounded Yahweh. They may have had no immediate wish to accept the theological and organisational precepts of those arriving with Cyrus's permission. And for many returning from Mesopotamia to the regions their forebears had seen fall under Babylonian rule, acquiring the right to own or use land to farm or raise livestock may have presented further challenges.

Historical scholarship and the archaeological evidence support an image of pre-exile Judah with fluctuating loyalty to the Yahweh cult, within a monolatrous or polytheistic framework. The departure of the most literate classes, including the religious and political elite, and the diminution of the role and population of Jerusalem, allowed the next two to three generations of less literate and non-elite Judaeans under Babylonian control to continue their own beliefs in the same pattern. So when a group of descendants of the exiles came into the land again in the late 6th century, they needed to take a completely new approach and emphasise the role they were creating for Jerusalem, the Temple, and themselves as religious and social leaders, by creating both ritual practices and developing religious literature that traced the history of Yahwism, of Judah and Israel in a manner that served the new context and goals. However, the biblical book Ezra notes that in 5th-century Yehud mixed marriages had become common between non-Jews and those of Jewish descent, including priests, officials and community leaders.[65]

Of the population of the area of Judah at the eve of the Babylonian conquest, estimated at about 110,000, perhaps a quarter lived in and around Jerusalem. There have been different estimates for the population of the town itself, in a range from 5,000 up to as many as 30,000 or more. A recent reassessment, area by area, concluded the figure of 6,000 was realistic.[66] As discussed below, Yehud in the Persian period (within a slightly smaller area than Judah) may have had only 20,000 to 30,000 residents, with fewer than 1 in 10 based in Jerusalem.[67] When Babylonians moved the administrative centre of Judah to Mizpah after the attack and destruction of the Temple, Jerusalem seems to have fallen to a much reduced size, with just a small number of residents remaining where the capital of Judah had been.

The population of Yehud grew in the later Persian period, after the mid-5th century, and many locations were first occupied or reoccupied only under Hellenistic rule. In total, 105 sites have been dated to the Persian period in Yehud and 237 to the Hellenistic period, though there is continuity in material culture.[68] Demographic shifts to the north of Yehud were balanced by some gradual reductions in population in the southern highlands.

An emphasis of the new Jerusalem leadership, and one in the development of the Tanakh, was the unity of the two Yawhist communities of the former northern and southern kingdoms. As noted above, the term 'Israel' was used in biblical texts to apply no longer just to the northern kingdom but to all those who followed the redefined Jewish religion.

Emphasis on a tradition of the area of 12 tribes of Israel and Judah ruled as a united monarchy under David and Solomon, with Jerusalem becoming capital of the kingdom, served to strengthen the claims of the new leadership. Modern scholarship has raised doubts on the existence, or at least the power and spread, of such an ancient united monarchy dominating the future areas of Israel, Judah and beyond. The lack of collaborative textual evidence outside of the later Tanakh books casts doubt on the traditional image, and archaeological evidence suggests more modest political units.[69] When claims are periodically made to identify archaeological finds with the activities of David or of Solomon these are challenged with equal vigour. The image of the united monarchy served to give historical authenticity to later wishes by those in Jerusalem to establish religious authority over the area of Samaria/Israel.

In the model suggested by critical scholarship, Saul is likely to have led a chiefdom in the central highlands about 1000 BCE. David may well have expanded his political power base into Jerusalem, in the part now called the City of David, and also to have spread control northwards, but probably not to the extent implied in the Tanakh. The dating of archaeological sites attributed to the rule of his son Solomon has been challenged and the extent of his rule as stated in the Tanakh seems clearly exaggerated. The biblical description of his palace reflects the style of Achaemenid building.[70]

In 515 – that is, 71 years after the Temple's destruction – a new 'Second Temple' in Jerusalem was recorded as completed, during the long reign of Persian monarch Darius I and with support from his administration. With the arrival from the Persian royal court of Nehemiah as governor, recorded as 70 years after that, Jerusalem would become a more substantial town.

Yehud remained under Persian control from 539 to Alexander's conquest of the Levant in 332 BCE – some two centuries. The Hellenistic era of Ptolemaic and Seleucid rule that followed Alexander would itself last almost two centuries years before Hasmonean rule gave the area Jewish control.

A significant body of scholarship since the 1980s has challenged the view that Jewish monotheism emerged in exile and was developed immediately afterwards, in the early Persian period. This 'minimalist' line of argument would put the monotheistic movement later in the Persian period or even in the Hellenistic period, from the late 4th century, with much more substantial writing, rewriting and editing to create the books of the Tanakh.[71] Historians arguing along these lines have suggested that there was minimal or no evidence for monotheistic beliefs in the pre-exilic period, meaning that the biblical texts are largely devoid of an historical basis.

Critical scholarship has also challenged the validity of the books of Ezra and Nehemiah as an explanation for Second Temple Judaism, arguing that the growing power of the priesthood in the period of Persian Yehud required the construction of a narrative of exile and return that belied a *locally* based emergence of their position and ideas.[72] In this argument, the books, compiled into final form well after the events described, placed into the framework of a theological journey a series of historical narratives that included information of greater historical reliability alongside contradictions (three different accounts of the building of the Temple) and improbable accounts of the Persian administration's support and involvement in the process of developing the Judaean religious infrastructure.[73]

The geography of the Judaean world

The physical setting for the emergence of Jewish monotheism is the lands of the Neo-Babylonian and Persian Empires: empires whose boundaries fluctuated over time, not least during conflict with neighbours to the west such as Egypt and later with the Greek world, from which the Macedonian rulers emerged to replace Persian power.

A dominant geographical feature of the region is the stretch of productive land which lent itself to intensive settlement – the 'Fertile Crescent' wrapped around the arid zone that stretched north from the Arabian Peninsula.[74] This was the region that supported the civilisations of Mesopotamia, southern Anatolia and the Levant, and whose control provided the economic strength that maintained political power and attracted invaders.

Cultural linkages in prehistory and history are therefore along the routes round the Fertile Crescent and its river valleys rather than across the arid lands. The Levant at the west of the Fertile Crescent included Phoenicia and the kingdoms of Israel and Judah; in the east were the centres of those who conquered Palestine. East and west were linked by routes which took groups from Israel and Judah into exile and brought some of them back again.

From Jerusalem to Babylon the direct distance is 520 miles (840 km). But that line, across the empty wastes of the Syrian Desert, was not the journey of either armies or migrants. The route for humans to travel between Jerusalem and Babylon is much longer. Those travelling north from Jerusalem would sometimes first cross the Jordan Valley. What is today called the King's Highway travels north–south to the east of the Jordan River, heading to Damascus. From there, there have been trade routes to the northern Euphrates through the oasis of Tadmur (Palmyra), and an individual or family could travel a route between oases, a journey between Jerusalem and Babylon of about 850 miles (1,350 km). But a large group of exiled civilians, requiring food and water along the way, like soldiers moving in the other direction, would follow a route further north in the Levant, along the Orontes Valley, then east to the Euphrates and Upper Mesopotamia, and south-east along the Euphrates to Babylon, a journey closer to 1,020 miles (1,650 km). A travelling distance of this dimension emphasises the significance of 'exile' and Babylon to the Judaean families who experienced it.

The floodplain of Mesopotamia contained rich alluvial soils with pro-ductive cultivable lands along both the Euphrates and the Tigris, extended by irrigation, which benefited from the variable and unpredictable level of rainfall brought down the rivers from their sources in southern Anatolia. Cereals, fruit and vegetables supplied the urban centres. Grazing land extended beyond and between the arable areas. The city of Babylon lay where the two rivers came closest and provided a continuous area of cultivable land and therefore the densest occupation. It is assumed the Judaean exiles were settled in this region.

As emphasised in the previous chapter, the land areas of Palestine are modest, even if they loom large in narratives of world history. Its historical geography, though, is very varied. Lower Galilee and especially the Jezreel Valley at its south have agriculturally productive land through which ran the historically important route of the Via Maris. To the south, the Palestine region is distinguished by ecological zones running from north to south, divided primarily by the Judaean hills, up to the borders of the Negev Desert. The coastal plain is 210 miles long (340 km) and includes the most productive and adaptable arable land, on which cereals, orchards and vegetable crops can thrive.[75] This coastal plain narrows from 25 miles (40 km) in the south to 3 miles (5 km) in the north.

The western foothills of the Judaean range (the Shephelah), a zone about 40 miles (65 km) long and 8 miles (12 km) wide, are marked by changes in natural vegetation as well as topography, with fertile soils historically well suited for olive and vine cultivation. The Shephelah rises from about 300 to 1,300 feet (100–400 m) above sea level.

The Judaean hills proper, rising to 3,200 feet (1,000 m), have more broken topography, with terra rossa soils that allow cultivation, especially where terracing is possible. But in the higher and more broken land the areas for such cultivation are more restricted and in history encouraged pastoral activity

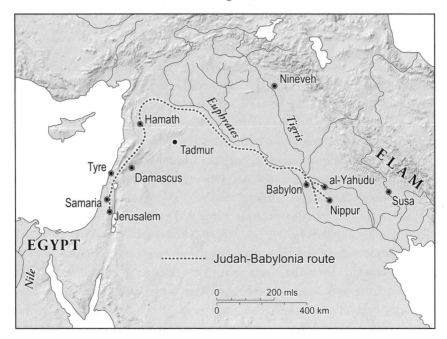

11. The route between Judah and Babylonia

alongside olives and wines, with cereals favoured in select parts of the north. Annual rainfall increases from 400–500 mm in the foothills to 800 mm in the highest areas, but with a reduction towards the south.[76] The descent from the Judaean hills to the Jordan Valley is marked by arid landforms in the southern part where it reaches the Dead Sea, unlike the fertile Jordan Valley to the north. Between the Dead Sea and Jerusalem, lying high and at the centre of the range of Judaean hills, land was forbidding and unproductive to all but determined nomadic pastoralists. There are oases at Jericho and at Ein Gedi.

The lands in Palestine which the Persian Empire acquired through its Babylonian conquests included valuable trade routes to Egypt, Anatolia and the Mediterranean,[77] routes which ran north–south through the Levant and to coastal ports.

Probably reflecting the pattern of Neo-Babylonian administration, the Persian satrapy of 'Across/Beyond the River' (i.e. west of the Euphrates) was split into different provinces, of which Yehud, based on the former Judah, was one. As these were all under a single rule there is no reason to believe there were fixed borders to these provinces, rather than spheres of control from the various administrative nodes.[78] The destination of tax payments would imply the province of a family.

The Persians now possessed the coastal plain with its productive land for mixed agriculture, and the westward-sloping hills of the Shephelah. In the coastal zone there were fortresses, towns, administrative centres and harbours. They controlled Galilee and the more fertile regions of the Judaean hills in Samaria to the north, with their agriculturally productive advantages from rain and soil, which gave them produce for taxes and trade.[79]

But the steeper areas of the hills in the former southern kingdom of Judah, leading up to Jerusalem, provided less productive terrain for an agricultural surplus, and beyond Jerusalem lay the arid eastern slopes down to the Jordan Valley and the Dead Sea. So the upland area around and beyond the city of Jerusalem afforded little to focus the conquerors' interests and was an ideal area for a small group to settle and develop a religious cult without affecting the power or economy of the ruling nation.

Before the Babylonian conquest, the southern kingdom of Judah had boundaries broader than those of the Persian province of Yehud. Until the exilic period, the southern kingdom was defined as that of two tribes, Judah and to the north Benjamin, but the term 'Judah' was applied to the whole kingdom, and Jerusalem was its religious and political capital. The Jewish group who moved from Babylon to Yehud and Jerusalem identified the Persian province of Yehud with that former southern kingdom even if the administrative centre was now elsewhere.

The area of Yehud can be defined by what it was *not*. It seems that the province of Yehud was a small area, smaller than the kingdoms of either pre-exilic Judah or Israel, despite some biblical claims for a larger settlement.[80] A number of different details for borders have been suggested, but the modest size of Yehud seems clear, with Jerusalem as the geographic centre. The separate administrative unit of Samaria began just 15 miles (25 km) beyond Jerusalem to the north. These territories of the former northern kingdom of Israel were important to the Jewish traditions but no longer in the sphere of the Jewish religious leadership. An area 15 miles (24 km) south of Jerusalem was one into which residents of Edom had moved and which would gain the name Idumaea. The boundary at the east of Yehud was the River Jordan, beyond which lay Ammon and Moab.

West of the administrative boundaries of Yehud was the productive coastal plain. Most of the Shephelah was probably excluded from Yehud. In one interpretation, Yehud extended no further than Beth-Zur in the hills to the south and Azekah and the Ellah Valley in the Shephelah. Yehud included both arid and productive land, with zones ranging west from the desert terrain bounding the Dead Sea to the most fertile western areas bordering the other Persian provinces. Jerusalem itself sits on the central highlands, with the desert fringe starting immediately to its east. The arid zone itself, parallel to the Dead Sea, would be about 40% of the land area of the suggested Yehud province.[81]

Feasible estimates, using the coherence of both geographical zones and cultural archaeology, suggest a land area of about 730–770 square miles (1,900–2,000 km²).[82] This is a land area smaller than the country of Luxembourg and only about 50% larger than the city of Los Angeles. This modest size makes it all the more remarkable when we consider the major religious, cultural and literary achievements that came from Yehud.

Judah, Babylonia and exile in archaeology

The biblical narratives present the years from the 8th to the 5th centuries BCE as times of dramatic changes in Palestine: invasions and conquests by Assyrians and Babylonians, dispersal and replacement of the tribes of the northern kingdom of Israel, exile of substantial numbers from the southern kingdom of Judah, followed by liberation under Cyrus and a mass return of the exiled Judaean families, to resettle the land of Judah and the city of Jerusalem, rebuild the Temple and re-establish Judaism and the Jewish identity.

Archaeological analysis suggests a contrasting picture, with greater continuity and more gradual change in the daily lives of the rural peasantry, despite being part of different empires under different rulers. The biggest impact of changing politics lay in the towns and specifically in the religious centre of Jerusalem, whose archaeology displays shifting patterns.[83]

The region had seen worship of Baal, El (the original deity of Israel, though the term is also used to mean 'a god' in a general sense), Yahweh and Asherah, all of whom are mentioned in the biblical account of Judges.[84] The Ugaritic deity Anat is found in personal names in the Tanakh. The features of some other deities were merged into the characteristics of Yahweh. The Mesha Stele or Moabite Stone of *ca.* 840 BCE, found at Dhiban in Jordan, mentions Yahweh; it also contains a reference most, but not all, scholars consider refers to a victory over the 'House of David'.

The evidence from the pre-exilic kingdoms of Judah and Israel shows a Yahweh cult within a polytheistic framework, including 9th- and 8th-century inscriptions that refer to Asherah (a deity with cults elsewhere in the region) as the consort of Yahweh.[85] Personal names incorporating the deity Baal are also a feature of the 8th century. The relationship between the cults of Yahweh/El, Asherah, Baal, Astarte and sun and moon deities in Israel is hard to define but the biblical denunciations by prophets from the Yahweh cult provide some indicators. At a monumental temple at the site of Tel Moza, just to the south-west of Jerusalem, dated to the 10th to early 9th centuries BCE, cultic activities appear to have rivalled those of Jerusalem itself.[86]

The deity called Yahweh seems likely to have had the major cult centre in the northern kingdom, at Bethel. Unlike the later pattern of a concentrated cult centre, it seems that in Judah Yahweh had multiple sanctuaries in different locations, including one much further south, at Beersheba.[87] A reference to Yahweh appears in an inscription at Khirbet Beit Lei, in western Judah, dated to the 6th century.

Kuntillet 'Ajrud, at the north-west of the Sinai Peninsula, provided a snapshot of 8th-century BCE beliefs at a site occupied for only a short period. Here were remnants of cultic activities, images painted on pots and walls, and inscriptions with references to Yahweh 'and his Asherah', his divine consort, though the exact relationship between these items is uncertain.[88]

The large growth of rural settlements around Jerusalem in the 7th century may reflect the aftermath of the Assyrian destruction of the northern kingdom and the migration of some from Israel to Judah; challenges have been raised to this interpretation, however, with doubts over whether Jerusalem itself received a significant influx at this time.[89]

There are debates and disagreements on the effects of Babylonian rule of Judah on settlement and population. According to one view, Babylonian rule in the 6th century BCE had limited impact on peasant life and smaller settlements, and is not marked by significant changes to the material culture of Judah.[90] In line with this argument, the archaeological analysis of pottery from sites in Judah implies cultural continuity between the end of the 7th century and the 5th century, showing the limited impact that political events and shifts in empires had on the rural community, with changes marked only in the mid-5th century.[91]

An alternative (if minority) position argues that there was a marked cultural change with the typical four-roomed house and Judaean tomb style disappearing in the 6th century at the time of the Babylonian conquest.[92] The absence of specific cultural markers in the Neo-Babylonian period is seen as supporting this argument. If correct, the 6th-century population of Judah (including urban residents) may have fallen to a fraction of that of the pre-Babylonian period.[93]

Archaeological work suggests that during the Babylonian period a large population remained in what was called the tribal area of Benjamin in the northern Judaean hills, and the material culture of Benjamin continued without dramatic impact.[94] The archaeological pattern alongside reassessment of the historical picture has helped to erode further the 'myth of the empty land', a once strongly held image of a Judah depopulated by the Babylonians, an image from which most historians (though not all) have now departed.[95]

The archaeology of major settlement sites in Judah following the Babylonian conquest does suggest some urban depopulation. This was most dramatic in Jerusalem, emphasising the argument that the Babylonians sought to destroy its political and religious power but not the economy.

Mizpah took on the role of administrative capital. Mizpah is thought to be the excavated site of Tell en-Nasbeh, to the north-west of Jerusalem, with continuity in the material culture spread from pre-Babylonian into the Persian period. The site of Tell el-Ful was abandoned at the time of the conquest, but other sites, like el Jib (Gibeon), continued without loss of population.[96]

Despite extensive excavations in and around Jerusalem there is no archaeological access to the core of the city, the Temple Mount. It is not therefore possible to test David Finkelstein's radical hypothesis that the Temple Mount was the location of the 10th-century town to which biblical texts assigned the rule of a united kingdom.

South of the Temple Mount is the area called the Ophel and beyond that is the south-eastern hill, the ridge above the Kidron Valley conventionally if controversially named the 'City of David'. Visitors are shown 'the large stone structure' that the excavators claimed was the palace of King David.[97] It lacks features that suggest the ruler of a large and powerful kingdom, as biblical tradition had claimed. Nearby is a building with a burned destruction level considered to mark the 586 Babylonian conquest. A spring providing fresh water lies to the east of this ridge, while the larger area to the south-west of the Temple Mount, the Western Hill, falls partly within what would later be included within the walls of the Old City.

A major growth of Jerusalem was seen in the middle of the 9th century as the town doubled in size and expanded on and around the south-eastern hill, with some dramatic masonry constructions. In the later 8th and 7th centuries, the residential area of Jerusalem grew, with an extensive region of cultivation beyond it. In Jerusalem, city walls had been built on both the south-eastern hill and the western hill by the late 8th century – about the time of the successful Assyrian attack on Israel and presumably in anticipation of their assault on Judah. The walls proved successful: Sennacherib's siege of the city in about 701 failed to capture it. Other settlements which had built defensive walls did not fare so well and their walls once destroyed were not rebuilt and destruction by Assyrian forces had lasting impact on the region of Judah.[98]

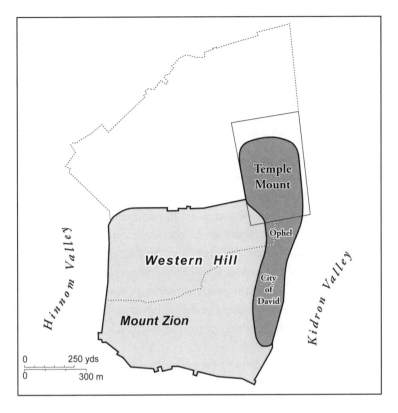

12. Jerusalem on the eve of the Babylonian conquest

Jerusalem as the political and religious centre of Judah remained the only settlement of any size, and at the time possibly the largest town in the Levant.[99] But, as noted above, estimates of its size range widely.

The devastation of Jerusalem at the hands of the Babylonians is indicated in the archaeology of the city. The scarcity of archaeological material from the period after the Babylonian destruction indicates how dramatic the change was. A find announced in 2019 was a bulla (seal) carrying a name, Nathan-Melech, also known in a biblical reference to an official of the reign of King Josiah (640–609 BCE). The bulla was found in the destruction level of a Jerusalem building just south of the Temple Mount, assumed to date from the Babylonian conquest of 586.

The city seems to have been largely emptied of its population, although this has been a matter of debate.[100] Even in the hinterland around the city there was a major decline in occupation between the end of the Judaean period and the start of Persian control. The destruction of the Temple in Jerusalem would have been more than a statement against a religious and state cult. We can envisage the Temple as a major economic factor in Judah: owner of lands, recipient and distributor of wealth. Therefore its destruction would have impacted the agricultural communities whose produce and skills it used.[101]

Persian Yehud, Jerusalem and archaeology

Archaeological work in Palestine, which began in earnest in the later 19th century, was commonly influenced by religious enthusiasms, and chose to focus on places and periods fed by those enthusiasms.[102] Ethnic and nationalist politics have sometimes played a similar role in more recent decades. Archaeological research in Jerusalem in particular remains a contested area between religion, politics and science. The Persian period of Palestine for long attracted minimal attention from archaeology compared with later or earlier periods, but there is still enough information from both excavations and surface survey to gain an image of the region at different stages of Persian Yehud.[103] So the Persian period is not quite the 'black hole in archaeology' that is at times implied.

The interpretation and dating of some of the material found in older investigations have been subject to challenge and debate. Early excavators were unwilling or unable to distinguish between occupation levels of early Yehud, later Yehud or even the Hellenistic period, and so reinterpretation of some of their conclusions is required.[104]

An overall indication is that there was no large-scale migration into Yehud after the Persian defeat of Babylonia: no 'mass return'. The conclusion is that 'The "Return to Zion" did not leave an impression in the archaeological data or in the demographic evidence'[105] and that 'The beginning of the Post-Exilic period does not exist from the archaeological point of view'.[106]

The first period of Persian Yehud, from 539 to *ca.* 450 BCE, appears from archaeological work to be a pattern of mainly small villages without walls or other fortifications, with Jerusalem the outlier (two or three times the size of any other settlement, but still small). There is little immediate change in the material culture at the beginning of the Persian period, only a gradual transition – while features such as shaft tombs, seals and coinage are found later under Persian rule.[107]

With the Neo-Babylonian conquest, Jerusalem lost its role both as a religious centre and an administrative capital and its population fell very dramatically. Its numbers began to grow again slowly with the move of Judaean families from Babylonia to Yehud after Cyrus's victory, but there was no immediate burst of settlement. The growth of Jerusalem progressed only slowly during the two centuries of Persian rule and the subsequent Hellenistic period.[108]

Estimates of the population of Jerusalem during the Persian period have seen dramatic downward revisions, mainly on the basis of archaeological work, with suggestions of a population of just a few thousand – or even, by some estimates, initially just a few hundred.[109] A revised estimate of the changing size of the population of Jerusalem over time has suggested that it had grown to about 8,000 by the end of the 8th century BCE, before a decline in the early 7th century and a rise to 6,000 on the eve of the Babylonian destruction; after this, it had few occupants, with perhaps 1,000 in the Persian period, rising to 2500–3,000 in Hellenistic Jerusalem, though some population growth has been argued from the mid-5th century. (Other estimates for the population at the end of the Persian period range from 500 to 4,500.[110]) If this is the total population, it needs dividing by at least three or four to suggest the numbers of families and heads of families: a small group of leading figures. The rise of the Hasmonean dynasty in the early 2nd century marked a period of growth of the city.[111]

The biblical account in Nehemiah implies Jerusalem was equipped with walls and became the administrative capital in the mid-5th century.[112] Even then, much of the area within the extended town walls may have been unoccupied. It is possible that the idea of walls around Jerusalem built by Nehemiah was a literary invention dating to the Hellenistic period, or even the Hasmonean.[113] There must have been visible walls, built before current memory, by the time the text of Nehemiah was finalised in the version we know: but these may have been constructions to mark a town boundary, not defensive fortifications. Indeed, they may have been reconstructions of early walls undertaken as a purely symbolic act.[114]

In the Persian period of Jerusalem, settlement existed east of the town walls, but was focussed in the Ophel hill area to the south of the Temple Mount and on the south-eastern hill (the so-called 'City of David'). Here, too, was dumped debris from quarrying work which probably reflected town development.[115] Excavations in the large archaeological site of the former Givati parking lot at the west of the City of David produced finds (announced to the media in June 2020) of simple housing built using rubble from the destroyed city; an official seal impression confirmed the dating and another seal with crude markings suggested a non-literate maker.

The Western Hill is considered to have been unoccupied in Persian-period Jerusalem, with only potsherds and some small finds located there,

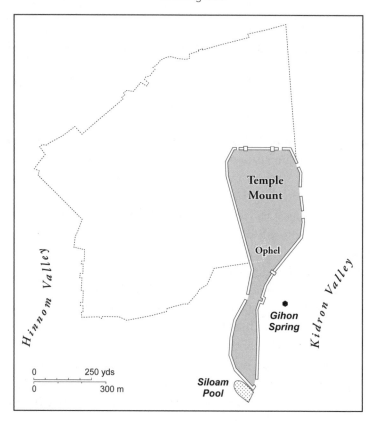

13. Jerusalem in the later Persian period

but no construction. Increased archaeological work on the Western Hill and elsewhere around Jerusalem have strengthened the image that this was not part of the town in the Persian period, and that the town itself was only a strip from the Temple Mount along the Ophel and the northern part of the 'City of David'. The lack of finds from the period on the Temple Mount itself reflects the limitations on archaeological work there.

If the population of the town in the Persian period was in the order of 1,000–1,500, in itself this does not contradict Jerusalem being a major centre of religious ritual, scribal endeavours and spiritual insights. But it does cast doubt on the image of Jerusalem becoming an important administrative centre. The Jerusalem of religious, political and demographic importance in 2nd-century BCE Hasmonean Judaea shrinks as we go back in time through Hellenistic, Persian and Neo-Babylonian times.

More than a third of excavated sites in Jerusalem's rural hinterland have Persian-period finds, with the majority of these village settlements.[116]

Specialist wine production has also been identified.[117] More dramatic is the site of Ramat Rahel (Ramat Rachel), 2½ miles (4 km) to the south of the Old City of Jerusalem, near the fertile Rephaim Valley.[118] The site lies on a high point between Bethlehem and Jerusalem, 2,625 feet (800 m) above sea level, in an ideally defensible position. Although Ramat Rahel is close to Jerusalem, the line of site between the two settlements is blocked by another ridge, giving today only a glimpse of the gilded roof of the Dome of the Rock.

The site had continuous occupation from the pre-exilic monarchical period of the 7th century BCE through to the end of the 4th century BCE. Excavations revealed a major residential building throughout this period, which has been described as a 'palace' with garden. Already an important institution in the period when Judah was dominated by Assyrian rule, it appears to have been a major administrative centre during Babylonian times. It was further expanded in the Persian period, with the development of a lavish garden, which included water pool, and it continued to be occupied in Hellenistic times.

Ramat Rahel has been suggested as the main centre for Persian administration after the mid-5th century.[119] The continuity of its use across periods of Assyrian vassalage, Neo-Babylonian and Persian rule, and continuity of finds in the Hellenistic era, suggests to the excavators a site of primary importance to foreigners rather than to Judaeans. The palace, in fact, faces *away* from Jerusalem, a feature which supports the image of a property occupied by outsiders. That interpretation would be supported by the site's destruction by the Hasmoneans, if it was seen as a symbol of the power and wealth of alien rulers.[120]

The form and impressions on the pottery found at the Persian palace suggest its role as a centre for the collection of agricultural produce, mainly olive oil and wine, presumably tribute paid from rural Judah to the state. Studies of the pollen from the Persian-period garden indicate both local trees (fig, grape, olive, willow, myrtle, as well as water lily) and exotic trees imported from other parts of the Persian Empire (citron, cedar, birch, Persian walnut).[121] This implies a residence to celebrate and impress, and the idea of Ramat Rahel as a centre controlled and occupied by the Persian administration, following a model of Neo-Babylonian and even Assyrian predecessors, parallel to local government.

A major role of the province was to provide tribute to the imperial power – tribute that gradually changed from products to coinage.[122] A number of sites (some being places mentioned in the biblical books of Ezra and Nehemiah) have produced seals from the Persian period stamped with the Aramaic *yhwd* or *yhd* – the provincial name; 60% of these are from Ramat Rahel, reinforcing the identity of its administrative role.[123] However, seals with inscriptions referring to Jerusalem – *yrslm* – seem to date only from Hellenistic times. The seals indicate the important factor of tax, payable to the Persian authorities.

The archaeology of Persian Yehud is marked by changes in the material record from about 450 BCE. These may imply greater 'Persianisation' and greater influence of Persian culture, reflecting changes which followed from the challenges to Persia's power over Egypt. From the mid-5th century, trade developed; the prosperous settlement at Tell Goren, at the oasis of Ein Gedi on the western side of the Dead Sea, 50 miles (80 km) by road from Jerusalem, had traded goods from Galilee, Jordan, Greece and Egypt.[124]

Sites described as fortresses were constructed in this period.[125] An alternative interpretation of Yehud has been proposed by Israeli archaeologist Avraham Faust. He noted how few villages seemed to be occupied during the Persian period, with only one site (Jerusalem) that could be called a town. In contrast are many sites which have been designated as fortifications or as administrative buildings, more than the administration of this small province would have required. His suggestion is that many of these 'forts' were in fact the centres of estates: lands provided either to groups of settlers or to those favoured by the political authorities.[126] But such a network of land grants would imply they were on agricultural land worth owning and that would need to be demonstrated.

While it has been difficult to distinguish clearly from site survey which sites were occupied or used in the earlier Persian period, numerous sites have been dated from regional survey to the century after *ca.* 450.[127] One calculation suggested that in this late period the population of Yehud almost doubled, from a little over 13,000 to *ca.* 20,000, though estimating total population numbers from archaeology is more difficult than tracing the trends in growth and development.[128] Jerusalem, with perhaps 10% of the total population of a small province of the Persian Empire, would be a settlement whose importance lay in its religious significance.

The archaeological evidence for neighbours of Yehud in the Persian period indicates their greater wealth and greater importance than Yehud, and probably a greater level of Persian administrative interest. Yehud, as a small territory with a small population and low productivity, could be left to develop its own religious style and leadership without causing major concern to the Achaemenid Empire. The coastal area which gave the Achaemenid Empire access to the Mediterranean was densely occupied. But, overall, the impression from archaeology is that material culture in the Levant was not

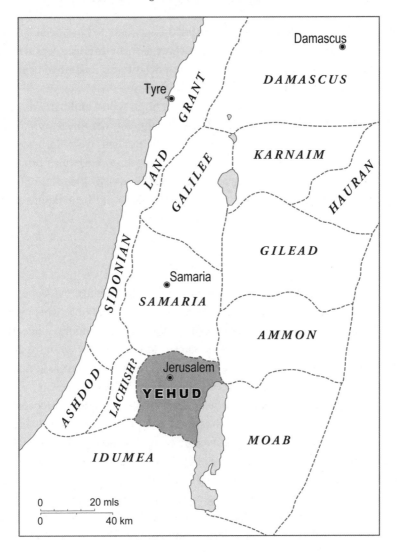

14. Yehud and the Levant in the Persian period

dramatically 'Persianised' after its conquest. Rule was important, taxation was important, but, given those factors, the Persian administration did not seek to intervene in the economic lives of its subject peoples.

The area of Samaria saw expansion in settlement, especially in the north, under Persian rule.[129] The destruction of some settlements in southern Samaria and also in northern Judah (Benjamin) about 480 BCE may imply internal conflict. Small settlements characterise the region in the period and suggest intensively occupied and productive land.[130] At the southern extent of Lower Galilee in the Jezreel Valley, Megiddo appears to have been a major settlement in the Persian period, and, further east, Beth-Shean was densely populated; to the north, Kedesh was an important administrative centre in the 5th century and later.[131]

The virtual absence of cultic objects from both Yehud and Samaria, contrasting with other areas of Persian Palestine, supports the image of religious development focussed on the strengthening Judaism from Jerusalem.[132] Altars and figurines from other cultic practices seem to have been produced from Phoenician workshops but reflect a diversity of divinities and religious allegiances. Nor did Mazdaism (or Zoroastrianism) as the religion of the ruling Persians show a presence in occupied Palestine.

Conclusions

This survey of sources, historical debates and archaeological evidence indicates that there remains a great deal we do *not* know about how, when, where and why Judaism became a monotheistic religion. Contemporary historical scholarship has served to cast doubt on many traditional accounts and assumptions, while archaeological work continues to erode some past assumptions but without fully delivering a detailed picture of period and place.

As with the spread of Islamic power, discussed in Chapter 3, archaeology shows that changes in empire and changes in ruler did not necessarily impact on the material culture, economic lives or ethnic identity of the population. Peasant farmers continued to grow their crops, herd their animals, build their village homes, practise their crafts and (as required) pay their taxes, most often in kind, to whoever might be the ruling administration of the time: Hellenistic Seleucid rulers, Achaemenid Persians, Neo-Babylonians, Assyrians, or local kings based in Jerusalem or Samaria.

Religion too can remain the same or change only slowly. Folk religion in the ancient Middle East could see communities pledging their religious loyalty to, and invite protection by, one particular deity or more (among all those thought to exist). That loyalty would distinguish them from adherents of other deities. They may have recognised their deity as identical to that with another name: Yahweh as Elohim or simply El. State religions throughout the ancient Middle East tied a ruler closely to the deity or deities whose cult they honoured and whose protection they required. Loyalty of many or most of their own subjects to the state cult had advantages to a small society, like Israel or Judah, but the local cults of subject peoples were of less importance and interest to the rulers of large empires.

What makes the emergence of 'post-exilic' monotheistic Judaism unusual is that it was not a religious cult tied to political power, actual or potential. That contrasts with contemporary cults of the region, and with the later emergence and power of Islam. Judaism was proclaimed as the religion of past rulers of Israel to the 8th century, of Judah to the early 6th century, and of a supposed united kingdom of the 10th century; it was the religion of the Maccabees and the Hasmonean dynasty from the mid-2nd century BCE. But between the 6th century and the mid-2nd century, within a minor colony of Persian Achaemenids, then Macedonian Ptolemies and Seleucids, the literary corpus of Judaism, the Tanakh, was brought into its familiar form, the rituals and social practices of Judaism were specified, a priestly elite without political power was established with Jerusalem as the centre of religious authority, and its Temple identified as the rebuilding of a construction created by King Solomon in a golden era of the past. Significantly, a widespread diaspora in the Persian Empire and its successors who identified as descendants of Judaeans acknowledged the position and literature of the Jerusalem Temple, even if some living close at hand – the Samaritans to the near north – did not.

The setting is further complicated by the archaeology of Jerusalem. Disputes over whether it was ever the centre of rule for a widespread kingdom are immaterial to the argument here.[133] After the fall of the northern kingdom of Israel to Assyria it was perhaps the largest town in the Levant region. But its final conquest by the Babylonians and destruction in 586 left it irrelevant in both administration and religion, with a much diminished population. It remained a small town in the period of Persian rule, growing only slowly, important as a religious centre around the Temple built or rebuilt there.

The Tanakh (or Old Testament) as we know it largely existed, in Greek and in Hebrew with some differences, by the Hasmonean period. How much of its editing was undertaken in the early or later Persian Yehud and how much in Hellenistic times cannot be stated with certainty. An anthology of widely differing books, including some of the finest literature of the ancient world, was brought together with redaction and editing of material from different sources. The unifying theme is a monotheistic outlook from a Jerusalem-based theocracy emphasising a special covenant and role for the followers of Yahweh. But because the Tanakh incorporates material from different sources, oral and written, old and new, it does not present a single coherent narrative of history or theology.

The vast sweep of debate in historical and religious scholarship has largely considered how to disentangle the different sources used in the Tanakh, and how much credence to give to statements within its texts. Some histories of the Jewish people choose to start only in or about the Persian period.[134] At the other extreme are volumes which present as history the narratives from Abraham to the exile, with relatively little interest in the period of Persian Yehud, which is all important for the origins of monotheism.

Because the books of the Tanakh were selected, partly integrated, edited and copied but not rewritten into a single continuous account, our judgements on what history to draw from them remain subjective. We know that the Genesis stories of creation and a universal flood are legends; that the Exodus story of a large migration escaping Egypt and a military conquest of Canaan are myths; that the narrative of King Solomon ruling a rich and powerful land stretching between the borders of Egypt and Mesopotamia is an invention.[135] From archaeology we know that the Babylonian conquest of Judah was not followed either by the emptying of the land nor by a mass return from Babylonia after Cyrus's victory. But beyond that, the timing and stages of a translation from Yawhist polytheism and Yahwist monolatry to a monotheistic religion cannot be placed more confidently than the 6th, 5th, 4th and perhaps into the 3rd centuries BCE. Those leading this movement added to the store of myths, legends, histories and prophetic declamations a particular emphasis on the Babylonian exile and the return to Judah of descendants of those in exile.

The Tanakh texts make it clear that before the Babylonian conquest, and the exile of the Judaean elite, dedication to Yahweh had frequently been flawed: divine warning, primarily through the words of powerful prophets, addressed this issue. They indicate that pre-exilic Judah and the northern kingdom of Israel contained the worship of many different gods beyond Yahweh, and blame the fall of their rulers on deviation from the cult of Yahweh. Some individuals could be described as polytheistic, others with variable loyalties as monolatrous, with adherence to one deity existing among others. There is argument about how useful is the term 'monotheism' but in the contemporary sense of only one existing deity (even if accompanied by minor supernatural figures like angels) it seems valid to place this concept no earlier than the 6th century BCE.

A significant body of scholars use the biblical texts to place the beginnings of a monotheistic outlook in the reign of Josiah, king of Judah *ca.* 640–609 – when regional politics had seen the defeat of Israel, a move of peoples from Israel to Judah, and a threat remaining to Judah itself. In this model Josiah led an emphasis on adherence to 'Yahweh alone', and drafts of written texts were prepared in his reign, and retained in the possession of the Babylonian exiles, which would later be incorporated into the Tanakh. But other scholars consider the presentation of Josiah as the reformist adherent of Yahweh as a later construction, taking newly developed ideals and projecting them back into the Judaean monarchical period.[136] If Josiah had lasting importance, it lay in establishing Jerusalem as the centre of Yahwist religion, which set the stage for its reclamation and development in post-exilic Yehud.

Previous chapters noted the impact of powerful religious leaders, who believed they were receiving divine messages and had the responsibility to build a body of followers to whom they should pass on these divine messages. In the Tanakh we have texts assigned to prophets from pre-exilic, exilic and post-exilic times, with more than one voice included under the name of a single individual in some cases. We can assume that such prophets – Deutero-Isaiah being a prominent example – were highly influential in creating the Judaic theology of a single all-powerful god, as would be presented in the practice and texts of Jewish religion. Other anonymous voices, including those scribes who worked to bring together the books of the Tanakh, share the credit for formulating the movement – a role which belongs to named individuals like Yeshua, Muhammad and Joseph Smith, Jun. in previous chapters of this book.

The Jewish world of Yehud saw a consolidation of religion, a consolidation of religious leadership, but essentially a consolidation of *identity* – Jewishness, the greater Israelite identity. The community was to be bound together by legal rules, by matrimonial rules, by rules of purity, by rituals and practices that included festivals, circumcision, Sabbath observance, and a focus on Jerusalem and its Temple that includes tithes, visits (pilgrimage) and a sense of its centrality.[137] The context is all the more remarkable given the small size and relative poverty of the geographical setting of Yehud, an unimportant landlocked minor province of the Persian Empire. As with Mormonism, Islam and Christianity, a marginal context could provide the location for a challenging world view.

But the setting in which monotheistic Judaism was formulated lay in a place ruled and controlled by outsiders, Achaemenid Persians, whose affiliation was also to a dominant deity, and whose religion we know as Zoroastrianism or Mazdaism.

Chapter 6

Ahura Mazda and the enigmas of Zoroastrian origins

The religion that is today called Zoroastrianism is considered by many to be the oldest of the religions with a single creator divinity at the centre of its beliefs, before the monotheism of Judaism, Christianity and Islam. This divinity was called Ahura Mazda (Wise Lord), from which comes an alternative name for the religion, Mazdaism. The primary religious texts, the Gathas, identify a prophet, Zarathushtra (in more familiar form, Zoroaster), as their author, and he has therefore been widely considered as founder of the religion. While Zoroastrian traditions place the prophet's life in the late 7th to early 6th centuries BCE, for some modern scholars Zoroastrianism, the prophet and his texts stretch further back still, into the 2nd millennium BCE. The origins and spread of Zoroastrianism present many intriguing questions, with passionate disputes and widely differing claims for evidence of the Ahura Mazda cult, the antiquity of the practices, texts and prophet of Zoroastrianism, and the places of its development. Examining the history of these religious beliefs reveals many enigmas. Following the Muslim Arabians' conquests of the Sasanian Empire, Zoroastrian priests committed to writing the sacred texts of the Avesta. A millennium earlier the inscriptions of Achaemenid Persian rulers show they were worshippers of Ahura Mazda, but with no mention of Zarathushtra. The question arises of what impact the religion of their Persian rulers had on the Jerusalem elite who developed and formalised monotheistic Judaism: scholars have identified passages in the later writings of Judaism and early Christianity that echo Zoroastrian ideas. There is a broad consensus that places Zoroastrianism's early stages in Central Asia, where history and archaeology provide a background to the societies where it may have evolved. Yet mysteries remain about the beginnings of this ancient religion.

Discussions of 'Zoroastrian origins' by non-Zoroastrians have been influenced by models taken from other faiths. As western scholars began to study Zoroastrianism, parallels were drawn with those religions that had a founding figure (Jesus Christ or Muhammad – we could add Joseph Smith,

Jun.) and a founding document (the Qur'an, the New Testament – and again, *The Book of Mormon*). An historical examination suggests a better parallel for the development of Zoroastrianism lies in Judaism and the long history and changing patterns of the Yahweh cult, from which familiar forms of Judaism eventually emerged. The cults of Ahura Mazda, the development of Zoroastrian practices and the role of the texts ascribed to the prophet Zarathushtra are similarly diverse and complex.

Modern followers of the faith have come to accept the use of the term 'Zoroastrianism', although this refers to the prophet associated with texts fundamental to the faith, rather than the deity they acknowledge as omniscient. For long they had described themselves as *wehdenan* – followers of the good religion. Similarly, adherents of Islam were long described by outsiders not as Muslims but as 'Mohammedans' (with various spellings), which likewise refers to the prophet rather than the faith. The first historical records of the worship of Ahura Mazda, the inscriptions of Persian Achaemenid rulers of the 6th to 4th centuries BCE, neither mention the prophet Zarathushtra nor cite the sacred texts of the Avesta, so it seems best to refer to the royal cult of that period as Mazdaism.

The co-editor of a recent survey volume on Zoroastrianism observes that a focus on Zarathushtra as prophetic author is relatively modern.[1] Only after the 1860s, when German scholar Martin Haug distinguished the Gathas and other Old Avestan texts from those we call Young Avestan, did the identity of Zarathushtra as author of the Gathas loom larger than his role as a prophet within the whole scriptural canon of the Avesta.

An estimate from 2012 counted about 120,000 members of Zoroastrian communities in the modern world.[2] The largest group are the 60,000 Parsis in India, the majority in Mumbai. The name 'Parsi' reflects their historic origins in Persia, where recent Iranian censuses suggest a total of 25,000 remain. An estimated 20,000 Zoroastrians live in North America and 5,000 in Britain.

As in all religious movements, the beliefs, religious practices and traditions of origin in Mazdaism and Zoroastrianism have varied, evolved and changed over the very many centuries and different contexts of its followers. It simplifies history but confuses our understanding if we assume there is something specific called 'Zoroastrianism' founded by one prophet at one time with a basic text, like Islam, and then search for when and where we can locate it. We cannot expect that model to apply to 'the religion' of groups in the modern, medieval and ancient world: to Zoroastrians under Muslim rule, to Sasanians and Parthians, to rulers and ruled in Achaemenid times and to pastoralist communities of Iran and Central Asia of uncertain antiquity.

Religions develop in their beliefs, their organisation, their activities and their perceptions of the history of their faith and the meanings of their texts.

To Mormons, the prophet Zarathushtra may be among those who received a message from God.[3] Early Islam initially took a pragmatic approach to the religion of those it had conquered in its defeat of the largely Zoroastrian Sasanian Empire. The Qur'an does not include references to Ahura Mazda or Zoroastrianism, nor does it mention Zarathushtra as it does Christian and Jewish prophets; there is just a reference to *majus* or Magians, who would be judged, like those of other religions, on the day of resurrection.[4] But the early Muslim Arabian conquerors accepted the continuation of the religious practices of Zoroastrian subjects in the territories seized from the Sasanians on the same basis as the Christian and Jewish communities they now controlled, and subject to the same payment of tax. Such acceptance of their religious practices defused resistance and the risk of rebellion.

The fire temples which were central to Zoroastrian ritual continued to operate, though it seems this tolerance did not extend to Muslims sharing holy spaces with them, as they did with Christians and Jews.[5] The Islamisation of the eastern territories developed later, in Umayyad and 'Abbasid times, yet even then, the governing Muslims made significant use of the skills of Zoroastrians in administration. Meanwhile, Muslim scholars debated whether Zoroastrians could be considered, like Jews and Christians, as 'people of the book'. It seems very likely that the texts of the Avesta were committed to writing by Zoroastrian priests for the first time only after the Muslim conquests. The broad Quranic reference to the line of prophets who had been sent to humanity before Muhammad ibn 'Abdullah would come to be interpreted as including Zarathushtra.

The New Testament mention of *magoi* from the east who visited the nativity of Yeshua in Bethlehem would seem to convey the image of priests from the Persian religion, using the Greek word which applied to Medes, Persians, astrologers and (our derived word) magicians.[6]

Christian theology describes a struggle between the forces of good and evil, with Satan as the supernatural personification of evil an important part of Christian teaching. The image of such a character as Satan (or Greek *diabolos*) is emphasised in non-canonical Jewish work written in the 3rd and 2nd centuries BCE, when the significantly but not exclusively Zoroastrian Parthian (Arsacid) rulers controlled Iran and Mesopotamia. Fundamental to the Zoroastrian tradition is the conflict between the creator divinity, Ahura Mazda, and the embodiment of evil, Angra Mainyu (also known as Ahriman), who was neither created by Ahura Mazda nor subordinate to him – hence the term 'dualism' (rather than monotheism) is often applied to Zoroastrianism; however, Angra Mainyu is not significant in the earliest texts, receiving only brief mentions in the Gathas, which described evil as 'the Lie'.[7] This influenced the later Jewish image of Satan but Judaism and Christianity avoided the risk of dualism by placing their deity as the creator of everything. Elements of Zoroastrian world views have been identified both in the Essene texts of Qumran and in Gnostic Christian writings. An influential variant of Zoroastrianism during the Sasanian period, Zurvanism, appears to have placed the two divine figures of good and evil on an equal footing, and may reflect a long heritage.

Judaeans of the 6th century BCE exiled to Babylonia were living in a world of polytheism, with Marduk the patron god of Babylon city. The liberator Cyrus the Great, the *messiah* of Deutero-Isaiah, allowed the people he ruled to follow their own gods, and Cyrus may have been a Mazdaist as his successor Achaemenid rulers clearly were.

The Jerusalem elite developed the practices of Judaism and edited religious texts into the books of the Tanakh while under the political rule and administrative control of these Mazdaist adherents whose king they acknowledged had freed them from the Babylonian yoke. Many would only move to Jerusalem and Yehud from Babylonia after spending some generations there under Persian rule. Yet these texts make no direct or implied mention of Ahura Mazda, either positively as an alternative to polytheism or negatively as a foreign cult. They chose not to contrast or compare their image of Yahweh with their rulers' image of Ahura Mazda; instead they contrasted their monotheism to the failure of past societies and rulers of Israel and Judah to adhere to the Yahweh cult, denouncing worship of Baal and other deities. Other ancient empires and rulers were condemned but not the Persians. Unlike in the eastern regions of Achaemenid rule, the Persian administration did not construct markers of the rulers' religion in provinces to the west such as Yehud. Aspects of these Mazdaist beliefs, though not imposed on their subject peoples, would have been known to the group working and editing in Jerusalem.

Scholars have examined the Old Testament, the Tanakh texts, to identify possible influences from the assumed beliefs of Mazdaism or Zoroastrianism of the time.[8] The Deutero-Isaiah text describes a single creator god and attributes to him both good and evil, which has echoes of the fundamental Zoroastrian texts, the Gathas. Trito-Isaiah, assigned to the period of Persian Yehud, may have more of an echo of Ahura Mazda. The Book of Ezra seems to have phrasing reminiscent of the Cyrus Cylinder mentioned in Chapter 5. The Priestly Code in the Torah (Pentateuch) has parallels in Zoroastrian teaching. The late Book of Daniel, written in the common language of the Middle East, Aramaic, includes themes seen as influenced by Zoroastrian models (and it also includes Persian loan words). It has an apocalyptic vision like late Jewish texts omitted from the canon of the Tanakh: 1 Enoch, 2 Enoch and Jubilees.

While the model of Yahweh's relation to his chosen people was unique to Judaism, the broader cosmological framework suggests awareness of the religion of the Persian rulers. But if the questions and issues in that belief system influenced the thinking of Jewish religious leaders, the answers they gave were distinct. As a modern leading Old Testament theologian noted:

> The development within Jewish religion of such matters as angels, dualism, eschatology, and the resurrection of the body is commonly attributed to the impact of Iranian religion. This would not be surprising, at least in theory; for the Jews lived about two centuries under the Pax Persica, and some of their most important books were written in that time.[9]

The source documents

What is the history of the sacred texts associated with Zoroatrianism? Can we assign a date to their creation and to Zarathushtra as author of the Gathas?

There have been widely different suggestions for the date of the prophet Zarathushtra and the antiquity of the texts which formed the canon of Zoroastrian beliefs and practices. The Gathas are 17 poetic compositions in the Old Iranian Avestan language; they are considered to originate with Zarathushtra himself.[10] The doyenne of western Zoroastrian history in a general survey confidently assigned 1400–1200 BCE to the prophet's life, while shifting to a suggestion of 1700–1500 BCE a few pages later.[11] One distinguished linguist went as far as the assertion that 'the Zoroastrian texts were composed in the Late Bronze Age and faithfully transmitted orally up to their first writing down during the Sasanian Empire' (i.e. a period of perhaps a millennium and a half!).[12] By contrast, a tradition among Sasanian Zoroastrians, recorded in writing in the Islamic period, placed Zarathushtra's birth at 628 or 618 BCE, and a broadly similar dating of late 7th to early 6th centuries BCE for his life matches some earlier assumptions in classical, Jewish and Christian sources.[13] However, limited reliance should be put on such secondary sources – indeed, it has been suggested that the 6th-century date derives from ancient Greek imagination rather than any historical confidence within the

Zoroastrian community.[14] Other Greek writers, including Aristotle, placed Zoroaster (as the classical writers spelled him) millennia earlier.

While some leading modern authorities have accepted the later date, other equally distinguished specialists are persuaded by the arguments that place Zarathushtra back into the 2nd millennium BCE. Although the scholars in any generation who are fully literate in the Old Iranian and later Persian languages may be few in number and widely scattered, there is no shortage of passion in their disagreements over interpretations of Zoroastrian texts and origins.[15] But deductions from linguistic analysis have to be considered alongside the nature of real social processes in human history and pre-history. For our understanding of the origins of Mazdaism and development of Zoroastrianism we need to consider direct historical and archaeological evidence, and also trace the history of the key texts, to address these enigmas.

It is unusual to find scholarship arguing for an *earlier* date for religious traditions than that accepted by its adherents; the reverse is a more predictable response of critical history. A common feature of a religious movement is to claim antiquity for its origins, and for its foundational documents, which a critical historical analysis might question. The Mormons consider the golden plates containing *The Book of Mormon* to have been hidden away about 421 CE, and that they are a record of even earlier texts, some of which date back to 600 BCE and before. For Islam, while the Qur'an is accepted as a document brought together not long after Muhammad ibn 'Abdullah's life, many of the accounts of the words and actions of the Islamic prophet detailed in the *hadith* were acknowledged by 'Abbasid Muslim scholars as inauthentic. Authorships of Christian documents from the later 1st and 2nd centuries were attributed to contemporaries and followers of Yeshua from his lifetime and non-canonical works continued to receive such attribution. And in the Tanakh of the Jewish faith, the tradition developed that the five books of the Torah had been composed by Moses, leader of the Israelites out of Egypt, which would imply an origin in the 13th century BCE.

In the assessment of historical sources (as in the interpretation of archaeological finds) academic caution and the search for the simplest of explanations would lead to the preference for a later date for a text, an event, an archaeological structure or a belief system, until an earlier date can be demonstrated; once an earlier date is proven, it demands acceptance.

The religious texts of the Zoroastrian tradition, the Avesta (in the original language, Avestan, and the Middle Persian translations), need interrogating to examine their sources in the light of our contemporary knowledge and debates. We can step stage by stage backwards through the history of the texts and then consider the other evidence of early Zoroastrianism and Mazdaism. Questions of language and interpretations by linguists come to the forefront in this debate.

Manuscripts of the Avesta were collected by western libraries in the 18th and 19th centuries.[16] Indeed, the Middle Persian and Avestan texts we possess are mainly copies made in the 17th, 18th and 19th centuries. Loyalty to the authenticity of the texts as foundational religious documents must be measured alongside the presence over the centuries of copyist errors in languages that were not those of the transcribers, and this led therefore to some differences between the manuscripts. Oral transmission long remained important to Zoroastrian priests. However, the Middle Persian in these texts is similar in style to other Sasanian sources, and this supports the broad authenticity of their contents.

Material earlier than the 17th century is very rare. A manuscript from India now in the British Library, dated to 1323 CE, presents the religious text of the *Videvdad*, written in the Young Avestan language, together with translation and commentary in Middle Persian; there are other manuscripts from the same source in Copenhagen, Oxford and Cambay. Dating to the 9th (or possibly 10th) century is a text from the Ashem Vohu prayer of Avesta translated into the Central Asian language of Sogdian, found at Dunhuang on the Silk Road in north-western China and also held in the British Library.[17] Beyond these manuscripts, the dating of Zoroastrian texts is based upon interpretations of their contents, on linguistic analysis, and on textual references.

The Zoroastrian literature we possess is based on materials put in writing by Zoroastrian communities in the greater Iran region when it was under Islamic control. They had been under Islamic rule after the 7th-century defeat of the Sasanian rulers, and there was a gradual increase in conversion to Islam, especially under the 'Abbasids, who ruled from Baghdad after 750.[18] The incentive for Zoroastrian priests to formalise, record and transmit religious texts would have been increased by such a situation, since the temptation to convert to Islam brought secular advantage. Such conversion in rural areas seems to have been slower than among urban elites, where it reached a peak in the 9th century. While Zoroastrian authorities denounced acceptance of Islam in the strongest terms, they invited renunciation and a return to the faith; however, abandonment of Islam by converts met strong penalties from the Muslim state.[19]

The 'New Persian' language developed over the 8th and 9th centuries, and was written in an Arabic-related script.[20] (In New Persian, the prophet's name was presented as Zardusht, so believers became Zardushtis.) But Middle

Persian (Pahlavi), the language of the Sasanians and since the 3rd century BCE their Parthian predecessors, continued in use as a religious language of Zoroastrianism into the 10th or 11th centuries. In fact, little in Middle Persian has survived other than the Zoroastrian texts, and literature from the Sasanian period is best reflected in later Arabic and Syriac translations from Middle Persian.

The Zoroastrian *Denkard* of the 10th century – that is, 200–300 years into the period of Islamic rule – described the beliefs and customs of the religion and included quotations from many Zoroastrian texts, some of which did not survive into our 18th- and 19th-century manuscripts. The contents of the *Denkard* indicate that the sacred texts had been put into writing in Middle Persian by the 9th century at the latest; this formalised what had survived as oral literature for an unknown extent of time, including the texts seen as dating from the life of Zarathushtra. The tradition of copying the Avesta – not only the original texts, but also translations and commentaries – continued in Zoroastrian communities. New religious works, specifically commentaries on the Avestan literature known as *Zand* (or *Zend*), had been composed in Middle Persian. Our manuscripts are copies of works that combine the commentaries of the *Zand* with the Zoroastrian texts in both the Avestan language and in Middle Persian translations.

Different dates have been suggested for the first commitment of the text and translation of the Avesta to written form. While this had been undertaken by the 9th century CE, some suggest that the start of written records of the Avestan texts can be dated back to the 6th or 7th centuries CE, which would imply it was a response to the initial challenge of Muslim rule.[21] There are scholars who would place the initiative to establish a written version back further, under Sasanian rule, and even the 4th century CE, within the long reign of Shapur II (309–379). If no Zoroastrian texts or commentaries were put into writing earlier than the Islamic period, all the earlier dating of the original texts belongs in the debated hypotheses of specialists in Persian and Old Iranian languages.

It seems likely that the translations we possess from the sacred texts of the Avesta into Middle Persian date from early in the Sasanian period (i.e. from the 3rd century CE) rather than under Parthian rule. These translations were initially only for oral transmission, thus making their contents comprehensible to the broader community.[22] This implies that priests were able to understand and interpret a set of complex texts of great antiquity in the Avestan language and establish a contemporary translation that was theologically sound and authentic. That in itself presents a challenge to those who place the composition of the Gathas of Zarathushtra up to a millennium and a half earlier.

No manuscripts or inscriptions in the Avestan language exist other than the Zoroastrian scriptures. The script in which the Avestan oral literature was recorded appears to have been created by priestly scribes, who added new characters to those of Middle Persian.[23] Significantly, this 'new' script was not used for any other form of writing, secular or commercial, political or religious: 'Avestan' was exclusively the language of the Avesta; linguists who study the Avesta have the Middle Persian translations to use.

The Avesta texts would have been transmitted orally, emphasising their status as sacred compositions.[24] Throughout Zoroastrian history, priests would have learned to repeat the words of the Avesta in the original language and use it in Zoroastrian ritual just as non-Arabic speakers have learned passages of the Qur'an.

The language style of those texts considered to date from the time of Zarathushtra is described as 'Old Avestan', in which the Gathas were written, with other (though possibly contemporary) texts classified as 'Young Avestan' distinguished by the differences in linguistic style, theological emphasis and assumed context of composition. Young Avestan works include the Yashts (dedicatory verses to divinity or divine concepts), the recitals of the *Visperad* and the religious code of the *Videvdad* (*Vendidad*). They can also be described as incorporating 'pagan' material.[25] There is no external evidence to place texts as older or younger: these are classifications based on their stylistic differences as well as their contents, and therefore an alternative description of them is 'Gathic Avestan' and 'Standard Avestan'.[26] In fact, texts described as Old Avestan and Young Avestan have only been found together, combined into the sacred literature of Zoroastrianism, where the Old is wrapped into the Young, with the two elements separated out only in modern times.

When Mazdaism first enters history, in the Achaemenid era of the 6th to 4th centuries BCE, Old Persian was the spoken tongue of the rulers and the written language of Achaemenid inscriptions and documents, and Aramaic the lingua franca of the empire. Avestan and Old Persian are together described as the Old Iranian languages, part of the Indo-European language group.

Some of the Young Avestan texts acknowledge the presence of divinities other than Ahura Mazda; they are also addressed in Yasht hymns. This could imply these core texts of Zoroastrianism are effectively polytheistic.[27] The Avestan 'Hymn to Mithra' is the longest of the Yashts. These materials may incorporate earlier belief systems while now emphasising the worshipping Ahura Mazda ahead of other gods. That would be comparable to Tanakh texts that show a history of Yahweh worship operating while other deities were considered to exist, and loyalty to one or another deity could fluctuate.

The Gathas, in Old Avestan style, are 17 poetic hymns attributed to Zarathushtra. Set in 1,300 lines, they total only 6,000 words (compared with the 77,000 words of the Qur'an and the 65,000 words of the four canonical gospels combined). Some are addressed to Ahura Mazda and some expound the worship of Ahura Mazda to others. They are generally considered to be a single composition; however, they are spoken in different voices – Zarathushtra appearing both as 'I' and as the figure addressed. This has led to a challenge to the concept of a single authorship by a single prophet, with an argument advanced for a collective authorship by Mazdaist priests.[28]

Also in the language of Old Avestan but in prose is the *Yasna Haptanghaiti* (Liturgy of the Seven Chapters) and two holy prayers relating to the Gathas. The *Yasna Haptanghaiti*, with only 850 words in total, appears to include a slightly different theological emphasis, which some consider makes it an earlier document that the Gathas, but there are strong arguments that they belong together as complementary texts, composed at the same time and even by the same individual.[29] We thus have the possibility that everything which historians and linguists have described as an 'Old Avestan' *language* is in the linguistic style associated with one religious leader whom we know as Zarathushtra, at one time, for one purpose.

While traditional approaches in modern scholarship often treated Avestan texts as though they were formal written compositions, because that is how the copies have come down to us, their oral nature is now more fully emphasised.[30] The texts – especially those which were part of ritual practice – would be transmitted, adapted, separated, combined and adjusted. The selection and order of elements in the Avesta would be made to suit each ritual occasion; the Young Avestan materials especially fit such a model. The Gathas, attributed to a single author, may have seen less adjustment in time, as they played a different role in Zoroastrian practice: 'not very different, just more complex'.[31]

The theological context of the two groups may be different but the age difference is unproven.[32] Some specialists see the Old Avestan and Young Avestan texts as broadly contemporary, representing different aspects of an emerging religion.[33] To others, the differences in linguistic style, theological nature and not least their implied social setting mark them as having widely different origins in time and place. One supporter of early dates placed Young Avestan in the early and middle 1st millennium BCE, with Old Avestan perhaps dated to the later 2nd millennium BCE. Others suggest a 400-year gap between the two groups, or at least 'several centuries'.[34]

But if the Young Avestan texts do post-date the Old Avestan, the difference between the groups may not require such a long interval; written language can change readily with context. The 'archaic' style of the texts in 'Old Avestan' could arguably be deliberately adopted for these central religious oral verses, just as *The Book of Mormon* established its authority with archaisms, and the inclusion of an archaic style may have been part of the editing of the Tanakh. Some Young Avestan texts have been noted to imitate Old Avestan.[35] Another interpretation has suggested that at least a portion of the 'Young Avestan' works were composed by Zoroastrian priests during and even after the Achaemenid period, when Avestan existed only as a sacred language: works transmitted orally until later Sasanian times. There are many uncertainties.

It therefore seems possible (though far from certain) that the different core texts of Zoroastrianism were brought together during the period of the powerful Achaemenid Empire when Mazdaism served as the religion of the rulers. But it would be many centuries later, within the late Sasanian period, that a canon of acknowledged religious books was formalised.[36] The literary history alone does not tell us how old are the Gathas and when was the date of a prophet known as Zarathushtra. Since Avestan is related to the Old Persian of the Achaemenids, in a world of different communities, economies, languages and dialects, it requires a great deal of confidence in the linguistic evidence to push far back into prehistory a set of texts we first encounter when translated by priests in or after the 3rd century CE.

The social context presented in the Old Avestan Gathas is a world of pastoralists, especially herders of cattle. By contrast, Young Avestan texts, with their somewhat different theology, feature that of settled agriculture.[37] Does this mark a difference in origin, or are the Gathas consciously set in a less complex world of nomadic peoples, just as the Christian gospels ignored the Hellenistic cities of Sepphoris and Tiberias and focussed on the peasant and fishing lives of Galilee? Do they reflect an origin outside of the core of powerful empires, as most scholars believe?

Linguists have led the debates about the early history of Zoroastrianism. They confirm the links between the Middle Persian translations of the manuscripts and the few other Sasanian texts. They describe the Avestan spoken language, as written down in a script specifically developed by Zoroastrian priests only in the Sasanian period, as an archaic language related to the Old Persian used in the Achaemenid inscriptions but distinct from it. And more significantly, they draw parallels between the language and the literary structure of the Avestan texts and the other ancient religious texts in an

Indo-European language, the Vedic works in Sanskrit, such as the Rigveda, which represent literary materials in Hinduism. These are texts whose dating, like that of the Avesta, is open to debate, with one suggestion giving both a date of around 1200 BCE.[38] The Rigveda itself was an orally transmitted text before being written down some time between the 7th and 3rd centuries BCE and available to us only in copies from a millennium and a half later. Fire played an important role in Vedic texts as it did in the Zoroastrian tradition. If there were a common ancestor for both in the Indo-European speakers of the steppe region of Eurasia, with its harsh winters, it is unsurprising that fire was central to ritual and religion.

We can obtain information on the worship of Ahura Mazda from the history and archaeology of societies where it was an official cult of dynasties – Achaemenid, Parthian and Sasanian – ruling empires whose citizens were adherents to a range of different cults and beliefs. Their images and inscriptions give central importance to the deity Ahura Mazda but include no reference to the prophet Zarathushtra. The pastoralist framework of the Gathas seems to put them within societies very different from that of the great urban-based empires.

The debates about the date of the Old Avestan texts, and their assumed author, need not be debates about the origins of a cult of Ahura Mazda. For as in Judaism the cult of Yahweh predated the texts of the Tanakh and began in a polytheistic world, so Ahura Mazda may have been a deity in Central Asia long before the Gathas. But the theological and literary power of the Old Avestan texts mark a key moment in the evolution of the religion that would be called Zoroastrianism.

Historical Mazdaism

When do we first see the cult of Ahura Mazda in historical records? The search for signs of early Zoroastrianism focusses on images and textual mentions of its deity, and evidence of what became acknowledged as Zoroastrian practice. This includes rites of fire and fire temples in which a sacred flame was kept alight; rituals of purity in fire temples, which contrasted with those of other religious loyalties; and a pattern of treatment of the dead that involved neither inhumation nor cremation, but the exposure of the corpse until the bones, stripped by the action of vultures and dried by the sun, could be collected and placed in an ossuary. But none of these are prescribed by the Old Avestan texts and we cannot assert at what stage of the religion's development they became an essential part of the Zoroastrian practice and identity.

As noted above, describing something as 'Zoroastrianism' or 'Mazdaism' in the ancient world risks combining very different phenomena, and religious observances of the ruled (even within the major Achaemenid cities) may not have followed the practices of the rulers. Variations in religious practice were likely across the regions controlled by their rulers, who did not seek to replace their subjects' religious practices and beliefs with their own cult.[39] While the Achaemenids allowed the worship of Yahweh to develop and thrive in Yehud, as discussed in the previous chapter, no signs of the Persian rulers' cult of Ahura Mazda have been discovered in the archaeology of the Levant region during the two centuries of their control. Respect for local cults was politically advantageous to the rulers from the east.

The Achaemenid dynasty, between the 6th century BCE and their defeat by Alexander in 331, was different from the Parthians (Arcasids), *ca.* 247 BCE to 224 CE, and their successors, the Sasanians, before the Muslim conquests after 642 CE. Zoroastrianism under Muslim rule can be seen as different again. But they have in common that their inscriptions feature Ahura Mazda but make no mention of Zarathushtra.

At Naqsh-e Rustam, near Persepolis, a relief has an inscription that identifies Ahura Mazda presenting a ring that symbolises kingship to Sasanian king Ardashir (r. 224–241 CE). This labelling may post-date the carving of a scene in which a priest rather than a god is portrayed.[40]

The influential Zoroastrian priest Kartir in 3rd-century CE Sasanian Iran is known from his inscription at Naqsh-e Rajab, north of Persepolis.[41] The text (which echoes much in the earlier Achaemenid inscriptions) affirms his loyalty to the kings he served, notes his ritual duties and his acts to benefit Ahura Mazda and other divinities and oppose Ahriman (Angra Mainyu). But this too makes no mention of Zarathushtra nor includes quotes from the Avesta.

Zarathushtra and magi are featured in many writings of the classical Greek world – to which Persia had been a fascination (and a threat). Mazdaism may well have been the largest religious allegiance in the Persian Empire at the conquest by Alexander. Later Greek, Roman and Byzantine authors approached Zarathushtra in different lights: to some he was a religious prophet or priest, while to others he was a philosopher and contributor to secular knowledge, with new narratives developed about his life and role.[42]

The central role of Ahura Mazda in the state and religion of Achaemenid rulers is attested by many pieces of evidence. However, it seems difficult to confirm the presence of Mazdaism before the reign of Darius I (r. 522–486 BCE), and even then the details of religious practices are unclear; the worship of Ahura Mazda may have been previously one of many active cults.

Fire-holders made from white stone were discovered in fragments at the palace of Cyrus's capital city, Pasargadae. Also at Pasargadae are two limestone platforms with stone structures interpreted as locations for fire altars by comparison with images of Achaemenid reliefs (on Darius I's tomb he stands before a fire-holder).[43] This suggests the possibility but not certainty that Cyrus was an adherent of the Ahura Mazda cult, since his reign lacks other evidence for it. We do not know the true nature and cultic context of the Pasargadae platforms.[44] Similar possible temples from the Achaemenid era are known at Susa, at Erebuni (Arinberd) in Armenia and at Fratadara in Persepolis. However, the fire temple, which became a central feature of Zoroastrian worship, has no descriptive term in the Avestan-language texts.[45]

In the Council Hall of the royal capital of Darius I at Persepolis, a distinct carving showing Ahura Mazda is above the doorway to the main gallery of the building. The inscriptions of Darius I in Old Persian with cuneiform script at Elvend and at Naqsh-e Rustam make clear and public his adherence to the divine being Ahura Mazda, and the contract between god and king. An inscription carved at an unreadably high level on the rock face of a cliff at Behistun, in western Iran, seems to be addressed to the divine, not to the king's subjects. Ahura Mazda is 'the great god', one who provides for the happiness of humankind and who established the universe (or 'who created this empire' – an alternative reading).[46] The king owes his power specifically to Ahura Mazda, whom the inscriptions place above 'the other gods' – a contrast with monotheism. Also at Behistun, Darius recorded how he had taken power from one of the magi, Gaumata, who had pretended to be from the royal family; the Elamite-language version in the Behistun inscription records Ahura Mazda as 'the god of the Aryans'.

Darius's son and successor Xerxes I (r. 486–485 BCE) similarly placed Ahura Mazda ahead of other divinities in his inscriptions, which demonstrates differences from the belief system of the Zoroastrian texts.[47] At Persepolis an inscription from Xerxes' reign proclaims 'The man who has respect for the law which Ahura Mazda has established, and worships Ahura Mazda with due order and rites, he becomes happy when living and blessed when dead'.

Further Achaemenid rulers maintained the prominence of Ahura Mazda. However, their texts acknowledged the existence of other gods, whether intended in order to reconcile and not alienate subject peoples, or as an integral feature of contemporary Mazdaism.[48] An inscription of the late ruler Artaxerxes III (r. 359–338 BCE) at the palace in Susa acknowledged three deities, with a request 'may Ahura Mazda, Anahita and Mithra protect me

Key dates	
628 (618) BCE	Traditional date of Zarathushtra's birth
625	Median king Cyaxares's rule begins
609	Median victory over Assyria
585	Death of Cyaxares; accession of Astyages
560	Cyrus's rule begins
551 (541)	Traditional date for Zarathushtra's death
550	Victory of Cyrus over Medes
530	Death of Cyrus; accession of Cambyses
522	Death of Cambyses; accession of Darius I
515	Darius's conquest of the Indus Valley
486	Death of Darius I; accession of Xerxes I
331	Defeat of Persian Empire by Alexander
247	Parthian (Arcasid) rule begins (traditional date)
224 CE	Sasanian dynasty replaces Parthian
636	Muslim victory over Sasanians at al-Qadisiyyah

against evil'.[49] The last deity appears in the Vedic texts of India as Mitra and has an association with fire; by contrast, the important deity Indra of the Vedic texts is characterised as a demon in the Avesta. Mithra, like other names from the Avesta, is a common part of personal names in the Achaemenid era.[50] Persian names of the period also link to Avestan words, as they do in the later Parthian Empire.

Parallels with sections of the Avesta have been identified in the Achaemenid royal inscriptions and the religious activities of the Achaemenid kings from Darius I on. So 'there are passages in the inscriptions that are so close to Avestan texts as *almost* to rule out coincidence'.[51] These have led many scholars to concede that the Achaemenids could indeed be called Zoroastrians, though the debate continues.

In addition to the inscriptions, we possess from Persepolis an administrative archive of clay tablets from the reigns of Darius I, Xerxes I and Artaxerxes I, using cuneiform to write in the Elamite language (rather than the unrelated Old Persian), and some with Aramaic annotations or seals.[52] They include records of supplies for the cult of Ahura Mazda and for cults of deities worshipped by other communities within the Achaemenid Empire, and also references to 'guardians of fire'. Yet they make no reference to fire worship as such; they also mention libation services – offerings to water.[53]

Strikingly, these texts make no mention of Zarathushtra. This would support the idea that the worship of Ahura Mazda in the Achaemenid cities and the prophetic writings of Zarathushtra were not linked; emphasis was on a great god, not on a great prophet and his texts.[54] But a comparison with early Islam could raise other possibilities; as noted in Chapter 3, the earliest inscriptions of the Muslim empire made no mention of the Prophet Muhammad.

A further distance of the Achaemenid imperial practice of Mazdaism from later Zoroastrian teaching is the burial of kings and others from the elite in tombs – dramatic public statements of status – rather than the exposure of the bodies seen in later Zoroastrianism. The Medes from whom the Achaemenids seized power had also practised inhumation.

The first direct evidence of Mazdaism as state cult thus comes from the Achaemenid rulers of Darius I onwards.[55] It lacks key elements that we associate with later Zoroastrianism: post-mortem exposure, definitive monotheism or dualism, mentions of Zarathushtra or direct quotes from Avestan texts in inscriptions. We remain uncertain how closely the use of 'fire temples' in Achaemenid Iran correlates with later Zoroastrian practices. If the religion had old established roots and firmly established orthodox theology and practices, we might have expected these signs. If, however, there was a diversity of practices across a broad region it would not be surprising for a ruling dynasty to select and emphasise those which suited political power and purpose.

The date for Zarathushtra was calculated by Sasanian Zoroastrians in relation to the conquest of Alexander, which implies 628 or 618 BCE for his birth. This might appear rather too exact but a late 7th-century date does match the images assumed by non-Zoroastrian sources.[56] The tradition that he lived for 77 years would place his death at *ca.* 551 or 541 BCE, the time when Cyrus the Great conquered the Central Asian area of Sogdiana (Sogdia), a place which features in Young Avestan texts.

A key point in the development of Zarathushtra's prophecy is dated to his 30th year (thus *ca.* 598–588 BCE), which implies this stage in the worship of Ahura Mazda had been reached two or three generations before Darius's reign, when the Medes were the rulers of an empire stretching east from their Iranian base. These traditional dates for Zarathushtra's active prophesying sit during the final reign of Median king Cyaxares (Uvaxshtra) (r. 625–585 BCE) and that of Astyages (r. 585–550 BCE), who fell to the power of Cyrus.

The core area from which Median power developed was west of modern Tehran, and both final Median rulers were born in Ecbatana in western Iran. The rise of Medea had been marked by their conquest of Nineveh in northern Mesopotamia in 612 and the subsequent collapse of Assyrian power, a westward shift in Iranian rule and focus; yet the Medes also extended their rule to the poorer, more sparsely populated regions eastwards, to control significant areas across eastern Iran.

If the early 6th-century date for Zarathushtra's prophecy is accepted, we have a possible image of the form of Zoroastrianism associated with his texts emerging in an area marginal to the major centres of power, as with the religions described in previous chapters, and at a time of major political upheavals.

The Medes, like the Achaemenid Persians, were speakers of an Indo-European language. Some consider Median religious affiliation had elements of Zoroastrianism, while others challenge this.[57] But it may be a false question: in a range of Indo-European religious affiliations, elements of Mazdaism could have been present in Median society and the rituals of their magi priests without their being followers of Zarathushtra or aware of Avestan religious texts.

A find at the late 8th-century Median site of Nush-i Jan raises the question of the antiquity of the fire cult. In a building described as a fire temple, a mud-brick altar covered with plaster had a shallow depression on a stepped top, most likely to hold fire for ceremonies but not enough to maintain the permanent fire known in later Zoroastrianism. These ceremonies seem to have been associated with a different cult.[58] Even earlier, one possible if isolated early reference to Ahura Mazda lies in an Assyrian text of about 1000 BCE with a name interpreted as Asara Mazas.[59]

Overall, the evidence for Mazdaism is strong in the Achaemenid era, though not as early as Cyrus's reign. The history and archaeology of the Median and Achaemenid Persian Empires based in western Iran are well enough known. We can study their capital cities of Ecbatana on the Iranian Plateau at the east of the northern Zagros Mountains, Susa, facing towards the Tigris on the west of the central Zagros, Pasargadae and Persepolis, at the south of the Zagros. But these areas of western Iran receive no mentions in the Avestan texts, which refer only to places in eastern Iran, Afghanistan and Central Asia. This is the broad region within which linguists place the languages and origin of the Old and Young Avestan texts, and the historical prophet Zarathushtra.

The geographical setting

The wealthiest area and the ancient urban development of Iran lay to the west, where the Zagros Mountains separate the arid interior of Iran from the Mesopotamian plain. But if Zarathushtra and the Avestan texts do not belong in the imperial civilisations of Medes and Achaemenids based in western Iran, and may not even have been known there, we must look away from the Zagros Mountains, across the desert regions of Iran, beyond the Elburz Mountains, which extend along the south of the Caspian Sea, and focus on Central Asia, eastern Iran and western Afghanistan. The prehistory and history of these regions have gradually become better known, but do they set a framework in which we can confidently place the prophet of Zoroastrianism?

Their geography is complex. Places had different names in ancient and more recent history, alternative names in different modern states, and with varying spelling of many of these names when transliterated into Roman characters, as noted below.

The Central Asian region lies south of the Eurasian steppe, and is dominated by deserts and mountains. The Kyzyl-kum (Qizil-qum) and the Kara-kum (Gara-gum, Qara-qum) Deserts are separated by the Amu-Darya River (the Oxus of classical reference), which today ends at the Aral Sea; the Syr-Darya River reaches the Aral Sea further north. Between the Aral Sea and the Caspian Sea is the Ust-Yurt Plateau. The deserts can support some nomadic pastoralism.

Apart from the nomadic groups, the historically settled populations of Central Asia in limited to regions where water was adequate for agriculture.[60] The area of Chach, near modern Tashkent, lies around tributaries north of the Syr-Darya; Ferghana lies on the middle of the Syr-Darya River, east of the Kyzyl-kum Desert; Khorezm (Chores/Coram/Khwarazm, ancient Chorasmia) lies on the area of the lower Amu-Darya River; the Sogdiana region is around modern Samarqand (on the Zerafshan and Qashqa-Darya river valleys); and the Balkh region (including ancient Bactria) is to the south of where the Amu-Darya rises. At the south-east of the Kara-kum Desert, the area around Merv (Marv) on the inland delta of the Murghab (Murgap) River was the location of ancient Margiana.

On the south side of the Kara-kum Desert is the Kopet Dagh mountain range, running from north-west to south-east for *ca.* 300 miles (480 km) and about 40 miles (65 km) wide, reaching 9,750 feet (3,000 m) in height.[61] To the south of the Kopet Dagh, the Atrek (Atrak) River flows westward into the Caspian Sea, and the Herat River (Hari-rud or Tejen/Tedzhen) comes from the south to evaporate in the Tejen oasis, to the south of Margiana. The Atrek is the main line of communication in the region and has long been a context for exchange between agricultural and pastoralist products. To the south of the Atrek are hills of North Khorasan and beyond that the sweep of the arid Kavir Desert and Lut Desert of Iran. Culturally, the area of western Khorasan has been markedly different from eastern Khorasan.[62]

East of the Lut Desert, in the borderlands of Iran and Afghanistan, is the Sistan (Seistan) region, including Lake Hamun and the Helmand river basin on its east side, an area which has a history of wheat production with more cereals and vegetable crops in recent times, to which irrigation is an important contributor. Pastoralist grazing is also a feature of this region.[63]

The majority of Iran cannot be cultivated, and where it can, the management of water is crucial, hence the long-established *qanat* system of underground channels and wells to complement what was available from the river systems. Pastoralists had greater mobility and so could follow seasonal variations in available fodder and natural water on an established route. Half a century ago they were estimated to number 1–2 million, from a population of 20 million within Iran, and they had encountered decades of conflict with the central government.[64]

Place and the Avestan texts

Where should we look for the origin of the Avestan texts, and the authorship of the Old Avestan Gathas? What is the local religious background in which this developed and what were the geographical, social and cultural contexts? Can we see other early evidence of the worship of Ahura Mazda? Modern interpretations which accept an historical Zarathushtra have proposed different locations for the prophet within this region, some favouring Sistan and others the region beyond the border of north-eastern Iran, within the area of today's Turkmenistan, Uzbekistan, Tajikistan and southern Kazakhstan.[65] The name Zarathushtra itself may mean something like 'he who can manage camels'.[66]

The Old Avestan texts do not provide a geographical framework of reference. Their contents are set in a social framework in which cattle were central, with a symbolic role as well as being economic providers of milk, meat and leather.[67] (Cattle also had a significant role in the Indo-Aryan Vedic texts.) Sheep and goat were kept, and both horses and dogs were part of the social world. Significantly, the Old Avestan materials associated with Zarathushtra himself do not mention crop agriculture, while references in the Young Avestan items imply a society with agriculture maintained by irrigation and ploughing to produce crops that included barley and wheat. This difference could have different explanations. It could reflect stages of the development of the religion: the Old in a pastoralist community, where agriculture was not feasible, the Young in a more settled (though apparently still not urbanised) setting. Or if the texts are broadly contemporary, those created in the style described as Old Avestan could be archaic both in literary form and in the deliberate use of images of a traditional society distinct from that of their construction.

Even if the Old Avestan texts were composed in a society of nomadic pastoralists, this does not imply or require that such a society preceded or lay outside of the world controlled by large empires. Throughout the history of Iran and Central Asia from the 3rd millennium BCE to today, settled farmers have existed alongside, interacted and traded with nomadic pastoralist groups.

Within the Young Avestan texts, with their general setting of agricultural communities, there are fuller geographical references. But some of these are clearly mythological, in a framework similar to some of the Vedic myths. A specific geography in the *Videvdad* (*Vendidad*) lists 16 districts to the east and north-east of Iran created by Ahura Mazda, which may imply either the reality or the hope of Zoroastrian influence at the time of composition, or a 'mythological and symbolic' country, or later additions reflecting the spread of the religion.[68] These districts cover a broad area, extending from Sogdiana (the Samarqand region of eastern Uzbekistan) to what is probably north-eastern Punjab in India.[69]

While the dating of the *Videvdad* is uncertain and contested, it is clear that it saw revision and editing over the centuries before the versions we possess.[70] This means it cannot be used to specify a location for Zoroastrian origins rather than for Zoroastrian growth and development, although some scholars have used the texts to advance hypothetical constructions of Zoroastrian development.[71] One major survey of the prehistoric cultures of the region considers that the Gathas place Zarathushtra specifically at a time when the settled agriculturalists and nomadic pastoralists were coming together in a common culture, *ca.* 1000–800 BCE.[72]

Similar in nature, text in the Young Avestan Yashts describes the area occupied by 'the Aryans', from the mythical Mount Hara, across eastern Iran and north to Sogdiana, and another text extends to the Hindu Kush.[73]

Did the description of an Aryan area under Ahura Mazda reflect a long tradition of the Mazdaist religion? Did it reflect areas that had become Zoroastrian only after Achaemenid conquest? Or did it incorporate other legends of ethnic identity, such do the travels in many regions narrated in the Pentateuch, and which in later tradition would be identified with specific sites?

The Zamyad Yasht mentions a more specific geography, focussing on Sistan, the region around the lower Helmand River and Lake Hamun (perhaps the Lake Kayansih that myths would state preserved the seed of Zarathushtra): 'in Avestan geography no other region has received such treatment'.[74]

Core to the Gathas is the arrival of Zarathushtra at the court of a local ruler, Vishtaspa, who features also in a number of the Young Avestan texts. Vishtaspa accepted the prophet's message to become major patron and sponsor of the religion. Text in the Yashts places Zarathushtra's royal patron Vishtaspa in Sistan, and later myths and narratives would develop around both Vishtaspa and Sistan. One scholarly supporter of a later date for Zoroastrian origins suggests Zarathushtra migrated to Sistan from the Sogdiana region.[75] 'Vishtaspa' is also considered to be the name of the father of Darius I, Hystaspes in Greek, as well as that of one of Darius's sons. Such a shared name could indicate that they were specifically named after the major figure in the Avesta, unless the Gathas were created during the Achaemenid period and the character was named after the historical dynastic figure. This is a complex question.

The town of Raga (Rhaga, Ray) at the southern edge of modern Tehran was the eastern town of Median power and became the administrative capital of the Parthians. This later role may have influenced its absorption into Zoroastrian tradition with the legend that placed Zarathushtra himself there. By contrast, later Zoroastrian communities claimed other areas as the heartland of the tradition; some of the priestly group whom classical writers called the magi placed Azerbaijan as Zarathushtra's homeland.[76] Modern Russian nationalists have focussed on the Urals, where they have named Arkhaim as the birthplace of Zarathushtra and Sintashta as his burial place.[77]

Searching through prehistory

The contents of the Avesta suggest a context away from urban settings; the place names in the texts lie in Central Asia, eastern Iran and western Afghanistan. Does the archaeology of those areas provide clues to the early Zoroastrian religion in that area, or to a possible location of a prophet Zarathushtra?

With written records of the cult of Ahura Mazda emerging only in the Achaemenid era, we rely on archaeology to consider the framework in which the religion may have emerged and developed. The inscriptions and carved reliefs of Achaemenid kings help us see a Mazdaism in the historical period but there are no divine images from earlier societies of eastern Iran or Central Asia. The spread of Achaemenid power helped spread the adoption of the beliefs of the rulers in certain regions.

As the religion had developed by Sasanian times, its form and ritual involved specific practices: worship of Ahura Mazda, exposure of the dead (rather than cremation or burial) and the use of fire temples, with an emphasis

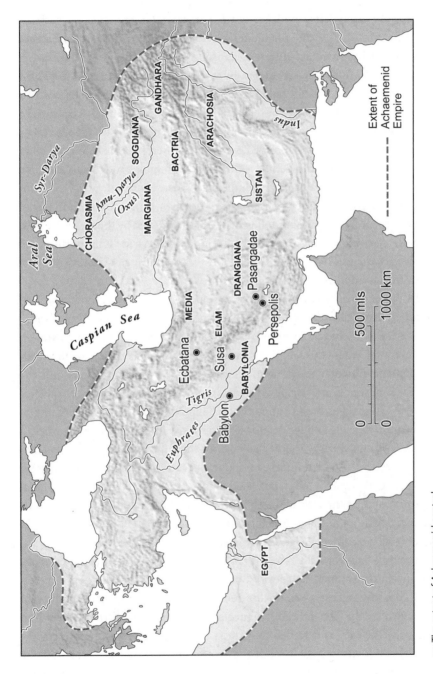

15. The extent of Achaemenid control

on purity in the fire temple rituals. These would be useful indicators of early Zoroastrianism, yet their absence cannot be taken as proof of absence of the religion. We can look for evidence of what are later recognised as Zoroastrian practices, and we can note practices which contrast with Zoroastrian images of ritual purity, or attest different approaches to worship and death. Yet because we do not know the stages by which Zoroastrian rituals developed within the religion, we can only suggest circumstantial indicators of where a form of Zoroastrianism may have existed in prehistoric Central Asia, eastern Iran or western Afghanistan. Use of fire at temples in later Central Asian pre-history is not in itself evidence of Zoroastrian adherence, fire being a feature in many forms of religious activity. Although fire temples and rituals are not a feature of Old Avestan texts, fire is important in the Gathas.

The archaeology of prehistoric Bronze Age then Iron Age communities of eastern Iran and Central Asia, followed by their conquest by the Achaemenids, provides a setting to consider possible times and places for Zarathushtra and the development of Mazdaist practices, even though it may not resolve the questions raised by historians and linguists.

Discussions of prehistory involve discussions of linguistic change and diffusion, especially about how Indo-European languages spread southward. The source of the Indo-European group is agreed to be in the Eurasian steppe, but how and when the languages spread (and the correlation of this with archaeological evidence) remain debated. Linguistic comparisons and the presence, absence or sharing of key terms are indicators of relationships between language groups, but cultural change need not follow the shifts in dominant language, and we cannot with certainty link linguistic categories to groups distinguished by the archaeology of their material culture and settlement patterns.[78] A small number of migrants can influence language change without an equivalent and correlated impact on the economy or material culture visible in the archaeological record. The history of the world records dramatic changes in the dominant language arising from the arrival of influential (and typically male) traders, migrants, armies and colonisers.

The link between Old Iranian languages (Avestan, Old Persian, Median) and the Indo-Aryan languages of South Asia is sufficiently strong to assert their common ancestry within the Indo-European group. Speakers of what developed as the Old Iranian languages may have entered the greater Iran region in the late 2nd millennium BCE, bringing with them some cosmic and religious views seen in both the Avesta and the Sanskrit Vedas of the Indo-Aryans.[79] This means that the deity Ahura Mazda and other divine figures mentioned in the Avestan texts may have their origins in early migrant groups well before the religious texts associated with Zarathushtra. This is a parallel with the development of the Yahweh cult in Palestine, with a possible ancestry late in the Bronze Age of the Middle East.

Large population movements, small migrations, or just the transmission of religious affiliations and ideas require specific paths to travel, and these would follow water courses or trade routes, from areas of sustainable settlement through regions of adequate fresh water to other places suitable for settlement. A feasible geographical setting is required for any interpretation or description of a diffusion in human prehistory, whether this is the spread of a language, an economy, material culture, a gene pool, a religion, or a combination of these transmitted together.

A migration of early Indo-Europeans into western Iran via the Caucasus west of the Caspian Sea, although geographically possible, is thought unlikely.[80] The probable routes for the movement of Indo-European languages, people and associated ideas passed into Iran through the zone south of the Aral Sea, east of the Caspian Sea and west of the Hindu Kush. Within this zone, the Kyzyl-kum and Kara-kum Deserts of Turkmenistan limit likely routes for population expansion and migration. The Amu-darya River from Balkh (Bactria) to the Aral Sea marks a change in environment. A path by which Indo-European populations could migrate into eastern Iran lay south of the Kopet Dagh, following the Atrek River and then the Hari-rud (Herat River) River, which continues a route into Afghanistan. The Atrek alone could bring people into northern Iran, and from western Afghanistan populations (or transmitted cultural elements) could extend south to the border region of Sistan (Seistan), east of Iran's Lut Desert. Linguistic arguments suggest that the eastern Iranian-speakers moved along the Herat River before reaching easternmost Iran and western Afghanistan (Arachosia and Sistan).[81]

The Bronze Age Andronovo cultural complex of the steppe to the north is widely considered to be the source from which migrants speaking ancestral Iranian languages and the Indo-Aryan languages of the Indian sub-continent originated.[82] It is found across a large region of western China, southern Russia and Central Asia, with different areas dated to between the early 2nd millennium and as late as *ca.* 900 BCE. Andronovo traditions included cremation with pit fires, in contrast with later Zoroastrian practice. Reconstruction of the ancestral language of the Indo-Aryans and Indo-Iranians suggests they had no word for 'iron', implying migrations from the Russian steppe before they had developed use of this material.[83]

These migrations therefore belong within the Bronze Age, with the Indo-Iranians in the middle to later centuries of the 2nd millennium BCE spreading southward around or across the Central Asian deserts, into the areas then occupied by the advanced sedentary Bronze Age agriculturalists of the Bactria-Margiana Archaeological Complex (BMAC).[84] The BMAC, sometimes called the 'Oxus civilisation', dates from *ca.* 2400 to the middle of the 2nd millennium BCE. The decline of the BMAC may reflect environmental rather than just demographic causes. It was centred on the upper stretches of the Amu-Darya River and the Murghab river delta, developing urban settlements and a wide trading network. Some have advanced the suggestion that the BMAC groups were themselves of Indo-European origin, even linking the early Iranians to the Complex.[85]

Excavations by Russian archaeologists have exposed BMAC sites where the dead were buried rather than exposed.[86] Temples in the sites of Togolok-21 and Gunur (Gonur) have both round and rectangular fire altars, though these are not a universal feature in Margiana. Fire was a feature of temples at Jarkutan and Dashli-3 in Bactria. This has led some archaeologists to suggest (without any widespread acceptance) an early development of Zoroastrianism in this region.[87]

However, this would place the emergence of the religion in a more urbanised setting than is conventionally assumed. The contrast between the reference frame of the Avesta and the urban civilisation of BMAC is as great as the contrast between the Avestan worlds and Median and Achaemenid urban life. Advocates of the ambitious argument to place Zarathushtra back into the later Bronze Age would need to assign him to one of these dominant cultural groups, and migrants from the Andronovo culture gain more support than a BMAC context.[88]

The Iron Age of Central Asia after the later 2nd millennium BCE provides the setting in which a more cautious view would place Zarathushtra and the Avesta, and the societies that included the pastoralism of the Old Avestan texts and the mixed agriculture of the Young Avestan.[89]

Conventionally, the eastward expansion of the Achaemenid Empire from the mid-6th century BCE marks a chronological break in Iron Age prehistory. But rule from western Iran had only a partial impact on the archaeology of Central Asia; much continuity in material culture shows societies and economies operating in traditional Iron Age mode despite being nominally part of the great empire.[90] It is, however, easier to find signs of Zoroastrianism after the defeat of Achaemenid power by Alexander in 331 BCE than before.

The historian Herodotus, writing in Greek but born in the Persian Empire *ca.* 484 BCE, recorded a geography of territories under Persian control, and these can be compared with information on the Achaemenid inscriptions and reliefs. The Achaemenid provinces of the empire included Parthava, Drangiana, Karmania (south-central Iran), Maka (on the Persian Gulf), Margiana (Merv oasis), Areia, Arachosia and Bactria.[91] Further away from the centre of the empire were Sogdiana, Chorasmia and Gandhara. To the north of the Oxus was Sogdiana (around modern Samarkand), with Chorasmia lying further down the Oxus. Archaeology has sought evidence of possible Zoroastrian practices across this region.

The oasis region of ancient **Chorasmia** (Khorezm) lies in western Uzbekistan and the border region of Turkmenistan. The Amu-Darya (Oxus) River running between the Kara-kum and the Kyzyl-kum Deserts today becomes a delta as it approaches the Aral Sea. Iron Age settlement began around the 9th century BCE, with a cultural change from the 7th century until the Achaemenid control of the region in the 6th century. Suggestions that Chorasmia had earlier importance in Zoroastrianism have gained little support from linguists or archaeologists. This pre-Achaemenid Iron Age is marked by canals and fortified sites, which were long thought to mark settlements, but it seems possible that the fortifications (constructed of mud brick) marked open space, perhaps used periodically by an elite, with settlements lying outside them. Nomadic pastoralism operated alongside settled agriculture.[92]

The site of Kuizely-gyr is among the largest of the fortified sites from the pre-Achaemenid period, covering 65 acres (26 hectares). Within the walls was a large building containing a platform on which ritual fires had been made, but the area lacked domestic occupation.[93] Its use as a cattle kraal by largely nomadic pastoralists therefore seems possible.

Chorasmia was free from external control after Alexander's defeat of the Achaemenids. It became a major centre of Zoroastrianism, developing its own local characteristics. The large fortified site of Akchakhan-kala was the royal seat of the Chorasmian kingdom that emerged after the fall of Achaemenid power. There were 'fire features' in the period of the main kingdom (late 3rd or early 2nd century BCE to the 2nd century CE, after which Sasanian rule overtook the region). A ceremonial complex included areas for presumed royal rituals, with an entrance marked by fire torches, as well as fire altars.[94] A throne leg from such an altar echoes elements of Achaemenid ancestry.[95]

Painted murals from the kingdom depict 'Avestan gods': one huge crowned figure, 20 feet (6 m) tall, is thought to be a deity and was accompanied by two 'bird-priests' represented in a style that appeared later in Sogdiana.[96] This mural is dated between the 1st century BCE and the early 1st century CE. Ossuaries at the site and elsewhere in Chorasmia suggest that exposure of the dead was undertaken.

A dramatic platform excavated at the site of Angka Malaya has been interpreted as a dedicated Zoroastrian funerary building, used from the 1st to 4th centuries CE.[97] At Tash-k'irman-tepe a large platform from the 4th century BCE supported chambers within which were fire altars as well as ash, suggesting it was a fire temple.[98] We thus have a clearly developed locally strong set of practices we would call Zoroastrian, yet they are not matched in the culture of other Central Asian or eastern Iranian localities.

The **Sogdiana** area lies between the Amu-Darya and Syr-Darya rivers and includes modern Samarqand and Bukhara.[99] Sogdiana is listed in the Avestan *Videvdad* as an Achaemenid possession in the Behistun inscription of Darius I. The area had supported prosperous Bronze Age societies before the transition to the Iron Age by the early 1st millennium BCE.

A number of pre-Achaemenid and Achaemenid period 'platforms' found at sites in Sogdiana and to the south in the Bactria–Margiana area have been interpreted as having religious purposes: temples sometimes built over pits contained 'ritual' deposits with surfaces on which fire was placed. These were, however, very varied in form and context, which suggests a range of practices in a period of religious diversity. What seems absent is a fixed form of religious temple extending throughout the Iron Age. This could represent a period in which Mazdaism/Zoroastrianism was developing and changing.[100]

Kok-Tepe, 19 miles (30 km) north of Samarqand, has Bronze Age and Iron Age settlement. Monumental architecture began by the 8th to 7th centuries BCE, and included a fireplace within a courtyard, interpreted as having a ritual or religious function, with the burnt material removed to a corner tower. This settlement was destroyed in apparent invasions of nomadic people in the 6th century BCE, before Achaemenid conquest.[101] Two platforms were then constructed over ritual fireplaces and pits. This change would suggest the religion of the Achaemenids was not that of those nomadic occupiers they displaced.

The large settlement of Kyzyltepa, south-east of Samarqand, of some 50 acres (20 hectares), sat at the border of agricultural communities and nomadic pastoralists, spanning the pre-Achaemenid Iron Age and the Achaemenid period.[102] Crops included barley, wheat, millet and pulses. Animal remains (whether from local stock or trade with nomadic herders) were dominated by sheep and goats, but with an equivalent contribution of meat from cattle. Pigs, horses and donkeys were present and some camels, cats and dogs.[103] A monumental structure of the Achaemenid period comprising a large tower with a platform on the top suggests the possibility of a surface for fire in a religious ritual.

Following Achaemenid conquest of Sogdiana in the mid-6th century BCE, which became the furthest area of the empire in the north-east, they established the settlement of Cyropolis (Kyreschata). But, overall, Achaemenid conquest did not dramatically alter the local cultural norms of Sogdiana, which was marginal to Achaemenid wealth and ambitions.[104]

Sogdian archaeological finds do not provide firm evidence for Zoroastrianism before the Achaemenid conquest, although fire was part of religious rituals. Sogdiana would become an important centre of Zoroastrianism after the Achaemenid period.[105] It was a major territory along the Silk Road, and Sogdian influences extended eastward, to China. At Yerkurgan (Er-kurgan), north-west of the modern town of Karshi in southeast Uzbekistan, is a high tower typical of Zoroastrian exposure of the dead, dated no earlier than the 1st century BCE.[106] A temple from the 3rd to 4th centuries CE was later discovered at the town, which became the capital of early medieval southern Sogdiana.

Sogdiana's crucial development as a strongly Zoroastrian centre in the centuries after Achaemenid rule might account for the tradition that placed Zarathushtra himself in this region. Such a phenomenon would be comparable to the claims for localised apostolic visits by later Christian communities in India and western Europe.

Further south, the **Margiana** area around the inland Murghab delta in Turkmenistan, and the neighbouring relatively fertile **Bactria** region around Balkh in northern Afghanistan and southern Uzbekistan were marked, as noted above, by the prosperous Bronze Age BMAC tradition in the 2nd millennium.

The term 'Yaz culture' is applied to the Iron Age sequence in Margiana and Bactria that followed the BMAC from the later 2nd millennium BCE until the Achaemenid conquests. If archaeological change were correlated with linguistic change in Central Asia, then the emergence of the Yaz communities might be an indication of the arrival of Iranian languages from the north. In Margiana, Iron Age settlement was based around oases, and included constructions of a defensive nature.

Significantly, there seem to be no significant changes in economic strategies and resource use between the later 2nd-millennium Early Iron Age (Yaz 1), 1st-millennium Middle Iron Age (Yaz 2) and the Achaemenid period.[107] Settled communities relied on sheep, goats and cattle throughout this period, together with cereal crops. However, the area did see significant Achaemenid construction, including some that suggests palaces. The Oxus treasure found in the 1870s demonstrates the value of Bactria to the

Persian Empire.[108] To the west, the Dakhistan cultures near the south-east of the Caspian Sea, with fortified settlements, appeared distinct from the Yaz culture. Archaeological work in Areia (Haraiva) to the south of Margiana in the Hari (Herat) River valley of Afghanistan awaits more peaceful times.

The absence of burials from the earliest Iron Age sites in Margiana and Bactria stimulated the idea that this reflected the exposure of the dead as seen in later Zoroastrian practice, therefore providing an argument to identify Zoroastrianism in this early period. However, the practice of burial is found in *later* Yaz stages, which would seem to undermine this suggestion. The diversity of practices around the dead in the archaeology of the Iron Age of Central Asia implies there was no established and unified religious practice that could be identified as a coherent religion.[109]

The **Sistan** region of easternmost Iran and western Afghanistan, the historical area of Drangiana or Sarangians, was featured in the Young Avestan texts as a location of Zarathushtra and his patron Vishtaspa and some modern scholars have accepted this as historically possible or even probable. However, this prominence in Zoroastrian narratives may follow rather than precede the Achaemenid conquest of the region.

Bronze Age Sistan was studied in detail at the substantial urban settlement site of Shahr-i Sokta, which was occupied through the 3rd millennium BCE and then again from *ca.* 1850–1700 BCE.[110] There seems very limited occupation of the region between the Bronze Age and Achaemenid settlement. This 'gap' indicates, at the least, that the region was not one of significant cultural development during the pre-Achaemenid Iron Age, possibly because of climatic change that followed the Bronze Age decline.[111] An alternative explanation might be that, in a context of climatic and social decline, only nomadic pastoralists utilised the region and they have not yet been identified in archaeological survey.

If we accept that the Gathas were composed within a nomadic pastoralist community, then an archaeologically invisible context like that of pre-Achaemenid Sistan could apply.[112] But it is not the land of a regal Vishtaspa.

The large urban settlement of Dahan-e Ghulaman, constructed by the Achaemenids most probably as the administrative centre for the region they conquered, has been described as 'magnificent mud brick architecture in the desert terrace'. Here a religious structure is interpreted as a fire temple. Significantly, it did not follow the orthodox practices and purity laws associated with later Zoroastrianism, as animal remains were mixed with the ashes.[113]

The impact of Achaemenid occupation seems to have transformed Sistan from a minimally inhabited backwater into a substantial complex society. That changed world provided a context in which Zoroastrianism could flourish and develop, which helped create the image of Sistan as a place of importance to the Zoroastrian tradition. A fire temple uncovered by archaeological work at Kuh-e Khajeh shows the rituals established by the Parthian period.

Conclusions

As archaeological field survey, excavation, interpretation and reinterpretation of finds continue to expand, and explore areas such as western Afghanistan, we may expect changes to the pattern of knowledge outlined above. Overall, an impression from the region is that during and after the Achaemenid Empire, versions of what would later be called Zoroastrianism flourished in the areas that had fallen under Persian rule from the 5th century BCE. Before then there are elements that resemble aspects of the religion but no firm evidence for the unified practices that would become considered basic to Zoroastrianism. This diversity might suggest that it was not until Parthian or Sasanian times that the key practices we associate with the religion had become established orthodoxies. Importantly, the Gathas lack any reference to exposure of the dead or fire temples.

Questions of dating the emergence of Mazdaism, or Zoroastrianism, of the Avestan texts and of the prophet Zarathushtra involve complex arguments about language with diverse assumptions. Archaeology and history can set a framework for these debates but not resolve the issues. Sometimes it appears that the more we study, the less we know.

The arguments are least productive if it is assumed there was a single religion called Zoroastrianism, formed with a pioneering prophet, with a founding text of prophetic literature created in Old Avestan, and a set of practices requiring adherence. That is the model of Mormonism, Islam and Christianity. More useful is an historical analogy with the Yahweh cult and Judaism: diverse contemporary practices across a large region over many centuries, including a literature of oral traditions that developed, changed and was redacted, and a set of beliefs, varying with time, place and society, with differences between the religion of the elites, rural and urban groups.

It would therefore be quite possible (though far from certain) to assign an early date to the worship of Ahura Mazda, while giving a relatively late date to Old Avestan literature, with Zarathushtra creating theological develop-ment within an already existing, even strong, cult. We can consider a deity, Ahura Mazda, to have been worshipped in areas of Central Asia and greater Iran, perhaps for an extended period before the inscriptions in the reign of

Achaemenid Darius I and his successors that show an adherence of the rulers to Ahura Mazda. We can envisage magi – priests from Iran – performing different roles in different times and places.

The sacred texts of India, the Vedic literature in the Indo-Aryan language of Sanskrit, have been compared to the Old Avestan texts both in forms of expression and in linguistic elements.[114] Fire is a theme common to the literature of Indo-Aryan Rigveda and Old Iranian Avesta. Fire was a feature of rituals of Medes and Achaemenids, of the Central Asian Iron Age and beyond. Tracing this to a common source of Indo-European speakers of the steppe shows us only a stage in the development of religious practices. Mitra or Mithra exists in both traditions; Indra was treated differently in each; Ahura Mazda is not known in the Vedic literature. There are some similarities between mythical elements in Vedic and Avestan texts: ideas of the divisions of the earth, its mountains and seas. But specialists do not suggest the Vedic texts could have influenced the composition of the Gathas by emulation of style or content. One scholar has argued that the origins of Buddhism lay in a reaction against the influence of Zoroastrianism in the areas of western India conquered by the Achaemenids.[115]

Tracing the evolution of the Avestan texts is made more complex not only by their intrinsic nature, but by their first commitment to writing more than a millennium after the Achaemenid era, in a language exclusive to them (although related to Old Persian), and only alongside Middle Persian translations. The language difference of so-called Old and Young Avestan seems to tell us little about their relative age, though their theological differences show that Ahura Mazda worship included a diversity of beliefs.

Like the Homeric epics, the Old Avestan text of the Gathas is traditionally associated with one author, Zarathushtra, whose name does not occur in the Achaemenid or even Sasanian inscriptions. As with the study of Homer, there are some who consider the Gathas a collective oral literature, but most see them as originating with one author.

An unconvincing argument suggests that since the Young Avestan texts refer to settled agriculture and Old Avestan to pastoral activities, one must derive from a rural agriculturalist settlement and the other from specialist nomadic pastoralist communities, both well beyond the time and place of advanced cultures. In turn, this interpretation is used to push their origins (and Zarathushtra's dates) far back, and sometimes into the deep prehistory of the Eurasian Bronze Age.

There are challenges to this approach. The broadest reach of even the powerful Achaemenid Empire include urban, semi-urban, rural farming and nomadic groups, all contemporary, and all with a variable level of interaction. A community with an emphasis on sheep, goat or cattle pastoralism would readily be found within a complex empire. Indeed, it was still to be found in modern Iran. A description of Iran in the 1960s stated:

> The life of Iran is dominated above all by the disparity between the nomadic peoples and those who have settled – between the shifting habitat of the former and the permanent homes of the latter.[116]

Another reservation about such contextual dating of the Avestan texts is by comparison with the texts of other religions we have discussed, which did not reflect the dominant culture and structure of the society in which they were introduced. Joseph Smith, Jun.'s *The Book of Mormon* presents a world very far from that of the United States in the 19th century, and indeed very far from that of pioneering white farming families. The Qur'an has its own regional focus, even though Muhammad ibn 'Abdullah had worked for many years on trade routes to the sophisticated cities of the Levant. The books of the Tanakh, edited and brought together within Persian Yehud, referred back to a Babylonian exile but said little about the contemporary cities and palaces of the Persian Empire. And, as emphasised in Chapter 4, the gospel accounts of Yeshua that form the basis of Christianity bypass the fact that he grew up within walking distance of a major sophisticated city of the Hellenistic-Roman world and began his preaching close to another. Religious texts focus on what they want to say and present a context for this message that suits their purpose.

Such an approach does not demonstrate that Zarathushtra and the Gathas are necessarily late, but it does question the proposals for a very early date based on content and apparent context. The remaining arguments for the antiquity of the Gathas are therefore linguistic. Since Old and Young Avestan are Old Iranian languages related (but not identical) to Old Persian, it is impossible to be certain if they are contemporary with each other and with Old Persian, or were regional languages, or if they were earlier or even later in time. Comparisons between the Vedic Rigveda and the Avesta have formed a large part of these discussions, and appear to present a stronger case for placing the texts much earlier than the 7th–6th century BCE dates found in Zoroastrian tradition.

This would help resolve the issue if it were not for the wide disagreements between distinguished scholars with expertise in the study of Indo-Iranian and other Indo-Aryan languages. Some would see some or most Young Avestan texts as dating centuries before the Achaemenid era, but others as contemporary with the Achaemenids, and, with the Old Avestan, much earlier. A few would see even the Old Avestan texts as dating from the 7th to 6th centuries BCE. This would make them regional variants of the Mazdaist religion with a local language distinct from but related to that of western Iran. Non-linguists cannot confidently resolve these debates.

It is difficult to subscribe to an image of a founding prophet creating texts in the late Bronze Age of Central Asia, that is, before 1200 BCE, and these texts being transmitted orally in the language of that time for 2,000 years before being accurately translated and committed to writing. If such an early date for a foundational prophet of Zoroastrianism and his texts were correct, then their absence from the iconography of Persian worshippers of Ahura Mazda would need explaining, as would the diversity of religious and burial practices across the Central Asia region.

Indications in the texts would allow southern Central Asia, eastern Iran or western Afghanistan as the location of their origin and Zarathushtra. As noted above, a number of individual locations mentioned in the Avesta did become centres of the Zoroastrian religion; the question remains of whether the final version we possess of the texts include at least some of those places because of their adoption of Zoroastrianism.

So, enigmas remain. A conservative approach would consider a later date for the authorship of the Gathas as safer than an earlier date, whether within the pre-Achaemenid Iron Age, or in those areas conquered by the Persian Empire, or even after that empire had lost its power. But we should be fully prepared to adopt an earlier date if the evidence were conclusive. If such a later date were assumed for Zarathushtra and the composition of the Gathas, it would still be reasonable to consider that there was a long extent of religious development of the worship of Ahura Mazda behind them, with Zarathushtra as a reforming prophet at some place and time unknown, and the development over time of a range of orally transmitted sacred texts. An analogy for this would be the history of Judaism, with parallels in the prophets of Israel and Judah and the long evolution of the Yahweh cult.

Whatever the level of influence of Mazdaism or Zoroastrian ideas on passages in the Tanakh, these were in the background as the religion of the Persian rulers of the areas where monotheistic Judaism developed. The cosmology of later Judaism is found in Christianity, and Jewish themes are notable in the texts of Islam. Modern religions such as that of the Mormons incorporate both a Jewish Old Testament and a Christian New Testament background. While there is no simple linear development in the religions that extended from the Mazdaism of Iran or a Zoroastrianism of Central Asia or the early forms of Judaism in Palestine, the links between these multiple religions extend across a vast stretch of time and place to provide the mono-theistic tradition.

Chapter 7

Prophets, religions and history: some conclusions

This book has not set out to demonstrate a broad-ranging theory or to test a set of hypotheses on the early history of religions. It has not addressed the broad questions of why religion has played such an important part in social and individual life. It focusses on the context in which individual religious movements first developed. It has not sought to prove a point, beyond the unexceptional observation that history written from the conventions of critical scholarship will differ from that written when advancing or supporting an individual religion.

Each reader will reach different conclusions when considering and comparing the different religious traditions and will, hopefully, be stimulated to read more of the debates and competing interpretations, including those in the bibliography and notes. There is much we do not know about how an individual religious movement began and why some continued and developed while others did not. If everything was clear and certain we would not need any more research by historians, linguists, archaeologists and those who study theology and the history of ideas. We may rarely have the benefit of a completely new ancient document but a brilliant new insight can change the focus of the debate. In archaeology, with its constant field research, a single excavation, even a single find, can challenge our assumptions.

But there remains a large gap – a binary divide – between those who consider that such debates are about the results of human agency, the norm of secular historical discourse, and those who choose to say that if we do not know something for certain, then the view involving divine and supernatural agency that arises from faith and adherence to (their own) religion remains valid.

A number of discussion points, themes and ideas do emerge from the history of the religious movements' origins outlined in the previous chapters. These focussed on movements which were or became part of the monotheistic tradition, and the presence in the narratives of 'prophets', even if, as with Judaism and Zoroastrianism, some of those figures were seen as part of the deeper past. Such individuals were thought to have a special link to the divine. Individual religious reformers were important in the development of religions elsewhere, such as Siddhartha Gautama (the Buddha), but not in the same role of receiving and transmitting a direct divine message or text.

Visions and cults

With other major religions, those included in this book – Mormonism, Islam, Christianity, Judaism and Zoroastrianism – all succeeded in attracting significant numbers of adherents across many regions and persisting through time to the present day, although not without significant divisions and schisms. Far more numerous are the sects and cults whose impact was smaller or short term, and even greater the number of preachers and visionaries whose ideas and activities had no impact beyond their own lifetime.

There have been many new religious movements through to the lifetimes of readers of this book, almost all beginning with the words and activities of a single individual. A founding figure is a norm: 'new religions are rarely initiated by a committee.'[1] What makes someone's religious experience, and personal belief in a message from a supernatural source, lead to a following, develop as a cult or sect, and even become a lasting religious movement?

We can repeat here the observation in the introductory chapter. Everyone considers the majority of people in the world, past and present, to be misguided in their religious ideas and affiliations; but they make an exception for their own beliefs and the group of co-believers who share these. People see the prophets of other religions as false prophets and their rituals as ineffectual, and often consider their texts to be of human rather than divine inspiration. The commentator from a non-religious standpoint extends this perspective without the exception. It is a rare individual who can consider every faith, movement, prophecy and text as a different but equally valid expression of the divine.

Many individuals have perceived that they were receiving a message from God or a god, from a messenger of God (or indeed of Satan), that they were communicating with another supernatural being, or with the spirit of a deceased individual. These may be told or decide that they must spread the message they have received.

Followers of established religions may be advised of the need to seek guidance from God – which presumes they will indeed receive such guidance. 'God spoke to me' is not a rare claim. Many evangelical Christians, for example, affirm they were instructed by God to spread the word. If such guidance is broadly within the context of a locally conventional religion, it may thrive without being seen as a challenge to the establishment and may serve to reinforce that religious faith.

The Tanakh or Old Testament presents the words and deeds of the prophets as core to the message of Yahweh to guide his chosen people. Christian visionaries, when accepted by the authorities, may become saints, while those not so accepted are historically condemned as heretics.

The Maid of Orleans, Jeanne d'Arc (Joan of Arc, 1412–1431), stated that her visions and messages from angels and saints began when she was 13; French royal support led her to play a pivotal role in French resistance to the English during the Hundred Years War, before English-backed authorities had her burned for heresy. But the Maid of Kent, Elizabeth Barton (1506–1534), whose public prophesying began at the age of 19, met a reaction that resulted in her execution once she announced that messages from God were critical of the policies of King Henry VIII. Modern visions continue in all times and places. The second Prime Minister of Australia, Alfred Deakin (1856–1919), was an adherent of the Spiritualist movement and his connection with otherworld spirits included taking dictation in his youth from John Bunyan, author of *A Pilgrim's Progress* (1678).[2]

The vast majority of people who have what others would describe as a religious delusion do not secure a following. This book has mentioned that Joseph Smith, Jun. in the United States, Yeshua in Palestine and Muhammad ibn 'Abdullah in Arabia shared time and place with other prophets and preachers whose ideas failed to achieve the same lasting impact. The stories of the Tanakh (Old Testament) prophets present them as defenders of Yahweh against the cults, priests and prophets of other competing deities. Since the later 19th century, and especially in 'western' urban societies, many visions, inspirations and interpretations have led to a substantial growth in cults of varied success, reflecting in part a tolerance for challenges to dominant established religions – or a confidence these would not be affected.

It therefore seems artificial to speak of 'prophets who fail'. There is a vast spectrum, ranging from the individual whose impetus to preach a message goes no further than their immediate family, to those who acquire a temporary following for part of their lifetime, to cults which are successful for a longer period before they fade away. Prophets who fail vastly exceed prophets whose legacy continues.

Within different communities of past and present, the response to and tolerance of individuals who claim to experience supernatural communication differ widely, from reverence as a shaman to expulsion (or death) as a heretic. In the urbanised modern world, such visions may be ignored, acknowledged by some, or lead to medical attention.

The standard reference work in professional clinical psychiatry, the *Diagnostic and Statistical Manual of Mental Disorders* (DSM-5), includes a classification of 'Delusional Disorder: Grandiose Type', which usually refers to an individual's belief that they possess an unrecognised talent:[3]

> In grandiose type, the central theme of the delusion is the conviction of having some great talent or insight or of having made some important discovery. Less commonly, the individual may have the delusion of having a special relationship with a prominent individual or of being a prominent person (in which case the actual individual may be regarded as an impostor). Grandiose delusions may have a religious content.

But DSM-5 notes elsewhere:

> Ideas that appear to be delusional in one culture (e.g., witchcraft) may be commonly held in another. In some cultures, visual or auditory hallucinations with a religious content (e.g., hearing God's voice) are a normal part of religious experience.

We do not know how many people experience what they perceive as a divine message, but we can use a very tentative example. Delusional disorders of all kinds are estimated in DSM-5 to have a lifetime frequency of 1 in 500 individuals (a figure based on patients in western societies and particularly US experience). If only 1 in 10 of these had a religious content, only 1 in 50 of those persisted enough to secure family belief in their experience, and only 1 in 50 of those announced their vision further and secured any following, that would imply that there are in the world at least 600 people who are or will develop as religious visionaries or prophets. This proportion, applied to an estimated total of humans since the origins of agriculture, gives us a minimum of 8,000 individuals.

Such a large figure can be compared to estimates of the number of New Religious Movements (NRMs), which have increased especially since the 1960s, inspiring a burgeoning academic field of study. A review in 1999 suggested there were then 600 NRMs in Britain and 2,000 in the United States.[4] The statistical difficulty is, of course, how to distinguish between a small variant of an established sect or religious group and a quite new movement. A catalogue of the more established and successful NRMs classified the majority of them as derived from major established religions, even if some are western developments claiming Asian religious affiliation and heritage.[5] Some can be considered as quite independent, like Subud in Indonesia (originating in the 1920s), Rastafarianism (from the 1930s), or movements such as Scientology (from the 1950s) and Transcendental Meditation (also the 1950s).

An estimate of worldwide totals of religious adherents for 2010 suggested there were 63 million in NRMs. That would be 0.9% of the world population, compared with 32.8% Christians, 22.5% Muslims (up from 12.6% a century earlier), 13.8% Hindus and 11.8% agnostics/atheists (up from a tiny 0.2% a century earlier).[6]

Without influencing and retaining followers there is no movement. Studies of NRMs reject the idea that those who join cults do so because of mental health issues, although they may address the stresses in life by choosing such an affiliation.[7] A person's behaviours may change after they have joined a cult and new stresses are found around the decision to leave. The psychology of mass movements demonstrates many contexts in which people may join a cult, and the appeal of a new and direct solution to the many challenges of life – whether a religious, political or social programme and community – is readily understandable. It is especially appealing when presented in a well crafted narrative by an individual charismatic figure who presents without doubt and reduces complexity. The greater the isolation of a group, the greater is the confidence of its members; condemnation by the wider society may strengthen and serve to encourage its survival.

A visionary must convince others, a process that develops stage by stage and gradually changes the leader's view of their own role. For NRMs these stages have been classified as an Initial Discovery Moment, followed by the Public Sphere Entry Moment, then the Expansion/Consolidation Moment.[8] The term 'charisma' seems most appropriate here – charisma may be reported by cult members as an aura around a leader. Studies of charisma in religion refer back to the classic work of sociologist Max Weber.[9]

The psychiatrist Anthony Storr applied the term 'gurus' to a range of influential people whose belief in themselves and the ideas they proselytise lead them to acquire a cult following.[10] His category ranges from Carl Jung and Sigmund Freud, classed as secular gurus, to Jim Jones and David Koresh, leaders of extreme religious cults, both of whom led their followers into violent deaths, and to less threatening figures such as George Gurdjieff and Rudolf Steiner. Storr notes that gurus commonly claim to have been granted an individual spiritual insight from God or other non-human source, and find that belief reinforced by the support of others: dedicated followers whom they lead with single-minded determination.

From a psychiatrist's viewpoint the unusual perspectives that come from gurus and prophets may emerge from a period of stress, mental or indeed physical.[11] But that does not mean they need have psychiatric problems or that what they say is delusional in a clinical sense.

Critics often suggest that such 'gurus' are fraudulent in their presentations. Adherents of one religious movement have frequently made such an assessment of those from another. But if a tentatively advanced set of beliefs is endorsed by an ever-increasing number of believers, any uncertainties the progenitor may have had would seem to be removed and the question of authenticity becomes less important. The support of others provides reassurance that the insights have come from God or another divine source. To transform a personal vision into public proclamation requires self-confidence, and the reaction of a wider audience can reinforce such self-confidence.

Prophets and success

Some themes appear to achieve impact for a religious message, but they are not universal. Continuity of religious experiences can be an important contributor, although only a single 'vision' can be important. Paulos (St Paul) experienced the appearance of Yeshua once, 'on the road to Damascus', and no further such contact appears in the biblical narrative. By contrast, the dictation of the Qur'an by the angel Jibril to the Prophet Muhammad ibn 'Abdullah took place in multiple stages over 23 years. Joseph Smith, Jun. had several encounters with the angel Moroni. Visions of Mary, the mother of Yeshua, have been relatively common in the history of Roman Catholic Christianity, with some people experiencing multiple apparitions; there have been an estimated 21,000 sightings since the 4th century.[12]

Family attitude can be a key factor in an individual's decision to take their vision further, and family involvement in a new movement can be central to its spread. If an individual declares they have divine instructions to teach a new set of beliefs, the response of their immediate family may determine the outcome. The inspiration may go no further if a family successfully discourages the seer from acting on their visions, or refers them for help and advice to an elder or priest or counsellor or psychiatrist – whatever fits the culture. But if family, friends and a large number of adult followers accept the validity of claims to a religious message, then for psychiatry to categorise it as delusion is a challenge to the terminology; psychiatrists refer to a shared delusion (usually within a family) as *folie à deux*. But when family members believe, support and encourage the seer's belief it can move to the next stage.

Joseph Smith, Jun. had substantial support from his family in the formation of the Latter-day Saints. His wife, Emma, was persuaded of his divine role and message; his father, Joseph Smith Sr, was cited as one of the witnesses of the golden plates and was an active leader of the new church; his mother, Lucy, was a Mormon leader who wrote a biography of her son and his visions; his brother, Hyrum, followed Joseph so strongly they met death in the same incident. However, sons of Joseph Smith, Jun. were involved in arguments about succession in Mormon leadership and became leaders of the break-away Reorganized Church of Jesus Christ of Latter-day Saints.

In the historical traditions, Muhammad ibn 'Abdullah's first converts were his wife, Khadija, her children, and his young cousin (and later son-in-law) 'Ali ibn Abi-Talib. As Islam grew, the extended family played an important role in the political and religious aspects of the movement. The first four caliphs after the Prophet's death were respectively his father-in-law Abu Bakr, another father-in-law, 'Umar, his son-in-law 'Uthman, and then 'Ali ibn Abi-Talib.

Mary the mother of Yeshua (Jesus) plays a major role in the Christian narrative, including the Catholic and Orthodox belief in her bodily assumption to heaven. Her support in life for Yeshua's mission is implied though rarely stated: the gospels record her at the Temple when a young Yeshua was questioning teachers, and she is placed at the miracle of turning water into wine. Yeshua's mother and brothers are described as standing outside while he was preaching.[13] James is mentioned in the New Testament as the brother of Yeshua and is identified in early Christian tradition as a key leader of the emerging Christian movement in Jerusalem.

The Tanakh narrative of exiles returning to Jerusalem from Babylonia also implies families who stayed together and then moved back to re-establish the Yahweh cult in the light of their identity maintained in exile. By contrast, the tradition of Zarathushtra had him develop his prophetic role after he had moved away from his family. And the narrative of Siddhartha Gautama in the formation of the Buddhist faith was marked by his renunciation of the elite role intended for him by his father, and turning his back on his family.

So, family support can be important in the first stage of expounding a prophetic message, but not universally. Many modern NRMs originate when someone is brought up in a deeply religious family and makes a break both from their family and from its affiliation.

Women were important supporters of the founders of Mormonism, Islam and Christianity in the traditions of those religions. The majority of religious leaders through history have been men, reflecting the overall patriarchy of their societies. But a sense of revelation of the divine – and the imperative to share that more widely – is not exclusively male, although we should not generalise from individual examples. Modern NRMs include cults in which women are the leaders, some in response to male leadership in conventional religion. Leading authority in the Church of Jesus Christ of Latter-day Saints has remained in the hands of men but the time and region of its origin saw influential women in religious innovation. Ann Lee (1736–1784) preached her revelations in England and the United States, where her followers, the Shakers, continued their faith into the 20th century. Ellen White (1827–1915) proclaimed her visions of God as one of the founders of the Seventh-day Adventists. Cora Scott (1840–1923) was one of the influential figures in the founding of the 19th-century Spiritualist movement. Helena Blavatsky (1831–1891) founded the Theosophical Society in 1875, though citing Asian sources and not identifying as a prophet.

The very numerous women saints recognised by the Roman Catholic Church include many who proclaimed direct communication from God and his angels, although this did not give them positions of authority in the Church outside of the convent. In the Tanakh several women are identified as a prophet (*nebi'ah*), with Miriam, Deborah, Huldah and Noadiah named. In Islam the famous 8th-century figure of Rabi'a al-'Adawiyya al-Qaysiyya was an influential mystic and ascetic. But generally it appears that the occurrence and frequency of women prophets and leaders of religious innovations were determined, and limited, not by divine choice but by the cultural norms of society.

The power of words appears all important in religious movements. Oratory, the ability to convey the content of personal religious inspiration and bring together a community of followers, commonly forms a significant part of the appeal of an NRM leader. Successful preachers of modern times have been able to hold an audience for hours at a time; and foundational texts of ancient religions may have been memorised and only later recorded in writing. As described in previous chapters, Mormonism began with the dictation of *The Book of Mormon* and continued with the organisational work and new works and revelations by Joseph Smith, Jun. The Qu'ran was proclaimed by the Prophet as the religious texts of the new movement and written down by others, and the work of Muhammad ibn 'Abdullah in organising a community of believers and then a military force implies the power of his own charismatic oratory. Yeshua wrote nothing, and though the text of the gospels is not considered stylistically fine Greek, the record of his preaching is their core; Paulos's letters show his inspirational control of words. The

Tanakh includes some of the most powerful and magnificent literature of the pre-classical ancient world. The Avesta was learned and transmitted as an oral text for many centuries before it was committed to written form. Words convey spiritual authority, whether declaimed as the word of God, presented as historical documents, written as religious guidance or spoken repeatedly to guide and encourage followers of a new cult or faith.

Another source of strength in presenting a new movement is the linkage to an existing religious heritage. Of course, many who preach a religious message claim it is the authentic version of an established religion: to Luther and Calvin and the pioneers of European Protestantism, theirs was the true Christianity rather than the corruption and misguidance they perceived in the contemporary Roman Catholic Church. Islamic fundamentalist groups of the modern era strengthen their claims for political authority by asserting that they are following precepts of a true original Islam that has been abandoned by others in the Muslim *ummah*. For NRMs, authority often comes from building on the heritage of early religion, whether stated or not. It is more persuasive to state that a body of new religious teaching is firmly grounded in what went before, and then build upon it.

Mormonism – the Church of Jesus Christ of Latter-day Saints – was presented as a denomination of the Christian faith, and *The Book of Mormon* has many echoes of the Old Testament. Christianity began as a development within Judaism and its axial moment – the crucifixion – took place in the Temple city of Judaism. The influence of and links to Judaism in the Qur'an are manifest and Islam considered there was a succession of prophets with important messages from God, with Isa (Jesus, Yeshua) the last prophet before Muhammad ibn 'Abdullah. The monotheistic Judaism of Yehud built clearly and deliberately on the traditions of earlier Yahwism, which presented a long history of Israel's relations with Yahweh. There is no concession to the influences on passages in Tanakh from Zoroastrianism/Mazdaism, or in Genesis from pre-Achaemenid Babylonian myth. The long (if difficult to trace) development of the Zoroastrian religion appears to have built on elements from earlier cults.

As mentioned in Chapter 6, elements in the Avesta of the Zoroastrians are comparable to the Vedas of the Indian subcontinent, both initially oral texts and appearing to reflect their common Indo-Iranian background. But the Indian religions developed in a different direction, with those we subsume under the name Hinduism, as well as Jainism, both of which recognise many male and female deities. The emergence of Buddhism from the 5th century BCE is traced to an individual initiator, Siddhartha Gautama, whose teaching and beliefs evolved without a direct message from the divine of the kind seen in the prophetic tradition of the monotheistic faiths. Similarly, the message conveyed by the 16th-century CE founders of Sikhism, Guru Nanak and his successors, were derived from inner contemplation rather than the external impact of a deity. In Japan, the Shinto religion, with its adherence to many gods or spirits, has continued alongside Buddhism since the latter's introduction in the 6th century CE. The religious traditions of China are similarly complex. The development of Taoism is associated with a teacher, Lao Tzu, somewhere in the 6th to 4th centuries BCE, and while historical detail for such an individual is obscure, the traditions indicate a source of his teachings from his inner life rather than external revelations. Even more different from the prophets of 'Abrahamic' monotheism, Confucianism derives its teaching from K'ung Fu-tzu in the 6th to 5th centuries BCE in China, with a derivation some would describe as secular, but certainly not derived from a supernatural experience. In the modern era, the teaching of Li Hongzhi, founder of the Falun Gong movement, which grew rapidly in China in the 1990s, is described as deriving from human teachers and inner revelations, not divinities.

By contrast, the Baha'i faith, which emerged within the Muslim world of Iran and Iraq in the mid-19th century, had its origins in the teaching of a prophet, Siyyid 'Alí Muhammad Shirazi, whose inspirations were in many ways closer to those of earlier prophets in the monotheistic tradition: he identified himself as the messenger of God. So while many religions had significant individuals in their formation, there is a substantial difference between the prophetic tradition in the monotheistic religions and the influential figures in the major religions of South and East Asia.

Contexts

One shared feature of the origins all five movements described in the previous chapters is that they began in the periphery of a major civilisation but not in its core. They were the product of locations marginal to the dominant imperial cultures, though not in areas beyond their influence. These were not the products of the great cities of the era, but nor were they generated in total isolation from these.

Thus Mormonism in western New York State began away from the great cities of the relatively new nation of the United States, in a region of fast economic growth as land was cleared for farms, where townships developed and the Erie Canal promised increasing prices for traded produce. This was not the land of pioneers on the frontier. Islam found itself an initial base in Medina (Yathrib), on trading routes between southern Arabia and the cities of the Levant, and the smaller settlement of Mecca; Arabs had served as mercenaries in the Sasanian and Byzantine Empires yet the Hijaz had not been part by either. Christianity came from rural parts (not even the towns) of an area, Galilee, relatively productive in agricultural land but certainly not central to the Roman occupation of the east Mediterranean (it was ruled by client kings appointed by Rome). The development of the Judaism we see in the Tanakh (Old Testament), Second Temple and evolution of Jewish ritual and priesthood was centred on a small town in a relatively unproductive area of the Persian Empire. Wherever in the complex of Mazdaist religion we place Zarathushtra and the Avesta, they were not from any of the urban centres of Iran or Central Asia.

By comparison, Confucius is thought to have come from a region beyond the direct rule of the Chinese Zhou dynasty in the 6th to 5th centuries BCE. The origins of Buddhism lie with Siddhartha Gautama in an area of north-eastern India marginal to significant contemporary power centres also in the 6th to 5th centuries BCE. Guru Nanak, founder figure of Sikhism in the 15th to 16th centuries CE, travelled widely in and beyond areas under the control of Muslim rulers, yet his origins were not at the centres of political power.

Some modern religious movements can be seen to have emerged in more central urban locations; for example, Theosophy in 19th-century New York City (though its founder, Helena Blavatsky, had travelled in Asia from her native Russia), as well as the many NRMs which developed in California in the 1970s and 1980s. So, marginality may not be an essential characteristic.

Another common (but not universal) pattern of the religious movements described in this book is that they began in one place but thrived in a quite different area. The strength of the Mormons lay not in New York State and its neighbours but far away, at the Great Salt Lake. Islam began in the Hijaz region of the Arabian Peninsular but established its centre of rule well beyond, though with Arabia remaining the centre for religious pilgrimage. Christianity had its origins in Galilee and Judah but it was in the towns and cities of the Roman Empire elsewhere that its following developed. The emergence of a strict monotheism in Judaism has often been attributed to the period of Babylonian exile, although its growth took place subsequently, indeed in the Judah area of Palestine (Yehud). But despite the development of Jerusalem as the central town of Jewish monotheism, Jews remained scattered throughout the countries of the Middle East and then more widely through the successor Roman Empire. Whatever the time and place of Zarathushtra and the origin of the texts associated with him, with a putative location in Central Asia, it was the imperial centres of Achaemenids, Parthian and Sasanians which presented the power of Mazdaism. And Buddhism, despite its origins in India, would thrive instead in lands to the south, east and north.

Though cults, sects and religions may emerge at times of political and social stress, in their initial stages they can also provide alternatives to paths of political opposition. As a result, the history of religions is not always a history of the persecution of new unorthodoxies. While the Californian and other NRMs can be described as part of alternative cultures, few would characterise them as threats to the stability of western capitalism. The very existence of religious movements outside of the dominant institutions can allow the state to condemn them as subversive, the position of Falun Gong in China being an example.

The Church of Jesus Christ of Latter-day Saints was no threat to the United States while it was one of many competing evangelical movements in the 'Burned-over District' of western New York State. The Mormons sought no confrontation with the US government, but escaped local community opposition by moving westward. They became of political concern when the United States acquired land formerly claimed by Mexico and had to engage with the Mormon settlers around the Great Salt Lake.

Despite the execution of its founding prophet and some of his followers, no political rebellion was preached by the early Christians. Christianity remained no real threat to the Roman Empire for some two and a half centuries, despite many individuals being punished for their refusal to acknowledge official cults.

In the small Persian province of Yehud, the development of the theology and priesthood of Judaism was not going to affect the power of the Achaemenid rulers. The Jerusalem Judaists operated peaceably under Persian and Hellenistic rule without challenging the political status quo.

An exception lies with Islam, where the early militarisation of the faithful developed into a successful military force that overthrew existing empires in the name of the new religion. The early history of Islam within Arabia, where religious and political identities united to create a military force, brings religious innovation more into the sphere of social revolution. Other religions would await later stages in their development before they were used by states and rulers as means to unify and to wage wars. Religious affiliations throughout human history have served communities to define their own identity and distinguish it from those they sought to conquer.

A common feature of ancient and modern cults is the tendency to schisms. No matter how powerful the message of a founder prophet and the strength of a foundational text, religious movements may rapidly fragment under competing ideologies, or competing leadership, and commonly a combination of the two. They share this characteristic with many modern political parties and movements, and, as in politics, a small organisation can split just as readily as a large one. Many if not most NRMs can trace their origin to separation from another NRM or a traditional sect. The Mormons divided into rival groups of Latter-day Saints almost immediately on the death of the founder. The split over the leadership of the Islamic world was seen less than 40 years after the death of the Prophet – and would eventually lead to the fatal division between Sunni and Sh'ia. The Book of Acts in the New Testament recounts the division between those who wanted the Christian movement to follow Jewish prescriptions and those who thought gentile converts need not, and the two millennia of history of Christianity is dominated by its divisions.

One of the means by which religions develop their strength is by invention: as time moves on, their narratives of foundation expand, their traditions become more ambitious, their documents more numerous. Because so much of its history is recorded in contemporary print, this is less a feature of Mormonism. But other chapters of this book have drawn attention to questions of sources and their reliability. Islam developed stories of miraculous events in the life of the Prophet, and so many legends of his life that a medieval industry developed to try to trace which were more authentic. Christian documents continued to be produced and attributed to names of early followers of Yeshua. Over many centuries, stories of the travels of the early disciples and saints and the distribution of their relics became a major feature of the Church; it contributed to a rebellion in the form of Protestantism, which now paid greater attention to another source of myth, that of the biblical narrative. The redactors of the Tanakh pulled together a huge range of myth, legend, history and literature while ignoring contradiction and incompatibilities. Religions outside of those described in this book have their own foundational myths and augmented narratives, of course. The potential of the invention of tradition is unending.

This book has reviewed what we can know of the beginnings of some religions when we bypass the narratives derived exclusively from traditions and look to critical scholarly history alongside some of the results of scientific archaeology. The ideas and understanding we have today will be refined, improved and replaced as information is revealed and debates and discussions continue on important issues. Religion has been, and remains, one of the most powerful forces in human history.

Acknowledgements

A primary acknowledgement is due to the many authors and researchers whose work I have cited in this book or otherwise consulted.

I have appreciated assistance, advice and input from a number of friends and colleagues, ranging from practical suggestions to reviews of draft chapters, even when they might disagree with my general approach. I should stress that none of these shares responsibility for the interpretations and perspectives presented in this book, nor my errors and omissions. They include: Matthew Adams, Alison Betts, Stephen Bourke, Michael Cook, Fred Donner, James Fraser, Raphael Greenberg, Oystein LaBianca, Oded Lipschits, Bill Loader, Jamie Lovell, Craigie Macfie, Frances Mayall, Jeremy Mynott, John Palmer, Daniel Potts, Garry Trompf, Ian Tyrrell, Alan Walmsley, Alan Williams, Wolfgang Zwickel and anonymous publisher's readers; with acknowledgements for indirect help to Anurag Acharya, David Meadows, Alex Verstak and Jimmy Wales. Not least, my thanks to Marguerite, Frances and Tim for their support, encouragement and ideas.

I have benefited from the online resources of University of New South Wales Library and the physical resources and staff of libraries at ACU, Albright Institute, Moore College, Rockefeller Museum, State Library of NSW, University of Sydney and UNSW.

Emma Brennan and her colleagues at Manchester University Press, including Alun Richards and Lianne Slavin, have brought a combination of enthusiasm and professionalism to this project, doubly appreciated as it was undertaken during the rigours and restrictions of a coronavirus lockdown.

I am especially grateful for the major contribution to this book from Ralph Footring, who has brought a wise, thoughtful and experienced eye to the text as its copy-editor, and has brought a constructive and flexible approach to the design and layout of the final volume.

For redrawing the maps in this book I am indebted to Don Shewan.

Sources for the data in the maps include:

1 The Landscape of Mormon origins: W.H. McIntosh et al., *History of Wayne County, New York*, Philadelphia: Everts, Ensign & Everts, 1877, facing p. 18.

2 Territory of the Iroquois, 1771: Guy Johnson, *Map of the Country of the VI. Nations proper with part of the adjacent colonies*, 1771.

3 Places of the main Mormon migrations to 1847: R.H. Jackson, 'Mormon perception and settlement', *Annals of the Association of American Geographers* 68 (1978): 317–334; *Cambridge Modern History Atlas*, Cambridge: Cambridge University Press, 1912, pl. 72.

4 Native American and Mormon settlements near the Great Salt Lake: W.L. D'Azevedo (ed.), *Handbook of North American Indians, Vol. 11: Great Basin*, Smithsonian Institution, 1986, p. 264, fig. 1 (after J.H. Steward).

5 The Middle East *ca.* 600 CE: J.L. Bacharach, *A Middle East Handbook*, Cambridge: Cambridge University Press, 1984, p. 90, fig. 8.

6 A reconstruction of pre-Islamic Arabian trade routes: D.T. Potts, 'Trans-Arabian routes of the pre-Islamic period', in F.E. Peters (ed.), *The Arabs and Arabia on the Eve of Islam*, Aldershot: Ashgate, 1999, p. 56, fig. 1.

7 Early campaigns of the Arab armies: F.M. Donner, *Muḥammad and the Believers: at the origins of Islam*, Cambridge, MA: Harvard University Press, 2010, p. 120, map 4; R. Lawless, in G. Blake, J. Dewdney and J. Mitchell (eds), *The Cambridge Atlas of the Middle East and North Africa*, Cambridge: Cambridge University Press, 1987, p. 28.

8 Palestine in the early 1st century CE: K.C. Hanson and D.E. Oakman, *Palestine in the Time of Jesus*, 2nd edition, Minneapolis, MN: Fortress Press, 2008, p. ix.

9 Jerusalem in the early 1st century CE: H. Geva, 'On the "New City" of Second Temple period Jerusalem: the archaeological evidence', in K. Galor and G. Avni (eds), *Unearthing Jerusalem: 150 years of archaeological research in the Holy City*, Winona Lake, IN: Eisenbrauns, 2011: 295–312, p. 300; H. Geva, 'Jerusalem's population in antiquity: a minimalist view', *Tel Aviv* 41 (2014): 131–160, fig. 6.

10 Journeys of Paulos according to Acts: www1.antiochian.org/node/36121 and www.conformingtojesus.com/charts-maps/en/paul's_journeys_map.htm

11 The route between Judah and Babylonia: M. Cogan, *Bound for Exile: Israelites and Judeans under imperial yoke*, Jerusalem: Carta, 2013.

12 Jerusalem on the eve of the Babylonian conquest: A. Faust 'Society and culture', in Z.I. Farber and J.L. Wright (eds), *Archaeology and History of Eighth-Century Judah*, Atlanta, GA: SBL Press, 2018, p. 181.

13 Jerusalem in the later Persian period: C.E. Carter, *The Emergence of Yehud in the Persian Period: a social and demographic study*, Sheffield: Sheffield Academic Press, 1999, p. 149, fig. 14.

14 Yehud and the Levant in the Persian period: C.E. Carter, *The Emergence of Yehud in the Persian Period: a social and demographic study*, Sheffield: Sheffield Academic Press, 1999, p. 291, fig. 26.

15 The extent of Achaemenid control:
www.iranchamber.com/history/achaemenids/achaemenids.php

Notes

The following abbreviations are used in the notes below:

AAE   *Arabian Archaeology and Epigraphy* journal

ALUP   *Arabic Literature to the End of the Umayyad Period*, edited by A.F.L. Beeston, T.M. Johnstone, R.B. Serjeant and G.R. Smith (Cambridge: Cambridge University Press, 1983)

CCQ   *The Cambridge Companion to the Qur'an*, edited by J.D. McAuliffe (New York: Cambridge University Press, 2006)

CHC   *The Cambridge History of Christianity, Vol. 1: Origins to Constantine*, edited by M.M. Mitchell and F.M. Young (Cambridge: Cambridge University Press, 2006)

CHI   *The Cambridge History of Iran* (Cambridge: Cambridge University Press): *Vol. 1: The Land of Iran*, edited by W.B. Fisher (1968); *Vol. 2: The Median and Achaemenid Periods*, edited by I. Gershevitch (1985); *Vol. 3: The Seleucid, Parthian and Sasanid Periods*, edited by I. Yarshater (1983)

CHJ   *The Cambridge History of Judaism* (Cambridge: Cambridge University Press): *Vol. 1: Introduction. The Persian Period*, edited by W.D. Davies and L. Finkelstein (1984); *Vol. 3: The Early Roman Period*, edited by W. Horbury, W.D. Davies and J. Sturdy (1999); *Vol. 4, The Late Roman-Rabbinic Period*, edited by S.T. Katz (2006)

EncyclIran *Encyclopædia Iranica* online at www.iranicaonline.org/

JJFC   *Judah and the Judeans in the Fourth Century BCE*, edited by O. Lipschits, G.N. Knoppers and R. Albertz (Winona Lake, IN: Eisenbrauns, 2007)

JJNBP   *Judah and the Judeans in the Neo-Babylonian Period*, edited by O. Lipschits and J. Blenkinsopp (Winona Lake, IN: Eisenbrauns, 2003)

JJPP   *Judah and the Judeans in the Persian Period*, edited by O. Lipschits and M. Oeming (Winona Lake, IN: Eisenbrauns, 2006)

OHECA   *The Oxford Handbook of Early Christian Archaeology*, edited by W.R. Caraher, T.W. Davis and D.K. Pettegrew (Oxford: Oxford University Press, 2019)

OHECS   *The Oxford Handbook of Early Christian Studies*, edited by S.A. Harvey and D.G. Hunter (Oxford: Oxford University Press, 2008)

PSAS   *Proceedings of the Seminar for Arabian Studies* journal

WBCZ   *The Wiley Blackwell Companion to Zoroastrianism*, edited by M. Stausberg and Y.S.-D. Vevaina (Chichester: Wiley Blackwell, 2015)

1. Introduction: approaching religions' history

1 A thoughtful attempt at this, bringing together the author's long engagement with the issue, is E. Anati, *The Origins of Religion: a study in conceptual anthropology*, Brescia: Atelier, 2020.

2 L. Smith, *Biographical sketches of Joseph Smith the prophet and his progenitors for many generations*, Liverpool: Orson Pratt, 1853, p. 37.

3 F. M. Donner, 'The historian, the believer, and the Qur'ān', in G.S. Reynolds (ed.), *New Perspectives on the Qur'an, The Qurǎan in Its Historical Context*, Abingdon: Routledge, 2012: 47–59.

4 K. A. Appiah, *The Lies That Bind: Rethinking Identity*, London: Profile Books, 2018, p. 36.

5 A. de Botton, *Religion for Atheists*, London: Hamish Hamilton, 2012, pp. 23–96.

6 Information taken from www.pewresearch.org/fact-tank/2018/12/05/how-do-european-countries-differ-in-religious-commitment ; www.pewresearch.org/fact-tank/2019/07/01/5-facts-about-religion-in-canada ; www.pewforum.org/religious-landscape-study/attendance-at-religious-services

7 B. Nongbri, *God's Library: the archaeology of the earliest Christian manuscripts*, New Haven, CT: Yale University Press, 2018.

8 R. Derricourt, *Inventing Africa: history, archaeology and ideas*, London: Pluto, 2011; and *Antiquity Imagined: the remarkable legacy of Egypt and the ancient Near East*, London: Tauris, 2015. Journal papers include R. Derricourt, 'Pseudoarchaeology: the concept and its limitations', *Antiquity* 86 (2012): 524–531; 'Pyramidologies of Egypt: a typological review', *Cambridge Archaeological Journal* 22 (2012): 353–363.

9 J. Droogan, *Religion, Material Culture and Archaeology*, London: Bloomsbury, 2013.

10 Derricourt, 'Pseudoarchaeology'.

11 R. W. Stump, *The Geography of Religion: faith, place and space*, Lanham, MD: Rowman & Littlefield, 2008.

2. Frontiers of place and belief: Mormon origins and journeys

1 B. Lowe, 'A brief history of Palmyra', at www.palmyrany.com/about/1800.htm ; F.M. Brodie, *No Man Knows My History: the life of Joseph Smith the Mormon prophet*, 2nd edition, New York: Knopf, 1971, p. 9.

2 R.L. Bushman, *Joseph Smith and the Beginnings of Mormonism*, Urbana, IL: University of Illinois Press, 1984, pp. 59–60; R.L. Bushman, *Joseph Smith: rough stone rolling*, New York: Knopf, 2006, pp. 31–33; Brodie, *No Man Knows*, pp. 10–11.

3 Brodie, *No Man Knows*, p. 410.

4 Brodie, *No Man Knows*, pp. 427–429; Bushman, *Joseph Smith and the Beginnings*, p. 75.

5 Brodie, *No Man Knows*, p. 53; Bushman, *Joseph Smith and the Beginnings*, p. 86 (the price was $200); Bushman, *Joseph Smith: rough stone*, p. 63.

6 J. Smith, 'Church history', *Times and Seasons* (Nauvoo, IL) 3 (9), 1 March 1842: 706–771, p. 706; see also 'First vision accounts' at www.lds.org/topics/first-vision-accounts?lang=eng

7 'Published volumes' at www.josephsmithpapers.org/articles/published-volumes

8 *Bicentennial Edition, Statistics of the United States, Colonial Times to 1970*, Washington, DC: US Census Bureau, 1975; R. Gallman, 'Economic growth and structural change in the long nineteenth century', in S. Engerman and R. Gallman (eds), *The Cambridge Economic History of the United States, Vol. 2: The Long Nineteenth Century*, Cambridge: Cambridge University Press, 2000: 1–56, pp. 7, 50. US average annual economic growth rates have been calculated as 4.0% from 1810 to 1820, and 3.8% from 1820 to 1830; and gross national product (not adjusted for inflation) increased by a factor of three from 1800 to 1830.

9 T. O'Dea, *The Mormons*, Chicago, IL: University of Chicago Press, 1957, p. 10.

10 D.W. Howe, *What God Hath Wrought: the transformation of America 1815–1848*, New York: Oxford University Press, 2007, p. 140.

11 J. Atack, F. Bateman and W. Parker, 'Northern agriculture and the westward movement', in S. Engerman and R. Gallman (eds), *The Cambridge Economic History of the United States, Vol. 2*, Cambridge: Cambridge University Press, 2000, p. 294.

12 W.H. McIntosh et al., *History of Wayne County, New York*, Philadelphia, PA: Everts, Ensign & Everts, 1877, p. 14.

13 Y.-C. Wang, 'Spatial patterns and vegetation–site relationships of the pre-settlement forests in western New York, USA', *Journal of Biogeography* 34 (2007): 500–513.

14 F. Milliken, *History of Ontario County, New York and Its People, Vol. 1*, New York: Lewis Historical, 1911, pp. 38, 41, 45, 47–48.

15 McIntosh et al., *History of Wayne County*, p. 134; H.G. Spafford, *A Gazetteer of the State of New-York; carefully written from original and authentic materials*, Albany, NY: Southwick, 1813, p. 271. In 1803 Palmyra had 82 registered voters on the roll.

16 Spafford, *A Gazetteer*, p. 270.

17 J. Fowler, *Journal of a Tour in the State of New York, in the Year 1830*, London: Whittaker, Treacher, & Arnot, 1831, p. 101.

18 M.P. Leone, *Roots of Modern Mormonism*, Cambridge, MA: Harvard University Press, 1979, p. 16.

19 S.C. Harper, 'Infallible proofs, both human and divine: the persuasiveness of Mormonism for early converts', *Religion and American Culture* 10 (2000): 99–118.

20 Howe, *What God Hath Wrought*, p. 37.

21 McIntosh et al., *History of Wayne County*, pp. 147–149.

22 P.E. Johnson, *A Shopkeeper's Millennium: society and revivals in Rochester, New York 1815–1837*, New York: Hill & Wang, 1978, p. 4.

23 W.R. Cross, *The Burned-over District: the social and intellectual history of enthusiastic religion in western New York, 1800–1850*, Ithaca, NY: Cornell University Press, 1950; Rachel Cope, 'From smouldering fires to revitalizing showers:

a historiographical overview of revivalism in nineteenth-century New York', *Wesley and Methodist Studies* 4 (2012): 25–49.

24 Howe, *What God Hath Wrought*, p. 218.

25 Cross, *The Burned-over District*, pp. 11, 13, 40, 70, 76.

26 Cross, *The Burned-over District*.

27 P.E. Johnson and S. Wilentz, *The Kingdom of Matthias*, Oxford: Oxford University Press, 1995, pp. 3–6.

28 D.W. Howe, 'Emergent Mormonism in context', in T.L. Givens and P.L. Barlow (eds), *The Oxford Handbook to Mormonism*, Oxford: Oxford University Press, 2015: 24–36.

29 As argued by Johnson, *A Shopkeeper's Millennium*, pp. 135–137.

30 A phrase of Cross, *The Burned-over District*, p. 268.

31 R. Derricourt, *Antiquity Imagined: the remarkable legacy of Egypt and the ancient Near East*, London: Tauris, 2015, pp. 211–219.

32 P.C. Olive, *The Lost Lands of the Book of Mormon*, Springville, UT: Cedar Fort, 2013.

33 Brodie, *No Man Knows*, pp. 34–37; Milliken, *History, Vol. 1*, pp. 1–11.

34 S.W. Manning et al., 'Radiocarbon re-dating of contact-era Iroquoian history in northeastern North America', *Science Advances* 4(12) (2018): EAAV0280.

35 W. Engelbrecht, 'The Iroquois: archaeological patterning on the tribal level', *World Archaeology* 6 (1974): 52–65, p. 55.

36 B.G. Trigger (ed.), *Handbook of North American Indians, Vol. 15: Northeast*, Washington, DC: Smithsonian Institution, 1978, p. 421.

37 G. Johnson, *Map of the Country of the VI. Nations proper with part of the adjacent colonies*, 1771. Map 2 (p. 32) is based on this.

38 J. Rossen (ed.), *Corey Village and the Cayuga World*, Syracuse, NY: Syracuse University Press, 2015, pp. 22–32.

39 A. Taylor, 'The divided ground: Upper Canada, New York, and the Iroquois Six Nations, 1783–1815', *Journal of the Early Republic* 22 (2002): 55–75, p. 58.

40 T.J. Shannon, *Iroquois Diplomacy in the Early American Frontier*, New York: Penguin, 2008, p. 197.

41 R.L. Bushman, 'Joseph Smith and his vision', in Givens and Barlow, *The Oxford Handbook*.

42 O'Dea, *The Mormons*, p. 41.

43 For example R.V. Francaviglia, 'Geography and Mormon identity', in Givens and Barlow, *The Oxford Handbook*.

44 Adam-ondi-Ahman at www.lds.org/scriptures/history-photos/photo-10?lang=eng

45 Brodie, *No Man Knows*, p. 149.

46 B.C. Pykles, *Excavating Nauvoo: the Mormons and the rise of historical archaeology in America*, Lincoln, NE: University of Nebraska Press, 2010, pp. 129–191.

47 Howe, *What God Hath Wrought*, ch. 18.

48 Brodie, *No Man Knows*, pp. 358–359.

49 M.S. De Pillis, 'The social sources of Mormonism', *Church History* 37 (1968): 50–79.

50 O'Dea, *The Mormons*, p. 97.

51 O'Dea, *The Mormons*, pp. 198–201, 256.

52 R.H. Jackson, 'Mormon perception and settlement', *Annals of the Association of American Geographers* 68 (1978): 317–334, pp. 321–322.

53 L.J. Arrington, *Brigham Young: American Moses*, New York: Knopf, 1985, pp. 145–146.

54 Jackson, 'Mormon perception', p. 330.

55 T.G. Alexander, 'Brigham Young and the transformation of Utah wilderness, 1847–58', *Journal of Mormon History* 41 (2015): 103–124.

56 Arrington, *Brigham Young*, p. 130.

57 Alexander, 'Brigham Young', p. 108.

58 F. Piercy, *Route from Liverpool to Great Salt Lake Valley*, Liverpool: Richards, 1865, opp. p. 108.

59 D.W. Meinig, 'The Mormon culture region: strategies and patterns in the geography of the American West, 1847–1964', *Annals of the Association of American Geographers* 55 (1965): 191–210, p. 202, fig. 3; T. Carter, *Building Zion: the material world of Mormon settlement* (Minneapolis, MN: University of Minnesota Press, 2015); L.J. Arrington, 'Economic history of a Mormon valley', *Pacific Northwest Quarterly* 46 (1955): 97–107; D. Bedford, 'Utah's Great Salt Lake: a complex environmental-societal system', *Geographical Review* 95 (2005): 73–96.

60 Jackson, 'Mormon perception', pp. 328ff.

61 Meinig, 'The Mormon culture region'.

62 Material on Indian–Mormon relations includes R.W. Walker, 'Toward a reconstruction of Mormon and Indian relations, 1847–1877', *Brigham Young University Studies* 29 (1989): 23–42; M.W. Dougherty, 'Imagining Lamanites and feeling Mormon', *Journal of Mormon History* 43 (2017): 22–45; H.A. Christy, 'Open hand and mailed fist: Mormon–Indian relations in Utah, 1847–1852,' *Utah Historical Quarterly* 46 (1978): 216–235; J. Brooks, 'Indian relations on the Mormon frontier,' *Utah Historical Quarterly* 12 (1944): 1–48.

63 C.I. Malouf and J. Findlay, 'Euro-American impact before 1870', in W.L. D'Azevedo (ed.), *Handbook of North American Indians, Vol. 11: Great Basin*, Washington, DC: Smithsonian Institution, 1986, p. 508; J. Farmer, *On Zion's Mount: Mormons, Indians and the American landscape*, Cambridge, MA: Harvard University Press, 2008, p. 13.

64 Arrington, *Brigham Young*, pp. 210, 214.

65 D.K. Grayson, *The Great Basin: a natural prehistory*, Berkeley, CA: University of California Press, 2011, pp. 328–331.

66 J. Coltrain and S. Leavitt, 'Climate and diet in Fremont prehistory: economic variability and abandonment of maize agriculture in the Great Salt Lake Basin', *American Antiquity* 67 (2002): 453–485.

67 Grayson, *The Great Basin*, pp. 262–264, 317–318, 327.

68 J.H. Steward, 'Linguistic distributions and political groups of the Great Basin Shoshoneans', *American Anthropologist* 39 (1937): 625–634; J.H. Steward, 'Basin-plateau Aboriginal sociopolitical groups', *Bureau of American Ethnology Bulletin* 120 (1938): 1–346, p. 178, fig. 12, p. 220.

69 S.R. Simms and M.E. Stuart, 'Ancient American Indian life in the Great Salt Lake wetlands: archaeological and biological evidence', in J.W. Gwynn (ed.),

Great Salt Lake: an overview of change, Salt Lake City, UT: Utah Geological Survey, 2002: 71–83, pp. 71, 80.

70 Farmer, *On Zion's Mount*, p. 50.

71 D.H. Thomas, L.S.A. Pendleton and S.C. Cappennari, 'Western Shoshone', in d'Azavedo, *Handbook, Vol. 11*: 262–283, p. 264, fig. 1.

72 Farmer, *On Zion's Mount*, p. 41.

73 J.C. Janetski, 'Utah Lake: its role in the prehistory of the Utah Valley', *Utah Historical Quarterly* 58 (1990): 5–31.

74 D.G. Callaway, J.C. Janetski and O.C. Stewart, 'Ute', in d'Azevedo, *Handbook, Vol. 11*: 336–367, p. 337, fig. 1; Farmer, *On Zion's Mount*, pp. 26–27.

75 Janetski, 'Utah Lake', p. 26; M.K. Knoll, 'Settlement location as a reflection of economic strategies by the late prehistoric fishermen of Utah Lake', *Utah Archaeology* 15 (2002): 85–98.

76 Farmer, *On Zion's Mount*, pp. 19, 26, 69, 78.

77 For example, W.P. Reeve, *Making Space on the Western Frontier: Mormons, miners and southern Paiutes*, Urbana IL: University of Illinois Press, 2006.

78 R. White, *'It's your misfortune and none of my own': a history of the American West*, Norman, OK: University of Oklahoma Press, 1991, p. 164. The Mormon migration into American Indian territory has been discussed in its wider context in W. Nugent, 'Tanner lecture: the Mormons and America's empires', *Journal of Mormon History* 36 (2010): 1–27.

79 Mormon responses to this analogy are predictably hostile: see A.H. Green, 'The Muhammad–Joseph Smith comparison: subjective metaphor or a sociology of prophethood?', in J.S. Palmer (ed.), *Mormons and Muslims: spiritual foundations and modern manifestations*, Provo, UT: Religious Studies Center, Brigham Young University, 2002: 111–133; A.H. Green and L.P. Goldrup, 'Joseph Smith, an American Muhammad? An essay on the perils of historical analogy', *Dialogue* 6 (1971): 46–58. Such hostile comparisons continue: e.g. A.J. Schmidt, *The American Muhammad: Joseph Smith, founder of Mormonism*, St Louis, MO: Concordia, 2013.

80 E. Meyer, *Ursprung und Geschichte der Mormonen*, Halle: Niemeyer, 1912.

3. Vision, faith and conquest: the source and power of Islam

1 C.F. Robinson, *Islamic Historiography*, Cambridge: Cambridge University Press, 2003, p. 14.

2 J. Jomier, 'Aspects of the Quran today', *ALUP*: 260–270, pp. 264–265.

3 E. Said, *Orientalism*, London: Routledge, 1978.

4 R.G. Hoyland, *In God's Path: the Arab conquests and the creation of an Islamic empire*, New York: Oxford University Press, 2015, p. 38.

5 D.T. Potts, *The Arabian Gulf in Antiquity, Vol. 2*, Oxford: Oxford University Press, 1990, pp. 257–259, 341.

6 J.A. Langfeldt, 'Recently discovered early Christian monuments in northeastern Arabia', *AAE* 5 (1994): 32–60. A Christian church building that appears to both pre-date and post-date the arrival of Islam has been found at Jubail on the Arabian Gulf coast, and this serves as a reminder that the pattern of

communities with different religions long remained in the region despite it being part of the Islamic world.

7 C.F. Robinson (ed.), *The New Cambridge History of Islam, Vol. 1: The Formation of the Islamic World, Sixth to Eleventh Centuries*, Cambridge: Cambridge University Press, 2010, p. 3.

8 P. Crone, 'What do we actually know about Mohammed?' (2008), at www.opendemocracy.net/en/mohammed_3866jsp/

9 Robinson, *Islamic Historiography*, p. 7.

10 H. Modarressi, 'Early debates on the integrity of the Qur'an: a brief survey', *Studia Islamica* 77 (1993): 5-39.

11 M. Rodinson, *Mohammed*, London: Penguin, 1971, p. 217.

12 R.B. Serjeant, 'Early Arabic prose', in *ALUP*: 114-153, p. 114.

13 R.G. Hoyland, *Arabia and the Arabs from the Bronze Age to the Coming of Islam*, London: Routledge, 2001, pp. 36, 64; A. Avanzini, A. Prioletta and I. Rossi, 'The Digital Archive for the Study of Pre-Islamic Arabian Inscriptions: an ERC project', *PSAS* 44 (2014): 15-24. The major project on the inscriptions Avanzini et al. describe is detailed online at the Digital Archive for the Study of pre-Islamic Arabian Inscriptions at dasi.cnr.it . In south-west Arabia alone, some 10,000 inscriptions are known on rocks, and there are 20,000 inscriptions to the north, at the other end of the desert region.

14 A.F.L. Beeston, 'Background topics', in *ALUP*: 1-26, pp. 3-4, 7.

15 R. Paret, 'The Qur'an – I', in *ALUP*: 186-227, pp. 196-197.

16 A. Jones, 'The Qur'an – II', in *ALUP*: 228-245, p. 235; P. Crone and M. Cook, *Hagarism: the making of the Islamic world*, Cambridge: Cambridge University Press, 1977, pp. 3, 18.

17 Jones, 'The Qur'an – II', p. 244.

18 Jones, 'The Qur'an – II', p. 240; Modarressi, 'Early debates'.

19 F.M. Donner in *CCQ*, p. 35; discussed by H. Motzki in *CCQ*, pp. 65-66.

20 J. Wansbrough, *Quranic Studies: sources and method of scriptural interpretation*, Oxford: Oxford University Press, 1977; J. Wansbrough, *The Sectarian Milieu: content and composition of Islamic salvation history*, Oxford: Oxford University Press, 1978.

21 E.A. Rezvan, 'The Mingana folios in their historical context', *Manuscripta Orientalia* 21 (2015): 32-38; T.F.G. Higham et al., 'Radiocarbon dates from the Oxford AMS system: Archaeometry Datelist 36', *Archaeometry* 60 (2018): 628-640, p. 634, with an uncalibrated C14 date of 1456 ± 21 BP, equivalent to 568-645 at 94.5% probability.

22 A. Hilali, 'Le palimpseste de Ṣan'ā' et la canonisation du Coran: nouveaux éléments', *Cahiers du Centre Gustave Glotz* 21 (2010): 443-448; B. Sadeghi and M. Goudarzi, 'Ṣan'ā' 1 and the origins of the Qur'an', *Der Islam* 87 (2012): 1-129; B. Sadeghi and U. Bergmann, 'The codex of a companion of the Prophet and the Qur'an of the Prophet', *Arabica* 57 (2010): 343-436; A. Hilali, *The Sanaa Palimpsest: the transmission of the Qur'an in the first centuries AH*, Oxford: Oxford University Press, 2017. The date was 1407 ± 36 BP.

23 M.A. Rauf, '*Ḥadīth* literature – I', in *ALUP*: 271-288, pp. 271, 272, 274; N.J. Coulson, 'European criticism of *Ḥadīth* literature', in *ALUP*: 317-321, pp. 317, 319-320;

G.H.A. Juynboll, *Muslim Tradition: studies in chronology, provenance and authorship of early hadith*, Cambridge: Cambridge University Press, 1983, p. 28.

24 Juynboll, *Muslim tradition*, pp. 23, 39; F.M. Donner, *Narratives of Islamic Origins: the beginnings of Islamic historical writing*, Princeton, NJ: Darwin Press, 1998, p. 14.

25 M. Lecker, 'Glimpses of Muḥammad's Medinan decade', in J.E. Brockropp (ed.), *The Cambridge Companion to Muhammad* (New York: Cambridge University Press, 2010): 61–79, p. 61.

26 M.J. Kister, 'The *sirah* literature', in *ALUP*: 352–367, p. 367.

27 M. Cook, *Muḥammad*, Oxford: Oxford University Press, 1983, pp. 63–64; R. Derricourt, *Antiquity Imagined: the remarkable legacy of Egypt and the ancient Near East*, London: Tauris, 2015, pp. 220–250.

28 C. Cahen, 'History and historians', in M.J.L. Young, J.D. Latham and R.B. Serjeant (eds), *Religion, Learning and Science in the ʿAbbasid Period*, Cambridge University Press, 1990: 188–233.

29 Robinson, *Islamic Historiography*, p. 12. Donner, *Narratives*, pp. 5–31 discusses these different approaches.

30 Rodinson, *Mohammed*, p. xi.

31 Robinson, *Islamic Historiography*, pp. 125–126.

32 Robinson, *Islamic Historiography*, p. 121.

33 Serjeant in *ALUP*, pp. 141–142.

34 Serjeant in *ALUP*, p. 356.

35 Donner, *Narratives*, p. 282.

36 F.M. Donner in *CCQ*, p. 34.

37 F.M. Donner, *Muhammad and the Believers: at the origins of Islam*, Cambridge, MA: Harvard University Press, 2010, p. 51.

38 U. Rubin, *The Eye of the Beholder: the life of Muḥammad as viewed by the early Muslims*, Princeton, NJ: Darwin Press, 1995, pp. 189–214.

39 J. Retsö, *The Arabs in Antiquity: their history from the Assyrians to the Umayyads*, London: Routledge, 2003, pp. 97, 99, 621ff; P. Schadler, 'Changing identities? Arabs and Ishmaelites', in G. Fisher (ed.), *Arabs and Empires Before Islam*, Oxford: Oxford University Press, 2015: 367–372, p. 367.

40 F.M. Donner, 'Talking about Islam's origins', *Bulletin of the School of Oriental and African Studies* 81 (2018): 1–23; P. Webb, *Imagining the Arabs: Arab identity and the rise of Islam*, Edinburgh: Edinburgh University Press, 2016.

41 R.G. Hoyland, *Seeing Islam as Others Saw It*, Princeton, NJ: Darwin Press, 1997, pp. 57, 58, 117.

42 C.E. Bosworth, 'Iran and the Arabs before Islam', in *CHI* 3: 593–612, pp. 600–601; Hoyland, *Arabia*, p. 79.

43 I. Toral-Niehoff, *Al-ḥīra: Eine arabische Kulturmetropole im spätantiken Kontext*, Leiden: Brill, 2013.

44 G. Bar-Oz et al., 'Ancient trash mounds unravel urban collapse a century before the end of Byzantine hegemony in the southern Levant', *Proceedings of the National Academy of Sciences* 116 (2019): 8239–8248.

45 Hoyland, *Arabia*, pp. 66, 170.

46 Discussed in detail in Potts, *The Arabian Gulf*.

47 M.C.A. Macdonald, 'Arabs and empires before the sixth century', in Fisher (ed.), *Arabs and Empires*: 11–89, p. 57.

48 D. Kennet, 'The decline of eastern Arabia in the Sasanian period', *AAE* 18 (2007): 86–122, pp. 87–88.

49 A.A. Ezzah, 'The political situation in eastern Arabia at the advent of Islam', *PSAS* 9 (1979): 53–64.

50 Hoyland, *Arabia*, p. 40ff; M.C. Macdonald, 'Reflections on the linguistic map of pre-Islamic Arabia', *AAE* 11 (2000): 28–79.

51 B. Vogt, 'Towards a new dating of the Great Dam of Mārib: preliminary results of the 2002 fieldwork of the German Institute of Archaeology', *PSAS* 34 (2004): 377–388.

52 2 Chronicles 9: 9.

53 Hoyland, *Arabia*, pp. 44, 47.

54 Hoyland, *Arabia*, pp. 233, 235–236.

55 J. Schiettecatte and M. Arbach, 'The political map of Arabia and the Middle East in the third century AD revealed by a Sabaean inscription', *AAE* 27 (2016): 176–196.

56 C.J. Robin, 'Ḥimyar, Aksūm, and Arabia Deserta in late antiquity: the epigraphic evidence', in Fisher (ed.), *Arabs and Empires*: 127–171, pp. 129–130.

57 Qur'an 34: 15–17.

58 Fisher (ed.), *Arabs and Empires*, p. 14.

59 D.T. Potts, 'Trans-Arabian routes of the pre-Islamic period', in F.E. Peters (ed.), *The Arabs and Arabia on the Eve of Islam*, Aldershot: Ashgate, 1999: 126–162, p. 155.

60 Rodinson, *Mohammed*, pp. 35–36.

61 P. Crone, *Meccan Trade and the Rise of Islam*, Princeton, NJ: Princeton University Press, 1987.

62 Hoyland, *Arabia*, pp. 58, 109–110.

63 Hoyland, *Arabia*, p. 139.

64 P. Crone, 'The religion of the Qur'ānic pagans: God and the lesser deities', *Arabica* 57 (2010): 151–200.

65 G.R. Hawting, *The Idea of Idolatry and the Emergence of Islam*, Cambridge: Cambridge University Press, 1999, pp. xiii, 150–151.

66 Qur'an 22: 17.

67 J. Neusner, 'Jews in Iran', in *CHI* 3: 909–923; J.P. Asmussen, 'Christians in Iran', in *CHI* 3: 924–948.

68 P. Brown, *The World of Late Antiquity from Marcus Aurelius to Muḥammad*, London: Thames & Hudson, 1971, p. 172.

69 D. Nicolle, *Historical Atlas of the Islamic World*, London: Mercury, 2004, pp. 24–25.

70 Nicolle, *Historical Atlas*, pp. 22–23.

71 Hoyland, *Arabia*, pp. 146–147; Y. Tobi, 'The Jews of Yemen in light of the excavation of the Jewish synagogue in Qanī'', *PSAS* 43 (2013): 349–356.

72 F.E. Peters, *Muhammad and the Origins of Islam*, Albany, NY: State University of New York Press, 1994, p. 192; M. Gil, 'The origin of the Jews of Medina', in Peters (ed.), *The Arabs and Arabia*, 145–166, reprinted from *Jerusalem Studies in Arabic and Islam* 10 (1987): 65–96.

73 P. Crone, 'Jewish Christianity and the Qur'ān (Part Two)', *Journal of Near Eastern Studies* 75 (2016): 1–21, pp. 20–21.

74 Peters, *Muhammad*, pp. 260–261.

75 Crone, 'What do we actually know?'

76 Serjeant in *ALUP*, pp. 127–128.

77 Rodinson, *Mohammed*, pp. 66–67.

78 Peters, *Muhammad*, pp. 121–127.

79 Rodinson, *Mohammed*, pp. 121–122.

80 Donner, *Muhammad*, p. 69.

81 A. Borrut and F.M. Donner, 'Introduction', in A. Borrut and F.M. Donner (eds), *Christians and Others in the Umayyad State*, Chicago, IL: Oriental Institute, 2016: 1–10, p. 3.

82 Donner, *Muhammad*, pp. 107ff, 194.

83 Donner, *Muhammad*, p. 206.

84 Crone and Cook, *Hagarism*.

85 Hoyland, *Seeing Islam*, pp. 687–703, especially p. 695; R. Hoyland 'New documentary texts and the early Islamic state', *Bulletin of the School of Oriental and African Studies* 69 (2006): 395–416, p. 407.

86 Crone and Cook, *Hagarism*, p. 8; Hoyland, *Seeing Islam*, p. 696; Donner, *Narratives*, p. 88.

87 J. Johns, 'Archaeology and the history of early Islam: the first seventy years', *Journal of the Economic and Social History of the Orient* 46 (2003): 411–436, p. 416.

88 Hoyland, 'New documentary texts', p. 397.

89 E. Rutter, 'The Hejaz', *Geographical Journal* 77 (1931): 97–108, p. 97.

90 G.R. Hawting, 'The origin of Jedda and the problem of al-Shu'ayba', *Arabica* 31 (1984): 318–326; T. Power, 'The origin and development of the Sudanese ports ('Aydhâb, Bâ/di', Sawâkin) in the early Islamic period', *Arabian Humanities* 15 (2008): 92–110; G. Rentz, 'Hidjaz', in B. Lewis (ed.), *Encyclopedia of Islam, Vol. 3*, Leiden: Brill, 1971: 362–364, p. 362.

91 M.M. Abd El-Ghani, 'Vegetation along a transect in the Hijaz mountains (Saudi Arabia)', *Journal of Arid Environments* 32 (1996): 289–304.

92 R.B. Winder, 'al-Madīna', in C.E. Bosworth et al. (eds), *Encyclopedia of Islam, Vol. 5*, Leiden: Brill, 1986: 994–1007; S.b.A. al-Rāshid, 'Sadd Al-Khanaq: an early Umayyad dam near Medina, Saudi Arabia', *PSAS* 38 (2008): 265–275.

93 D.A. King, 'Makka', in C.E. Bosworth et al. (eds), *Encyclopedia of Islam, Vol. 6*, Leiden: Brill, 1991: 144–187, p. 144.

94 Fisher, *Arabs and Empires*.

95 Crone, 'What do we actually know'; Crone, *Meccan Trade*.

96 Crone, 'What do we actually know'. See also Crone, *Meccan Trade*, pp. 6–7; G.W. Heck, '"Arabia without spices": an alternate hypothesis', *Journal of the American Oriental Society* 123 (2003): 547–576.

97 Crone, *Meccan Trade*, pp. 44–45, 50.

98 Crone, *Meccan Trade*, pp. 107–108, 133, 149.

99 Peters, *Muhammad*, pp. 72–75. Or even trading leather to the Byzantine army: P. Crone, 'Quraysh and the Roman army: making sense of the Meccan leather trade', *Bulletin of the School of Oriental and African Studies* 70 (2007): 63–88.

100 Hoyland, *Arabia*, p. 180; H. Munt, 'Ka'ba', in *Encyclopedia of Islam* online, and references.

101 Peters, *Muhammad*, p. 116.

102 Crone, *Meccan Trade*, pp. 172, 185.

103 A. de Maigret, *Arabia Felix: an exploration of the archaeological history of Yemen*, London: Stacey International, 2002, pp. 54ff; M. Milwright, *An Introduction to Islamic Archaeology*, Edinburgh: Edinburgh University Press, 2010, p. 11.

104 C. Morley, 'The Arabian frontier: a keystone of the Sasanian Empire', in E.W. Sauer (ed.), *Sasanian Persia: between Rome and the steppes of Eurasia*, Edinburgh: Edinburgh University Press, 2017: 268–283, pp. 268, 270, 273.

105 Potts, *The Arabian Gulf*, vol. 2, pp. 209, 296; D. Kennet, 'On the eve of Islam: archaeological evidence from eastern Arabia', *Antiquity* 79 (2005): 107–118; Kennet, 'The decline of eastern Arabia'; N.S. al-Jahwari et al., 'Fulayj: a late Sasanian fort on the Arabian coast', *Antiquity* 92 (2018): 724–741; Morley, 'The Arabian frontier', p. 276.

106 A. Benoist, M. Mouton and J. Schiettecatte, 'The artefacts from the fort at Mleiha: distribution, origins, trade and dating', *PSAS* 33 (2003): 59–76; M. Mouton et al., 'Building H at Mleiha: new evidence of the late pre-Islamic period D phase (PIR.D) in the Oman Peninsula (second to mid-third century AD)', *PSAS* 42 (2012): 205–221.

107 Kennet, 'On the eve of Islam', p. 115; A. Kutterer et al., 'Late pre-Islamic burials at Mleiha, Emirate of Sharjah (UAE)', *AAE* 25 (2014): 175–185, p. 184.

108 D. Kennet, 'Transformations in late Sasanian and early Islamic Eastern Arabia: the evidence from Kush', in J. Schiettecatte and C. Robin (eds), *L'Arabie à la veille de l'Islam: bilan clinique*, Paris: De Boccard, 2009: 135–161.

109 A. Petersen, 'Islamic urbanism in eastern Arabia: the case of the Al-'Ayn-al-Buraymī oasis', *PSAS* 39 (2009): 307–320; T. Power et al., 'First preliminary report on the Buraimi oasis landscape archaeology project', *PSAS* 45 (2015): 233–252; G.R.D. King, 'Settlement in western and central Arabia and the Gulf in the sixth-eighth centuries A.D.', in G.R.D. King and A. Cameron (eds), *The Byzantine and Early Islamic Near East: land use and settlement patterns*, Princeton NJ: Darwin Press, 1994: 181–212.

110 R. Carter, 'Christianity in the Gulf during the first centuries of Islam', *AAE* 19 (2008): 71–108; R. Payne, 'Monks, dinars and date palms: hagiographical production and the expansion of monastic institutions in the early Islamic Persian Gulf', *AAE* 22 (2011): 97–111.

111 Carter, 'Christianity', p. 106. Twenty Christian dioceses east of the Oxus River (Amu Darya) were recorded in the mid-7th century: Hoyland, *In God's Path*, p. 14.

112 al-Jahwari et al., 'Fulayj'.

113 D. Moez, 'Entre foi et compromis tribal', *Chroniques yéménites* 14 (2007): 36–62; D. Moez, *La rive orientale de la péninsule Arabique aux premiers siècles de l'Islam: entre système tribal et dynamism commercial*, PhD thesis, Université Paris I, 2009.

114 T.J. Wilkinson, C. Edens and M. Gibson, 'The archaeology of the Yemen High Plains: a preliminary chronology', *AAE* 8 (1997): 99–142.

115 J.A. Harrell, 'Building and ornamental stones of the Awam (Mahram Bilqis) Temple in Marib, Yemen', *AAE* 18 (2007): 182–192.

116 T.J. Wilkinson and C. Edens, 'Survey and excavation in the Central Highlands of Yemen: results of the Dhamār Survey Project, 1996 and 1998', *AAE* 10 (1999): 1–33; E. Barbanes, 'Domestic and defensive architecture on the Yemen plateau: eighth century BCE–sixth century CE', *AAE* 11 (2000): 207–222; M. Gibson and T.J. Wilkinson, 'The Dhamār Plain, Yemen: a preliminary study of the archaeological landscape', *PSAS* 25 (1995): 159–83.

117 Barbanes, 'Domestic and defensive', p. 218.

118 King, 'Settlement', pp. 201–205.

119 M.B. Piotrovsky, 'Late ancient and early mediaeval Yemen: settlement traditions and innovations', in King and Cameron (eds), *Byzantine and Early Islamic Near East*: 213–229, pp. 215–216.

120 J.-F. Breton, 'Preliminary notes on the development of Shabwa', *PSAS* 33 (2003): 199–213.

121 A.V. Sedov and A. Bâtâyi', 'Temples of ancient Hadramawt', *PSAS* 24 (1994): 183–96; A. Benoist et al., 'Building G at Makaynūn: a late pre-Islamic settlement above the ruins of a South Arabian town', *AAE* 25 (2014): 80–95; M.A. Mouton et al., 'Makaynūn, an ancient south Arabian site in the Ḥaḍramawt', *PSAS* 36 (2006): 229–242; A. Benoist et al., 'Chronologie et évolution de l'architecture à Makaynūn: la formation d'un centre urbain à l'époque sudarabique dans le ḥaḍramawt', *PSAS* 37 (2007): 17–35.

122 A.V. Sedov, 'Bi'r Hamad: a pre-Islamic settlement in the western Wādī Hadramawt', *AAE* 6 (1995): 103–115; A. Sedov and A. As-Saqqaf, 'Al-Guraf in the Wâdî 'Idim', *AAE* 7 (1996): 52–62.

123 D.P. Hansen, E.L. Ochsenschlager and S. Al-Radi, 'Excavations at Jujah, Shibam, Wadi Hadhramawt', *AAE* 15 (2004): 43–67.

124 M. Mouton, P. Sanlaville and J. Suire, 'A new map of Qâni' (Yemen)', *AAE* 19 (2008): 198–209.

125 A. Rougeulle and A. Benoist, 'Notes on pre- and early Islamic harbours of Ḥaḍramawt (Yemen)', *PSAS* 31 (2001): 203–214.

126 M.G. Esposti and A. Pavan, 'Water and power in south Arabia: the excavation of "Monumental Building 1" (MB1) at Sumhuram (Sultanate of Oman)', *AAE* 31 (2020): 393–421.

127 S. Kay, 'Some ancient dams of the Hijaz', *PSAS* 8 (1978): 68–68; S.b.A. al-Rāshid, 'The development of archaeology in Saudi Arabia', *PSAS* 35 (2005): 207–214, p. 208.

128 M. Guagnin et al., 'An illustrated prehistory of the Jubbah oasis: reconstructing Holocene occupation patterns in north-western Saudi Arabia from rock art and inscriptions', *AAE* 28 (2017): 138–152, p. 148.

129 F.C.W. Courtenay-Thompson, 'Rock engravings near Madinah, Saudi Arabia', *PSAS* 5 (1975): 22–32; A. b. A. a-Sabali al-Zahrani et al., 'Preliminary report on the archaeological survey of Madinah region 1410 AH / 2000 AD', *Atlal* 17 (2002): 29–40.

130 A.b.I. Ghabban and R. Hoyland, 'The inscription of Zuhayr, the oldest Islamic inscription (24 AH/AD 644–645), the rise of the Arabic script and the nature of the early Islamic state', *AAE* 19 (2008): 210–237.

131 G. Bawden, 'Continuity and disruption in the ancient Hejaz: an assessment of

current archaeological strategies', *AAE* 3 (1992): 1–22; P.J. Parr, 'The early history of the Hejaz: a response to Garth Bawden', *AAE* 4 (1993): 48–58.

132 F.W. Weigel, 'Dwelling(s) in a north-west Arabian oasis: decoding residential architecture at Taymā'', *AAE* 30 (2019): 103–133.

133 F. Tourtet and F. Weigel, 'Taymā' in the Nabataean kingdom and in *Provincia Arabia*', *PSAS* 45 (2015): 385–404.

134 Al-Hijr Archaeological Site (Madâin Sâlih), online at whc.unesco.org/en/list/1293

135 Donner, *Muhammad*, p. 104; D. Whitcomb, 'Urbanism in Arabia', *AAE* 7 (1996): 38–51, p. 44, citing S.b.A. al-Rāshid, *Al-Rabadhah: a portrait of early Islamic civilisation in Saudi Arabia,* London: Longman, 1986; see also S.b.A. al-Rāshid, 'Lights on the history and archaeology of Al-Rabadhah (locally called Abu Salim)', *PSAS* 9 (1979): 88–101; S.b.A. al-Rāshid, 'The discovery of al-Rabadha: a city in the early days of Islam', in A.I. al-Ghabban et al. (eds), *Roads of Arabia: archaeology and history of the Kingdom of Saudi Arabia*, Paris: Somogy/Musée du Louvre, 2010: 433–451.

136 Hoyland, *Arabia*, pp. 111–112; G.W. Heck, 'Gold mining in Arabia and the rise of the Islamic state', *Journal of the Economic and Social History of the Orient* 42 (1999): 364–395.

137 Heck, '"Arabia without spices"'; A. Peli, 'Les mines de la péninsule Arabique d'après les auteurs arabes (VIIe–XIIe siècles)', *Chroniques yéménites* 13 (2006).

138 Milwright, *An Introduction*, p. 25.

139 King, 'Settlement', pp. 185–186, 187–197.

140 Rodinson, *Mohammed*, pp. 18–19.

141 Macdonald, 'Arabs and empires', pp. 82–83, 85; Hoyland, *Arabia*, pp. 238–239.

142 G. Fisher, *Between Empires: Arabs, Romans and Sasanians in late antiquity,* Oxford: Oxford University Press, 2011, p. 210; Hoyland, *In God's Path*, p. 23.

143 Hoyland, *Arabia*, p. 243.

144 F. Donner, *The Early Islamic Conquests*, Princeton, NJ: Princeton University Press, 1981, pp. 86, 101; P. Crone and M. Hinds, *God's Caliph: religious authority in the first centuries of Islam*, Cambridge: Cambridge University Press, 1986, pp. 2, 117.

145 Hoyland, *In God's Path*, p. 158.

146 Retsö, *The Arabs in Antiquity*, p. 621.

147 I. Lapidus, *A History of Islamic Societies*, 2nd edition, Cambridge: Cambridge University Press, 2002, p. 43.

148 Donner, *The Early Islamic Conquests,* p. 173; R.N. Frye, 'The political history of Iran under the Sasanians', in *CHI* 3: 116–180, pp. 172–175.

149 Hoyland, *In God's Path*, p. 56.

150 P. Pourshariati, *Decline and Fall of the Sasanian Empire: the Sasanian–Parthian confederacy and the Arab conquest of Iran*, London: Tauris, 2017, pp. 282–283.

151 P.G. Forand, 'The status of the land and inhabitants of the Sawad during the first two centuries of Islam', *Journal of the Economic and Social History of the Orient* 14 (1971): 25–37, p. 30.

152 For a detailed account of these conquests see Hoyland, *In God's Path*.

153   S.T. Parker, *Romans and Saracens: a history of the Arabian frontier*, Winona Lake, IL: American School of Oriental Research, 1986, pp. 149, 152.

154   Parker, *Romans and Saracens*, p. 154.

155   C.F. Robinson, 'The rise of Islam, 600–705', in Robinson (ed.), *The New Cambridge History of Islam, Vol. 1* 171–225, p. 197; Donner, *The Early Islamic Conquests*, p. 220; G. Martinez-Gros, 'Arab conquests (630–750 AD)', in al-Ghabban et al. (eds), *Roads of Arabia*: 111–117.

156   A. Walmsley, *Early Islamic Syria: an archaeological assessment*, London: Duckworth, 2007, pp. 47–48.

157   P.-L. Gatier, 'Villages du Proche-Orient Protobyzantine (4ème-7ème s.): étude régional', in King and Cameron (eds), *Byzantine and Early Islamic Near East*: 17–48; Walmsley, *Early Islamic Syria*, pp. 31–47.

158   Milwright, *An Introduction*, p. 29.

159   Walmsley, *Early Islamic Syria*, pp. 77–78; C. Foss, 'Syria in transition, AD 550–750: an archaeological approach', in A. Cameron (ed.), *Late Antiquity on the Eve of Islam*, Farnham: Ashgate, 2012: 171–276, p. 266.

160   H. Kennedy, 'Islam', in G.W. Bowerstock, P. Brown and O. Grabar (eds), *Late Antiquity: a guide to the postclassical world*, Cambridge MA: Harvard University Press, 1999: 219–237, p. 224; X. de Planhol, *The World of Islam*, Ithaca, NY: Cornell University Press, 1959, p. 3; Milwright, *An Introduction*, p. 24.

161   Walmsley, *Early Islamic Syria*, pp. 77–78; Milwright, *An Introduction*, pp. 34–35.

162   D. Whitcomb, *Ayla: art and industry in the Islamic port of Aqaba*, Chicago, IL: Oriental Institute, 1994, pp. 6–10; Y. Rapuano, 'An early Islamic settlement and a possible open-air mosque at Eilat', *'Atiqot* 75 (2013): 129–165.

163   N. Luz, 'The construction of an Islamic city in Palestine: the case of Umayyad al-Ramla', *Journal of the Royal Asiatic Society* 7 (1997): 27–54.

164   H. Geva, 'Jerusalem's population in antiquity: a minimalist view', *Tel Aviv* 41 (2014): 131–160.

165   Donner, *The Early Islamic Conquests*, pp. 151–152.

166   M. Sharon, 'Witnessed by three disciples of the Prophet: the Jerusalem 32 inscription from 32 AH / 652 CE', *Israel Exploration Journal* 68 (2018): 100–111.

167   G. Avni, *The Byzantine–Islamic Transition in Palestine: an archaeological approach*, Oxford: Oxford University Press, 2014, pp. 107–159.

168   O. Amichay et al., 'A bazaar assemblage: reconstructing consumption, production and trade from mineralised seeds in Abbasid Jerusalem', *Antiquity* 93 (2019): 199–217, pp. 207–208.

169   J. Magness, *The Archaeology of the Early Islamic Settlement in Palestine*, Winona Lake, IN: Eisenbrauns, 2003, pp. 194–196.

170   Whitcomb, 'Urbanism in Arabia', p. 39.

171   Y. Tsafrir and G. Foerster, 'From Scythopolis to Baysan – changing concepts of urbanism', in King and Cameron (eds), *Byzantine and Early Islamic Near East*: 95–115, p. 111; Avni, *The Byzantine–Islamic Transition*, pp. 55–71.

172   D. Whitcomb, 'Khirbet al-Karak identified with Sinnabra', *Al-'Usur Al-Wusta*, 14 (2002): 1–6; D. Whitcomb, 'Notes for an archaeology of Mu'āwiya: material culture in the transitional period of believers', in Borrut and Donner (eds),

Christians and Others: 11–28, p. 13; R. Greenberg, O. Tal and T. Da'adli, *Bet Yeraḥ, Vol. III. Hellenistic Philoteria and Islamic al-Sinnabra,* Jerusalem: Israel Antiquities Authority, 2017.

173 Avni, *The Byzantine–Islamic Transition*, pp. 71–90.

174 Magness, *The Archaeology*, pp. 1–2, 196, 206–216.

175 I.W.N. Jones et al., 'Khirbat al-Mana'iyya: an early Islamic-period copper-smelting site in south-eastern Wadi 'Araba, Jordan', *AAE* 28 (2017):297–314.

176 Avni, *The Byzantine–Islamic Transition*, pp. 93–8.

177 Walmsley, *Early Islamic Syria*, p. 55; A. Walmsley, 'The social and economic regime at Fihl (Pella) and neighbouring centres, between the 7th and 9th centuries', in P. Canival and J.-P. Rey-Coquais (eds), *La Syrie de Byzance à l'Islam VIIe-VIIIe siècle: actes du colloque,* Damascus: Institut Français de Damas, 1992: 249–261; Avni, *The Byzantine–Islamic Transition.*

178 Whitcomb, 'Urbanism in Arabia', pp. 38–39.

179 D. Orssaud, 'Le passage de la céramique Byzantine et las céramique islamique', in Canival and Rey-Coquais (eds), *La Syrie*: 219–228; J.P. Sodini et al., 'Déhès (Syrie du nord): campagnes I–III (1976–1978)', *Syria* 57 (1980): 1–301.

180 D. Genequand, 'The archaeological evidence for the Jafnids and Nasrids', in Fisher (ed.), *Arabs and Empires*: 172–203, pp. 188–207.

181 H.I. Macadam, 'Settlement and settlement patterns in northern and central Transjordania, ca. 550–ca. 750', in King and Cameron (eds), *Byzantine and Early Islamic Near East*: 49–93, pp. 59, 91.

182 A. Zeyadeh, 'Settlement patterns, an archaeological perspective: case studies from northern Palestine and Jordan', in King and Cameron (eds), *Byzantine and Early Islamic Near East*: 117–131, p. 131; Milwright, *An Introduction*, pp. 137–138.

183 Kennedy, 'Islam', p. 233.

184 Sodini et al., 'Déhès', p. 295.

185 Walmsley, *Early Islamic Syria*, p. 115.

186 P. Niewöhner (ed.), *The Archaeology of Byzantine Anatolia: from the end of late antiquity until the coming of the Turks,* Oxford: Oxford University Press, 2017.

187 P. Niewöhner, 'Urbanism', in Niewöhner (ed.), *The Archaeology*, pp. 50–51.

188 Magness, *The Archaeology*; Walmsley, *Early Islamic*; Avni, *The Byzantine–Islamic Transition.*

189 Kennedy, 'Islam', pp. 229–232.

190 M. Milwright, 'Archaeology and material culture', in Robinson (ed.), *New Cambridge History of Islam, Vol. 1*: 664–682, p. 666; see also Milwright, *An Introduction*, pp. 44–45, 52–53.

191 Johns, 'Archaeology and the history of early Islam'.

192 Avni, *The Byzantine–Islamic Transition*, pp. 21–22.

193 Avni, *The Byzantine–Islamic Transition*, pp. 6–8.

194 Avni, *The Byzantine–Islamic Transition*, pp. 352–353.

195 Borrut and Donner, 'Introduction'.

4. Rural Galilee to imperial cities: the beginnings and spread of Christianity

1 A brief account of developing views is in F. Young, 'Prelude: Jesus Christ, foundation of Christianity', in *CHC* 1: 1–34.

2 K. Hopkins, 'Christian number and its implications', *Journal of Early Christian Studies* 6 (1998): 185–226, pp. 211–213.

3 For example, the sympathetic review of a critical study by the then Archbishop of Canterbury, Rowan Williams, '*Christian Beginnings* by Geza Vermes – review', www.theguardian.com/books/2012/jul/11/christian-beginnings-geza-vermes-review

4 See for example R. Carrier, *Proving History: Bayes's theorem and the quest for the historical Jesus*, Amherst, NY: Prometheus Books, 2012; and R. Carrier, *On the Historicity of Jesus: why we might have reason for doubt,* Sheffield: Sheffield Phoenix Press, 2014. Responses to this minority view include M. Casey, *Jesus: evidence and argument or mythical myths?*, London: Bloomsbury, 2014; and B.D. Ehrman, *Did Jesus Exist? The historical argument for Jesus of Nazareth*, New York: Harper, 2012.

5 S. Amorai-Stark et al., 'An inscribed copper-alloy finger ring from Herodium depicting a krater', *Israel Exploration Journal* 68 (2018): 208–222.

6 Győző Vörös, in his report *Machaerus III: the golden jubilee of the archaeological excavations. Final report on the Herodian Citadel (1968–2018)*, Milan: Edizioni Terra Santa, 2019, identified a possible area of the royal chamber. Interestingly, pig bones were found in Herodian levels at the site.

7 Census: Luke 2:2. Age of Jesus: Luke 3:23. John the Baptist: Luke 3:1.

8 A papyrus with a fragment of Mark's gospel had been rumoured to be from the 1st century but its formal publication dated it as early 3rd or possibly late 2nd century: P.J. Parsons and N. Gonis (eds), *The Oxyrhynchus Papyri LXXXIII*, London: Egypt Exploration Society, 2018, p. 5.

9 B. Nongbri, *God's Library: the archaeology of the earliest Christian manuscripts*, New Haven, CT: Yale University Press, 2018, pp. 55, 268.

10 J. Barton, *A History of the Bible: the book and its faiths*, London: Allen Lane, 2019, p. 199.

11 Comparative table in *The Cambridge Annotated Study Bible: New Revised Standard Version*, Cambridge: Cambridge University Press, 1993, pp. 327–335.

12 B.D. Ehrman, *Misquoting Jesus: the story behind who changed the Bible and why*, New York: HarperCollins, 2005.

13 B.D. Ehrman (ed. and tr.), *The Apostolic Fathers*, Cambridge, MA: Harvard University Press, 2003, pp. 24–26, 159.

14 T. Burke and B. Landau (eds), *New Testament Apocrypha: more non-canonical scriptures*, Grand Rapids, MI: Eerdmans, 2016, vol. 1, p. xxvii.

15 On oral traditions of the narrative of Yeshua's death, see B.D. Ehrman, *Jesus Before the Gospels: how the earliest Christians remembered, changed, and invented their stories of the Savior*, New York: HarperCollins, 2016.

16 G. Vermes, *The Changing Face of Jesus*, London: Allen Lane, 2000, pp. 258–262.

17 Acts 15:1–21; Galatians 2:7–14.

18 H.-J. Klauck, *Apocryphal Gospels: an introduction*, London: Clark, 2003; B.D. Ehrman and Z. Pleše, *The Apocryphal Gospels: texts and translations*, New York: Oxford University Press, 2011; B.D. Ehrman, *Lost Christianities: the battles for scripture and the faiths we never knew*, New York: Oxford University Press, 2003, pp. xi–xv.

19 Perceptions of Gnosticism are largely through the prism of early Christian critics. See for example R.M. Grant (ed.), *Gnosticism: an anthology*, London: Collins, 1961.

20 Geza Vermes, *Christian Beginnings: from Nazareth to Nicaea AD 30–325*, London: Penguin, 2012, pp. 136–147.

21 1 and 2 Corinthians, Galatians, Philemon, Philippians, Romans, 1 Thessalonians, and possibly Colossians and 2 Thessalonians.

22 D.B. Capes, 'Jesus tradition in Paul', in C.A. Evans (ed.), *Encyclopedia of the Historical Jesus*, New York: Routledge, 2008: 446–449.

23 Romans 1:4, 1:13, 8:34; 1 Corinthians 1:23, 2:2, 6:14, 11:23–5, 15:4–7; 2 Corinthians 13:4; Galatians 1:18–19, 2:7–13, 3:1. Possible quotations are 1 Corinthians 7:10–11 and 2 Corinthians 12:8–9.

24 The major historical sources remain the writings of Josephus: *The Jewish War* (written about 75 CE) and *Antiquities of the Jews* (from the mid-90s).

25 E. Gabba, 'The social, economic and political history of Palestine 63 BCE–CE 70', in *CHJ* 3: 94–167, pp. 97, 114, 117, 123.

26 E.W. Stegemann and W. Stegemann, *The Jesus Movement: a social history of its first century*, Minneapolis, MN: Fortress Press, 1999, pp. 99, 111–112, 133–134, 139–141.

27 Gabba, 'The social', pp. 126–127, 133–134, 139, 152.

28 S. Schwartz, 'Political, social, and economic life in the land of Israel, 66–c. 235', in *CHJ* 4: 23–52, p. 23.

29 R.A. Horsley, 'Popular messianic movements around the time of Jesus', *Catholic Biblical Quarterly* 46 (1984): 471–495; R.A. Horsley, 'Jesus and Galilee: the contingencies of a renewal movement', in E.M. Meyers (ed.), *Galilee Through the Centuries: confluence of cultures*, Winona Lake, IN: Eisenbrauns, 1999: 57–74, p. 74.

30 Stegemann and Stegemann, *The Jesus Movement*, pp. 144–149, 162, 171–173, 182–183.

31 Williams, '*Christian Beginnings* by Geza Vermes – review'.

32 B.D. Ehrman, *Jesus: apocalyptic prophet of the new millennium*, New York: Oxford University Press, 1999; Geza Vermes, *The Authentic Gospel of Jesus*, London: Allen Lane, 2003, pp. 38–39.

33 B.D. Ehrman, *How Jesus Became God: the exaltation of a Jewish preacher from Galilee*, New York: Harper, 2014.

34 Gabba, 'The social', pp. 145–146.

35 M. Goodman, 'Galilean Judaism and Judaean Judaism', in *CHJ* 3: 596–617, pp. 608–609; Vermes, *The Changing Face*, pp. 240–246.

36 Vermes, *The Changing Face*, pp. 240–241; Vermes, *Christian Beginnings*, pp. 18–27.

37 R. Gray, *Prophetic Figures in Late Second Temple Jewish Palestine: the evidence from Josephus*, New York: Oxford University Press, 1993, pp. 158–163 (on Jesus son of Ananias).

38 See for example G. Vermes's books *Jesus the Jew: a historian's reading of the gospels*, London: SCM Press, 1973; *The Religion of Jesus the Jew*, Minneapolis, MN: Fortress Press, 1993; *Jesus and the World of Judaism*, London: SCM Press, 1983; *The Changing Face of Jesus*, London: Allen Lane, 2000; *The Authentic Gospel of Jesus*, London: Allen Lane, 2003. Quote from Vermes, *The Changing Face*, p. 147.

39 Vermes, *The Changing Face*, p. 224.

40 Gabba, 'The social', pp. 111–113.

41 J.F. Strange, 'First century Galilee from archaeology and from the texts', in D.R. Edwards and C.T. McCollough (eds), *Archaeology and the Galilee: texts and contexts in Greco-Roman and Byzantine periods*, Atlanta, GA: Scholars Press, 1997: 39–48.

42 Goodman, 'Galilean Judaism and Judaean Judaism', p. 601; D. Gurevich, 'The water pools and the pilgrimage to Jerusalem in the late Second Temple period', *Palestine Exploration Quarterly* 149 (2017): 103–134.

43 Josephus, *Antiquities of the Jews*, Book 18, 5:2.

44 Matthew 4:23–25; Luke 6:17–19.

45 S. Freyne, 'Galilee and Judaea in the first century', in *CHC 1*: 35–52, p. 51.

46 Acts 9:31.

47 J. Finegan, *The Archeology of the New Testament: the life of Jesus and the beginning of the early church*, Princeton, NJ: Princeton University Press, 1969, pp. 88–108.

48 J.D. Crossan and J.L. Reed, *Excavating Jesus: beneath the stones, beneath the texts*, London: SPCK, 2001, pp. 2–3.

49 M. Avian, 'First century Jewish Galilee: an archaeological perspective', in D.R. Edwards (ed.), *Religion and Society in Roman Palestine*, New York: Routledge, 2004: 7–27; M. Aviam, 'The transformation from Galil Ha-Goyim to Jewish Galilee', in D.A. Fiensy and J.R. Strange (eds), *Galilee in the Late Second Temple and Mishnaic Period, Vol. 2: The Archaeological Record from Cities, Towns and Villages*, Minneapolis, MN: Fortress Press, 2015: 9–21, pp. 16–19.

50 J.L. Reed, *Archaeology and the Galilean Jesus: a re-examination of the evidence*, Harrisburg, PA: Trinity, 2000, pp. 39–41.

51 E.P. Sanders, 'Jesus' relation to Sepphoris', in R.M. Nagy (ed.), *Sepphoris in Galilee: crosscurrents of culture*, Winona Lake, IN: Eisenbrauns, 1996: 75–79.

52 J.F. Strange, 'The Eastern Basilica building', in Nagy (ed.), *Sepphoris*: 117–121; R.A. Horsley, *Archaeology, History and Society in Galilee*, Valley Forge, PA: Trinity, 1996, p. 51; Crossan and Reed, *Excavating Jesus*, p. 65; D. Adan-Bayewitz et al., 'Preferential distribution of lamps from the Jerusalem area in the late Second Temple period', *Bulletin of the American School of Oriental Research* 350 (2008): 37–85.

53 Reed, *Archaeology and the Galilean Jesus*, p. 80; E. Meyers, 'Jesus and his Galilean context', in Edwards and McCollough (eds), *Archaeology and the Galilee*: 57–66, p. 59.

54 Sanders, 'Jesus' relation to Sepphoris'; J.F. Strange et al., 'Sepphoris', in Fiensy and Strange (eds), *Galilee*: 22–87; K. Cytryn-Silverman, 'Tiberias, from its foundation to the end of the early Islamic period', in Fiensy and Strange (eds), *Galilee*: 186–210.

55 John 6:23.

56 For conflicting views, see H.C. Kee, 'Early Christianity in the Galilee', in L.I. Levine (ed.), *The Galilee in Late Antiquity*, New York: Jewish Theological Seminary of America, 1992: 3–22, p. 15; R.A. Horsley, 'Jesus and Galilee', pp. 59–60; A. Berlin, cited in J. Magness, *Stone and Dung, Oil and Spit: Jewish daily life in the time of Jesus*, Grand Rapids, MI: Eerdmans, 2011, p. 61.

57 Reed, *Archaeology and the Galilean Jesus*, p. 44.

58 K.R. Dark, 'Roman-period and Byzantine landscapes between Sepphoris and Nazareth', *Palestine Exploration Quarterly* 140 (2008): 87–102; K. Dark, 'Early Roman-period Nazareth and the Sisters of Nazareth Convent', *Antiquaries Journal* 92 (2012): 37–64.

59 Horsley, *Archaeology, History and Society*, pp. 73ff.

60 J.F. Strange, 'Nazareth', in Fiensy and Strange (eds), *Galilee*: 167–180; J.F. Strange, 'Archaeology of the gospels', in *OHECA*, pp. 38–39; Crossan and Reed, *Excavating Jesus*, pp. 15–36.

61 Reed, *Archaeology and the Galilean Jesus*, p. 83; K. Dark, *Roman-Period and Byzantine Nazareth and Its Hinterland*, London: Routledge, 2020. Other estimates have ranged from 400 to 1500 or even 2000.

62 K. Dark, 'Has Jesus' Nazareth house been found?', *Biblical Archaeology Review* 41 (2015): 54–63.

63 Crossan and Reed, *Excavating Jesus*, p. 35.

64 M. Avian, 'Yodefat – Jotapata: a Jewish Galilean town at the end of the Second Temple period: the results of an archaeological project', in Fiensy and Strange (eds), *Galilee*: 109–126; Avian, 'First century', pp. 16–17.

65 Avian, 'Yodefat', pp. 114–115.

66 Reed, *Archaeology and the Galilean Jesus*, pp. 83, 139–169; Horsley, *Archaeology, History and Society*, pp. 112–116; Crossan and Reed, *Excavating Jesus*, pp. 81–97.

67 Crossan and Reed, *Excavating Jesus*, pp. 92–96.

68 R. Bauckham and S. de Luca, 'Magdala as we now know it', *Early Christianity* 6 (2015): 91–118; S. de Luca and A. Lena, 'Magdala/Taricheae', in Fiensy and Strange (eds), *Galilee*: 280–342; C.A. Evans, *Jesus and the Remains of His Day: studies in Jesus and the evidence of material culture*, Peabody, MA: Hendrickson, 2015, pp. 17–28.

69 S. Wachsmann, K. Raveh and O. Cohen, 'The Kinneret boat project Part I. The excavation and conservation of the Kinneret boat', *International Journal of Nautical Archaeology* 16 (1987): 233–245.

70 R. Arav and R.A. Freund (eds), *Bethsaida: a city by the north shore of the sea of Galilee*, Kirkville, MI: Truman State University Press, vol. 2 (1999), pp. 107–108, vol. 4 (2009), p. xxii;. M. Appold, 'Bethsaida and a first-century house church?', in Arava and Freund (eds), *Bethsaida*, vol. 2: 373–396, has an unconvincing argument that Bethsaida was a major centre of active Christianity.

71 R. Avav and C.E. Savage, 'Bethsaida', in Fiensy and Strange (eds), *Galilee: 258–279*, pp. 266–269; Evans, *Jesus*, pp. 5–17; C.E. Savage, *Biblical Bethsaida: an archaeological study of the first century*, Lanham, MD: Rowman & Littlefield, 2011, pp. 14, 135.

72 Meyers, 'Jesus and his Galilean context', pp. 58–59.

73 Savage, *Biblical Bethsaida*, p. 142.

74 M. Moreland, 'The Galilean response to earliest Christianity', in Edwards (ed.), *Religion and Society*: 37–48.

75 J. Marcus, 'Jewish Christianity', in *CHC 1*: 85–102, p. 99; E. Schürer, *The History of the Jewish People in the Age of Jesus Christ*, revised edition, Edinburgh: Edinburgh University Press, 4 volumes, 1973–1987, vol. 3:i, p. 498; C. Koester, 'The origin and significance of the flight to Pella tradition', *Catholic Biblical Quarterly* 51 (1989): 90–106.

76 J.L. Kelley, *The Church of the Holy Sepulchre in Text and Archaeology*, Oxford: Archaeopress, 2019; S. Gibson and J.E. Taylor, *Beneath the Church of the Holy Sepulchre, Jerusalem: the archaeology and early history of traditional Golgotha*, London: Palestine Exploration Fund, 1994, pp. 24, 48, 51; M. Biddle, *The Tomb of Christ*, Stroud: Sutton, 1999, pp. 1, 53, 57. Useful reconstructions accompany the article by K. Romey, 'The search for the real Jesus', *National Geographic*, December 2017: 34–69.

77 K.J. Conant, 'The Original Buildings at the Holy Sepulchre in Jerusalem', *Speculum* 31 (1956): 1–48; R. Ousterhout, 'Rebuilding the Temple: Constantine Monomachus and the Holy Sepulchre', Journal *of the Society of Architectural Historians* 48 (1989): 66–78.

78 G. Avni and G. Seligman, 'Between the Temple Mount/Haram el-Sharif and the Holy Sepulchre: archaeological involvement in Jerusalem's holy places', *Journal of Mediterranean Archaeology* 19 (2006): 259–288; M. Biddle, M Cooper and S. Robson, 'The tomb of Christ, Jerusalem: a photogrammetric survey', *Photogrammetric Record* 14 (1992): 25–43; Kelley, *Church of the Holy Sepulchre*; A. Moropoulou et al., 'OSL mortar dating to elucidate the construction history of the Tomb Chamber of the Holy Aedicule of the Holy Sepulchre in Jerusalem', *Journal of Archaeological Science: Reports* 19 (2018): 80–91.

79 Biddle, *The Tomb of Christ*, p. 58; K. Galor and H. Bloedhorn, *The Archaeology of Jerusalem: from the origins to the Ottomans*, New Haven, CT: Yale University Press, 2013, pp. 71–74.

80 Gibson and Taylor, *Beneath the Church*, p. 63.

81 Magness, *Stone and Dung*, p. 156; Galor and Bloedhorn, *The Archaeology*, pp. 97–108.

82 L.W. Raḥmani, 'Ossuaries and ossilegium (bone-gathering) in the late Second Temple Period', in H. Geva (ed.), *Ancient Jerusalem Revealed*, Jerusalem: Israel Exploration Society, 2000 (1994): 191–205, pp. 195–196; Galor and Bloedhorn, *The Archaeology*, p. 106.

83 Magness, *Stone and Dung*, pp. 164–172.

84 Kelley, *Church of the Holy Sepulchre*, p. 73.

85 S. Kochav, 'The search for a Protestant Holy Sepulchre: the Garden Tomb in

nineteenth-century Jerusalem', *Journal of Ecclesiastical History* 46 (1995): 278–301.

86 J.H. Charlesworth (ed.), *The Tomb of Jesus and His Family? Exploring ancient Jewish tombs near Jerusalem's walls*, Grand Rapids, MI: Eerdmans, 2013; Evans, *Jesus and the Remains of His Day*, pp. 181–196; Magness, *Stone and Dung*, pp. 172–174; S. Gibson, 'Is the Talpiot tomb really the tomb of Jesus?', *Near Eastern Archaeology* 69 (2006): 118–124.

87 Galor and Bloedhorn, *The Archaeology*, p. 65; H. Geva, 'Jerusalem's population in antiquity: a minimalist view', *Tel Aviv* 41 (2014): 131–160.

88 M. Brishi and S. Gibson, 'Excavations along the western and southern walls of the Old City of Jerusalem', in H. Geva (ed.), *Ancient Jerusalem Revealed*, Jerusalem: Israel Exploration Society, 1994: 147–155, pp. 151–153; H. Geva, 'Excavations at the Citadel of Jerusalem, 1976–1980', in Geva (ed.), *Ancient Jerusalem*: 156–167, pp. 160–162; R. Sivan and G. Solar, 'Excavations in the Jerusalem Citadel, 1980–1988', in Geva (ed.), *Ancient Jerusalem*: 168–176.

89 J. Patrich, 'The structure of the Second Temple – a new reconstruction', in Geva (ed.), *Ancient Jerusalem*: 260–271; Galor and Bloedhorn, *The Archaeology*, pp. 76–80.

90 G. Barkay and Z. Dvira, 'Relics in rubble: the Temple Mount sifting project', *Biblical Archaeology Review* 42 (2016): 44–64; Y. Baruch, R. Reich and D. Sandhaus, 'A decade of archaeological exploration on the Temple Mount', *Tel Aviv* 45 (2018): 3–22; Crossan and Reed, *Excavating Jesus*, pp. 193–201.

91 Y. Baruch and R. Reich, 'Excavations near the Triple Gate of the Temple Mount, Jerusalem', *'Atiqot* 85 (2016): 37–95, p. 90.

92 R. Reich et al., 'Faunal remains from the 1994–1996 excavations at the Temple Mount, Jerusalem', *'Atiqot* 80 (2015): 19–34, pp. 21–22, 29, 32.

93 R. Reich and E. Shukron, 'The Jerusalem city-dump in the Late Second Temple period', *Zeitschrift des Deutschen Palästina-Vereins* 119 (2003): 12–18.

94 G. Bar-Oz et al., '"Holy garbage": a quantitative study of the city-dump of early Roman Jerusalem', *Levant* 39 (2007), 1–12.

95 A. Spiciarich, Y. Gadot and L. Sapir-Hen, 'The faunal evidence from early Roman Jerusalem: the people behind the garbage', *Tel Aviv* 4 (2017): 98–117.

96 A stable-isotope-based study of a probably 1st-century CE burial in a chamber near Nablus some 30 miles (50 km) north of Jerusalem noted a largely plant based diet, thought to be legumes, wheat, olives and grapes: L.A. Alsaud et al., 'Stable isotope dietary analysis on human remains: a case study at Khirbet Aqabet al Qadi burial chamber, Nablus, Palestine', *Radiocarbon* 61 (2019): 1107–1120.

97 G. Hartman et al., 'The pilgrimage economy of early Roman Jerusalem (1st century BCE–70 CE) reconstructed from the δ 15N and δ 13C values of goat and sheep remains', *Journal of Archaeological Science* 40 (2013): 4369–4376; Y. Magen, 'Jerusalem as a center of the stone vessel industry during the Second Temple period', in Geva (ed.), *Ancient Jerusalem*: 244–256, p. 256.

98 J. Magness, *Stone and Dung*, pp. 9–10, 56–58; Crossan and Reed, *Excavating Jesus*, pp. 202–207.

99 Galor and Bloedhorn, *The Archaeology*, pp. 88–95.

100 M. Humphries, 'Material evidence (1): archaeology', in *OHECS*: 87–103, pp. 87–88.

101 J. Marcus, 'Jewish Christianity', in *CHC 1*: 85–102.

102 R. Derricourt, *Antiquity Imagined: the remarkable legacy of Egypt and the ancient Near East*, London: Tauris, 2015, pp. 220–250.

103 Galatians 1:7.

104 Galatians 1:11–12.

105 Galatians 1:15–20, 1:17, 2:7–9.

106 M.M. Mitchell, 'Gentile Christianity', in *CHC 1*: 103–124, p. 106.

107 W.A. Meeks, *The First Urban Christians: the social world of the Apostle Paul*, New Haven, CT: Yale University Press, 2003, p. 9.

108 W.D. Davies, 'Paul: from the Jewish point of view', in *CHJ 3*: 678–730, pp. 680–681.

109 B.A. Pearson, 'Earliest Christianity in Egypt', in J.E. Goehring and J.A. Timbie (eds), *The World of Early Egyptian Christianity: language, literature, and social*, Washington, DC: Catholic University of America Press, 2007: 97–112. Although Christianity probably developed within the city's large Jewish community, an alternative view sees a break between Jewish Christianity in Alexandria and the Christian traditions reflecting a Greek heritage.

110 Meeks, *The First Urban Christians*, p. 40.

111 Galatians 1:17–21; Acts 11:19–30.

112 Acts 13–14; 16–18; 19–21; 27–28.

113 E.M. Smallwood, 'The diaspora in the Roman period before CE 70', in *CHJ 3*: 168–191.

114 R. Stark, *The Rise of Christianity: a sociologist reconsiders history*, Princeton, NJ: Princeton University Press, 1996, pp. 47, 49.

115 Stegemann and Stegemann, *The Jesus Movement*, p. 235; W. Scheidel, 'Progress and problems in Roman demography', in W. Scheidel (ed.), *Debating Roman Demography*, Leiden: Brill, 2001: 1–81, pp. 52, 57, 63; J.W. Hanson, *An Urban Geography of the Roman World 100 BC to AD 300*, Oxford: Archaeopress, 2016, pp. 66, 95.

116 M.D. Costa et al., 'A substantial prehistoric European ancestry amongst Ashkenazi maternal lineages', *Nature Communications* 4 (2013): 2543.

117 Schürer, *The History of the Jewish People*, vol. 3.i, pp. 3–86.

118 G.F. Snyder, *Ante Pacem: archaeological evidence of Christ before Constantine*, Macon, GA: Mercer University Press, 2003, pp. 2–3.

119 W.R. Caraher and D.K. Pettegrew, 'The archaeology of early Christianity: the history, methods, and state of a field', in *OHECA*: 1–22; W.H.C. Frend, *The Archaeology of Early Christianity*, London: Cassell, 1996 and Minneapolis, MN: Fortress Press, 1996 (a survey of research up to the mid-1990s).

120 K. Bowes, 'Early Christian archaeology: a state of the field', *Religion Compass* 2 (2008): 575–619.

121 Caraher and Pettegrew, 'The archaeology of early Christianity'.

122 M. Humphries, 'Material evidence (1): archaeology', in *OHECS*: 87–103, p. 96.

123 S. Huebner, *Papyri and the Social World of the New Testament*, Cambridge: Cambridge University Press, 2019, p. 214.

124 Snyder, *Ante Pacem*, pp. 2–3.

125 Hopkins, 'Christian number', pp. 192, 200–202; Stark, *The Rise of Christianity*, pp. 4–13. The derived figure is a trend of 3.4% growth per annum.

126 Horsley, *Archaeology, History and Society*, p. 108.

127 Meeks, *The First Urban Christians*.

128 B.S. Billings, 'From house church to tenement church: domestic space and the development of early urban Christianity – the example of Ephesus', *Journal of Theological Studies* 62 (2011): 541–569.

129 R. Hachlili, 'The origin of the synagogue: a re-assessment', *Journal for the Study of Judaism in the Persian, Hellenistic, and Roman Period* 28 (1997): 34–47, pp. 41–43; Horsley, *Archaeology, History and Society*, p. 132; J.H. Charlesworth (ed.), *Jesus and Archaeology*, Grand Rapids, MI: 2006, pp. 27–29; L.D. Matassa, *Invention of the First-Century Synagogue*, Atlanta, GA: SBL Press, 2018; Strange, 'Archaeology of the gospels'.

130 L.M. White, *The Social Origins of Christian Architecture, Vol. 2: Texts and Monuments for the Christian* Domus Ecclesiae *in Its Environment*, Valley Forge, PA: Trinity Press, 1997, pp. 123–135.

131 Y. Tepper and L. di Segni, *A Christian Prayer Hall of the Third Century* CE *at Kefar 'Othnay (Legio)*, Jerusalem: Israel Antiquities Authority, 2006, p. 36; J.E. Taylor, 'Christian archaeology in Palestine: the Roman and Byzantine periods', in *OHECA*: 369–389, pp. 371–372.

132 Billings, 'From house church', pp. 548, 569.

133 Tabbernee, 'Epigraphy', p. 127; W.M. Calder, 'Early-Christian epitaphs from Phrygia', *Anatolian Studies* 5 (1955): 25–38.

134 C.W. Concannon, 'The archaeology of the Pauline mission', in M. Harding and A. Nobbs (eds), *All Things to all Cultures: Paul among Jews, Christians and Romans*, Grand Rapids, MI: Eerdmans, 2013: 57–83.

135 G. Downey, 'The size of the population of Antioch', *Transactions and Proceedings of the American Philological Association* 89 (1958): 84–91; Hanson, *An Urban Geography*, pp. 66–67, 119–121.

136 A. De Giorgi, 'The formation of a Roman landscape: the case of Antioch', *Journal of Roman Archaeology* 20 (2007): 283–298; A. De Giorgi, 'Antioch, Apamea, and the Tetrapolis, archaeology of', in C. Smith (ed.), *Encyclopedia of Global Archaeology*, New York: Springer, 2014: 284–289.

137 J. Hanson, 'The urban system of Roman Asia Minor and wider urban connectivity', in A. Bowman and A. Wilson (eds), *Settlement, Urbanization, and Population*, Oxford: Oxford University Press, 2011: 230–272, pp. 255–258; Hanson, *An Urban Geography*, pp. 66–67, 119–120.

138 J. Murphy-O'Connor, *St Paul's Ephesus*, Collegeville, MN: Liturgical Press, 2008, pp. 186–200.

139 Snyder, *Ante Pacem*, p. 215.

140 L.V. Rutgers, *Subterranean Rome*, Leuven: Peeters, 2000, pp. 86, 89.

141 Rutgers, *Subterranean Rome*, pp. 53, 67, 98; Tabbernee, 'Epigraphy', in *OHECS*, pp. 127, 135; Frend, *The Archaeology of Early Christianity*, pp. 160–167, 247, 344–345, 370; V.F. Nicolai, 'The catacombs', in *OHECA*: 67–88.

142 Derricourt, *Antiquity Imagined*, pp. 224–229.

143 Frend, *The Archaeology of Early Christianity*, pp. 267–275.

5. Scribes, priests and exiles under foreign rule: the emergence of monotheistic Judaism

1 N. Macdonald, *Deuteronomy and the Meaning of Monotheism*, Tubingen: Mohr Siebeck, 2003, pp. 6–7, 28, 53, 55; J.F.A. Sawyer, 'Biblical alternatives to monotheism', *Theology* 87 (1984): 172–180, p. 173.

2 O. Lipschits, 'Persian-period Judah: a new perspective', in L. Jonker (ed.), *Texts, Contexts and Readings in Postexilic Literature*, Tubingen: Siebeck, 2011: 187–211.

3 Z.I. Farber, 'Religion in eighth-century Judah: an overview', in Z.I. Farber and J.L. Wright (eds), *Archaeology and History of Eighth-Century Judah*, Atlanta, GA: SBL Press, 2018: 431–453, p. 431.

4 Isaiah 40:28, 44:6.

5 R. Gnuse, 'The emergence of monotheism in Ancient Israel: a survey of recent scholarship', *Religion* 29 (1999): 315–336, pp. 318–325.

6 Farber, 'Religion in eighth-century Judah', pp. 431–436.

7 M. Leuenberger, 'Where does Yhwh come from?', *The Ancient Near East Today* 7 (2019), online.

8 Gnuse, 'The emergence of monotheism', p. 316. The theological implications of the exile, as reflected in the Tanakh, are discussed in R. Albertz, *Israel in Exile: literature of the sixth century B.C.E.*, Atlanta, GA: Society of Biblical Literature, 2003.

9 J.B. Pritchard (ed.), *The Ancient Near East: an anthology of texts and pictures*, Princeton, NJ: Princeton University Press, 2011, pp. 282–284.

10 L. Pearce and C. Wunsch, *Documents of Judean Exiles and West Semites in Babylonia in the Collection of David Sofer*, Bethesda, ML: CDL Press, 2014; L.E. Pearce, 'New evidence for Judeans in Babylonia', in *JJPP*: 399–411. The tablets are on extended loan to the Bible Lands Museum, Jerusalem.

11 L.L. Grabbe, *A History of the Jews and Judaism in the Second Temple Period, Vol. 1: Yehud: a history of the Persian province of Judah*, London: Clark, 2004, pp. 337–341.

12 I. Finkelstein, 'Persian period Jerusalem and Yehud: a rejoinder', *Journal of Hebrew Scriptures* 9 (2009), article 24, p. 3.

13 T.C. Mitchell, 'The Babylonian exile and the restoration of the Jews in Palestine', in J. Boardman et al. (eds), *Cambridge Ancient History, Vol. 3, Part 2: The Assyrian and Babylonian Empires and Other States of the Near East, from the Eighth to the Sixth Centuries BC*, 2nd edition, Cambridge: Cambridge University Press, 1992: 410–460, p. 440.

14 Grabbe, *A History of the Jews 1*, pp. 238–261.

15 C. Rollston, 'Scripture and inscriptions: eighth-century Israel and Judah in writing', in Farber and Wright (eds), *Archaeology and History*: 457–473, pp. 471–472.

16 K. Schmid, 'The biblical writings in the late eighth century BCE', in Farber and Wright (eds), *Archaeology and History*: 489–502, p. 489; J. Schaper, 'The literary history of the Hebrew Bible', in J.C. Paget and J. Schaper (eds), *The New Cambridge History of the Bible, Vol. 1: From the Beginnings to 600*, Cambridge: Cambridge University Press, 2013: 105–144, p. 110.

17 S. Faigenbaum-Golovin et al., 'Algorithms reveal literacy level in biblical Judah', *Proceedings of the National Academy of Sciences* 113 (2016): 4664–4669.

18 Macdonald, *Deuteronomy*, pp. 34, 209.

19 M. Liverani, *Israel's History and the History of Israel*, London: Equinox, 2005, pp. 238–240, 260–261, 274, 279.

20 R. Hendel and J. Joosten, *How Old is the Hebrew Bible?*, New Haven CT: Yale University Press, 2018.

21 J.L. Berquist, 'Prophesy in Persian Yehud', in C.J. Sharp (ed.), *Oxford Handbook of the Prophets*, Oxford: Oxford University Press, 2016: 55–66, pp. 62–64.

22 J. Middlemas, 'Prophesy and diaspora', in Sharp, *Oxford Handbook of the Prophets*: 37–54.

23 J.L. Wright, 'A new model for the composition of Ezra-Nehemiah', in *JJFC*: 333–348.

24 These debates are discussed in D. Banks, *Writing the History of Israel*, New York: Clark, 2006; and L.L. Grabbe, *Ancient Israel: what do we know and how do we know it?*, 2nd edition, London: Clark, 2017, pp. 21–36.

25 J. Schaper, 'The literary history of the Hebrew Bible', in Paget and Schaper (eds), *The New Cambridge History 1*: 105–144, p. 144.

26 E. Stern, 'From many gods to the One God: the archaeological evidence', in R.G. Kratz and H. Spieckermann (eds), *One God – One Cult – One Nation: archaeological and biblical perspective*, Berlin: de Gruyter, 2010: 395–403.

27 N. Na'aman, 'Provincial system and settlement pattern in southern Syria and Palestine in the New Assyrian period', in M. Liverani (ed.), *Neo-Assyrian Geography*, Rome: Universita di Roma 'La Sapienza', 1995: 103–115, p. 110.

28 I. Finkelstein and N.A. Silberman, *The Bible Unearthed: archaeology's new vision of ancient Israel and the origin of its sacred texts*, New York: Simon & Schuster, 2001; Itach, 'The kingdom of Israel'; Liverani, *Israel's History*, p. 121; W.G. Dever, *Beyond the Texts: an archaeological portrait of ancient Israel and Judah*, Atlanta, GA: Society for Biblical Literature Press, 2017, pp. 451–453.

29 R. Derricourt, *Antiquity Imagined: the remarkable legacy of Egypt and the ancient Near East*, London: Tauris, 2015, pp. 211–219.

30 G.N. Knoppers, 'In search of post-exilic Israel: Samaria after the fall of the northern kingdom', in J. Day (ed.), *In Search of Pre-Exilic Israel*, London: Clark, 2004: 150–180, pp. 170–171; G. Itach, 'The kingdom of Israel in the eighth century: from a regional power to Assyrian provinces', in Farber and Wright (eds), *Archaeology and History*: 35–56, p. 71.

31 Knoppers, 'In search', p. 151.

32 A.D. Crown, 'Redating the schism between the Judaeans and the Samaritans', *Jewish Quarterly Review* 82 (1991): 17–50; Y. Magen, 'The dating of the first phase of the Samaritan temple on Mount Gerizim in light of the archaeological evidence', in *JJFC*: 157–212, p. 158.

33 These effects are discussed by contributors to Farber and Wright (eds), *Archaeology and History*.

34 Grabbe, *A History of the Jews 1*, pp. 168–169; R.G. Kratz, 'Prophetic discourse on Israel', in Farber and Wright (eds), *Archaeology and History*: 503–515.

35 Liverani, *Israel's History*, p. 171.

36 Grabbe, *Ancient Israel*, pp. 167, 169.

37 A. Faust, 'Society and culture in the Kingdom of Judah during the eighth century', in Farber and Wright (eds), *Archaeology and History*: 179–204, p. 180.

38 2 Kings 24:14–16.

39 2 Kings 25:11–12; Jeremiah 52:30, in a text which numbers the three deportations as 3,023 + 832 + 745 = 4,600. For discussion see B. Porten, 'Exile, Babylonian', in *Encyclopedia Judaica*, 2nd edition, New York: Macmillan, 2006, vol. 6, pp. 608–611.

40 H.M. Barstad, 'After the "Myth of the Empty Land": major challenges in the study of Neo-Babylonian Judah', in *JJNBP*: 3–20, p. 11.

41 Ezra 4:1–23. And as in the Tanakh book of the prophet Malachi, some criticism continued.

42 D.M. Carr, *The Formation of the Hebrew Bible: a new reconstruction*, New York: Oxford University Press, 2011, pp. 225–251, gives a useful overview of the issues.

43 Porten, 'Exile'.

44 Mitchell, 'The Babylonian exile', pp. 418–420.

45 B. Becking, 'Global warming and the Babylonian exile', in J.J. Ahn and J. Middlemas (eds), *By the Irrigation Canals of Babylon: approaches to the study of exile*, New York: Clark, 2012: 49–59.

46 D. Langgut and O. Lipschits, 'Dry climate during the early Persian period and its impact on the establishment of Idumea', *Transeuphratène* 49 (2017): 135–162.

47 Mitchell, 'The Babylonian exile', pp. 421–422.

48 M. Nissinen, '(How) does the book of Ezekiel reveal its Babylonian context?', *Die Welt Des Orients* 45 (2015): 85–98.

49 Isaiah 49.

50 Carr, *The Formation*, p. 234.

51 Jeremiah 29: 1–10.

52 Carr, *The Formation*, pp. 229–231.

53 Ezekiel 1:3, 3:15.

54 Isaiah 40:3, 40:9, 40:18–20, 44:28.

55 A.L. Oppenheim, 'The Babylonian evidence of Achaemenian rule in Mesopotamia', in I. Gershevitch (ed.), *Cambridge History of Iran, Vol. 2: The Median and Achaemenian Periods*, Cambridge: Cambridge University Press, 1985: 529–587.

56 Isaiah 45:1.

57 Mitchell, 'The Babylonian exile', pp. 426–428, 430–440.

58 Liverani, *Israel's History*, p. 253.

59 I. Finkelstein, 'Archaeology and the list of returnees in the books of Ezra and Nehemiah', *Palestine Exploration Quarterly* 140 (2008): 7–16.

60 J.L. Berquist (ed.), *Approaching Yehud: new approaches to the study of the Persian period*, Atlanta, GA: Society of Biblical Literature, 2007, p. 3.

61 Mitchell, 'The Babylonian exile', pp. 429–430.

62 S.G. Rosenberg, 'The Jewish temple at Elephantine', *Near Eastern Archaeology* 67 (2004): 4–13; G. Granerød, 'Canon and archive: Yahwism in Elephantine and Āl-Yāhūdu as a challenge to the canonical history of Judean religion in the Persian period', *Journal of Biblical Literature* 138 (2019): 345–364.

63 Nehemiah 7:66–7.

64 Knoppers, 'In search', p. 172. A cuneiform tablet, dated to the Achaemenid period, from Mikhmoret on the Mediterranean coast indicates the presence in the 6th century of ethnically Babylonian people settled there: I. Spar, S.M. Paley and R.R. Stieglitz, 'A cuneiform contract fragment from Tel Mikhmoret', *Israel Exploration Journal* 68 (2018): 182–191.

65 Ezra 9:1–2.

66 M.L. Steiner, *Excavations by Kathleen M. Kenyon in Jerusalem 1961–1967, Vol. 3: The Settlement in the Bronze and Iron Ages*, London: Sheffield Academic Press, 2001, pp. 109–111; Dever, *Beyond the Texts*, p. 548; Grabbe, *Ancient Israel*, p. 213; H. Geva, 'Jerusalem's population in antiquity: a minimalist view', *Tel Aviv* 41 (2014): 131–160, pp. 139, 141.

67 J. Kessler, 'Diaspora and homeland in the early Achaemenid period', in Berquist, *Approaching Yehud*: 137–166, pp. 139–140; O. Lipschits, *The Fall and Rise of Jerusalem: Judah under Babylonian rule*, Winona Lake, IN: Eisenbrauns, 2005, p. 270; O. Lipschits, 'Achaemenid imperial politics', in *JJPP*: 19–52, p. 32. Nehemiah 7:4 notes the emptiness of Jerusalem, a reference to *ca.* 445 BCE. C.E. Carter, *The Emergence of Yehud in the Persian Period: a social and demographic study*, Sheffield: Sheffield Academic Press, 1999, p. 201, suggests 20,650 for the later Persian period but only 13,350 for the earlier Persian Yehud.

68 O. Lipschits and O. Tal, 'The settlement archaeology of the province of Judah: a case study', in *JJFC*: 33–52, p. 39.

69 Liverani, *Israel's History*, pp. 88–91; I. Finkelstein and N.A. Silberman, *David and Solomon: in search of the Bible's sacred kings and the roots of the western tradition*, New York: Free Press, and London: Simon & Schuster, 2006.

70 Liverani, *Israel's History*, pp. 88–91, 92–96, 96–101, 326–328.

71 Gnuse, 'The emergence of monotheism', pp. 325–328.

72 Carter, *The Emergence*, pp. 39–42.

73 Grabbe, *A History of the Jews 1*, pp. 270, 279.

74 D. Baly, 'The geography of Palestine and the Levant in relation to its history', in *CHJ* 1: 1–24.

75 E. Orni and E. Efrat, *Geography of Israel*, 3rd edition, Jerusalem: Israel Universities Press, 1973, p. 35.

76 Orni and Efrat, *Geography*, pp. 58–68.

77 Mitchell, 'The Babylonian exile', pp. 435–436.

78 J.W. Betlyon, 'A people transformed: Palestine in the Persian period', *Near Eastern Archaeology* 68 (2005): 4–58, p. 9.

79 Liverani, *Israel's History*, pp. 272–273; Grabbe, *A History of the Jews 1*, p. 198.

80 Carter, *The Emergence*, p. 76.

81 Langgut and Lipschits, 'Dry climate'; Carter, *The Emergence*, pp. 91, 112.

82 Carter, *The Emergence*, p. 102; Grabbe, *A History of the Jews 1*, p. 139.

83 O. Lipschits, 'Shedding new light on the dark years of the "Exilic Period"', in B.E. Kelle, F.R. Ames and J.L. Wright (eds), *Interpreting Exile: displacement and deportation in biblical and modern contexts*, Leiden: Brill, 2012: 57–90.

84 M.S. Smith, *The Early History of God: Yahweh and the other deities in ancient Israel*, New York: Harper & Row, 1990, pp. xxiii–xxiv, 22, 61ff., 125–144.

85 Gnuse, 'The emergence of monotheism', pp. 317–318; W.G. Dever, *Did God Have a Wife? Archaeology and folk religion in ancient Israel*, Grand Rapids, MI: Eerdmans, 2005; J.M. Hadley, *The Cult of Asherah in Ancient Israel and Judah: evidence for a Hebrew goddess*, Cambridge: Cambridge University Press, 2000.

86 'Newly discovered temple near Jerusalem calls into question Biblical depictions', at english.tau.ac.il/news/new_temple

87 Grabbe, *Ancient Israel*, pp. 150ff; Stern, 'From many gods'; N. Na'aman, 'In search of the temples of YHWH of Samaria and YHWH of Teman', *Journal of Ancient Near Eastern Religions* 17 (2017): 76–95.

88 B.A. Strawn and J.M. LeMon, 'Religion in eighth-century Judah: the case of Kuntillet 'Ajrud (and beyond)', in Farber and Wright (eds), *Archaeology and History*: 379–400; L. Singer-Avitz, 'The date of Kuntillet 'Ajrud', *Tel Aviv* 33 (2006): 196–228.

89 Y. Gadot, 'In the valley of the king: Jerusalem's rural hinterland in the 8th–4th centuries BCE', *Tel Aviv* 42 (2015): 3–26; E.A. Knauf, 'Was there a refugee crisis in the 8th/7th centuries BCE?', in O. Lipschits, Y. Gadot and M.J. Adams (eds), *Rethinking Israel: studies in the history and archaeology of ancient Israel in honour of Israel Finkelstein*, Winona Lake, IN: Eisenbrauns, 2017: 159–172; N. Na'aman, 'Dismissing the myth of a flood of Israelite refugees in the late eighth century BCE', *Zeitschrift für die Alttestamentliche Wissenschaft* 126 (2014): 1–14; A. Faust, *The Archaeology of Israelite Society in Iron Age II*, Winona Lake, IN: Eisenbrauns, 2012, p. 268.

90 Carter, *The Emergence*, p. 1168; Carter lists six excavated sites from the Neo-Babylonian period: Bethel, El-Jib, Tell el-Ful, Tell en-Nasbeh, Horvat Zimri and Khirbet er-Ras.

91 Lipschits, *The Fall and Rise*, pp. 192ff; H.M. Barstad, *History and the Hebrew Bible*, Tubingen: Mohr Siebeck, 2008, pp. 111–117.

92 A. Faust, *Judah in the Neo-Babylonian Period: the archaeology of desolation*, Atlanta, GA: Society of Biblical Literature, 2012, pp. 3ff., 147, 244–245, 247.

93 By one estimate the population of Judah may have fallen from around 110,000 to 40,000: Lipschits, 'Shedding new light', p. 78. The latter figure can be contrasted with the estimate of Carter, *The Emergence*, p. 201, of 13,350 for Yehud in the early Persian period.

94 E. Stern, *Material Culture of the Land of the Bible in the Persian Period*, Warminster: Aris & Phillips, 1982, p. 229.

95 *JJNBP*, pp. ix–x; Barstad, 'After the "Myth"'; Barstad, *History and the Hebrew Bible*, pp. 90–134.

96 Grabbe, *A History of the Jews 1*, pp. 23–24; Lipschits, 'Persian-period Judah', p. 191; Lipschits, *The Fall and Rise*, pp. 181–183; O. Lipschits, 'The history of the Benjamin region under Babylonian rule', *Tel Aviv* 26 (1999): 155–190.

97 I. Finkelstein et al., 'Has King David's palace in Jerusalem been found?', *Tel Aviv* 34 (2007): 142–194.

98 See for example A. Faust and H. Katz, 'A Canaanite town, a Judahite centre, and a Persian period fort: excavating over two thousand years of history at Tel 'Eton', *Near Eastern Archaeology* 78 (2015): 88–102, p. 95. After the destruction of *ca.* 701, the site was not rebuilt until late Persian period of the 4th century BCE.

99 Mitchell, 'The Babylonian exile', p. 415; Faust, 'Society and culture', pp. 181–182; Steiner, *Excavations by Kathleen M. Kenyon*, pp. 109–111; Dever, *Beyond the Texts*, p. 548.

100 Lipschits, *The Fall and Rise,* pp. 210–211, 217, 262, 270; Grabbe, *A History of the Jews 1*, p. 25.

101 Barstad, *History and the Hebrew Bible*, p. 127.

102 For example K. Galor, 'King Herod in Jerusalem: the politics of cultural heritage', *Jerusalem Quarterly* 62 (2015): 65–80; see Derricourt, *Antiquity Imagined*, pp. 191–210.

103 Carter, *The Emergence*, is a useful outline of information available by the 1990s; for a later survey see J.W. Betlyon, 'A people transformed: Palestine in the Persian period', *Near Eastern Archaeology* 68 (2005): 4–58 (pp. 20–26 for Judah and Benjamin). Sites from both Judah and Samaria are described in Grabbe, *A History of the Jews 1*, pp. 22–53. Carter, *The Emergence,* p. 118, lists (and describes finds from) Jerusalem, Ketef Hinnom, Mamilla, Khirbet er-Ras, Wadi Salim, Ramat Rahel, Jericho and Tel Goren (Ein Gedi) before the mid-5th century.

104 Stern, *Material Culture*, p. vii.

105 Lipschits, *The Fall and Rise*, p. 267.

106 Lipschits, 'Persian-period Judah', p. 195.

107 Carter, *The Emergence,* pp. 214ff, 246; Z. Zevit, 'Is there an archaeological case for phantom settlement in the Persian period?', *Palestine Exploration Quarterly* 141 (2009): 124–137. Very useful maps are in N. Shalom and O. Lipschits, 'Judah during the transition between the Persian and Early Hellenistic periods: regional processes', in W. Held (ed.), *The Transition from the Achaemenid to the Hellenistic Period in the Levant, Cyprus and Cilicia: cultural interruption or continuity?*, Marburg: Archäologischen Seminars der Philipps-Universität Marburg, 2020: 7–26.

108 Carter, *The Emergence,* pp. 134–148.

109 O. Lipschits, 'Persian period finds from Jerusalem: facts and interpretations', *Journal of Hebrew Scriptures* 2 (2010), article 20.

110 Geva, 'Jerusalem's population', pp. 142–143.

111 Lipschits, 'Persian period finds', pp. 17, 20; Geva, 'Jerusalem's population'.

112 B. Becking, '"We all returned as one": critical notes on the myth of the mass return', in *JJPP*: 3–18, pp. 9–10; Lipschits, 'Achaemenid imperial policy', p. 34.

113 C.E. Carter, '(Re)Defining "Israel": the legacy of the Neo Babylonian and Persian periods', in S. Niditch (ed.), *The Wiley Blackwell Companion to Ancient Israel*, Chichester: Wiley Blackwell, 2016: 215–240, p. 226; Finkelstein, 'Persian period Jerusalem'.

114 D. Ussishkin, 'On Nehemiah's city wall and the size of Jerusalem during the Persian period: an archaeologist's view', in I. Kalimi (ed.), *New Perspectives on Ezra–Nehemiah: history and historiography, text, literature, and interpretation*, Winona Lake, IN: Eisenbrauns, 2012: 101–130; I. Finkelstein, 'Jerusalem in the Persian (and early Hellenistic) period and the wall of Nehemiah', *Journal for the Study of the Old Testament* 32 (2008): 501–520.

115 D. Ussishkin, 'The borders and *de facto* size of Jerusalem in the Persian period', in *JJPP*: 147–166, p. 164; Lipschits, 'Persian period finds'; Grabbe, *A History of*

the Jews 1, p. 25; N. Avigad, *Discovering Jerusalem*, Oxford: Basil Blackwell, 1984, p. 62; Stern, *Material Culture*, pp. 34–35.

116 Gadot, 'In the valley', p. 19. On the rural economy of Yehud see O. Lipschits, 'The rural economy of Judah during the Persian period and the settlement history of the district system' in M.L. Miller, E.B. Zvi and G.N. Knoppers (eds), *The Economy of Ancient Judah in Its Historical Context*, Winona Lake IN: Eisenbrauns, 2015: 233–261. To the southwest of Jerusalem's Old City, just before the Hinnom valley, is the archaeological site of Ketef Hinnom. This location reflects continuity of use across the exilic and post-exilic periods, with caves containing family burials extending through the period of the Babylonian conquest of Jerusalem. Cave 24 at the site had material from pre-exilic to early Persian periods, with reuse in the 1st century BCE. There was also cultural continuity at Mamilla Street sites just west of the Old City.

117 Wine production continuing from before and through the Persian period, from the 7th to 4th centuries BCE, was a feature of the site of Rogem Gannim, 3 miles west of Jerusalem's Old City. This appears to have been an example of economic specialisation: R. Greenberg and G. Cinamon, 'Excavations at Rogem Gannim, Jerusalem: installations of the Iron Age, Persian, Roman and Islamic periods', *'Atiqot* 66 (2011): 79–106.

118 O. Lipschits et al., *What Are the Stones Whispering? Ramat Rahel: 3000 years of forgotten history*, Winona Lake IN: Eisenbrauns, 2017; O. Lipschits et al., 'Palace and village, paradise and oblivion: unraveling the riddles of Ramat Raḥel', *Near Eastern Archaeology* 74 (2011): 2–49.

119 Lipschits, *The Fall and Rise*, p. 212; Carter, *The Emergence*, pp. 150–153; Stern, *Material Culture*, pp. 35–36; Grabbe, *A History of the Jews 1*, p. 26.

120 Lipschits et al., *What Are the Stones*, p. 166.

121 D. Langgut et al., 'Fossil pollen reveals the secrets of the royal Persian garden at Ramat Rahel, Jerusalem', *Palynology* 37 (2013): 115–129.

122 Carter, *The Emergence*, p. 281.

123 Lipschits et al., 'Palace and village', p. 34; Stern, *Material Culture*, pp. 202–214, 237.

124 Stern, *Material Culture*, pp. 38–39; S.T. Stub, 'Life in a busy oasis', *Archaeology* May 2019. Excavations indicated substantial abandonment after destruction at the time of the Babylonian conquest, before revival in the Persian period. Late Persian-period settlement featured houses close together on narrow lanes; one large house with three wings and built over three terraces had walls of large stones with plaster on both walls and floors.

125 Carter, *The Emergence*, pp. 116, 183; Stern, *Material Culture,* pp. 253, 255.

126 A. Faust, 'Forts or agricultural estates? Persian period settlement in the territory of the former kingdom of Judah', *Palestine Exploration Quarterly* 150 (2018): 34–59, pp. 49, 51.

127 Carter, *The Emergence*, p. 187, fig. 17 for later Persian sites and p. 210, fig. 18 for earlier Persian period sites.

128 Carter, *The Emergence*, p. 201.

129 G.N. Knoppers, 'Revisiting the Samarian question in the Persian period', in *JJPP*: 265–289, pp. 268–269.

130 The town of Samaria itself saw substantial destruction by the Macedonians after a revolt at the time of Alexander's conquests. As a result, locating the archaeology of Persian settlement has been problematic. It is suggested, however, that Samaria may have become the largest town in Achaemenid Palestine; Shechem was the other large Samarian town. Stern, *Material Culture*, p. 29; A. Zertal, 'The province of Samaria (Assyrian *Samerina*) in the Late Iron Age (Iron Age III)', in *JJNBP*: 377–412.

131 Stern, *Material Culture*, pp. 5–9, 240; S.C. Herbert and A.M. Berlin, 'A new administrative center for Persian and Hellenistic Galilee: preliminary report of the University of Michigan/University of Minnesota excavations at Kedesh', *Bulletin of the American Schools of Oriental Research* 329 (2003): 13–59.

132 Stern, *Material Culture*, p. 158.

133 Finkelstein and Silberman, *David and Solomon*.

134 For example Davies and Finkelstein (eds), *CHJ 1*; S. Schama, *The Story of the Jews: finding the words 1000 BC–1492 AD*, New York: HarperCollins, 2013.

135 Grabbe, *Ancient Israel*; Finkelstein and Silberman, *The Bible Unearthed*.

136 J. Pakkala, 'Why the cult reform in Judah probably did not happen', in Kratz and Spieckermann (eds), *One God*: 201–235; T. Römer, 'The rise and fall of Josiah', in Lipschits et al. (eds), *Rethinking Israel*: 329–340, p. 337.

137 Liverani, *Israel's History*, pp. 342–360.

6. Ahura Mazda and the enigmas of Zoroastrian origins

1 M. Stausberg, 'Zarathustra: post-Gathic trajectories', in *WBCZ*: 69–81, p. 70.

2 R. Rivetna, 'The Zarathushti world, a 2012 demographic picture', *FEZANA Journal* (fall 2013); J. Rose, *Zoroastrianism: an introduction*, London: Tauris, 2011, p. xxii.

3 www.churchofjesuschrist.org/study/ensign/1971/11/zoroastrianism?lang=eng

4 Qur'an 22:17.

5 Rose, *Zoroastrianism*, p. 163.

6 Matthew 2:1–2; N. Cohn, *Cosmos, Change and the World to Come*, 2nd edition, New Haven, CT: Yale University Press, 2001, p. 228, suggests the author of Matthew may have been familiar with Zoroastrians.

7 M. Schwartz, 'The religion of Achaemenian Iran', *CHI 2*: 664–697, p. 681; M. Boyce, *A History of Zoroastrianism, Vol. 1: The Early Period* (Leiden: Brill, 1975, revised 1996), p. 193.

8 Rose, *Zoroastrianism*, p. 42; M. Boyce, *A History of Zoroastrianism*, Vol. 2: *Under the Achaemenians*, Leiden: Brill, 1982, pp. 44–47, 191–195; Cohn, *Cosmos*, pp. 163–164, 222–227.

9 J. Barr, 'The question of religious influence: the case of Zoroastrianism, Judaism, and Christianity', *Journal of the American Academy of Religion* 53 (1985): 201–235, p. 201.

10 Later documents continued to be attributed to Zarathushtra from Hellenistic times onwards: see M. Stausberg, 'A name for all and no one: Zoroaster as a figure of authorization and a screen of ascription', in J.R. Lewis and O. Hammer

(eds), *The Invention of Sacred Tradition*, Cambridge: Cambridge University Press, 2007, pp. 177–198.

11 M. Boyce, *Zoroastrians: their religious beliefs and practices*, 2nd edition, London: Routledge & Kegan Paul, 1986, pp. 2, 18. She also described its origins in the 'largely Stone-Age culture' of the Iranian Bronze Age: Boyce, *A History 2*, p. 1.

12 M. Witzel, 'Iranian migration', in D.T. Potts (ed.), *The Oxford Handbook of Ancient Iran*, Oxford: Oxford University Press, 2013, p. 425.

13 Complex arguments in defence of the 6th- to 5th-century BCE dates are in E. Gershevitch, 'Approaches to Zoroaster's Gathas', *Iran* 33 (1995): 1–29; and G. Gnoli, *Zoroaster in History*, New York: Bibliotheca Persica Press, 2000 (reversing his earlier opinions). A more straightforward argument is A. Soudavar, 'The formation of Achaemenid imperial ideology and its impact on the Avesta', in J. Curtis and St.J. Simpson (eds), *The World of Achaemenid Persia: history, art and society in Iran and the ancient Near East*, London: Tauris, 2010: 111–138.

14 P. Kingsley, 'The Greek origin of the sixth-century dating of Zoroaster', *Bulletin of the School of Oriental and African Studies* 53 (1990): 245–265.

15 M. Stausberg, 'On the state and prospects of the study of Zoroastrianism', *Numen* 55 (2008): 561–600, p. 568.

16 Avestan digital archive at www.heritageinstitute.com/zoroastrianism/scriptures/manuscripts.htm ; U. Sims-Williams, 'Zoroastrian manuscripts in the British Library, London', in A. Cantera (ed.), *The Transmission of the Avesta*, Wiesbaden: Harrassowitz, 2012: 173–194 (a special issue of *Iranica* 20 (2012)). Avestan manuscripts are being digitised at ada.geschkult.fu-berlin.de

17 P. O. Skjærvø and D.J. Sheffield, 'Zoroastrian scriptures', in Z.R. Kassam, Y.K. Kornberg and J. Bagli (eds), *Islam, Judaism and Zoroastrianism*, Dordrecht: Springer, 2018: 790–814, p. 799; www.bl.uk/collection-items/videvdad; www.bl.uk/collection-items/zoroastrian-prayer

18 J.K. Choksy, 'Zoroastrians in Muslim Iran: selected problems of coexistence and interaction during the early medieval period', *Iranian Studies* 20 (1987): 17–30, pp. 20–21.

19 Choksy, 'Zoroastrians', p. 26.

20 M. Macuch, 'Pahlavi literature', in R.E. Emmerick and M. Macuch (eds), *A History of Persian Literature, Vol. 17: The Literature of Pre-Islamic Iran*, London: Tauris, 2009: 116–196, p. 116; D.J. Sheffield, 'Primary sources: New Persian', in *WBCZ*: 529–542.

21 Macuch, 'Pahlavi literature'; M. Stausberg, 'The invention of a canon: the case of Zoroastrianism', in A. van der Kooij and K. van der Toorn (eds), *Canonization and Decanonization*. Leiden: Brill, 1998: 257–277, p. 262.

22 Rose, *Zoroastrianism*, pp. 243–245, has a useful checklist of texts.

23 Stausberg, 'The invention', p. 262.

24 Skjærvø and Sheffield, 'Zoroastrian scriptures', and the list by M.Á. Andrés-Toledo, 'Primary sources: Avestan and Pahlavi', in *WBCZ*: 517–528.

25 Boyce, *A History 1*, p. 20.

26 Gershevitch, 'Approaches', p. 3.

27 Schwartz, 'The religion', p. 667.

28 A. Hintze, 'On the literary structure of the Older Avesta', *Bulletin of the School of Oriental and African Studies* 65 (2002): 31–51, p. 35; J. Kellens and E. Pirart, *Les textes vieil-avestiques*, 3 vols, Wiesbaden: Reichert, 1988–1991.

29 Hintze, 'On the literary structure', pp. 46, 50.

30 P.O. Skjærvø, 'The Zoroastrian oral tradition as reflected in the texts', in Cantera (ed.), *The Transmission*: 3–48.

31 Skjærvø, 'The Zoroastrian oral tradition', p. 7.

32 Schwartz, 'The religion', pp. 664–665.

33 Gershevitch, 'Approaches', p. 3; Gnoli, *Zoroaster in History*, pp. 23–24.

34 A. Hintze, 'Avestan literature', in Emmerick and Macuch (eds), *A History 17*: 1–71, p. 26; F. Grenet, 'Zarathustra's time and homeland: geographical perspectives', in *WBCZ*: 21–29, p. 22.

35 Hintze, 'Avestan literature', p. 28; A. Hintze, 'Zarathustra's time and homeland: linguistic perspectives', in *WBCZ*: 31–38, p. 35.

36 Schwartz, 'The religion', p. 664.

37 M. Schwartz, 'The Old Eastern Iranian world view according to the Avesta', in *CHI* 2: 640–663, pp. 657–663.

38 Hintze, 'Avestan literature', p. 26.

39 Rose, *Zoroastrianism*, p. 102; P. Pourshariati, *Decline and Fall of the Sasanian Empire: the Sasanian–Parthian confederacy and the Arab conquest of Iran*, London: Tauris, 2017, pp. 321, 325–327.

40 B. Overlaet, 'And man created god? Kings, priests and gods on Sasanian investiture reliefs', *Iranica Antiqua* 48 (2013): 313–354.

41 P.O. Skjærvø, 'Kartir', *EncyclIran* (2011).

42 R. Beck, 'Zoroaster v. as perceived by the Greeks', *EncyclIran* (2012).

43 J.K. Choksy, 'Religious sites and physical structures', in *WBCZ*: 393–406, pp. 393–394.

44 Boyce, *A History* 2, p. 52; M. Shenkar, 'Temple architecture in the Iranian world before the Macedonian conquest', *Iran and the Caucasus* 11 (2007): 169–194, p. 177.

45 Boyce, *A History* 2, p. 222.

46 B. Lincoln, 'À la recherche du paradis perdu', *History of Religions* 43 (2003): 139–154, p. 154; Schwartz, 'The religion', pp. 684–685.

47 Schwartz, 'The religion', pp. 689–91; Boyce, *A History* 2, p. 176.

48 Rose, *Zoroastrianism*, pp. 31, 37; Schwarz, 'The religion', pp. 684–695.

49 Schwartz, 'The religion', p. 694.

50 Rose, *Zoroastrianism*, p. 35.

51 P.O. Skjærvø, 'Avestan quotations in Old Persian? Literary sources of the Old Persian inscriptions', *Irano-Judaica* 4 (1999): 1–15, p. 3; original emphasis. See also Skjærvø, 'Zoroastrian oral tradition', pp. 12–15; P.O. Skjærvø, 'Avesta and Zoroastrianism under the Achaemenids and early Sasanians', in Potts, *The Oxford Handbook*: 548–565, p. 562; P.O. Skjærvø, 'Achaemenid religion', *Religion Compass* 8 (2014): 175–187.

52 M. Dandamayev, 'Persepolis Elamite tablets', *EncyclIran* (2002).

53 Rose, *Zoroastrianism*, pp. 48, 52–53.

54 Lincoln, 'À la recherche', p. 140; O. Basirov, 'The Achaemenian practice of primary burial: an argument against their Zoroastrianism? Or a testimony of their religious tolerance?', in Curtis and Simpson (eds), *The World of Achaemenid Persia*: 75–83, p. 81.

55 Soudavar, 'The formation', pp. 134–136.

56 Gnoli, *Zoroaster in History*, p. 164.

57 M. Dandamayev and I. Medvedskaya, 'Media', *EncycIran* (2006).

58 Y. Yamamoto, 'The Zoroastrian temple cult of fire in archaeology and literature (I)', *Orient* 15 (1979): 19–53, pp. 33–34; M. Roaf and D. Stronach, 'Tepe Nush-i Jan, 1970: second interim report', *Iran* 11 (1973): 129–140, pp. 133–137; Shenkar, 'Temple architecture', pp. 172–173.

59 Witzel, 'Iranian migration', p. 435.

60 Y. Bregel, *An Historical Atlas of Central Asia*, Leiden: Brill, 2003, p. 2.

61 W.B. Fisher, 'Physical geography', in *CHI 1*: 3–110, pp. 65–66.

62 C.P. Thornton, 'The Bronze Age in northeastern Iran', in Potts, *The Oxford Handbook*: 180–199, p. 185.

63 Fisher, 'Physical geography', pp. 76–81; H. Bowen-Jones, 'Agriculture', in *CHI 1*: 565–598.

64 E. Sunderland, 'Pastoralism, nomadism and the social anthropology of Iran', *CHI 1*: 611–683, pp. 634ff.

65 M. Hutter, 'Zoroaster III. Zoroaster in the Avesta', *EncycIran* (2009).

66 Boyce, *A History 1*, p. 182.

67 Schwartz, 'The Old Eastern', pp. 657–658, 662–663.

68 Hutter, 'Zoroaster III'; Schwartz, 'The Old Eastern', pp. 640–641.

69 G. Gnoli, 'Avestan geography', *EncycIran* (2011).

70 W.M. Malandra, 'The *Videvdad*', *EncycIran* (2000).

71 For example, the suggestion that by the date of the last Young Avestan texts, the location of Zarathushtra was considered to be at the site of Darya-I Pand in Afghanistan: C. Rapin, 'Nomads and the shaping of Central Asia (from the early Iron Age to the Kushan period)', *Proceedings of the British Academy* 133 (2007): 29–72. p. 41, citing F. Grenet.

72 E.E. Kuz'mina, *The Origin of the Iranians*, Leiden: Brill, 2007, pp. 448–449.

73 Gnoli, 'Avestan geography'; Witzel, 'Iranian migration', p. 425, suggests the main focusses of the references are on the region of Bactria and, to the south, Arachosia in Afghanistan, with mentions of Hyrcania, at the south-east of the Caspian.

74 Gnoli, 'Avestan geography'.

75 Gershevitch, 'Approaches', p. 4.

76 Boyce, *A History 2*, pp. 8–9; Schwartz, 'The religion', p. 697.

77 C.C. Lamberg-Karlovsky et al., 'Archaeology and language: the Indo-Iranians', *Current Anthropology* 43 (2002): 63–88, p. 69.

78 The complexities of this issue are explored in Lamberg-Karlovsky et al., 'Archaeology and language'.

79 Witzel, 'Iranian migration', p. 434; A. Parpola, 'The Nâsatyas, the chariot and Proto-Aryan religion', *Journal of Indological Studies* 16–17 (2005): 1–63, pp. 24–29.

80 I.M. Diakonoff, 'Media', in *CHI* 2: 36–148, p. 52.

81 Witzel, 'Iranian migration', p. 437.

82 Kuz'mina, *The Origin of the Iranians*, pp. 299ff.

83 Witzel, 'Iranian migration', p. 428.

84 More nomadic groups associated with the Andronovo culture are identified further down the Amu-Darya River: S. Salvatori, 'Cultural variability in the Bronze Age Oxus civilisation and its relations with the surrounding regions of Central Asia and Iran', in S. Salvatori and M. Tozi (eds), *The Bronze Age and Early Iron Age in the Margiana lowlands*, Oxford: Archaeopress, 2008: 75–98.

85 Witzel, 'Iranian migration', p. 430; S. Salvatori, 'The Bronze Age in Margiana', in A. Gubaev, G.A. Koshelenko and M. Tosi (eds), *The Archaeological Map of the Murghab Delta. Preliminary Reports 1990–95*, Rome, IsIAO, 1998: 47–55; Rose, *Zoroastrianism*, p. 10.

86 V.I. Sarianidi, *Margiana and Protozoroastrism*, Athens: Kapon, 1998; V. Sarianidi, 'Temples of Bronze Age Margiana: traditions of ritual architecture', *Antiquity*, 68 (1994): 388–397; K. Jones-Bley, 'Long before Zarathustra (archaeological evidences of Protozoroastrianism in Bactria and Margiana)', *Journal of Indo-European Studies* 41 (2013): 527.

87 Sarianidi, *Margiana*, pp. 168–174.

88 Grenet, 'Zarathustra's time and homeland', p. 22; Soudavar, 'The formation', p. 113.

89 B. Genito, 'Eastern Iran in the Achaemenid period', in Potts, *The Oxford Handbook*: 622–637, p. 622.

90 Genito, 'Eastern Iran', p. 627.

91 J.M. Cook, 'The rise of the Achaemenids and establishment of their empire', in *CHI* 2: 200–291, pp. 244–256; Genito, 'Eastern Iran', pp. 622, 632.

92 M. Negus Cleary, 'Khorezmian walled sites of the seventh century BC–fourth century AD: urban settlements? Elite strongholds? Mobile centres?', *Iran* 51 (2013): 71–100; J. Dodson et al., 'The nature of fluctuating lakes in the southern Amu-dar'ya delta', *Palaeogeography, Palaeoclimatology, Palaeoecology* 437 (2015): 63–73, p. 72; M. Negus Cleary, 'Social complexity and political capitals in Ancient Eurasia', *Oxford Handbooks Online* (2018), doi 10.1093/oxfordhb/978019 9935413.013.19.

93 Negus Cleary, 'Social complexity'.

94 A. Betts et al., 'The Akchakhan-kala wall paintings: new perspectives on kingship and religion in ancient Chorasmia', *Journal of Inner Asian Art and Archaeology* 7 (2016): 125–165; A.V.G. Betts et al., 'The Karakalpak-Australian excavations in ancient Chorasmia, 2001–2005: interim report on the fortifications of Kazakl'i-Yatkan and regional survey', *Iran* 47 (2009): 33–55; M. Minardi, A.V.G. Betts and G. Khozhaniyazov, 'Columned halls in ancient Chorasmia', *Iran* 55 (2017): 208–226, p. 209.

95 F. Sinisi, A. Betts and G Khozhaniyazov, 'Royal fires in the ancient Iranian world: the evidence from Akchakhan-Kala, Chorasmia', *Parthica* 20 (2018): 9–30.

96 Betts et al., 'Akchakhan-kala wall paintings', p. 134.

97 M. Minardi and S. Amirov, 'The Zoroastrian funerary building of Angka Malaya', *Topoi* 21 (2017): 11–49.

98 S.W. Helms et al., 'The Krakalpak-Australian excavations in ancient Chorasmia: the northern frontier of the "civilised" ancient world', *Ancient Near Eastern Studies* 39 (2005): 3–43; A.V.G. Betts and V.N. Yagodin, 'The fire temple at Tash-k'irman Tepe, Chorasmia', *Proceedings of the British Academy* 133 (2007): 435–453.

99 B.I. Marshak, 'The archaeology of Sogdiana', *The Silk Road* 1.2 (2003): 3–8.

100 Discussed in Rapin, 'Nomads', pp. 39–42.

101 Rapin, 'Nomads', pp. 36–38.

102 X. Wu, N.F. Miller and P. Crabtree, 'Agro-pastoral strategies and food production on the Achaemenid frontier in Central Asia: a case study of Kyzyltepa in southern Uzbekistan', *Iran* 53 (2015): 93–117.

103 Wu et al., 'Agro-pastoral', pp. 96–105.

104 É. de La Vaissière, 'Sogdiana iii. History and archeology', *EncycIran* (2011); F. Grenet, 'Samarqand i. History and archaeology', *EncycIran* (2002); Marshak, 'The archaeology of Sogdiana', p. 4.

105 F. Grenet, 'Zoroastrianism in Central Asia', in *WBCZ*: 129–146.

106 I. Cesmeli, H. Gunozu and A. Raimkulov. 'The new archaeological discoveries in Sogdiana: the archaeological works in Yalpak Tepe Palace and Yerkurgan Central Temple (Kashkadarya-Uzbekistan / 2003–2013)', *Art-Sanat* 6 (2016): 11–83.

107 J. Lhuillier and M. Mashkour, 'Animal exploitation in the oases: an archaeozoological review of Iron Age sites in southern Central Asia', *Antiquity* 91 (2017): 655–673, p. 668.

108 Genito, 'Eastern Iran', pp. 630–631.

109 J. Bendezu-Sarmiento and J. Lhuillier, 'Sine Sepulchro cultural complex of Transoxiana (between 1500 and the middle of the 1st millennium BCE): funerary practices of the Iron Age in southern Central Asia: recent work, old data, and new hypotheses', *Archäologische Mitteilungen aus Iran und Turan* 43 (2013): 281–316.

110 S. Salvatori and M. Tosi, 'Shahr-i Sokhta revised sequence', *South Asian Archaeology* 1 (2001): 281–292.

111 G. Maresca, 'Between "early" and "late" Iron Age in south-eastern Iran: notes on the possibility to evaluate the "Achaemenid impact" on the area', *Vicino Oriente* 22 (2018): 197–211, pp. 201–203; M. Mortazavi, 'Mind the gap: continuity and change in Iranian Sistan archaeology', *Near Eastern Archaeology* 70 (2007): 109–110; M. Mortazavi, F.M. Negari and M. Khosravi, 'Step over the gap, not in it: a case study of Iranian Sistan archaeology', *Iranian Journal of Archaeological Studies* 5 (2015): 43–55; B. Barjasteh Delforooz, 'The role of natural phenomena in the rise and fall of urban areas in the Sistan Basin on the Iranian Plateau (Southern Delta)', in P. Sinclair et al. (eds), *The Urban Mind: cultural and environmental dynamics*, Uppsala: Department of Archaeology and Ancient History, Uppsala University, 2010: 221–242.

112 Mortazavi et al., 'Step over', p. 50.

113 Genito, 'Eastern Iran', p. 626; B. Genito, 'The Achaemenid Empire as seen as from its eastern periphery: the case of Dahan-i Ghulaman in Sistan. Forty years later, a revision of data', in P. Matthiae et al. (eds), *Proceedings of the 6th*

International Congress of the Archaeology of the Ancient Near East, Wiesbaden: Harrassowitz, 2010: vol. 1, pp. 77–92, p. 83; G. Gnoli, 'Dahan-e Golaman', *EncycIran* (1993).

114 Hintze, 'Zarathustra's time', pp. 33–34; Gnoli, 'Avestan geography'.

115 C.I. Beckwith, *Greek Buddha: Pyrrho's encounter with early Buddhism in Central Asia*, Princeton, NJ: Princeton University Press, 2017, pp. 177–179; see also E. Cortesi et al., 'Cultural relationships beyond the Iranian Plateau: the Helmand civilization, Baluchistan and the Indus Valley in the 3rd millennium BCE', *Paléorient* 34 (2008): 5–35. There had, of course, been trade links between eastern Iran and the Indus Valley since the 3rd millennium BCE.

116 X. de Planhol, 'Geography of settlement', in *CHI* 1: 409–467, p. 409.

7. Prophets, religions and history: some conclusions

1 E. Barker, *New Religious Movements: a practical introduction*, London: HMSO, 1989, p. 13.

2 A.J. Gabay, *The Mystic Life of Alfred Deakin*, Cambridge: Cambridge University Press, 1993.

3 *Diagnostic and Statistical Manual of Mental Disorders*, 5th edition, Arlington, VA: American Psychiatric Association, 2013.

4 G.D. Chryssides, *Exploring New Religions*, London: Cassell, 1999, p. 2.

5 C. Partridge (ed.), *New Religions: a guide. New religious movements, sects and alternative spiritualities*, New York: Oxford University Press, 2004.

6 T.M. Johnson and B.J. Grim, *The World's Religions in Figures*, Chichester: Wiley-Blackwell, 2013, p. 10.

7 L. Lilliston and G. Shepherd, 'New religious movements and mental health', in B. Wilson and J. Cresswell (eds), *New Religious Movements: challenge and response*, London: Routledge, 1999: 123–139.

8 D.G. Bromley, 'As it was in the beginning: developmental moments in the emergence of new religions', in J.R. Lewis and I. Tøllefsen (eds), *The Oxford Handbook of New Religions*, Oxford: Oxford University Press, 2016: vol 2, pp. 98–113.

9 E. Prophet, 'Charisma and authority in new religious movements', in Lewis and Tøllefsen (eds), *The Oxford Handbook*: 36–79.

10 A. Storr, *Feet of Clay: a study of gurus*, London: HarperCollins, 1996.

11 Storr, *Feet of Clay*, p. xiv.

12 S. Horsfall, 'The experience of Marian apparitions and the Mary cult', *Social Science Journal* 37 (2000): 375–384, p. 376.

13 Luke 2:41–51; John 2:1–12; Matthew 12:46–50.

Select bibliography

This bibliography lists some key sources and suggestions for further reading which include different perspectives and some older classic works. Further sources and references are in the notes.

Mormonism

The sources have been mined by numerous historians writing from Mormon, other Christian and secular perspectives. Much discussion focuses on the theological underpinnings of Mormonism, its organisational dimensions, or the demographics of the early adherents, rather than the world in which it emerged.

Full publication of papers relating to Joseph Smith, Jun. has been undertaken: www.josephsmithpapers.org/articles/published-volumes

Mormon beginnings

Arrington, Leonard J. and David Bitton, *The Mormon Experience: a history of the Latter-day Saints* (New York: Knopf, 1979).

Brodie, Fawn M., *No Man Knows My History: the life of Joseph Smith the Mormon prophet*, 2nd edition (New York: Knopf, 1971).

Brooke, John L., *The Refiner's Fire: the making of Mormon cosmology 1644–1844* (Cambridge: Cambridge University Press, 1994).

Bushman, Richard L., *Joseph Smith: rough stone rolling* (New York: Knopf, 2006).

Givens, Terryl L., *Wrestling the Angel. The Foundations of Mormon Thought: Cosmos, God, Humanity* (New York: Oxford University Press, 2014).

Givens, Terryl L. and P.L. Barlow (eds), *The Oxford Handbook to Mormonism* (Oxford: Oxford University Press, 2015), including D.W. Howe, 'Emergent Mormonism in context'; R.L. Bushman, 'Joseph Smith and his vision'; and R.V. Francaviglia, 'Geography and Mormon identity'.

Journal of Mormon History.

Neilson, Reid L. and Terryl Givens (eds), *Joseph Smith, Jr.: reappraisals after two centuries* (Oxford: Oxford University Press, 2009), including David J. Whittaker, 'Studying Joseph Smith Jr.: a guide to the sources'.

O'Dea, Thomas, *The Mormons* (Chicago, IL: University of Chicago Press, 1957).

Winn, Kenneth H., *Exiles in a Land of Liberty: Mormons in America, 1830–1846* (Chapel Hill, NC: University of North Carolina Press, 1989).

United States and New York State

Cross, Whitney R., *The Burned-Over District: the social and intellectual history of enthusiastic religion in western New York, 1800–1850* (Ithaca, NY: Cornell University Press, 1950).

Engerman, Stanley L. and Robert E. Gallman (eds), *The Cambridge Economic History of the United States, Vol. 2: The Long Nineteenth Century* (Cambridge: Cambridge University Press, 2000).

Howe, Daniel Walker, *What God Hath Wrought: the transformation of America 1815–1848* (New York: Oxford University Press, 2007).

Iroquois

Kerber, Jordan E. (ed.), *Archaeology of the Iroquois* (Syracuse, NY: Syracuse University Press, 2007).

Ritchie, William A., *The Archaeology of New York State* (Harrison, NY: Harbor City, 1980).

Shannon, Timothy J., *Iroquois Diplomacy in the Early American Frontier* (New York: Penguin, 2008).

Trigger, Bruce G. (ed.), *Handbook of North American Indians, Vol. 15: Northeast* (Washington, DC: Smithsonian Institution, 1978), including chapters by Elizabeth Tooker, James A. Tuck and B.G. Trigger.

Mormon settlement in Utah

Arrington, Leonard J., *Brigham Young: American Moses* (New York: Knopf, 1985).

Arrington, Leonard J., *Great Basin Kingdom: an economic history of the Latter-day Saints 1830–1900* (Urbana, IL: University of Illinois Press, new edition 2005).

Farmer, Jared, *On Zion's Mount: Mormons, Indians and the American landscape* (Cambridge, MA: Harvard University Press, 2008).

Turner, John G., *Brigham Young: pioneer prophet* (Cambridge, MA: Harvard University Press, 2012).

utahhistory.sdlhost.com

Native Americans in Utah

Cuch, Forrest S. (ed.), *History of Utah's American Indians* (Boulder, CO: University of Colorado Press, 2003), including Dennis R. Defa on the Gosiute and Clifford Duncan on the Ute.

D'Azevedo, Warren L. (ed.), *Handbook of North American Indians, Vol. 11: Great Basin* (Washington, DC: Smithsonian Institution 1986).

Grayson, Donald K., *The Great Basin: a natural prehistory* (Berkeley, CA: University of California Press, 2011).

Steward, Julian H., *Basin-Plateau Aboriginal Sociopolitical Groups* (1938, reprinted Salt Lake City, UT: University of Utah Press, 1970).

Papanikolas, Z. (ed.), *The Peoples of Utah* (Salt Lake City, UT: Utah State Historical Society, 1976), including Floyd A. O'Neil, 'The Utes, Southern Paiutes, and Gosiutes'.

Utah Archaeology (journal)

Islam

Materials included here represent a range of interpretations and viewpoints, and different stages in the development of debates, as outlined in the text and notes of Chapter 3.

General

Encyclopedia of Islam (Leiden: Brill, 2nd edition 1954–2005; 3rd edition 2007, with some online).

Nicolle, David, *Historical Atlas of the Islamic World* (London: Mercury, 2004).

Muhammad, the Qur'an and historical sources

Arberry, A.J., *The Koran Interpreted* (London: Allen & Unwin, 1955).

Armstrong, Karen, *Muhammad: prophet for our time* (London: Harper, 2006).

Asad, Muhammad, *The Message of the Qur'an* (1980, reprinted Bristol: Book Foundation, 2003).

Brockropp, J.E. (ed.), *The Cambridge Companion to Muhammad* (New York: Cambridge University Press, 2010).

Beeston, A.F.L., T.M. Johnstone, R.B. Serjeant and G.R. Smith (eds), *Arabic Literature to the End of the Umayyad Period* (Cambridge: Cambridge University Press, 1983).

Cook, Michael, *Muhammad* (Oxford: Oxford University Press, 1983).

Crone, Patricia, *Meccan Trade and the Rise of Islam* (Princeton, NJ: Princeton University Press, 1987).

Donner, Fred M., *Narratives of Islamic Origins: the beginnings of Islamic historical writing* (Princeton, NJ: Darwin Press, 1998).

McAuliffe, J.D. (ed.), *The Cambridge Companion to the Qur'an* (New York: Cambridge University Press, 2006) including F.M. Donner, 'The historical context'.

Peters, F.E., *Muhammad and the Origins of Islam* (Albany, NY: State University of New York Press, 1994).

Robinson, Chase F., *Islamic Historiography* (Cambridge: Cambridge University Press, 2003).

Robinson, Chase F. (ed.), *The New Cambridge History of Islam, Vol. 1: The Formation of the Islamic World, Sixth to Eleventh Centuries* (Cambridge: Cambridge University Press, 2010), including C.F. Robinson, 'The rise of Islam, 600–705'; and F.M. Donner, 'Modern approaches to early Islamic history'.

Rodinson, Maxime, *Mohammed* (London: Penguin, 1971).

Watt, W. Montgomery, *Muhammad at Mecca* (Oxford: Oxford University Press, 1953).

Watt, W. Montgomery, *Muhammad at Medina* (Oxford: Oxford University Press, 1956).

Watt, W. Montgomery, *Muhammad's Mecca: history in the Qur'an* (Edinburgh: Edinburgh University Press, 1988).

Young, M.J.L., J.D. Latham and R.B. Serjeant (eds), *Religion, Learning and Science in the 'Abbasid Period* (Cambridge: Cambridge University Press, 1990).

Arabia before Islam: history and archaeology

al-Ghabban, A.I. et al. (eds), *Roads of Arabia: archaeology and history of the Kingdom of Saudi Arabia* (Paris: Somogy/Musée du Louvre, 2010).

de Maigret, A. *Arabia Felix: an exploration of the archaeological history of Yemen* (London: Stacey International, 2002).

Fisher, Greg (ed.), *Arabs and Empires Before Islam* (Oxford: Oxford University Press, 2015).

Fisher, Greg, *Between Empires: Arabs, Romans and Sasanians in late antiquity* (Oxford: Oxford University Press, 2011).

Hoyland, Robert G., *Arabia and the Arabs from the Bronze Age to the Coming of Islam* (London: Routledge, 2001).

Magee, Peter, *The Archaeology of Prehistoric Arabia: adaptation and social formation from the neolithic to the Iron Age* (Cambridge: Cambridge University Press, 2014).

Potts, D.T., *The Arabian Gulf in Antiquity* (2 vols) (Oxford: Oxford University Press, 1990).

Islamic conquests and expansion: history and archaeology

Avni, Gideon, *The Byzantine–Islamic Transition in Palestine: an archaeological approach* (Oxford: Oxford University Press, 2014).

Crone, Patricia, *Slaves on Horses: the evolution of the Islamic polity* (Cambridge: Cambridge University Press, 1980).

Crone, Patricia and M. Hinds, *God's Caliph: religious authority in the first centuries of Islam* (Cambridge: Cambridge University Press, 1986).

Donner, Fred M., *Muhammad and the Believers: at the origins of Islam* (Cambridge, MA: Harvard University Press, 2010).

Donner, Fred M., *The Early Islamic Conquests* (Princeton, NJ: Princeton University Press, 1981).

Hawting, G.R., *The First Dynasty of Islam: the Umayyad Caliphate*, 2nd edition (London: Routledge, 2000).

Holland, Tom, *In the Shadow of the Sword: the battle for global empire and the end of the ancient world* (London: Hachette, 2012).

Hoyland, Robert G., *In God's Path: the Arab conquests and the creation of an Islamic empire* (New York: Oxford University Press, 2015).

Hoyland, Robert G., *Seeing Islam as Others Saw It* (Princeton, NJ: Darwin Press, 1997).

Insoll, Timothy, *The Archaeology of Islam* (Oxford: Blackwell, 1999).

King, G.R.D. and A. Cameron (eds), *The Byzantine and Early Islamic Near East: land use and settlement patterns* (Princeton, NJ: Darwin Press, 1994).

Lapidus, Ira, *A History of Islamic Societies*, 2nd edition (Cambridge: Cambridge University Press, 2002).

Madelung, Wilferd, *The Succession to Muhammad: a study of the early caliphate* (Cambridge: Cambridge University Press, 1997).

Magness, Jodi, *The Archaeology of the Early Islamic Settlement in Palestine* (Winona Lake, IN: Eisenbrauns, 2003).

Milwright, Marcus, *An Introduction to Islamic Archaeology* (Edinburgh: Edinburgh University Press, 2010).

Porter, Venetia (ed.), *Hajj: journey to the heart of Islam* (London: British Museum Press, 2012).

Robinson, Chase F. (ed.), *The New Cambridge History of Islam, Vol. 1: The Formation of the Islamic World, Sixth to Eleventh Centuries* (Cambridge: Cambridge University Press, 2010), including F. Robinson, 'The rise of Islam, 600–705'; and M. Milwright, 'Archaeology and material culture'.

Walmsley, Alan, *Early Islamic Syria: an archaeological assessment* (London: Duckworth, 2007).

Christianity

A large proportion of the numerous printed books on the origins or early history of Christianity is designed to argue a case for one or other Christian perspective, or as a polemic against all. Independent secular histories are a minority. There is also a very substantial literature on Paulos. A number of reference works present perspectives on interpretative issues.

General

Cambridge Annotated Study Bible: new revised standard version (Cambridge: Cambridge University Press, 1993).

Evans, Craig A. (ed.), *Encyclopedia of the Historical Jesus* (New York: Routledge, 2008).

Horbury, William, W.D. Davies and J. Sturdy (eds), *The Cambridge History of Judaism, Vol. 3: The Early Roman Period* (Cambridge: Cambridge University Press, 1999).

Katz, Steven T. (ed.), *The Cambridge History of Judaism, Vol. 4, The Late Roman-Rabbinic Period* (Cambridge: Cambridge University Press, 2006).

Mitchell, M.M. and F.M. Young (eds), *The Cambridge History of Christianity, Vol. 1: Origins to Constantine* (Cambridge: Cambridge University Press, 2006).

Schürer, Emil, *The History of the Jewish People in the Age of Jesus Christ*, revised edition (Edinburgh: Edinburgh University Press, four volumes, 1973–1987).

The Yeshua movement

Barton, John, *A History of the Bible: the book and its faiths* (London: Allen Lane, 2019).

Burke, Tony and Brent Landau (eds), *New Testament Apocrypha: more non-canonical scriptures.* (Grand Rapids, MI: Eerdmans, 2016).

Ehrman, Bart D., *How Jesus Became God: the exaltation of a Jewish preacher from Galilee* (New York: Harper, 2014).

Ehrman, Bart D., *Jesus: apocalyptic prophet of the new millennium* (New York: Oxford University Press, 1999).

Ehrman, Bart D. and Zlatko Pleše, *The Apocryphal Gospels: texts and translations* (New York: Oxford University Press, 2011).

Fredriksen, Paula, *When Christioans Were Jews: the first generation* (New Haven, CT: Yale University Press, 2018).

Klauck, Hans-Josef, *Apocryphal Gospels: an introduction* (London: Clark, 2003).

Stegemann, Ekkehard and Wolfgang Stegemann, *The Jesus Movement: a social history of its first century* (Minneapolis, MN: Fortress Press, 1999).

Vermes, Geza, *Christian Beginnings: from Nazareth to Nicaea AD 30–325* (London: Penguin, 2012).

Vermes, Geza, *The Changing Face of Jesus* (London: Allen Lane, 2000).

Paulos and later

Gager, John G., *Reinventing Paul* (Oxford: Oxford University Press, 2000).

Maccoby, Hyam, *The Mythmaker: Paul and the invention of Christianity* (London: Weidenfeld & Nicolson, 1986).

Meeks, Wayne A., *The First Urban Christians: the social world of the apostle Paul*, 2nd edition (New Haven, CT: Yale University Press, 2003).

Murphy-O'Connor, Jerome, *Paul: a critical life* (Oxford: Oxford University Press, 1997).

Murphy-O'Connor, Jerome, *Paul: his story* (Oxford: Oxford University Press, 2004).

Riesner, Rainer, *Paul's Early Period: chronology, mission strategy, theology* (Grand Rapids, MI: Eerdmans, 1998).

Sanders, E.P., *Paul: a very short introduction* (Oxford: Oxford University Press, 2001).

Archaeology

Caraher, W.R., T.W. Davis and D.K. Pettegrew (eds), *The Oxford Handbook of Early Christian Archaeology* (Oxford: Oxford University Press, 2019).

Crossan, John Dominic and Jonathan L. Reed, *Excavating Jesus: beneath the stones, beneath the texts* (London: SPCK, 2001).

Edwards, Douglas R. (ed.), *Religion and Society in Roman Palestine* (New York: Routledge, 2004), including M. Avian, 'First century Jewish Galilee: an archaeological perspective'.

Fiensy, David A. and James Riley Strange (eds), *Galilee in the Late Second Temple and Mishnaic Period, Vol. 2: The Archaeological Record from Cities, Towns and Villages* (Minneapolis, MN: Fortress Press, 2015).

Finegan, Jack, *The Archeology of the New Testament: the life of Jesus and the beginning of the early church*, revised edition (Princeton, NJ: Princeton University Press, 1969).

Frend, W.H.C., *The Archaeology of Early Christianity* (London: Cassell 1996; and Minneapolis, MN: Fortress Press, 1996).

Galor, Katharina and Hanswulf Bloedhorn, *The Archaeology of Jerusalem: from the origins to the Ottomans* (New Haven, CT: Yale University Press, 2013).

Geva, Hillel (ed.), *Ancient Jerusalem Revealed* (Jerusalem: Israel Exploration Society, 1994, new edition 2000).

Harvey, Susan Ashbrook and David G. Hunter (eds), *The Oxford Handbook of Early Christian Studies* (Oxford: Oxford University Press, 2008).

Horsley, Richard A., *Archaeology, History and Society in Galilee* (Valley Forge, PA: Trinity, 1996).

Horsley, Richard A., *Galilee: history, politics, people* (Valley Forge, PA: Trinity, 1995).

Kelley, Justin L., *The Church of the Holy Sepulchre in Text and Archaeology* (Oxford: Archaeopress, 2019).

Magness, Jodi, *Stone and Dung, Oil and Spit: Jewish daily life in the time of Jesus* (Grand Rapids, MI: Eerdmans, 2011).

McRay, John, *Archaeology and the New Testament* (Grand Rapids, MI: Baker Academic, 1991).

Reed, Jonathan L., *Archaeology and the Galilean Jesus: a re-examination of the evidence* (Harrisburg, PA: Trinity, 2000).

Snyder, Graydon F., *Ante Pacem: archaeological evidence of Christ before Constantine* (Macon, GA: Mercer University Press, 2003).

Stern, Ephraim (ed.), *The New Encyclopedia of Archaeological Excavations in the Holy Land* (Jerusalem: Carta, 2015).

Judaism

The literature on exilic and post-exilic ('Second Temple') Judaism includes work written from a range of different viewpoints. There are some useful basic reference sources which present overviews and perspectives.

Surveys and general reference

Boardman, John et al. (eds), *Cambridge Ancient History, Vol. 3, Part 2: The Assyrian and Babylonian Empires and Other States of the Near East, from the Eighth to the Sixth Centuries BC*, 2nd edition (Cambridge: Cambridge University Press, 1992), including T.C. Mitchell, 'The Babylonian exile and the restoration of the Jews in Palestine'.

Davies, W.D. and Louis Finkelstein (eds), *The Cambridge History of Judaism, Vol. 1: Introduction: The Persian Period* (Cambridge: Cambridge University Press, 1984).

Encyclopedia Judaica, 2nd edition (New York: Macmillan, 2006), including B. Porten, 'Exile, Babylonian'.

Farber, Zev I. and Jacob L. Wright (eds), *Archaeology and History of Eighth-Century Judah* (Atlanta, GA: SBL Press, 2018).

Lipschits, Oded and Joseph Blenkinsopp (eds), *Judah and the Judeans in the Neo-Babylonian Period* (Winona Lake, IN: Eisenbrauns, 2003).

Lipschits, Oded and Manfred Oeming (eds), *Judah and the Judeans in the Persian Period* (Winona Lake, IN: Eisenbrauns, 2006).

Lipschits, Oded, Gary N. Knoppers and Rainer Albertz (eds), *Judah and the Judeans in the Fourth Century BCE* (Winona Lake, IN: Eisenbrauns, 2007).

Liverani, Mario, *Israel's History and the History of Israel* (London: Equinox, 2005).

Römer, Thomas, *The Invention of God* (Cambridge, MA: Harvard University Press, 2015).

Sources

Cambridge Annotated Study Bible: New Revised Standard Version (Cambridge: Cambridge University Press, 1993).

Carr, David M., *The Formation of the Hebrew Bible: a new reconstruction* (New York: Oxford University Press, 2011).

Niditch, Susan (ed.), *The Wiley Blackwell Companion to Ancient Israel* (Chichester: Wiley Blackwell, 2016), including D.M. Carr, 'The formation of the Hebrew Bible'; and C.E. Carter, '(Re)Defining "Israel": the legacy of the Neo Babylonian and Persian period'.

Paget, James Carleton and Joachim Schaper (eds), *The New Cambridge History of the Bible, Vol. 1: From the Beginnings to 600* (Cambridge: Cambridge University Press, 2013), including J. Schaper, 'The literary history of the Hebrew Bible'.

Sharp, Carolyn J. (ed.), *The Oxford Handbook of the Prophets* (Oxford: Oxford University Press, 2016), including J.L. Berquist, 'Prophesy in Persian Yehud'.

Yehud

Albertz, Rainer, *Israel in Exile: literature of the sixth century B.C.E.* (Atlanta, GA: Society of Biblical Literature, 2003).

Carter, Charles E. *The Emergence of Yehud in the Persian Period: a social and demographic study* (Sheffield: Sheffield Academic Press, 1999).

Grabbe, Lester L., *A History of the Jews and Judaism in the Second Temple Period, Vol. 1: Yehud: a history of the Persian province of Judah* (London: Clark, 2004).

Grabbe, Lester L., *Ancient Israel: what do we know and how do we know it?*, 2nd edition (London: Clark, 2017).

Jonker, L. (ed.), *Texts, Contexts and Readings in Postexilic Literature* (Tubingen: Siebeck, 2011), including Oded Lipschits, 'Persian-period Judah: a new perspective'.

Archaeology

Dever, William G., *Beyond the Texts: an archaeological portrait of Ancient Israel and Judah* (Atlanta, GA: Society for Biblical Literature Press, 2017).

Finkelstein, Israel, 'Jerusalem in biblical times … 1350—100 B.C.E.', at www.youtube. com/watch?v=3Z-7qKFTOys

Finkelstein, Israel and Neil Asher Silberman, *The Bible Unearthed: archaeology's new vision of ancient Israel and the origin of its sacred texts* (New York: Simon & Schuster, 2001).

Finkelstein, Israel and Neil Asher Silberman, *David and Solomon: in search of the Bible's sacred kings and the roots of the western tradition* (New York: Free Press; and London: Simon & Schuster, 2006).

Lipschits, Oded, *The Fall and Rise of Jerusalem: Judah under Babylonian rule* (Winona Lake, IN: Eisenbrauns, 2005).

Lipschits, Oded, 'The myth of the empty land and the myth of the mass return', at www.youtube.com/watch?v=dJ3a9oTt5kk

Stern, Ephraim, *Material Culture of the Land of the Bible in the Persian Period* (Warminster: Aris & Phillips, 1982).

Stern, Ephraim, et al. (eds), *The New Encyclopedia of Archaeological Excavations in the Holy Land* (Jerusalem: Carta, 2015).

Zoroastrianism

While much of the literature on Zoroastrian origins is of a specialist nature there are some general resources, and some classic works still have value for reference.

Barthold, V.V., *An Historical Geography of Iran* (Princeton, NJ: Princeton University Press, 1984, translated from the Russia, originally 1903).

Bregel, Yuri, *An Historical Atlas of Central Asia* (Leiden: Brill, 2003).

Fisher, W.B. (ed.), *Cambridge History of Iran, Vol. 1: The Land of Iran* (Cambridge: Cambridge University Press, 1968).

Rose, Jenny, *Zoroastrianism: an introduction* (London: Tauris, 2011).

Stausberg, Michael and Yuhan Sohrab-Dinshaw Vevaina (eds), *The Wiley Blackwell Companion to Zoroastrianism* (Chichester: Wiley Blackell, 2015).

Texts

Emmerick, Ronald E. and Maria Macuch (eds), *The Literature of Pre-Islamic Iran (A History of Persian Literature Vol. 17)* (London: Tauris 2009), including A. Hintze, 'Avestan literature'; P. Huyse, 'Inscriptional literature in Old and Middle Iranian'; and M. Macuch, 'Pahlavi literature'.

Kassam, Z.R., Y.K. Kornberg and J. Bagli (eds), *Islam, Judaism and Zoroastrianism* (Dordrecht: Springer, 2018), including O. Skjærvø and D.J. Sheffield, 'Zoroastrian scriptures'.

Avesta-Zoroastrian Archives at www.avesta.org includes English-language versions of Zoroastrian texts online, although the translations are generally somewhat dated.

History

Boyce, Mary, *Zoroastrians: their religious beliefs and practices*, 2nd edition (London: Routledge & Kegan Paul 1986).

Boyce, Mary, *A History of Zoroastrianism, Vol. 1: The Early Period* (Leiden: Brill, vol. 1, 1975, revised 1996); *Vol. 2: Under the Achaemenians* (Leiden: Brill, 1982); with F. Grenet, Vol. 3: Zoroatstrianism under Macedonian and Roman Rule (Leiden: Brill, 1991).

Cohn, Norman, *Cosmos, Change and the World to Come*, 2nd edition (New Haven, CT: Yale University Press, 2001).

Curtis, John and St John Simpson (eds), *The World of Achaemenid Persia: history, art and society in Iran and the ancient Near East* (London: Tauris, 2010).

Encyclopædia Iranica online at www.iranicaonline.org

Gershevitch, Ilya (ed.), *The Cambridge History of Iran, Vol. 2: The Median and Achaemenid Periods* (Cambridge: Cambridge University Press, 1985), including M. Schwartz, 'The Old Eastern Iranian world view according to the Avesta'; and 'The religion of Achaemenian Iran'.

Kuhrt, Amélie, *The Persian Empire: a corpus of sources from the Achaemenid period* (London: Routledge, 2007).

Moazami, Mahnaz (ed.), *Zoroastrianism: a collection of articles from the Encyclopædia Iranica* (New York: Encyclopædia Iranica Foundation, 2016).

Potts, Daniel T. (ed.), *The Oxford Handbook of Ancient Iran* (Oxford: Oxford University Press, 2013).

Pourshariati, Parvaneh, *Decline and Fall of the Sasanian Empire: the Sasanian–Parthian confederacy and the Arab conquest of Iran* (London: Tauris, 2017).

Index